D1737150

LORD GREY OF THE REFORM BILL

Walter S. Colls. Sc.

Charles, 2 nd Earl Grey. K.G.
1764 – 1845.
From the picture by Sir Thomas Lawrence at Howick.
about 1827.

LORD GREY OF THE REFORM BILL

BEING THE

LIFE OF CHARLES, SECOND EARL GREY

BY

GEORGE MACAULAY TREVELYAN

LATE FELLOW OF TRINITY COLLEGE, CAMBRIDGE

AUTHOR OF
' GARIBALDI, ETC.,' ' LIFE OF JOHN BRIGHT '
' SCENES FROM ITALY'S WAR '

*WITH PORTRAITS AND OTHER
ILLUSTRATIONS*

GREENWOOD PRESS, PUBLISHERS
WESTPORT, CONNECTICUT

Originally published in 1920
by Longmans, Green and Company, London & New York

First Greenwood Reprinting 1970

Library of Congress Catalogue Card Number 76-110874

SBN 8371-4553-8

Printed in the United States of America

To the Memory of
ALBERT, FOURTH EARL GREY

PREFACE

When the late Earl Grey invited me, in 1913, to make use of the Howick Papers, in order to write the life of his grandfather, I asked him whether I might be allowed a freedom of historical comment more extensive than would be proper in the biography of a statesman recently dead. The permission was granted with characteristic readiness and generosity. My work was interrupted by an interval of more than four years of war, during which the late Lord Grey died, but his son, in the same spirit, desired me to complete the book.

The original biography of the Reform Bill Premier, begun by his children for the benefit of a generation that had known him, was suspended midway,[1] and the work had to be undertaken afresh. After the lapse of so many decades, the nature of the task had changed. A very different book is now wanted from that which would have been welcomed at a time when Russell, Palmerston, and other leading actors in the conflict of the great Reform Bill were still in public life, and when the clubs were full of men who remembered the Prince Regent and the Rotten Boroughs. Many debates, incidents, and intrigues that convulsed Brooks's, and were long held in memory there, have now lost the halo of traditional interest, without acquiring historical importance. The biographer, for example, is no longer called upon to narrate in detail the series of once famous negotiations by which Grey evaded office between 1809 and 1812. On the other hand, the trend and change of middle and working class opinion during the forty years of

---

[1] *Some Account of the Life and Opinions of Charles, Second Earl Grey*, by Lieut.-Gen. Hon. C. Grey, 1861, goes no further than the year 1817.

vii

the movement for Parliamentary Reform over which Grey presided, are of deeper interest than ever in the historical perspective of our own day, and give unity and permanent value to Lord Grey's career, as viewed down the lengthening ages.

For this reason I have not only used the rich treasury of the Howick Papers themselves, and the documents relative to my subject in Holland House and Lambton Castle, most kindly put at my disposition by Lord Ilchester and Lord Durham, but I have studied—among the Additional MSS. in the British Museum and among the Home Office Papers—the currents on which the ship of Reform was launched by Grey in the period of the first French Revolution, and the all-powerful but dangerous flood-tide on which he brought the vessel into harbour in 1832.

The object of the present volume is to recall the life of a great historical character to the public of our day. In an age when the law of perpetual and rapid change is accepted as inevitable, and the difficulty is to obtain progress without violence, there may be profit in the story of a statesman who, after a period of long stagnation and all too rigid conservatism, initiated in our country a yet longer period of orderly democratic progress, and at the critical moment of the transition averted civil war and saved the State from entering on the vicious circle of revolution and reaction.

I am grateful to Sir Algernon West for access to letters of Lady Grey, and to Lord Spencer for Grey's letters to Althorp. I am much indebted to Mr. and Mrs. Hammond for help and suggestions ; and to Lord Halifax for putting at my disposal, with indefatigable kindness, his traditional knowledge of the Grey family in that period, and of the circle in which they moved.

G. M. TREVELYAN.

December, 1919.

CONTENTS

BOOK I

THE FORMATION OF PARTIES

BOOK II

THE STAGNATION OF PARTIES

BOOK III

THE REFORM BILL

APPENDICES

ILLUSTRATIONS

LORD GREY
OF THE REFORM BILL

BOOK I

THE FORMATION OF PARTIES

CHAPTER I

BOYHOOD AND YOUTH—WHIG SOCIETY AND POLITICS
ON THE EVE OF THE FRENCH REVOLUTION

' At an age when most of those who distinguish themselves in life
are still contending for prizes and Fellowships at college, he had won
for himself a conspicuous place in Parliament. At twenty-three he had
been thought worthy to be ranked with the veteran statesmen who
appeared as the delegates of the British Commons at the bar of the
British nobility.'—MACAULAY ON CHARLES GREY.

THE map of Britain shows England thrusting up a
wedge far northward along its eastern coast, to touch
the Tweed and claim the Till. This extremity of
Northumberland consists of a long belt of low country
lying between the highest part of the Cheviots and the
Northern Sea, arable along the coast, but some miles
inland swelling up into moors. Moorland and arable
alike are dominated by great presences—to the west
the rounded mass of Cheviot Hill, and to the east the
ocean, seen from every piece of rising ground when

the day is clear, while the west wind is for ever tearing across, as a messenger between hills and sea. Since the days of Cuthbert on Holy Island it has been a fine coast for the breeding and rearing of men. It could not have been held for England without hard fighting, on a larger scale than in other parts of Northumberland, for it was a royal highroad of invasion between Scotland and England. Names such as Flodden and Etal, Bamborough and Dunstanborough, Alnwick and Warkworth recall, not the bickerings of border outlaws, but the strife of two great Kingdoms. In all this work the Greys had their full share. But, although they possessed land at Howick from 1319 onwards, they seem not to have lived there during the period of the Border Wars. Only when that rough school of heroism and romance was about to be closed for ever we find, at the end of Elizabeth's reign, the ' Greys of Howick ' setting up as a distinct local branch.

When George III came to the throne these Greys of Howick were a numerous clan. The eldest, Sir Henry, uncle to the Reform Bill Premier, lived as a bachelor in the old peel tower of Howick, near the sea, perhaps already meditating the more habitable mansion that twenty years later he built in a fortunate hour. The only one of Sir Henry's brothers who concerns our story was Charles Grey the elder, who had already been wounded at Minden, and was destined to notable military services in another hemisphere, which earned him in the end the title of first Earl Grey of Howick. But he always lived, as a cadet of the family, not at Howick, but five miles off at Fallodon, a small country house half-way between the moors and the sea, which his mother had brought into the Grey inheritance. Here, on March 13, 1764, his son Charles, the future Reform Bill Premier, was born, and not many weeks later, by the death of a baby brother, became the eldest of his generation.[1]

[1] See genealogical tree at end of book.

SIR HENRY GREY, of Howick, Bart., 1722-1808.
Uncle of the Prime Minister.

From a picture at Howick.

Both Fallodon, his parents' house, where he was born, and Howick, his uncle's house, which he himself was to inhabit for the last forty-four years of his life, were familiar ground to him in his childhood, and in his schoolboy holidays. Fallodon and Howick both breathe the spell of that windy land between hills and sea, which few cast off if they have been bred in it, least of all the Greys in the cherished intervals between one bout of public service and the next. But it was Howick that most won the heart of Charles Grey the younger. It stands, drawn back a mile from the shore, between the lonely ruins of Dunstanborough and the little port of Alnmouth. That coast, since celebrated by Turner and by Swinburne, was then bleakly unknown to good society, which had not yet developed a taste for such severe and distant joys. Their friends in London thought of the Greys, as old Chaucer thought of Alan de Strother, as coming from some place

'Fer in the North, I can not tellé where.'

It would have been happier for Grey if yet more of his boyhood had been passed in the kindly North. But the custom of the age prevailed even with the most loving of parents, and at six years old he was sent to an ill-chosen school at Marylebone. There he remained miserably for three years, suffering from a series of illnesses. The first of these overtook him immediately after his arrival in the South, and the poor little sick child, separated by four long days' posting from his parents' care, was put in the sole charge of a nurse who lived, as luck would have it, at Tyburn. The first day when the boy of six was well enough to be taken out of doors she took him across the road to see a batch of Jews hung for forgery, and lest he should miss any of the sight mounted him on the shoulders of a grenadier. The dying contortions of the wretches as they were one by one turned off the cart, left such an impress on a mind more than ordinarily sensitive that, in the reign of Victoria, the statesman who had passed the Reform Bill would wake sweating from a nightmare vision of this old horror of Hogarth's London.

At nine years old he was sent to Eton, and remained there till he was seventeen (1773-1781). It was here that he first touched the great world of politics and fashion, to which Eton was then an antechamber. Here he began a friendship of more than sixty years' duration with Richard, afterwards Marquis Wellesley, the half-ally of his later political life ; here he formed a yet closer personal attachment with his more short-lived brother Liberals, Sam Whitbread and William Lambton.[1] Canning was such a small boy when Grey left the school that we can hardly suppose that they had yet found occasion to dislike one another.

Grey, I believe, gained much from Eton, but, at the risk of alienating from him a powerful body of opinion, I must confess that he was not a good ' Old Etonian.' In the first year of his Reform Ministry he wrote to Wellesley on July 22, 1831, ' I am to be at Windsor on Sunday for [Eton] Speeches on Monday, where I have not been since I spoke myself fifty years ago.' He refused to send any of his numerous sons to a public school, on the ground that he himself had been taught nothing at the most famous of those establishments. This must be taken as a criticism directed at the limited aims of the curriculum and of the system, for he certainly got the best that Eton set out to provide. He succeeded there, socially and scholastically, and in those days athletic prowess was not indispensable.

Some of Grey's school verses won a place in the

---

[1] Grey was in the Sixth Form 1780-1 ; Wellesley in 1778 ; Whitbread in 1779-80 ; Lambton in 1782.

famous selection published some years later under the title 'Musae Etonenses.' Although, to judge by his strictures on the school course, he did not regard the writing of Latin verse as affording by itself a complete education, he was nevertheless much devoted to the lore of that peculiar art, which Milton did not disdain. In 1842 the octogenarian Marquis of Wellesley sent a volume containing his own Latin verses to Earl Grey, aged seventy-eight. The ex-Premier replied to the ex-Governor-General of India : ' I remember well admiring when at Eton the beautiful exercises which are contained in this collection, and which then made so great an impression on me that I could still repeat many of them by heart.' When we remember what had happened in the world in East and West during the sixty and odd years that Grey was carrying about Wellesley's Eton verses in his head, and what parts the two boys had played in preserving the *Imperium et Libertas* of modern Rome, we may think that the schoolrooms as well as the playing fields of Eton have had their part in English history.

The fact is that the Eton and Harrow education of that time was well directed towards a definite if insufficient end. It may have ill served some of the larger purposes of the community, but at least it forwarded the success in later life of the most important boys, those namely who were born to the purple of a seat in either House of Parliament, or who seemed likely by their talents to become recipients of a well-bestowed interest in a rotten borough. As Mr. Butler has admirably put it,[1] the system of these schools

aimed at the training of statesmen, at a time when statesmanship consisted largely in winning and retaining the confidence of an assembly of some six hundred gentlemen. Special attention was therefore paid to oratory, and oratory of a particular type—large, dignified, lofty, appealing to the sense of honour and

[1] *Passing of the Great Reform Bill,* J. R. Butler, p. 233.

responsibility of a particular class. Such was the object of the Speech-days so much in vogue, not less than of the specialized study of the Classics as the model of language and taste. Parliamentary eloquence was founded on the pure and lordly speech of the ancient poets and orators, who were freely quoted in the ordinary conversation of gentlemen ; Shakespeare was their only rival, but he was known with a thoroughness that would be rare to-day. Similarity of education combined with similarity of social position to produce a close society favourable to high spirit and intensity of life rather than to breadth of sympathy. For effective debate it is necessary that speakers and audience should share a common fund of experience and a common *hinterland* of thought.

Eton was a recruiting ground for Parliament, not only because of its peculiar education, but by reason of its personal connections. An ' Eton reputation ' was a long step towards a seat in the House. Grey might or might not have sat for Northumberland at twenty-two if he had never been at Eton, but it is in the highest degree unlikely that the friends and relations of the *bourgeois* Canning and Whitbread would have put those young gentlemen into the House so soon as they did, if Eton had not first proclaimed them as two of her chosen spirits.

It is indeed easy to point out the shortcomings of an education which Grey himself thought bad. And certainly, when the two Houses of public-schoolmen and classical scholars were asked by an untimely Fate to deal with the economic and social problems of the Industrial Revolution during a twenty years' war, the result for the community was as disastrous as might have been expected. But during the greater part of the eighteenth century, itself a ' classical ' period of stationary happiness for a considerable portion of the people of England, this close literary education had at least the merit of producing an aristocracy fit to set the fashion to other classes. Men of the world, but by no means ashamed of the things of the mind—

brought up to be proud of their knowledge of the Classics, Shakespeare, and Milton, and the histories of Greece, Rome, and Stuart England—the small group of families who governed the State with perhaps indifferent success, proved the best patrons of literature since the Athenian democracy. These aristocrats made the world, that doffed its hat to them, doff to the Muses also. For instance, while Grey was at Eton, the first volumes of Gibbon's History appeared ; at the high prices of that time they only sold 2,000 copies in the first year, but those copies, having been sold to the right kind of people, at once ensured to Gibbon an European reputation, and placed him, in the just regard of his contemporaries, by the side of Livy and Tacitus. Similarly, the great world of fashion and politics imposed on England the worship of Shakespeare ; it is due to the patrons of Garrick and Dr. Johnson that we still call the Elizabethan age, ' the age of Shakespeare,' as if letters were three parts of life. It was in this limited but truly civilised state of society and intellect, now very barely imaginable to us, that Grey was brought up, both at Eton and at home.

While his son was at Eton, General Charles Grey was earning fame as one of the best of our Generals in the war of the American Revolution. In a night onslaught at Paoli, near Valley Forge, he achieved all the conditions of successful surprise, and beat up Wayne's quarters with the cold steel. Among other expedients, he had caused the men whose muskets were loaded to knock out the flints, so as to prevent any chance explosion, a device which gained for the victor of Paoli the honourable nickname of ' no-flint Grey.' During the nineteenth century a portrait of Benjamin Franklin looked down from over the chimney-piece of Howick library at the domestic felicity of the Whig statesmen descended from this fine Tory soldier. When the British troops occupied Philadelphia, the portrait had been taken out of Franklin's house as the only permissible spoils of war, implying indeed a compliment to the worldwide fame of the philosophic rebel. The plunderer was no less interesting a person than the unfortunate Major André, then General Grey's aide-de-camp, who presented the picture to his chief. In the twentieth century Albert Earl Grey, Governor-General of Canada, gave back the portrait to the American people, who presented him instead with an excellent copy that now hangs in the same place at Howick.

In 1781 Grey left Eton for Trinity College, Cambridge. The eighteenth century was not a time of profound learning or of intellectual ferment at either University. The dons, as described by Gibbon for Oxford, and by Wordsworth for Cambridge, seem scarcely to have been libelled in Rowlandson's caricatures. They were little better than the other clerical sinecurists of that epoch, with some touch of eccentricity often added to distinguish the academician. On the walls of Trinity College there is a strange absence of portraits of great men of learning between Bentley and Porson. One must look before or after the sleepy century for true academic fame. Under such careless tutelage young men of family at least enjoyed themselves, continuing the lazy, lively existence, far from purely philistine, which they had begun at Eton or at Westminster.

Grey [1] consorted at Cambridge with his Eton friends, Lambton, of his own College, and the Johnian

---

[1] The *Dictionary of National Biography* incorrectly states that he was at King's, no doubt because he came so prominently from Eton. His real College is stated not only in a MS. by his son, but in Mr. Rouse Ball's monumental work, *Trinity College Admissions*, where we read, under the year 1781 :—' Grey, Charles, son of Charles Grey of Falladon (query Fallowdon), Northumberland. School, Eton (Mr. Davies). Age 17. Fellow-commoner, Nov. 12, 1781. Tutors, Mr. Therond and Mr. Cranke. Matriculated 1781. Did not graduate.' The Trinity registrar of that date was probably not the first, and certainly he was not the last, to boggle over the spelling of Fallodon.

CHARLES GREY at the time he left Eton.

From the picture by Romney at Howick.

Whitbread. It may have been in their company that he first developed a leaning towards what we now call Liberal opinions, which were a novelty in his father's house. At any rate, when the test of the French Revolution came, ten years later, this Eton and Cambridge trio figured together in the list, once of reproach, now of honour, of the Society of ' Friends of the People,' and stood together in Parliament for the down-trodden liberties of Englishmen till the death of Lambton in 1797 and of Whitbread in 1815. The brewer married Grey's sister ; and Lambton, the landed magnate of County Durham, was the father of Grey's son-in-law and Cabinet colleague, the famous Lord Durham of the Canadian report. During their Cambridge period the three friends were painted by Romney, each seated with a book in his hand, as if the three pictures formed one set ; they were done for the Head Master of Eton as ' leaving presents,' and hang in the Provost's Lodge with other fine portraits by Reynolds and Romney of the young men whom Eton delighted to honour.[1]

But it would be a mistake to imagine that these three scholars and future statesmen chose while at Cambridge ' to scorn delights and live laborious days,' like Pitt at Pembroke a few years before. They were devoted friends of the Falstaff of the University, Thomas Adkin of Corpus, a Bachelor of Arts, a little older than themselves, whose strange life and ready humour have been rescued from oblivion by Gunning. In his quarters at the White Bear Inn, known in his day as ' Adkin College,' nearly opposite Trinity, he used to entertain Grey and his other friends with Attic revelry, where much true wit degenerated, as night wore on, into Bacchanalian riot.

---

[1] For reproductions see Mr. Lionel Cust's *Eton Portraits*. The reproduction opposite is from the replica at Howick, where it forms one of a set of Romneys representing the four sons of General Grey.

Whenever the Proctors entered the Inn [writes Gunning] for the purpose of sending to their respective Colleges any undergraduates who might be found amongst so tumultuous an assemblage, they were immediately informed by the waiter that the noise proceeded from a private room where *Squire Adkin* was giving a dinner to a few friends.   Whether this was a sufficient answer to prevent the University officers entering the room, I am not able to say, *as the experiment was never made* ; but the waiters were always questioned as to there being any undergraduates in the party.   They never failed to answer, they could not tell, but imagined there were none, as they had seen neither caps nor gowns, and that the gentlemen were all in boots and leather breeches.[1]

The studies of Cambridge were in those days in somewhat too striking contrast to the rigorous classicism of Eton.   The only letter of Grey's of this period that has survived, written in his second term at Trinity, says :

You enquire how I like Cambridge.   I answer, very much. My only objection to it is that I think the study too confined. If a man is not a mathematician he is nobody.   Mathematicks and Philosophy supply the place of Classicks and all other studies ; though whatever mode is most agreeable to a young man he is at perfect liberty to pursue.

After school and college came, in those days, the third part of a gentleman's education—the Grand Tour. Foreign travel was then taken, not as now in sips periodically administered once or twice a year, but in one deep draught in early youth.   During most of the time between his departure from Trinity in 1784 and the beginning of his Parliamentary career in 1787, Grey was moving about through Southern France, Switzerland, and Italy, at first alone and later ' in the suite of Henry Duke of Cumberland.'   One long letter of his, that chance has preserved, gives us a glimpse of him,

---

[1] Gunning's *Cambridge*, i. 56–66 ; Broughton (Hobhouse), *Recollections*, i. 92.

like so many before and after, fascinated by Palladio's Theatre at Vicenza, astonished by the Roman amphitheatre at Verona, depressed by the gloom of Mantua, and preferring the scenery of Lago Maggiore even to the shores of Lake Leman. In the larger cities he had the opportunity of seeing much of foreign society, for travelling Englishmen then enjoyed the hospitality not only of the French but of the Italian Courts and salons. He came away with a lifelong skill in the language and literature of Italy. The Grand Tour helped to develop in him that excellent habit of mind whereby he always regarded foreign countries, not as pawns in the diplomatic game, but as places inhabited by human beings with rights and aspirations of their own.

In July 1786, while still abroad, he was returned at a by-election for the County of Northumberland, and he first took his seat in the new session of January 1787. The scarcity of family papers prior to 1792 makes it impossible to analyse with certainty the motives of his early political attachments. The difficulty is the greater because these motives, before the issues raised by the French Revolution sobered him for life, were probably not a little personal, and as much connected with Brooks's Club, Devonshire House, and the company of Charles Fox and his friends, as with any principle in politics. It is indeed hard to discern any principle, least of all of a Liberal character, in the actions of Opposition during the years when they were denouncing Pitt's Free Trade and pacific policy towards France, and plotting to climb back to power on the shoulders of the Prince Regent. Grey's father was, if anything, a supporter of Pitt, and the junior member for Northumberland had been returned at his first election with that delightful freedom from pledges and obligations which county members then so often enjoyed. Even after he had been taking a leading part in opposition for several months, Fox still denied to him the

title of ' party man.'[1] But it would appear that from
the moment he arrived in London he had gravitated
to the society of those who were working for Pitt's
overthrow. And, indeed, for good company and good
talk, no party was ever better worth joining than that
of Fox, Burke, Sheridan, and the authors of the *Rolliad*
when it was still swelling in size at every new edition.
Grey had soon adopted all the quarrels of his allies
with the light-hearted enthusiasm of two-and-twenty.

The only account of Grey's choice of a party which
has come down to us are the words which the famous
Lady Holland, then Lady Webster, wrote at the end
of 1793. They presumably represent some real tradition on the subject, but it must be remembered that
they were written seven years after the events related,
and at a period when the writer was not yet in the
heart of the Whig circle, and had at most but a slight
acquaintance with Grey. The first sentence sounds
absurd to those who know anything about the later
Grey, but may well have been less untrue about his
early youth :

Grey is a man of violent temper and unbounded ambition.
His connections were Ministerial, but on his return from abroad
both parties entertained hopes of him. His uncle, Sir Harry
[of Howick], is a rich, old, positive, singular man, leads a retired
life, but was always eager upon politics, particularly against the
Coalition—an infamous thing, by-the-bye. His father, Sir
Charles Grey, is attached to Government as a military man,
and is intimately connected with Colonel Barré and Lord Lans-
down, who at that time supported the Ministry. Grey was
elected whilst abroad, therefore not pledged to any particular

---

[1] ' Mr. Fox replied to what Mr. Pitt had said of Mr. Grey's being
a party man, and declared that the hon. gentleman was not of that
description, but he hoped by degrees he might become a party man '
(*Hansard*, xxvi. 1198, May 28, 1787). In a letter of 1782, at the
age of 18, Grey had spoken with pleasure of the advent of the Rockingham
ministry to power ; so he had not been, even at that early age, an adherent
of George III and Lord North.

party. The fashion was to be in Opposition; the Prince of Wales belonged to it, and he then was not disliked; all the beauty and wit of London were on that side, and the seduction of Devonshire House prevailed. Besides, Pitt's manner displeased him on his first speech, whereas Fox was all conciliation and encouragement.[1]

In view of the future, it was lucky that Grey fell under the influence of Fox. But in 1787 there was little reason for a Reformer to prefer Opposition to Government. The Rockingham or Foxite Whigs had delivered the country from North and the 'King's Friends' in 1782, put an end to the personal government of the Crown, and taken the first step, in Burke's Economic Reform Bill, towards the purification of English politics. But they then proceeded to deprive themselves, by a series of amazing blunders, of the opportunity to do any more good. When Rockingham died, Fox and Shelburne quarrelled, from incompatibility of temperament rather than on any public ground. To make good the loss of Shelburne's party, Fox entered into coalition with North. That easy-going nobleman, who had lost America rather than hurt George III's feelings, was still hated by that great majority of his fellow-countrymen who did not know by personal contact what a good-natured man he was. The coalition not only shocked the moral sense of the ordinary citizen, but alienated from the Whigs the one progressive element of that day, the Yorkshire Parliamentary Reformers led by Wyvill, who leaned for some years to come on the broken reed of Pitt's Liberal inclinations. The King, rising to his opportunity of revenge, tripped up the heels of his Ministers over their India Bill. Fox made mistake after mistake, and Pitt, the unerring tactician, soon established himself in the confidence of his countrymen, and began his long reign as Prime Minister. The King's personal rule was not restored, but

[1] *The Journal of Elizabeth, Lady Holland*, 1908, i. 100.

George III unfortunately retained in practice a veto on all great Liberal measures—Parliamentary Reform, Catholic Emancipation, and Abolition of Slave Trade. That power of veto was largely due to the weakness of Pitt, whose worst fault was unwillingness to risk a fall in order to pass the measures which he knew to be right, and who, as his friend Wilberforce learned bitterly to lament, preferred to govern the country by ' influence ' instead of by ' principle.' [1]   But at least he could govern.   In the ten years between the war of the American and the war of the French Revolution the country rose, in prosperity and in prestige, from the degradation to which George III had reduced it.   The wits of Brooks's jested about Pitt's youth.   But in fact he was prematurely old in spirit—cautious, dignified, formidable, experienced, laborious, wise ; but with a mind that, after a splendid springtime, too soon became closed to generous enthusiasms and new ideas, and ceased to understand human nature save as it is known to a shrewd and cynical Government Whip.   He was still being twitted as ' the schoolboy ' when he had acquired all the characteristics of the schoolmaster. While Fox always retained the faults and merits of youth, Pitt early acquired those of old age.

Pitt, in his studious years at Cambridge, had mastered the new doctrines of Adam Smith, and very shortly afterwards he was putting them into practice in his budgets.   It is true that his early Free Trade work was soon undone by the war taxation imposed by himself and his successors, and his *rapprochement* with France by the Commercial Treaty was the prelude to a twenty years' war.   But, shortlived as it proved to be, the Commercial Treaty of 1787 was, as Mr. Lecky says, ' probably the most valuable result of the legislation of Pitt.'   It was an admirable measure, both

---

[1] *Private Papers of W. Wilberforce*, Unwin, 1897, pp. 72-4.   A most remarkable passage.

commercially and as a means of putting an end to the traditional antagonism of England and France. The arguments of Opposition were directed, not so much against the commercial principles involved, on which Brooks's had no very clearly defined ideas, as against the political issue of improved relations with France. In so far as this criticism was more than factious, it was out of date. The traditional Whig hostility to the despotic and persecuting House of Bourbon had come down from William III through Chatham to Fox and Grey. But in 1787 the character of the French Monarchy, already staggering to its doom, was very different from what it had been in the time of the Dragonnades.[1]

On February 21, 1787, Grey rose to make his maiden speech against the Commercial Treaty. ' French perfidy ' was his theme, and the young orator could not refrain from ' *Timeo Danaos.* ' But it was a fine speech, and on the strength of it the House of Commons, then at the highwater-mark of its oratorical and debating genius, accepted the tyro as one of its leading men.

A new speaker [so Addington wrote to his father] presented himself to the House, and went through his first performance with an éclat which has not been equalled to my recollection. His name is Grey. He is not more than twenty-two years of age ; and he took his seat only in the present session. I do not go too far in declaring that in the advantage of figure, voice, elocution, and manner, he is not surpassed by any member of the House ; and I grieve to say that he was last night in the ranks of Opposition, from whence there is no chance of his being detached.

Thus, by a brilliant piece of invective on the wrong side of a question that he did not understand, the young man from Northumberland at twenty-two years of age

---

[1] On the fall of the Bastille, July 1789, Fox declares that ' all my prepossessions against French connections for this country will be at an end, and most part of my European system of politics will be altered,' if France ceases to be an absolutist Power. But the revolution that at once made Fox friendly to France, ere long made Pitt hostile.

became one of the most envied in that most enviable of all the aristocracies of history, the men and women who look out from the canvasses of Reynolds and Romney with a divine self-satisfaction, bred of unchallenged possession of all that was really best in a great civilisation, in the years when Rousseau was no more than a theory and Voltaire was still a fashion.

It is clear from Addington's letter that not a little of Grey's first success as an orator [1] was due to his appearance, to his manner, and to the general effect of his delivery. He was a handsome man. In the middle period of Grey's life, no less a judge than Byron spoke of 'his patrician thoroughbred look that I dote on.' In his old age, the Reform Premier is the most graceful figure among his colleagues in ' H. B.'s ' lifelike cartoons. In early youth, though many thought him ' supercilious,' he had, when he wished, the gift to please ; and before the domesticated period of his life began in 1794, he achieved successes such as fell to few in that world of *fin-de-siècle* gallantry. The men and women among whom he moved when he first came to London lacked both the virtues and the vices of the austere. They felt themselves above the censure of any class but their own, and they had not yet been frightened by the French Revolution or reclaimed by the Evangelical movement. But these days of unchartered freedom were already numbered. The change from the high society that Fox led to that of the generation which ostracised Byron, is an English version of the change from the Renaissance Courts of the early Cinquecento to the Italy of the Jesuit reaction.

---

[1] In a book of little value that belonged to Lord Macaulay occur the words, ' No member of either house of the British Parliament will be ranked amongst the orators of this country, *whom Lord North did not see*, or who did not see Lord North.' Macaulay has underscored the words here printed in italics, and written on the margin ' Lord North, poor man, was blind when Lord Grey came into Parliament.'

Within a few weeks of his entry into the House of Commons, his social success and his prominence in the Whig world had won him the always fatal privilege of intimacy with George, Prince of Wales. It is difficult to say whether the ladies or the statesmen who put their trust in that Prince fared the worst, though both ladies and statesmen courted their own discredit. In his youth he was the bane and disgrace of the Whigs, and in his old age of the Tories. And in each case the worst trouble arose from his conduct towards a wife.

The original connection of the Prince of Wales with the Whigs was due in part to his lively and dissolute manners, which fitted in better with Fox's and Sheridan's ideas of good company than with those of Pitt. There was also the natural tendency of an Opposition in disgrace at Court to fall back on the Heir Apparent ; Fox and the Prince of Wales both hated George III, and were hated by him. If and when the Prince of Wales became Regent or King, he could dismiss Pitt and call in Fox. Such action would probably create a Whig Parliamentary majority ; for, although the ' King's friends ' as such had disappeared from politics, it was calculated that some 185 members of the House of Commons were always ready to vote for any Government actually in power, if it was not peculiarly unpopular.[1] This calculation underlies the political history of the whole period.

So the Whigs shared the Carlton House revels, and championed the national payment of the Carlton House debts. This was bad, but there was worse to come. The Prince was passionately in love with Mrs. Fitzherbert, a Roman Catholic lady, at that time a widow. She would not yield to his wishes unless he married her. But even marriage was open to two objections— first, that if the Prince married a Roman Catholic he was liable to forfeit the succession to the Crown ; and

---

[1] *England under the Hanoverians*, Grant Robertson, p. 324, note.

second, that by the Royal Marriage Act he could not until he was twenty-five contract a legal union without the King's consent. Fox, in a letter of December 10, 1785, laid these considerations before the Prince, and urged him in the strongest terms ' not to think of marriage till you can marry legally. A mock marriage, for it can be no other, is neither honourable for any of the parties, nor, with respect to your Royal Highness, even safe.'

To this the Prince replied, on the next day :

Make yourself easy, my dear friend. Believe me the world will now soon be convinced that there not only is, but never was, any ground for these reports which of late have been so malevolently circulated.

Four days later [1] he secretly married Mrs. Fitzherbert. His arrangements for the marriage must have been far advanced when he wrote to his ' dear friend ' to induce him to believe that no such step would be taken.

As the King's consent had not been obtained, the union was not legal ; indeed, the Prince subsequently married another wife while Mrs. Fitzherbert was still alive. But since her Church recognised the ceremony as valid, Mrs. Fitzherbert chose to regard it as sufficient safeguard for her honour. Since the publication of the fact would endanger the Prince's succession to the Crown, she always observed a magnanimous silence. Her reticence and her sufferings atone for her mistake in consenting to a ceremony on terms so doubtful for herself and so dangerous for her husband.

More than a year later, at the end of April, 1787, the Prince, supported by the Whigs, was trying to get the Carlton House debts paid off by the nation. While the question was at issue, the Tory member Rolle, the exasperated hero of the *Rolliad*, raised in the House the rumour that the Prince was married to a Roman

---

[1] The marriage was on December 15, 1785, not, as has often been stated, on the 21st. See Wilkins, *Mrs. Fitzherbert*, i. 99.

Catholic. Fox 'denied it *in toto*, in point of fact as well as law,' and stated that he had ' direct authority ' for the denial. It is not known whether his sole authority was the Prince's letter of December 11, 1785, or whether he had received later reassurances by word of mouth from the Prince. In any case Fox when he spoke believed that he was telling the truth.

Never was man in such a predicament as Fox when he discovered that there had been a ceremony after all. If the truth were now made public the State would be convulsed and the Prince perhaps excluded from the succession. Meanwhile, Fox was responsible for the circulation of a false statement, closely affecting a lady's honour, for everyone knew that Mrs. Fitzherbert was now living with the Prince.

What precisely occurred between the Prince and the Whig leaders during the next few days and weeks is still obscure. What concerns us here is Grey's statement about himself, written late in life. He declares that the Prince sent for him after Fox's denial, and

in a long conversation which I had with him, in which he was dreadfully agitated, the object was to get me to say something in Parliament for the satisfaction of Mrs. Fitzherbert, which might take off the effect of Fox's declaration. I expressly told him how prejudicial a continuance of the discussion must be to him, and positively refused to do what he desired. He put an end to the conversation abruptly by saying, ' Well, if nobody else will, Sheridan must.' And the aged Earl Grey adds : ' He confessed it [the marriage] to me in the interview which I have mentioned.' [1]

¹ Fox, *Memoirs*, ii. 288-9, notes. See also Holland, *Memoirs of Whig Party*, ii. 139. When the story of this interview between Grey and the Prince was first alluded to in Moore's *Life of Sheridan* (1825), George IV, in talking to Croker, denied that he had seen Grey at all about the matter; but in the same conversation he denied that he had married Mrs. Fitzherbert (*Croker Papers*, i, 293, *et seq*.). So I fear that we must believe Grey, and that therefore Grey knew of the marriage in April 1787, prior to his denying it in the House of Commons in February 1789.

Fox and Coke of Norfolk quarrelled with the Prince, who had deceived them, and when the heir to the throne invited himself to visit Coke, at his famous Norfolk seat, the reply was : ' Holkham is open to strangers on Tuesdays.' Unfortunately for their happiness and good fame, the Whig chiefs after about a year renewed personal and political relations with the Prince, at his eager solicitation.[1] None of them, indeed, except Sheridan were ever again at ease in Carlton House. They now knew their man. As Grey wrote to Fox in later years, the Prince was ' the worst anchoring ground in Europe.' Unfortunately, they were tempted to trust to that anchorage, when the madness of George III in the winter of 1788 opened out the prospect of a Regency.

Never did Opposition appear in a worse light than during the Regency debates. The party that stood above all else for subordinating the authority of the Crown to that of the nation, proclaimed the doctrine that the Regency was vested in the Prince of Wales as of right, whatever Parliament might do. This mistake enabled Pitt to ' unwhig ' Fox, and gained for the Premier the support of democratic Reformers like Wyvill and Cartwright ; and on the same side were the Royalist, the Protestant, and the moral feelings of the nation. Pity for the afflicted King, and detestation of his dissolute son, were enhanced by renewed rumours that the latter was after all secretly married to a Papist.

The tone of the Opposition was as bad as its case. Burke's violence on behalf of the Prince was shocking, and already on both sides of the House men whispered that his noble mind was becoming unhinged. The *morale* of the Opposition leaders was not improved by the prospects of office approaching daily nearer as their unpopularity deepened. Georgiana, Duchess of Devonshire, the accomplished and beautiful woman who kept

---

[1] *Coke of Norfolk*, chapter xv.

the greatest of Whig houses open for the party chiefs,
has left in her private diary a day-to-day account of
the quarrelling that went on among her friends :[1]

1788. Nov. 23. I saw Grey and Sheridan. Sheridan
might certainly be Chancellor of the Exchequer if he chuses,
but prefers reaching it by degrees and when he has prov'd his
capability to ye public. He argued with Grey, who would only
accept the Chancellor of the Exchequer or Secretary of War.
Grey says he will give way to Ld. John [Cavendish], Charles
Fox, or Sheridan—but not to those Norfolks, Wyndhams, and
Pelhams.

Grey was only twenty-four ; when he was an older and
better man it was no longer his habit to stand out
selfishly for high office. Yet even now the benign
influence of Fox soon brought him to his bearings, for
in the following January Fox wrote to the Duke of
Portland that Grey ' would like ' the very much inferior
post of Vice-President of the Board of Trade in their
prospective Government.[2]

Pitt's measures for restricting the powers of the
Regent were bitterly resented by Opposition, and it is
arguable that they would have acted as improper limitations on the authority of the Regent's Cabinet. But it
was not held that they would prevent him from changing the Ministry, and in February 1789 Pitt was
preparing to resume his practice at the bar. There
still remained one desperate chance, that the marriage
of the Prince with Mrs. Fitzherbert might yet be
disclosed. On January 2 the Duchess of Devonshire
noted in her diary : ' A handbill was sent to Mrs.
Fitzherbert, telling her that to-morrow 500 libels would
be published declaring the Prince had forfeited his
right to the Crown by marrying her. Sheridan called
here at 2 in his way to the booksellers to suppress

[1] The diary is printed at the end of Mr. Sichel's *Life of Sheridan*.
[2] Fox, *Memoirs*, iv. 284.

it.' Meanwhile the indefatigable Rolle was perpetually bringing up the question in the House of Commons. Fox now knew that his own statement of two years before had been false, and he was not anxious either to repeat or to contradict it. After Rolle had in vain questioned him on January 19, he was perhaps glad to be too ill to attend the House for some weeks. He was absent on February 7, when Rolle raised in form the question of the Prince's rumoured marriage with a Papist. Sheridan and Grey both rose and denied the report ; Grey denied it twice in the same sitting, in even more explicit language than Sheridan ; and committed the absent Fox to full adherence to his own former statement.[1]

Documents may yet be discovered to throw light on this obscure business. Till then I can only guess that the Whig chiefs had agreed among themselves that, since Fox had been deceived into making the initial misstatement, it was too late to go back upon it now. They probably salved their consciences by remembering that the ceremony had been no legal marriage—though Fox had denied it ' in point of fact as well as law.' But the chief consideration presumably was that the truth, if confessed at this stage, would cause a national convulsion and exclude the Prince from the Regency and the Throne. Whatever their motives, Fox consented to the deception by his silence, and Grey by his speech. A few weeks later, by an event closely

[1] *Parliamentary History*, xxvii. pp. 1191-3.
Mr. Grey ' reprobated the rumours alluded to, as false, libellous and calumniatory ' ; and again, when he rose the second time : ' He repeated his reprobation of those reports as false, libellous and calumnious. . . . He assured the Committee that it was due to the character of his right hon. friend [Mr. Fox] to declare, that no consideration of health, or any other circumstance, would have prevented his attendance in his place, if he had not, at that moment, been fully satisfied that what he asserted on a former occasion, was strictly true. Had the case been otherwise, his right hon. friend would have been present even at the risk of his life.'

resembling an act of retributive justice on the part of Providence, the King unexpectedly recovered, and it was he and the Tories, not the Prince and the Whigs, who were to plague the British Islands for the next twenty years. In all his middle and later life Grey was regarded, alike by friends and enemies, as a man of scrupulous honour and veracity. ' Grey is truth itself,' wrote Fox to a friend in 1800, when a question of fact was at issue. ' Grey always at least tells the truth,' wrote the cynic Creevey. But all the meagre evidence that we have of Grey's early years confirms my belief that between the ages of twenty-two and twenty-five his character and principles were still unformed. It is impossible to imagine the Grey of 1800, of 1812, of 1827, or of 1834 intriguing for high office, deceiving the House of Commons, or being so much as accused of that ' violent temper and unbounded ambition ' which Lady Webster ascribed to him in youth. Few young men, except Charles Fox himself, were more severely tempted by the dazzling qualities of the company into which they were early introduced, and many statesmen of maturer age have tampered with the truth to avert a national convulsion. The evidence as to Grey's conduct and motives in this matter is insufficient and obscure. There may yet be some explanation which if discovered would exonerate him. But, as the evidence now stands, it appears that he floundered ; when the Prince sent for him and confessed the marriage, he was brought into deep waters before he had learnt to keep his feet.

Grey was from first to last on terms of intimate friendship with Fox and on bad terms with Sheridan ; with Burke he does not appear to have had any close relation at all. The Whig aristocrats are accused of keeping down Burke on account of his humble origin. If they did so they were to blame, though they were only carrying out Burke's own view of the Whig party, which he declared was and ought to be an ' aristocratic party,' in which the ' *new* men ' like himself ought to ' support those aristocratic principles, and the aristocratic interests connected with them.'[1]   But, in fact, the suspicion with which he was regarded in the party was due, at least in later years, rather to the violence and irresponsibility of his genius—qualities which were not, as in the case of Fox, redeemed by an irresistible charm.   After all, Burke did eventually break up the Whig party ; he was admitted into its bosom at least enough for that.   And even before the French Revolution, his habitual violence, as for instance in the Regency debates and the Warren Hastings trial, was the terror of his own side.   Bad as was the line adopted by Fox over the Regency, Burke had proposed a course yet more preposterous, and was deeply hurt when his extravagant advice was rejected.   ' Afterwards,' he complains, ' I was little consulted.'[2]

Genius, even of the first order, unless it is a genius essentially political rather than imaginative or philosophical, has no claim as of right to control the destinies of a party.   We may doubt whether, if Byron had survived, Grey would wisely have included him in the Reform Cabinet.   At the safe distance of five generations, Burke's imagination delights, elevates, and instructs us all.   But it was of that one-sided kind that ruins those who trust it in action.   As he grew older, it grew ever more splendid and ever more erratic. His imaginative conception of India deserves indeed all the gorgeous praise which has been bestowed on it ; but it was equalled by his total inability to grasp the character of Philip Francis, or the conditions under which Warren Hastings had been struggling to establish an Empire while serving a Company of

---

[1] Burke, *Correspondence*, 1844, iii. 388-9, January 1792.
[2] Burke, *Correspondence*, iii. 88-101, his letter to Windham of January 24, 1789.   Broughton (Hobhouse), *Recollections*, iii. 106.

traders. Burke's vision of the French Revolution was an equally striking and disastrous combination of prophetic insight and sheer blindness. The majority of the House of Commons, on both sides, felt the insanity of his genius growing as they listened to him year by year, and were ever more repelled by it, until the time came round when, being themselves shaken out of their customary good sense by the cataclysm of Old France, they and all Europe with them began to respond to his frenzied outcries for vengeance and for war.

In 1788 Grey had been associated with Burke, Fox, Sheridan, and the other managers of the ill-advised impeachment of Warren Hastings. The trial had only been going on for one of its seven years, when Fox and Grey already foresaw that Hastings would be acquitted, and desired to drop further proceedings. Pitt and the House of Commons, who had in the previous year consented to begin the impeachment and had named the Opposition chiefs as managers, in April 1789 passed a vote of censure on Burke for having called Warren Hastings the 'murderer' of Nuncomar. The whole course of the debate, and the refusal of the House to accompany the censure by any vote of encouragement or thanks, justified Fox in supposing that the impeachment was already thrown over by Pitt and his party, and that Hastings' acquittal was certain. Grey, writing to Allen in the year 1842, records that :

Fox and myself and others of the Committee of Managers felt very strongly the situation in which we were placed, and the little probability of bringing the trial to a successful issue.[1]

On the evening after the Commons' censure of Burke, Fox did not explain clearly to the other managers that he wanted to stop the trial ; but he seems to have

[1] In 1794 we read, in the betting book at Brooks's, in Grey's handwriting : ' Gen. Fitzpatrick bets Mr. Grey 10 guineas to 1 that Mr. Hastings is found guilty upon some part of the charges against him.'

expected that they would meet to settle the question early next day before the proceedings began.

The next morning [Grey continues] I went to Westminster Hall with Fox. On our way we of course talked the matter over, and the feeling of both remained as it had been the night before. On our arrival we found that the Managers had already been called over at the usual hour, and had proceeded to Westminster Hall. This of course decided the matter, though greatly to the disappointment both of Fox and myself, and we agreed to support Burke in the step he had taken.

If Fox had got up a little earlier than ' the usual hour ' that morning, Warren Hastings might have been spared the torture, and England the scandal, of six more years' trial. Lord Holland has left it on record that ' some slackness on the part of Grey and others ' in the prosecution of Hastings was one of the causes that alienated Burke from the party and fostered in him the suspicion that he was being neglected. This is borne out by Grey's narrative, which also proves that Fox himself was one of the ' others ' who became tired of the endless impeachment of a man already justly acquitted at the bar of opinion.[1]

In the spring of 1791 Pitt was preparing armaments against Russia, to prevent her from acquiring the district of Ocksakow from the Turks. Pitt's action is defended by his biographer,[2] because in Pitt's mind it formed part of a scheme to unite England with Prussia, and so to save Poland and the Baltic powers from Russian encroachment. But, unfortunately for the world, Prussia had far other views ; and our interference with Russia presented itself to the English people as a proposal for war, not on behalf of Poland, but on behalf of the Turk—' an anti-Crusade, for favouring barbarians and oppressing Christians,' as Burke called

[1] *Holland*, i. 9. Fox, *Memoirs*, ii. 355-9.
[2] Holland Rose, *Pitt and the National Revival*, chapters xxvi.-xxvii.

it in Gladstonian language. The Opposition for once was popular, since it resisted an adventure which interested but few people in our island. Grey took a leading part in the debates, and now acquired his profound hostility to the Turkish dominion in Europe, which served Greece well in 1830.[1] From this time forward till the end of his life Grey stands also as a firm advocate of peace. Of the eight resolutions that he moved on April 12, 1791, the first was : ' That it is at all times, and particularly under the present circumstances, the interest of this country to preserve peace.' He declared that to fight about Ocksakow was an abuse of the theory of the ' Balance of Power.'

Now that France has become no longer formidable, a rival is discovered in a corner of Europe. We are now to contend for forts on the Black Sea, as if we were fighting for our hearths and altars. This is a source of affliction to the peasant, and those who propose to lay new burdens on him for that purpose add insult to oppression.

The arguments are almost precisely those of John Bright in opposing the Crimean War, which is in turn defended on much the same grounds as Pitt's proposed interference about Ocksakow. In this speech of Grey's we seem to see the guiding principles of his life beginning to emerge out of the chaotic ambitions and partisanships of his early years.

---

1 See pp. 227–230, below.

CHAPTER II

THE FRIENDS OF THE PEOPLE

The trumpet of Liberty sounds through the world,
And the Universe starts at the sound ;
Her standard Philosophy's hand has unfurled,
And the nations are thronging around.

> *Chorus :* Fall, tyrants ! fall ! fall ! fall !
> These are the days of liberty !
> Fall, tyrants, fall !

Proud castles of despotism, dungeons and cells,
The tempest shall sweep you away.
From the east to the west the dread hurricane swells,
And the tyrants are filled with dismay.

Poor vassals who crawl by the Vistula's stream,
Hear ! hear the glad call and obey !
Rise, nations ! who worship the sun and the beams,
And drive your Pizarros away.

Shall Britons the chorus of Liberty hear
With a cold and insensible mind ?
No—the triumphs of freedom each Briton shall hear,
And contend for the rights of mankind.

(Written by Mr. John Taylor of Norwich, and first sung at the famous Whig banquet at Holkham given by Coke of Norfolk to celebrate the centenary of the English Revolution, Nov. 5, 1788.)

DURING the years immediately preceding the French Revolution, Pitt's enemies are too often found standing for no principle higher than factious opposition. But ' the times that try men's souls ' were now to prove that the Whig party was still the seed-bed of principles that contained the future ; while the forces on which Pitt depended for power had, when brought to the test, no thought or help for the new era, struggling to be born, except dull resistance to all change. As soon as the French Revolution and the democratic movement that answered to it in this island had made the issues real, the Tory party was found to be solid in favour of repressive measures and against Parliamentary Reform. The Whigs were divided, but owing mainly to Fox, and not a little to Grey, the nucleus of the party was secured for the cause of progress. It was Portland and the Burkite Whigs who seceded and merged their identity in the Tory ranks ; while the fifty M.P.'s and half-dozen peers who stood, disarmed and apparently helpless, beneath Fox's tattered banner, were constituting the party destined to reform England and govern her during the best half of the coming century. Their action, though it appeared to many then, and appears to some now, as unpatriotic and seditious, laid down the lines of modern politics in our island, and provided a Parliamentary channel through which the democratic ferment going on underground could in the end rise to the surface without a convulsion fatal to the commonwealth. The story of the anti-Jacobin and democratic movements of the 'nineties, and the position of the Foxite Whigs in relation to the two, is of greater interest than any part of our later political history until the Reform Bill itself. In the last decade of the eighteenth century, the times, if tragic, were great, and the leaders on each side, though far from impeccable, had the genius and the manhood to play great parts in the great manner.

Why was it that half the Whigs, in spite of the ' aristocratic ' character of their party, stood for liberty and enfranchisement when the rest of the upper classes were seized by a reactionary panic ? There was a soul in the Whig party that Carlton House could degrade but could not kill ; it was alive even during the winter

of the Regency debates. That soul was an idealised and
traditional love of liberty. Coleridge was surprised that
so aristocratic a lady as Georgiana, Duchess of Devonshire, should write verses to celebrate William Tell's
defiance of the tyrant.

> O Lady, nursed in pomp and pleasure !
> Whence learn'd you that heroic measure ?

So the poet asked. The true answer would have been
that the Duchess was bred in the Whig tradition, which
fostered an ideal passion for the overthrow of tyrants.

The tradition of the party started from the solid
achievement of the destruction of Stuart despotism.
This, to the Whigs, was the central event of history.
They seem to have regarded Hampden as the first
Whig, and Milton as the party laureate. Cromwell
was still ' a fiend hid in a cloud ' : the deed for which
they were constrained to condemn him was yet his dark
title to glory. He had ' ga'ed Kings to ken they had
a crick in their neck.' Whig tradition, so confident
on other subjects, never quite knew what to make of
Oliver. It was a relief to turn to the Revolution of
1688, and to celebrate that.

During the long, corrupting domination of the
party in the days of Walpole and his successors, the
Whig soul nearly died of fatness. But it was purified
and revived in the uphill battle against George III, by
the moral and intellectual splendour of Burke, and by
sympathy with the American Revolution. Whiggism
began to take on a less insular form, partly from the
act of looking across the Atlantic, partly under the
influence of the cosmopolitan ' Philosophy ' of that era.
Yet it always remained an unique British product. Its
religious toleration and dislike of ' priestcraft ' is Locke's
or Priestley's, not Voltaire's. Vague modern hopes of
liberty for all mankind blend with a hearty English
pride in ourselves, as the pioneers who had long ago
hewn out the path still to be traversed by less favoured

nations. When, in November 1788, the centenary of the British Revolution was celebrated by the party whose chief asset was that somewhat too immortal memory, the younger Whigs were generously stirred by the prologue to the French Revolution then enacting across the Channel. In accepting the invitation to the Centenary banquet at Holkham, Windham writes to Coke, ' a festival to celebrate the Revolution is a proper reception for a person just come from France.' [1]

It was at this banquet that the song, ' Fall, tyrants, fall ! ' was first sung.[2] The words, with their pathetic faith in the near future of mankind, perpetuate that fleeting hour of exaltation, when the traditions of the Whig party and the aspirations of the age of enlightenment seemed about to be realised together, first in France and then over all the world. Such were the ideas, or rather the ideals, which prepared the minds of Fox and Grey to sympathise with the French Revolution, to demand civic rights for Dissenters and Roman Catholics, to protect free speech and free association, and to support the movement for Parliamentary Reform even when it assumed the novel shape of a claim put forward by the working men.

The agitation for Parliamentary Reform in the last quarter of the eighteenth century falls into three periods, under the leadership of three distinct classes. First, there is the movement of the Yorkshire Freeholders, patronised by half the Whig party, which culminated in Pitt's Reform Bill of 1785 and declined after its rejection. Secondly, there is the movement led by the philosophic Dissenters, which we may call the ' Bastille' movement ; it was crushed by the Birmingham riots of 1791. The third movement was that of the working

---

[1] Oct. 18, 1788. *Coke of Norfolk*, p. 217. Windham at this time was what he himself would afterwards have called ' a Jacobin.'

[2] Printed at head of this chapter.

men of industrial London and the provinces, inspired by Paine, organised by Hardy in 1792, and forcibly suppressed by Pitt in the next half-dozen years. Contemporary with this last and most significant phase is the Parliamentary Whig movement led by Grey, protected by Fox, and organised in the short-lived but important Society of the Friends of the People.

The original Reform movement of the Yorkshire Freeholders had been Old English in its aims and methods. It was not cosmopolitan in its outlook ; nor was it ' democratic ' in the modern use of the word, for the economic changes of the Industrial Revolution had not then created the ' democracy ' that we know. It was an union under Whig aristocratic patronage of those old-fashioned ' freeholders,' the middle classes of town and country, who had beaten the Stuart Kings. They demanded Parliamentary Reform, not with a general view of elevating the lower class or of enriching the poor, but to attain good government for the nation as a whole. The movement had, in fact, been provoked by George III, and was intended to put an end to his personal rule exercised through the nominated and bribed majority of the House of Commons. The object was to restore the old English constitution, corrupted by time and evil counsellors.

It was almost as much a movement of occasion as of principle. When, therefore, the rule of the ' King's Friends ' came to an end, after 1782, and when the disasters and miseries of the American war were being repaired by the healing policy of Pitt as peace Minister, the agitation lost so much of its force that Pitt threw it over, after a half-hearted attempt at a Reform Bill in 1785. Wyvill and Major Cartwright, deeply disappointed by Pitt's desertion and by the collapse of their once powerful movement, survived to attach themselves to the more democratic aspirations of the coming epoch.

The second era of the Reform movement covers

the years immediately preceding and following the fall of the Bastille. The leadership lies with the philosophic Dissenters, Price and Priestley. Pitt not only dropped Parliamentary Reform, but in 1787, and again in 1789, he opposed the abolition of the Test and Corporation Acts which debarred Dissenters and Roman Catholics from civil rights. Fox, on the other hand, warmly espoused the cause of religious freedom, and asserted the modern principle that ' religion is not a proper test for a political institution.' In these Test Act debates, which precede the French Revolution, we have the first clear indication that Fox was capable of founding modern Liberalism, and Pitt that extravagant Toryism that was killed by the Reform Bill.

The leading Dissenters, now hopeless of relief from Pitt or from the existing House of Commons, began to agitate for Parliamentary Reform as a step necessary to their own civil enfranchisement. Dissenters and Parliamentary Reformers alike were alienated from Pitt and, in spite of the unsavoury memories of the Coalition and of the Regency debates, began with caution to draw towards Fox and the more liberal section of the Whigs. In this juncture of our affairs, the news from France began to affect the political imagination of Englishmen. France, not yet drenched with blood, had replaced a despotism by a constitutional monarchy, and was framing a code of laws which put men of every creed on the same platform of civil rights. The more progressive members of the Whig party, including Fox and Grey, were at one with the philosophic Dissenters in acclaiming the dawn of world-wide political enfranchisement and religious equality, while Burke, who already heard the fall of civilisation in the falling stones of the Bastille, flung himself against Price and the Unitarian Reformers with all the heaviest weapons of his splendid armoury.

Burke's ' Reflections on the French Revolution ' (Nov. 1790), whatever its author may have intended, appealed to passions only less cruel, and certainly more unprovoked, than those which he justly execrated in the French mob. It was an angel's trumpet, but it roused the fiends.

An unreasoned hatred of Dissenters, common in the higher orders of society and locally in the slum population, was stirred to fury as the result direct and indirect of the writings of Burke, who also denounced the Parliamentary Reformers and friends of the French Revolution. In the long battle between Reformers and anti-Reformers, that began with the Birmingham riots of 1791 and ended with the passing of Lord Grey's Reform Bill, the combatants drew much of their devotion and most of their cruelty from sectarian zeal—except in Scotland, where the fires of political hatred could be thrice heated without the bellows of religion. The more we study the local details of this forty years' war over which Grey spent his life so loftily presiding, the more does the sectarian aspect emerge. For example, the volumes in the British Museum of the correspondence of Reeves' ' Loyal ' Association of 1792 reveal how largely the Reform movement in particular towns and villages was an effort of Dissenters, and how much the counteracting ' loyalist ' movement was set on foot by churchmen and clergymen, in a panic of the old Dr. Sacheverel type, intensified by the news from France. In 1831 we find the same sectarian cleavage, except that then the Church clergy were deserted politically by their congregations, and the mob of Birmingham had gone round *en masse* to Reform.

The ministers of a State Church have a natural bent and perhaps an obligation to emphasise the conservative side of life. But the degree to which the Church clergy of that era were conservative is not easily credible to-day, when so many clergymen endeavour to see through the eyes of their parishioners in working-class districts, which their predecessors contemptuously left to the care of dissenting preachers.

In the sleepy days of the eighteenth century, laymen complacently regarded the parson as the chartered tithe-eater, and he often regarded himself primarily as the possessor of a snug freehold. When the old order began to change, when news came over of Church spoliation in France, and men discussed in alehouses what the community got from the parsons in return for so many tithe-sheaves and tithe-pigs, the clergy took serious alarm, and, as frightened men will do, too often made a virtue of the most unchristian actions against their neighbours. In the earlier age of good-nature and enlightenment, Dr. Johnson's attitude to Dissenters reads as an amusing idiosyncrasy ; when we see the word ' Dissenter ' coming below on the page, we know we are in for sport. But there was nothing amusing in the treatment of Dissenters in town and country during the iron age ushered in by the Birmingham riots of July 1791.

Priestley was a scientist of European reputation in an age when scientists were few. He was a man of blameless life and high public spirit. He was not a Republican, but he was a Dissenter—nay, a Unitarian —and he was now active in favour of Parliamentary Reform and Repeal of the Test Acts, and in public approval of the general course of the French Revolution up to the summer of 1791. Therefore his house and scientific instruments were destroyed by the ' Church and State ' mob of Birmingham, who had been incited against Nonconformists by sermons and pamphlets of the local clergy, and were personally encouraged on the night of riot by two J.P.'s. Dissenting chapels and the private houses of Dissenters as blameless and as unpolitical as the local historian William Hutton, were destroyed, with every appearance of connivance on the part of the Magistrates.[1]

[1] The most intimate account of the affair is in the *Life of W. Hutton*, 1816.

This action was hailed with delight by many who should have known better. The men who were rallying to protect ' property ' meant only the property of Churchmen, and those who denounced ' the swinish multitude ' in the abstract, rejoiced in the mob-law of Birmingham. The Marquis of Buckingham wrote to his brother Lord Grenville, the Foreign Secretary : ' I am not sorry for this excess, excessive as it has been '; and Lord Auckland, the British Ambassador at the Hague, wrote to him in a similar strain. Grenville himself expressed disapproval of the riots, but Pitt said nothing, and voted against Whitbread's motion for enquiry. Fox, with Grey and his Eton friends, Lambton and Whitbread, stood up in vain for justice. The motion for enquiry was lost by 189 votes to 46. In the course of the debate Grey said :

> It was not a political, but a religious mob, actuated by the most horrid and sanguinary spirit of bigotry and persecution. Many other houses belonging to persons known to entertain the same religious sentiments with Dr. Priestley were set on fire and destroyed amidst the acclamations of *Church and King for ever ! Down with the Presbyterians !* and the French Revolution appeared plainly to have been not the real cause but merely the pretext of these horrid devastations.

Such was the way in which the most learned and respectable men in England were treated if they happened to be Dissenters and to advocate Parliamentary Reform. The riots took place more than a year before the fall of the French Monarchy and the September massacres, and a year and a half before the outbreak of the war between England and France, which has been pleaded as a sufficient excuse for the whole spirit and system of persecution of Liberal opinions in this epoch. Indeed, more than six months after the Birmingham riots, Pitt declared in the House of Commons that we might ' reasonably expect fifteen years of peace.'

The spirit of religious and political bigotry was

now thoroughly aroused. The authorities, both local and central, smiled on outrage. More orthodox Dissenters were scarcely less obnoxious than Unitarians, and not a few were forced to abandon their business and follow Priestley across the Atlantic. The second phase of the Reform Movement, as championed by the Dissenters in the palmy days of the fall of the Bastille, may be said to have been put down before the end of 1791. Early in the following year a more significant agitation was begun by a class of men who had never yet acted in politics on their own behalf—the working men in the great towns.

The democratic movement in England—that is to say, the claim put forward by the common people themselves that they should choose their governors in order to improve their own conditions of life—owed its origin to the spectacle of the French Revolution and to the writings of Tom Paine. And the same causes that gave it birth proved in the first instance its undoing. The forcible suppression for so many years of the English movement was rendered possible by the course of the foreign revolution that aroused it, and by the impolitic and uncompromising logic of its first champion.

Paine was an English Quaker by origin. But he had early settled in America, where his pamphlet 'Common Sense' had done much to persuade the colonists to cut the knot of their difficulties with England by declaring themselves an independent republic. Paine was again in England, and as soon as he read Burke's 'Reflections on the French Revolution' he sat down to write a reply. The First Part of the 'Rights of Man' appeared in February 1791.

In answer to Burke's ultra-conservative doctrine, which tended to bind up the English constitution for ever by the pact of 1689, Paine stated the full democratic thesis : that government is derived from the people, can be altered at their will, and must be carried on for their benefit, through a system of popular representation. The pamphlet circulated by tens of thousands among classes who hitherto knew nothing of politics, save when at election time ' the quality ' dispensed beer and money to make a mob for the hustings. The idea that politics was an affair of the common people as such, and a means by which they could alleviate their poverty, was new and strange. But the events in France had roused our ancestors to unwonted mental activity, and in 1791-2 Burke and Paine were read and discussed with the simple eagerness natural to men plunged for the first time into political speculation. It was a fine and well-matched debate, in which the mind and character of Englishmen were expanding, certainly not all in one direction. But one of the two protagonists unworthily appealed to have his rival lynched : Burke declared that the proper way to reply to Paine was by ' criminal justice.'

Government, however, declined, in spite of much shrill advice, to prosecute the First Part of the ' Rights of Man,' where the author had not clearly drawn out all the inferences of his representative theory of government. But in the Second Part, published in February 1792, Paine's logical sword came right out of the scabbard. He claimed that all the hereditary elements in the constitution, both Monarchy and House of Lords, ought to be abolished, and the country governed by its representatives alone, sitting either in one or two Chambers. Government would then be carried on for the benefit of the mass of the people. Pensions on the taxes now granted to the rich would be diverted, and used, together with a graduated income-tax, to give education to the poor, old age pensions, and maternity benefit.

Far the greater number of Paine's ' criminal ' propositions are accomplished facts of the present day.

The only part of the ' Rights of Man ' that can possibly be called seditious lies in its Republicanism. Yet surely Major Cartwright put the true case, when he said at Horne Tooke's trial that he ' did not consider Paine's writings as a conspiracy to overthrow government, but as discussions on the subject of government.' Paine had not advised conspiracy or rebellion. The country would have sifted out for itself what it wanted in Paine's doctrine and rejected the rest, as indeed it has since done. But the controversy was cut short : the Government prosecuted and suppressed the ' Rights of Man,' and Paine, warned in time by his friend, the poet Blake, fled for his life to France, where he shortly got into trouble by denouncing the Terror and endeavouring to save the life of Louis XVI.

Paine had most rashly identified his theory of representative government with a scheme of rigid Republicanism. For many years to come this confusion continued in the common mind. Even Francis Place, speaking of the workmen's clubs of that era, writes, ' All the leading members of the London Corresponding Society were *Republicans ; that is, they were friendly to a representative form of government.*' This confusion of terms seems ridiculous to us, who are long accustomed to representative government in the form of a constitutional monarchy. But we can understand how the confusion came about, if we examine what was then the practice of the constitution, and what was the theory of it held by Paine's enemies. The royal and aristocratic party in England spoke of the existing constitution as the ' direct contrary ' of democratic or representative. For example, in 1794, Pitt's attorney-general, Sir John Scott, better known by his later title of Lord Eldon, tried to get Thomas Hardy, the founder of the Corresponding Society, condemned to death for high treason on the ground that the object of the Corresponding Society was ' to form a representative government in this country '—' *a representative government, the direct*

contrary of the government which is established here.[1] The
forms of our constitution have altered so little since then,
that we fail to remember how completely its spirit and
practice have changed, and hence we often misjudge
the men and controversies of that time.

In advising the English to abolish the form of
monarchy, Paine made a ruinous mistake ; he was too
much of an American, a theorist, a 'friend of the human
race,' and altogether too little of an Englishman to see
that his Republican logic would not apply to our island.
But the error was not as gratuitous as it would be to-day.
Monarchy in the reign of George III was very different
from monarchy in the reign of George V.   George III
had lost us America, and was destined to prevent the
reconciliation of Ireland.   He stood in the way of the
abolition of the slave trade, and of any chance of
parliamentary reform.   Grey was no Republican, but
there was probably a good deal in common between
what Grey said in private and what Paine said in public
about the powers enjoyed by the inhabitant of Buckingham Palace—'the gentleman at the end of the Mall,'
as he was called by the Whigs.[2]

The Whigs ultimately reduced the power of the
Crown by the Reform Bill, and by instilling their
doctrines into the youthful Queen Victoria.   But in
1792 they had no remedy.   Those of them who would
not follow Burke into the Tory camp found it impossible
to dissociate themselves in the public mind from Tom
Paine.   For years he stuck to everything Liberal like
a burr.   Either you were for 'the good old King,' or
else you were set down as a rebel and a Painite.   The
man in the street, as he gazed through the shop windows
at Gillray's cartoons, began to think of the Foxite
Whigs as people in red caps of liberty intent on beheading George III and setting up a ragged Republic.

---

[1] *State Trials*, xxiv. pp. 294–5.
[2] See *Creevey*, ed. 1903, i. 118–19.

At this stage in our affairs, in the early months of 1792, while the Second Part of the 'Rights of Man' was appearing, and men were choosing their sides at the dictation of the most extravagant hopes and fears about the new era, two societies sprang into being, the outcome of that year's turmoil of all England thinking. Thomas Hardy, the shoemaker, founded the Corresponding Society, while Grey and his young Parliamentary allies founded the Friends of the People. Both societies were short-lived, but one of them was the origin of the future Radical, and the other of the Whig-Liberal party. They stood for two principles of progress familiar in English history—the people helping themselves, and a minority of the governing class helping the people.

Thomas Hardy's Corresponding Society was the first political and educational club of working men. It supplied the natural leaders of that class with the opportunity to emerge and lead, with the means of study and debate, and with an embryo organisation. There was then little Trade Union life except of a purely economic character ; no Co-operative Society life, and no higher education for the working class ; and therefore the Corresponding Society was as important in its moral and intellectual as in its political aspects. If it had not been crushed by the authorities, it would have done a still greater work and would early have stimulated other movements in working-class life, that began many years too late. Its political programme was Universal Suffrage and Annual Parliaments—that, and nothing more.[1] Its members did, in fact, circulate Paine's works, and most of them were theoretically Republicans ; but it was Parliamentary Reform that they worked for as the practical object.

Hardy and his friends were Londoners. London was then more Radical than the North, perhaps because

---

[1] *Place Papers*, Add. MSS., B.M., *passim*, e.g. 35142, ff. 236–7 ; 27814, ff. 31–2. Wallas' *Place*, Veitch's *Genesis of Parliamentary Reform*, and P. A. Brown's *French Revolution in English History*, 1918.

the Westminster and Middlesex elections, held on a democratic franchise and enlivened by Wilkes and by Fox, had accustomed the inhabitants of the capital to watch real political contests, unknown in most towns before the Reform Bill. At this time the working men in Lancashire were still for ' Church and State ' ; the year after the Birmingham riots the Manchester mob imitatively wrecked houses of Dissenters and bourgeois Reformers. But the Tom Paine movement, working through the Corresponding Society and the somewhat more middle-class Society for Constitutional Information, acted from London, Sheffield, and Norwich on the rest of England, and sowed broadcast the ideas that re-emerged in the days of Peterloo as the Radical creed of the working men in Lancashire and the industrial north.

Such were the origins of the new Tory and of the Radical parties, between which Grey spent the rest of his life in steering a middle course. Under the impulse of the French Revolution, Burke had been able to indoctrinate the governing classes with the theory on which they acted for the next generation, namely, that the British Constitution was not only perfect, but unalterable ; and that everyone who advised his countrymen to alter it was a proper subject for ' criminal justice.' Meanwhile Paine and Hardy had roused a portion of the working classes to demand Universal Suffrage, with the avowed purpose of improving the lot of the poor, and a more vague intention of some day establishing a Republic. In the long middle years of his life, Grey with his Whig party was stranded so precisely midway between this new Toryism and this new Radicalism, that he had small influence on the course of affairs. But in 1792-7, and again in 1830-2, he was more nearly allied to the Radicals than to the Tories, and it was on those two occasions that he made history.

The action from which the rest of Grey's life flows, and from which the Whig-Liberal party takes its origin, was the founding of the Friends of the People in April 1792. It was this that broke up the old Whig party on domestic issues, a year before the war with France. There had been no split in 1791, when Burke renounced his friendship with Fox on the floor of the House, in a heated controversy on the merits of the French Revolution. At that time the majority of the Whig Members, preferring Fox to Burke personally, regarded the views of both on the French question as extravagant, and refused to quarrel among themselves about the internal affairs of a foreign country. The incident had left Burke more angry and more isolated than before.[1] That year he left Brooks's Club, to which all sections of the party belonged. The split in the party itself did not come till twelve months later, when Grey founded the Friends of the People. It was that act of Grey's which drove the anti-Reform section under the Duke of Portland to concert measures with Pitt against their fellow Whigs. Fox was thereby compelled to choose whether in the future he would work only with the Reformers or only with the anti-Reformers of his party. He had hoped against hope to avoid making the choice, but he had no doubt how to choose, if choose he must.

In this matter of the Friends of the People Grey did not follow Fox, but Fox followed Grey, to protect him from the consequences of an action of which Fox approved the purpose but disallowed the wisdom. This is the meaning of the passage in Lord Holland's ' Memoirs,' where ' the nephew of Fox and friend of Grey ' tells us that :

Mr. Grey felt additional attachment to Mr. Fox and zeal for his party, from an apprehension, suggested by his warm, susceptible, and generous temper, that much of the obloquy cast

[1] *Sir G. Elliot's Letters,* ii. pp. 7–9, 102–3.

on the party was founded on measures of which he had been the author, and from gratitude for the noble and unaffected disinterestedness and spirit with which Mr. Fox had vindicated his conduct and supported him against the aspersions even of some of his oldest adherents.

If Fox had declined to throw his shield over the Friends of the People, they and not the Portland Whigs would have had to go.   For Fox was the Whig party, with whomsoever he chose to abide.   In siding with Reform he destroyed his own career and his good name in the world, but he prevented the Whigs from becoming bottle-holders to the Tories, and so enabled England, many years after his own death, to obtain Reform without Revolution.

These transactions require to be followed in some detail.   Considering the importance in our political history of the founding of the Friends of the People, which broke up the Old and originated the New Whigs, it is curious how little record we have of the first conception of the plan.   Lord Lauderdale and Philip Francis were, with Grey, the moving spirits ; Grey put his name first on the list of the Associators [1] and acted as their Parliamentary spokesman.   But Grey himself has told us little about it.   In the very last years of his long life he repented of the action, on the ground that it had linked him with extremists, although he never repented of the principles of Parliamentary Reform, which alone the Society was founded to promote.   In his last illness (1845) he told his son that ' one word from Mr. Fox would have kept me out of all the mess of the Friends

---

[1] The ' Association ' and ' Associators ' are the words used for the Society of Friends of the People and its members in the correspondence and speeches of the year 1792.   It will be seen that the list of their names, about 150 in all, contains no one but ' gentlemen,' and that there were originally twenty-eight Members of Parliament, five of whom resigned in June.   Their full proceedings can be read in the *Wyvill Papers*, iii. Appendix, pp. 128-292 ;   pp. 128-31 give the list, and pp. 169-71 the five who were expunged from the list on resignation.

of the People, but he never spoke it.'[1] But when, still in the fulness of his powers, he was introducing the Reform Bill into the House of Lords as Prime Minister, in 1831, he had spoken to their lordships with pride of his connection with the Friends of the People as 'not at all inconsistent' with the great measure he was then proposing.[2]

We have two accounts of the inception of the Friends of the People prior to the official meeting at which it was constituted, on April 11. There is on the one hand the hostile tradition of Holland House that represents it as an after-dinner freak of irresponsible young aristocrats.[3] On the other hand there is the friendly narrative of Thomas Hardy the shoemaker, who had founded the Corresponding Society a few months before ; to him the foundation of the Friends of the People seemed the generous act of young men of rank, ready to lend a hand to the democratic movement beginning in the lower classes of society. The view of Lord and Lady Holland, and the view of Thomas Hardy, may both have some element of truth, but, as is often the case, the more sympathetic account has the most real insight. The list of some hundred and fifty original Associators contains many honoured names of men who were much more than boon companions engaged in a foolish freak.

The London Corresponding Society [wrote its founder, Hardy] were encouraged by such men [as the *Friends of the People*]

---

[1] On the other hand, in June 1792, only three months after the foundation of the Society, Mr. Thomas Pelham wrote to Lady Webster : 'Fox told me that he had never been consulted about it, and that, on the contrary, the Associators seemed determined *not to have any advice*, and particularly not to *have his*. This I know to be true, for Lauderdale told me that they were determined not to consult Fox until they saw the probability of success, in order that he might not be involved if they failed' (*Lady Holland's Journal*, i. p. 15, note).

[2] *Hansard*, Oct. 7, 1831, p. 313.

[3] Holland, *Memoirs*, i. 13–14 ; and *Lady Holland's Journal*, i. 101.

stepping forward in the same cause, professing to have the same object in view, which caused the people to flock in astonishing numbers to the *Corresponding Society* ; they began to be very sanguine in their hope of success by such a respectable number of members of the House of Commons coming voluntarily forward in that cause which we were embarked in. The society of *Friends of the People* were likewise encouraged to proceed by such large numbers of the industrious lower and middle classes of society which were associating in London and various parts of the country for a reform in Parliament.[1]

Thus for a short while shoemaker Hardy's club of working men, each paying a penny a week, and Grey's association of gentlemen, each paying two and a half guineas a year, grew and flourished by indirect mutual encouragement, though without any actual communication. And later in the year there grew up, in various cities of Great Britain, other democratic societies, answering in social and political character to the Corresponding Society rather than to Grey's association, but calling themselves ' Friends of the People,' in embarrassing compliment to that highly respectable body. The furious outburst of rage, in Parliament and among the upper classes generally, against Grey's association, can only be accounted for by the example these much-abused gentlemen set to the lower orders. For, apart from the moral support which their mere existence as a society lent to the more democratic clubs, there was nothing that differentiated the Friends of the People from the Reform associations to which Pitt and the Whig chiefs had belonged without censure a dozen years before. Not only did the Friends of the People not circulate Paine's writings, but they expressly repudiated his views.[2] Their two objects were :

First.—To restore the Freedom of Election, and a more equal Representation of the People in Parliament.

[1] *Place Papers*, Add. MSS., B.M., 27814, ff. 32–4.
[2] *Wyvill*, iii. Appendix, pp. 149–69.

Secondly.—To secure to the People a more frequent exercise of their Right of Electing their Representatives.

They never had, either officially or actually, any other object. The language of their Address to the People of Great Britain, adopted on April 26, was unexceptionable. After quoting as their predecessors in the movement ' Mr. Locke and Judge Blackstone, the late Earl of Chatham, the Duke of Richmond, Mr. Pitt, and Mr. Fox,' they proceed :

The example and situation of another Kingdom [France] are held out to deter us from innovations of any kind. We say that the Reforms we have in view are not innovations. Our intention is not to change, but to restore ; not to displace, but to reinstate the Constitution upon its true principles and original ground. We deny the existence of any resemblance whatever between the cases of the two Kingdoms ; and we utterly disclaim the necessity of resorting to similar remedies. Our general object is to recover and preserve the true balance of the Constitution. These are the Principles of our Association.

Resolved unanimously :

That a motion be made in the House of Commons, at an early period in the next Session of Parliament, for introducing a Parliamentary Reform.

Resolved unanimously :

That Charles Grey, Esq., be requested to make, and the Hon. Thomas Erskine to second, the above motion.[1]

Four days later (April 30, 1792) Grey rose in the House of Commons to give notice of the motion for a Reform of Parliament to be introduced for ' the next session.' Since a whole year was to elapse before he brought in his motion, he only said a few words in thus giving notice, and those words were certainly not provocative, except to persons who had come there to be provoked. He quoted Mr. Pitt as his predecessor in Parliamentary Reform. ' It is of the utmost importance,' he said, ' that the House should enjoy the good

---

[1] *Wyvill*, iii. Appendix, pp. 129, 139–44.

opinion of the public and possess their confidence as a true representation of the people.' ' The loss of that character might produce all the miseries of civil commotion.' If there were those who wished to excite such commotion, he disclaimed all connection with them, and believed that ' the evils threatening the constitution can only be removed by a timely and temperate Reform.'

It was then that Pitt first appeared in the full character of alarmist. As soon as Grey sat down, the Prime Minister was on his feet, talking of ' anarchy and confusion worse, if possible, than despotism itself.' Reform in Parliament might be well enough if everyone agreed to it, ' but I confess I am afraid, at this moment, that if agreed on by this House the security of all the blessings we enjoy will be shaken to the foundation.' Then he turned on the Friends of the People : ' I have seen with concern that the gentlemen of whom I speak who are Members of this House are connected with others who profess not Reform only but direct hostility to the very form of government. This affords suspicion that the motion for a Reform is nothing more than the preliminary to the overthrow of the whole system of government.'

There was yet no question of an approaching war with France ; it was not alluded to as a remote possibility, and Pitt had two months before declared his expectation of fifteen years' peace. In accusing Grey of the intention to ' overthrow the whole system of government,' because he made a proposal for Parliamentary Reform in the same spirit that he himself had made it seven years before, Pitt was acting as ' factiously ' in his own party interest as ever Fox had done, and with a want of generosity that Fox would never have displayed.

The moment that Pitt sat down Fox leapt up to defend Grey, and the split in the Whig party had begun. In the following month of May the divisions among the Whigs were further increased by a Royal Proclamation

drawn up by Pitt against ' seditious writings,' in terms
so indefinite that they might seem to apply either to
Tom Paine or to the Friends of the People or to both;[1]
all sections of Reformers were confounded together and
held up to public infamy.   ' You have seen the Proclamation, of course,' wrote the Archbishop of Canterbury
to Lord Auckland ; ' the prevailing opinion about it at
present is that it seems to admit more disposition in
the country to tumult than exists in fact.'   To this
alarmist Proclamation Pitt invited the Duke of Portland,
as Head of the Opposition, to lend his countenance and
support.   The Duke was the titular head of the party
that had hitherto been led by Fox.   He at once
acquainted the latter with Pitt's communication, but
Fox ' said he saw no danger to warrant any unusual
measure, and declined taking any part in support of
what is proposed, in Parliament or elsewhere.'   A
meeting of Opposition Members was therefore held
without Fox[2] at the Duke of Portland's mansion,
Burlington House, which became for the rest of the
year the stately scene of an historic tragedy—a great
party in dissolution.   When the Duke of Bedford came
to this meeting he looked round for Mr. Fox.   On being
informed he ' was not likely to come,' he drily observed,
' Then I am sure I have nothing to do here,' and left
the room.   So the house of Russell once more chose
the side of freedom and popular rights in a new age
and on new issues.   When the Duke took up his hat
and stalked out of Burlington House, he began a new
roll of honour for his family, though well-nigh forty
years were to pass before the famous night when his
nephew read the list of doomed boroughs, from the
bench where Pitt had once sat supreme.

[1] Add. MSS., B.M., 35154, ff. 29–31.
[2] *Elliot*, ii. 30; Holland, *Memoirs*, i. 15–16.   According to *Malmesbury* (ii. 424), Fox ' was present, but declared against ' the Proclamation.
There may have been two Burlington House meetings on the Proclamation—one with and one without Fox.

Those who remained in the room under Portland's chairmanship took the draft of the Government's Proclamation against 'seditious writings,' and at Sir Gilbert Elliot's suggestion made a number of alterations in it afterwards accepted by Pitt. Although the Portland Whigs did not take office for two more years, they had now practically joined the Ministerial party. They were well contented with their work.

You will perceive [wrote Sir Gilbert Elliot] that there is a schism in the party. I flatter myself I am in much the most numerous, as well as respectable, side. . . . What has passed on the subject of the Association [Friends of the People] and the Proclamation has obtained the greatest possible credit with the country and the House for the Portland part of our party, and will go further than anything that could have happened to reconcile both King and people to that branch of us.

He speaks of the other side as ' Grey and his party ' ; ' Fox,' he says, ' is in a difficult and uncomfortable position. He endeavours to trim, which is not natural to him and he does not do it well. He does not sign the Association on the one hand, but on the other he defends it.'

The position thus correctly described by Elliot was further emphasised by a debate in both Houses on the Proclamation, when Grey boldly defended the Friends of the People against an angry House. In the Lords' debate, the event of the evening was a generous pronouncement in favour of Grey by the ablest man in the Chamber, the Marquis of Lansdowne, better known and more disliked in Whig annals under the name of Lord Shelburne. He had long been connected with the Grey family and had taken a fancy for young Charles Grey, who now helped to effect a personal and political reconciliation between him and Fox.[1] If it had taken place ten years before, history would

---

[1] Holland, *Memoirs*, i. 43–5. *Parl. Hist.*, xxix. p. 1526.

have been very different. And so, at the end of May 1792, the session was wound up.

Grey thought all his life long, and his biographer may be allowed to think, that the fears to which Pitt so ably appealed were, as regards our island, wholly unfounded ; that our affairs had no analogy with those of France ; and that a moderate Reform of Parliament in the early 'nineties would have saved England from untold evils in the next forty years, and would have united her as one man against any possible foreign foe.[1] But the fears that prevented this consummation, though they often had a large alloy of base self-interest, and of purposeful exaggeration, were with many as genuine and deep as fears can be. Their nature and force must be understood by the reader who seeks the springs of action in this terrible period of our history. The prevailing panic finds fair expression in the private correspondence of two men as shrewd and as little given to lose their balance as Gibbon and his friend Lord Sheffield. On May 30, 1792, the historian, writing from Lausanne, comments on Grey's notice of motion for Parliamentary Reform :

I shuddered at Grey's motion, disliked the half-support of Fox, admired the firmness of Pitt's declaration, and excused the usual intemperance of Burke. Surely such men as Grey, Sheridan, Erskine have talents for mischief. . . . Do not suffer yourselves to be lulled into a false security ; remember the proud fabric of the French Monarchy. Not four years ago it stood founded, as it might seem, on the rock of time, force and opinion, supported by the triple Aristocracy of the Church, the Nobility and the Parliaments. They are crumbled into dust ; they are vanished from the earth. If this tremendous warning has no effect on the men of property in England ; if it does not open every eye and raise every arm, you will deserve your fate.

---

[1] This view was held in later years by Pitt's ' good angel ' Wilberforce. See *Private Papers of William Wilberforce* (1897), pp. 73-4, in his remarkable ' Sketch of Pitt.'

To this Lord Sheffield replies :

I am fully convinced that if our Good Old Island had been drawn into the torrent of the new philosophy, Holland, Germany, Spain, etc., would have followed her, and we should have seen all Europe involved in the extravagances of irreligion, immorality, anarchy, and barbarism. . . . The devastation of the Species might be repaired, and at the end of a couple of centuries it is possible that Science, the fine Arts, and the politeness and gentleness of Society might again have been brought to the point at which they now are. Perhaps you may recollect that on the Decline and Fall of the Roman Empire a greater number of centuries was necessary for restoration. I really believe there is nothing exaggerated in this speculation.

Having these opinions, I highly approved and cordially promoted the conduct of Opposition at such a crisis. They have come to the aid of Government fairly and unreservedly, and many even zealously, particularly the Dukes of Portland, Devonshire, Lord Fitzwilliam, Guildford, Spencer, Egremont, Ashburnham, Stormont, Loughborough, Windham of Norfolk, Sir Gilbert Elliot, in short almost everybody except about a score who had committed themselves with Mr. Grey, many of whom are heartily sick of the business. The attempt at an Association has in truth had an excellent effect. It has alarmed, roused, and combined men in support of the constitution and good order.

But 'the score who had committed themselves with Mr. Grey' had the future with them if they could wait so long, and in the meanwhile might console themselves with a monopoly of Charles Fox.

CHAPTER III

FOX, GREY, AND THE PARTY SPLIT—LOYALISTS AND
DEMOCRATS—WAR—JUNE 1792 TO FEBRUARY 1793

'I am not a friend to Paine's doctrines, but I am not to be deterred
by a name from acknowledging that I consider the rights of man as the
foundation of every government, and those who stand against those
rights as conspirators against the people.'—GREY in the House of
Commons, December 13, 1792.

GREY, who had posted north when the session ended,
was not present on the scene of affairs during the renewed party crisis of June and July, although the chief
point at issue was the attitude that Fox would adopt
towards him. It was characteristic, not indeed of the
ambitious youth of four years back, but of the Grey we
know so well in later life, thus to absent himself in
his beloved Northumberland, while his fate was being
decided in the south. If success had attended the efforts
made in midsummer, 1792, to attach Fox to Grey's
enemies, the Liberal elements in Parliament would
have been annihilated. Early in July we read that
'the Duke of Portland seems to consider the members
of the Association as persons entirely separated from
the party.'[1] It was Fox and his personal adherents
who turned the tables, and decided that the Duke
and his friends should be the outcasts from the Whig
organisation.

When Grey left for the north Fox was still hoping
to unite all sections, though he had shown his own

[1] *Elliot*, ii. 56.

preference for the advanced party.   But the Portland Whigs still hoped to win Fox for themselves.   They were none of them lacking in personal devotion to him, least of all the Duke of Portland, who, though he was more reactionary in his public views than any Whig except Burke, had a strong feeling of party loyalty and regarded with horror any prospect of a breach with Fox.   He eagerly caught at a suggestion thrown out by Pitt in June for a coalition ministry of all parties, excepting only the group led by Grey.   Pitt, perhaps, would have liked best to get the Portland Whigs without Fox, as he finally got them in 1794, but he knew that it was useless at present to ask them to come in without him, and he suggested, sincerely it may well be, though Fox did not believe it, that his rival might sit beside him in the Cabinet.   The negotiations never approached success, but they were important as a stage in the decomposition of the old Whig party.   Portland would not take office without Fox or with Grey.   Fox would not take office without Grey, or on anything except an equality with Pitt.[1]

The Portland Whigs hoped for the coalition of Fox and Pitt as a means of dividing Fox from Grey and so destroying the Friends of the People.[2]   But 'on going over the matter,' as Lord Malmesbury records, 'it became evident that the great obstacle would arise from Fox's being too much entangled with Grey, Lambton and that set of men who had lately separated themselves from the party.'

It was no mere personal quarrel.   If personalities had been the deciding factor, all who boasted the Whig name would have been delighted to serve together under Fox.   The issues were neither petty nor selfish.   The trouble was that while Fox was developing the creed of Liberalism, the Duke of Portland and his friends were

---

[1] *Malmesbury*, ii. 428, 431, 433.
[2] Fox, *Memoirs*, iii. 22-3.   Carlisle's letter.

on principle more opposed to change than Pitt himself. Portland and Malmesbury agreed together that they could join no Government unless they had security about ' Parliamentary Reform, the Abolition of the Slave Trade, the Repeal of the Test Act and the system to be observed relative to French politics. That on *all* these Fox differed from us, and Pitt on several.'[1]   These men, in fact, found even the Pitt of 1792 too Liberal for them, though he had given up Parliamentary Reform, had always been opposed to the repeal of the Test Act, and now offered them to compromise the Slave Trade question because the King ' did not like the measure.'[2] They had quarrelled with Grey and were regretfully breaking with Fox, because they conscientiously opposed any step in the direction of civil or religious liberty, and regarded the proposal to stop the Slave Trade with the same horror as the King himself.   It was on these great domestic issues that the old Whig party broke up in the summer of 1792, when no one expected and no one except Burke desired a war between England and France.

The abortive negotiations for a coalition were, in their most important aspect, an attempt to detach Fox from the progressive elements in the country, and to make him part of a National Conservative Bloc, which would, if he had joined it, have acquired a monopoly of both Houses of Parliament and of all recognised political institutions.   Grey and his friends could not have maintained themselves in politics without him. But although this scheme had great attractions for the Portland Whigs, Pitt's followers were naturally less eager to share office with such formidable rivals, and regarded Fox as a political suicide who had already

---

[1] *Malmesbury*, ii. 427, 430;   Fox, *Memoirs*, iii. 261-2.   *Elliot*, ii. 44, gives the same list of securities demanded by Portland, adding the ' Act against Unitarians,' which Portland considered as sacred as Rotten Boroughs, Test Act, and Slave Trade.

[2] *Malmesbury*, ii. 430.

taken up with Reform.   On June 27 Portland wrote
to Fox : [1]

> Lord Loughborough says Pitt declared in the most explicit
> terms his readiness and willingness to act with you ; that no
> objection whatever arose from him or from the Closet [viz. the
> King] to the arrangement which he had professed to wish. [But]
> on consulting with some of his most considerable and best friends,
> [Pitt] had met with strong prejudices against you, and particu-
> larly for your conduct respecting the Proclamation, that he there-
> fore had not mentioned the subject in the Closet.   And finding
> himself not pressed to form a new arrangement, he felt it most
> expedient and indeed incumbent upon him to proceed no further
> in the business.

With that the negotiation virtually ended.   We
may surmise that, had the proposal been referred to a
higher quarter, ' the Closet ' would not improbably
have closed itself against Fox, as on so many other
occasions.   Throughout July Pitt still declared himself anxious for a coalition, but Fox was no longer in
the mood to listen.   On July 21 he wrote to Lord
Portland: ' I own I cannot bring myself to think that
Pitt has ever meaned any thing but to make a division
among us.'

Meanwhile great events were taking place abroad.
The ' metaphysical war,' as Lord Lansdowne called it,
had begun between the despotic and the democratic
idea, each now fatally armed with sword and gun.   Both
sides had provoked the conflict.   The spoilers of Poland
had first begun to threaten the rebellious French nation ;
then the Girondin party had, with a light heart, taken
up the challenge and plunged their country, already
drifting to anarchy through intestine feuds, into a war
to be conducted by a King who was on the enemy's
side, with an army in a state of dissolution.   Having
led their country into this scrape the Girondins were

---

[1] Unpublished.

unable to deliver her, and had to make way, pitiably complaining, for men more forcible and more wicked. To save herself France went mad. Her first war measure was indeed sane enough—to overthrow the Monarchy which hampered her every movement of self-defence. This was done on August 10, to the accompaniment of the storming of the Tuileries and the slaughter of the Swiss Guard. Ere this the Austrian and Prussian armies had begun to move on Paris, followed by a train of French gentlemen whom *noblesse* obliged to join in the destruction of their country. At the end of July the Duke of Brunswick had issued his famous manifesto, announcing that he would raze the towns and massacre the people of France, if they continued to coerce their lawful monarch, or to resist his friends the invaders.

The division of English opinion about our own affairs was now deepened by opposite sympathies for and against Brunswick. The Pitt ministry had resisted the public and private appeals which Burke had been making to them for a year past to lead a crusade against the French Revolution. Burke was disappointed, but he tells us that ' every now and then I seemed to make an impression on them.' The Cabinet now hoped that Brunswick would do the work which they were unwilling themselves to undertake. Our Foreign Minister wrote :

I *fear* more from this weather in retarding the Duke of Brunswick's operations than from any resistance he seems likely to meet with from Dumourier's troops, if we may judge of them by the late specimen of their conduct.

Fox on the other hand regarded the defence of the French soil as the old issue of Marathon, Bannockburn, Morat, and his passion on the subject carried him yet further away from Portland and yet nearer to Grey. On September 3 he wrote to his nephew Lord Holland, to whom he always opened his heart :

I do not think near so ill of the business of the 10th of August as I did upon first hearing it.   If the King and his Ministers were really determined not to act in concert with the Assembly, and still more if they secretly favoured the Invasion of Barbarians, it was necessary, at any rate, to begin by getting rid of him and them.   However, it is impossible not to look with disgust at the bloody means which have been taken, even supposing the end to be good, and I cannot help fearing that we are not near the end of these trials and executions.   There is a want of dignity and propriety in everything they do.   And yet, with all their faults and all their nonsense, I do interest myself n their success in the greatest degree.

While Fox was writing this letter, he was still ignorant that the Parisians, beside themselves from terror of Brunswick's near approach, were permitting a gang of filthy rascals to perpetrate the ' September massacres.' As soon as Fox heard of it he wrote to Holland :

I had just made up my mind to the events of the 10th of August, when the horrid accounts of the 2nd of this month arrived, and I really consider the horrors of that day and night as the most heart-breaking event that ever happened to those who, like me, are fundamentally and unalterably attached to the true cause.   There is not, in my opinion, a shadow of excuse for this horrid massacre, nor even the possibility of extenuating it in the smallest degree.

The September massacres were indeed one of the worst blows that ever befell the cause of progress and freedom in our island.   They did for the English reaction what the Massacre of St. Bartholomew and the Revocation of the Edict of Nantes had done for English Protestantism.   What a ' Jesuit ' had seemed once, a ' Jacobin ' seemed now.   And every Reformer was a ' Jacobin,' morally guilty of the September massacres. Pity and righteous horror hardened the hearts and darkened the understandings of men.   It was in vain that Grey argued that the Russians and Prussians were committing the like atrocities in Poland, as mere lawless invaders without a shadow of excuse or right, and that the English Ministers would do nothing to stop them. Poland was far off and its names outlandish ; Paris was near and familiar, and many of those poor heads nodding on pikes had smiled in London drawing-rooms. ' I have scarce a thought for Poland,' we read in a letter of the time, ' France is nearer and more interesting.' So Brunswick's retreat from before Valmy was regarded as a disaster, probably by the majority of Englishmen, certainly by nine well-dressed persons out of ten ; but the new working-men's clubs openly rejoiced at the French victory, and their rejoicing seemed proof sufficient of their criminal temper and seditious intent. Grey, too, spoke of Brunswick's retreat as ' matter of joy and exultation.'

So, under evil auspices, the winter came on which decided for a generation the issue between the Reforming and Anti-reforming parties in England. It was the winter of two spontaneous popular movements in the country, one democratic and the other loyalist. The latter proved so much the stronger of the two, that the Radical movement was completely overwhelmed, and might after this winter have been safely left alone as a mere element of opinion working for the future. But the Government preferred to destroy it by statutory persecution, after it had been already conquered by popular disapproval and social boycott. The open contest between the two propagandas, before the unnecessary *coup-de-grâce* was given by Government, took place in the last months of 1792, under the influence of the recent events in France. During this contest of opinion, Grey found himself angrily condemned by the respectable for his sympathy with the working-men's clubs on the subject of Parliamentary Reform, but unable to work with those bodies on account of the Painite and Republican enthusiasm of so many of their members. His own letters of this year have not been preserved, but George Tierney's answer to one of them well describes the difficult position of the Friends of the People.

29th October 1792.

Dear Grey,—. . . As one of the Friends of the People, I must continue to be anxious for a Cabinet consultation somewhere We do not seem to be aware of the very critical situation in which we stand. The late events in France are to us most important, and much may depend on the use we make of them. As far as I can see, they have made one party here desperate and the other drunk. Many are become wild Republicans who a few months back were moderate Reformers, and numbers who six weeks ago were contented with plain, old-fashioned Toryism, have now worked themselves up into such apprehensions for the fate of Royalty as to be incapable of distinguishing between Reform and treason, and to threaten death and destruction to all who differ from them. In this extravagant ferment of men's opinions our task becomes every day more difficult. The Leveller and the Reformer, the King and the Tyrant, seem in the new vocabularies of Courtiers and Patriots to be confounded and considered as synonymous, and I much fear we shall neither gain proselytes from amongst those who seem attached to the very defects of the Constitution, or those who seek to overturn it altogether.

The Friends of the People were not, however, wasting their time. A committee of the association had during the summer been drawing up a masterly Report on the State of Parliamentary Representation of Great Britain, which remained until 1832 the great magazine of facts and arguments for reformers of every shade ; it appears from a passage in this letter that Tierney was responsible for much of the work. It was the well-conceived intention of the Friends of the People, actually carried out in the spring of the next year, that this damning report should first be published, proving statistically and *nominatim* that British representation was a farce, and that then, after the public had digested it for a couple of months, Grey should bring in his Reform motion, of which he had given notice on the

previous 30th of April.[1] Such, however, was the rage
in Parliamentary circles against Reform, and in particular against the Friends of the People, that some of
the members of that association were frightened by the
talk of the town, and urged that Grey had best let his
motion drop. But Grey, urged by Tierney and Erskine,
stood firm to his purpose. The Reformers indeed felt
that they were capturing the party, though losing the
country. In the party their position was stronger than
in the early summer, owing to the movement in their
direction of Fox and his personal *clientèle*. On November 15, 1792, Tierney writes to Grey :

> I yesterday saw Lord Robert Spencer, who assured me that
> Fox was disposed to come forward as stoutly as we could desire
> on the subject of Parliamentary Reform, but that he was anxious
> to know what plan of reform we intended to propose before he
> shewed himself. I assured him that we had no specific plan
> yet drawn out, and that we should esteem it a very particular
> favour if Fox would give us his ideas, as I was convinced the
> majority of our Society were above all things anxious to act
> cordially with him. Lord Robert thought the best way of
> settling all this would be for you to meet Fox immediately, and
> I must add I look upon it to be absolutely necessary that you
> should do so. I am quite satisfied that, if Fox does not come
> forth speedily in his true natural colours and speak boldly what
> I am certain he thinks, he will be lost.

Fox, indeed, was far from easy as to his own situation, but his difficulties still appeared to him in the form
of the problem how to keep Grey and Portland in the
same party. This he discusses in a series of letters to
his confidant Adair :

> I overheard you say to Sheridan [he writes on November 26]
> that there was much disposition on what is called the Aristo-
> cratic part of the Party to concede and conciliate. I must repeat
> that not one symptom of the kind has appeared to me. If any
> such disposition existed, I cannot help thinking that on the other

[1] See p. 47, above.

side *I* should have weight enough to produce a correspondent
disposition.   I am sure that Lauderdale, Grey, and Sheridan are
all manageable men, and the rascals of the Democratic party
(for there are such on all sides) have not set their wits to pervert *them*, in the way that those on the Aristocratic side have to
pervert the Duke of Portland, Fitzwilliam, Windham, etc.

Three days later Fox writes again to Adair :

> Though Parliamentary Reform was not, as Burke says, in
> the original contract, yet neither was opposition to it in that
> contract, and Grey had good reason to be surprised at so
> violent a schism arising from his undertaking what many of us
> had done before him.   Indeed the taking of such an alarm on
> such a ground, and running to Pitt upon it, were very bad
> symptoms.

While the Parliamentary Whigs were thus dividing
themselves, against the next session, into two clear
parties on the great issue, the country was deciding the
fate of Reform by an unmistakable demonstration of
opinion.   In November and December 1792—months
of most unaccustomed political activity in whole classes—
the popular reaction was organised by Reeves' ' Association for the Preservation of Liberty and Property.'
Hundreds of ' loyal ' resolutions were carried by public
bodies and public meetings, and sent up to Reeves.
The half-dozen volumes [1] of letters received by his
society in that strenuous winter is a record of much
honest zeal and much selfish fear ; of devoted work in
fair propaganda and odious delation against neighbours.
In all villages and most towns the Democrats were
effectually cowed.   Shopkeepers who showed Democratic sympathies were boycotted until they declared
their repentance.   Publicans who allowed Democratic
societies to meet under their roof were given notice to
turn them out or lose their licenses.   In the provincial
and London theatres, then the centre of a vigorous

---

[1] Add. MSS., B.M., 16919-16925.

popular life, both sides used to come to make their demonstrations, but ' God save the King ! ' easily drowned ' Millions, be free ! ' and the Democrats, who by no means represented the ' millions ' of whom they sang, generally went down fighting before the fists of the loyal-hearted pit and boxes. In the public holocausts on November 5, Tom Paine replaced his Popish predecessor, not only in the south, but ' at most of the towns and considerable villages of Northumberland and Durham.' [1]

While this storm of opinion was rising and blowing its first great gale throughout the island, the Democratic clubs in London showed more zeal than wisdom. They chose this November to send deputations to congratulate the Convention of France, and the ill-selected representatives of Hardy's Corresponding Society delighted the French legislators with the unpardonably foolish remark that ' it would not be extraordinary if in a much less space of time than can be imagined the French should send addresses of congratulation to a National Convention of England.' The French Jacobins, who knew as little of England as Burke did of their country, were thus encouraged in the belief that Britons were dying to throw off the yoke of tyranny. The success achieved by the Republican armies in this month in overrunning the Rhine country, Belgium and Savoy, had already made Jacobin France drunk with glory ; the idea of revolutionising all Europe was grateful at once to Gallic vanity and Democratic effervescence. On November 19 the French Convention declared its resolve to ' grant fraternity and assistance to all people who wish to

---

[1] *Dropmore Papers*, ii. 354–355. *Life of Henry Hunt*, i. 70–72. Conway's *Paine*, i. 370–371. *Holcroft* (ii. 151) tells us how ' language the most outrageous was employed to make those who were in the least suspected declare their creed ; and if it was not entirely accommodating, the peaceable citizen, after being entrapped, was insulted and turned, or frequently kicked, out of tap-rooms, coffee-houses, and public places.'

recover their liberty,' and though this decree was not aimed at England, and was little more serious than so many other pieces of Republican gasconade, it caused the utmost indignation in the now sensitive body of English Toryism. In many countries to which the French troops carried the tricolor, they were welcomed as deliverers by important classes of the community, and they never understood what a very different reception they would have met with in England, where even the Corresponding Society voted that all its members should take arms against the French if they landed.[1] The Jacobins were deceived, partly by their own conceit and ignorance, partly by the foolish conduct of the English Democrats in Paris in November 1792, partly by the Tory Press and Gillray's cartoons which represented Fox and his adherents as Jacobins bent on beheading George III. Our alarmists' outcries about the 'seditious sentiments' of the lower orders were taken by the French *au pied de la lettre*. In October 1793 a play was acted in Paris about the invasion of England. The plot was as follows :

'Grey proposes to go and welcome the French, a Republic is proclaimed, the heads of the Prince of Wales and Pitt are cut off and paraded through the streets. George III shut up in a carriage, is drawn to Bedlam by Burke, Grenville, and Chesterfield. Fox and Sheridan in red caps insult him.' In England this Parisian *revue* was seriously cast in Grey's teeth.[2] But the plot might have been, and probably was, culled from Gillray and the Tory Press, which from first to last did all they could to make the French believe that they would be welcomed in England by the chiefs of the Opposition and a large part of the community.

Pitt helped to increase this misconception, when on December 1, 1792, he issued a Proclamation to

---

[1] Add. MSS., B.M., 35143, ff. 60–61.

[2] Alger, *Englishmen in the French Revolution*, 141–2. *Life of Wilberforce*, ii. 427, 459.

call out the militia and summon Parliament a month
sooner than was expected, on the alleged ground that
'a spirit of tumult and disorder,' incited by seditious
persons in league with foreigners, 'had lately shown
itself in acts of riot and insurrection.' It was the
old story of the wolf and the lamb, for the only
mob violence that had taken place in connection
with the new democracy had been perpetrated by the
Royalist roughs of Birmingham and Manchester.
Ministers, when challenged to say where the 'insurrection' had shown its head, replied that there had
been a bread-riot at Perth, and that a mob had planted
a tree of liberty at Dundee. Sir Gilbert Elliot, though
he now supported Pitt, confessed to his wife that the
Proclamation of December 1 was not justifiable, that ' no
insurrection has taken place in England, which seems,
I think, rather more quiet than usual,' while the Scotch
' insurrections ' were ' ridiculous to those who live in
Scotland and know the truth.' A few days before,
Lord Grenville, Pitt's principal colleague, had confessed in a letter to his brother that the country was
perfectly quiet, and that the stories of riot when investi-
gated came to nothing.[1]

When, therefore, Fox heard of the Proclamation he
was moved to an access of fury which probably affected
his conduct during the important crisis of the next
month. The hasty scrawl he sent off to the Duke of
Portland on first hearing the news bears all the traces
of being written by a man beside himself with rage
against a mean but all-powerful enemy :

My dear Lord,—I send you inclosed a note I have just
received from Adam. If they mention danger of Insurrection,
or rather (as they must do to legalise their proceedings)[2] of *Rebel-*

---

[1] *Parl. Hist.*, xxx. 48. *Elliot*, ii. 80–1. Fox, *Mem.*, iii. 28–9.

[2] Viz., to legalise calling out the militia and the summons of Parliament without the legal length of notice. The Proclamation in fact
mentioned not mere ' danger ' but actuality of insurrection.

lion, surely the first measure all honest men ought to take is to impeach them for so wicked and detestable a falsehood.   I fairly own that *if* they have done this I shall grow savage, and not think a French *Lanterne* too bad for them.   Surely it is impossible if anything were impossible for such monsters, who for the purpose of weakening or destroying the honourable connection of the Whigs, would not scruple to run the risque of a Civil War.   I cannot trust myself to write any more for I confess I am too much affected.[1]

Ten days after writing this note, and two before Parliament met, Fox dined at Burlington House with the Duke of Portland's friends ; the conversation revealed that he was more than ever divided from them, not only on these home affairs but on the question now arising of peace or war with France.   When the Commons met on December 13, Fox appeared in close league with Grey's party, of which he is henceforth the acknowledged head.   The Liberal leader and his lieutenant denounced the fraud of Pitt's ' insurrection.' [2]   ' The behaviour of Fox rather afflicts than surprises me,' wrote Gibbon, when he heard the news ; ' *his inmost soul is deeply tinged with democracy.*'

The breach in the party was at length complete, although the Duke of Portland himself had not the heart to proclaim what everyone knew, that ' the Whig connection ' was dissolved.   When once he had gone over, the Duke made a very good Tory, and never came back again, as did some who were impatient with him this winter for his slowness in publicly repudiating

[1] Unpublished.

[2] Grey said : ' If the conduct of any set of men was calculated to excite insurrection it was that of Ministers, who, by proclamations calumniating whole descriptions of men as seditious, and announcing insurrections that never existed, filled the minds of the people with false alarms, and taught every man to distrust if not hate his neighbour.   The only instance like insurrection that had occurred, at Birmingham, and he was informed now at Manchester, were mobs on pretext of loyalty and order, directed solely against persons supposed inimical not to His Majesty but to his Ministers.'—*Parl. Hist.*, xxx. 83.

Fox. These mercurial spirits, such as Windham and Elliot, found it no light task to get Portland to move. They complained that he would sit ' not uttering one word, admitting all you say and sobbing grievously.' For hours together he would stare in front of him in a trance, while his followers lectured him on his duty. The operation might have been called ' hoisting the Duke,' for whenever they had lifted him to the level of promising to make his announcement, Fox would call at Burlington House or write him an appealing letter, and back he would slip once more. The poor man dumbly felt that he was, as he had been called, ' a good block to hang Whigs on,' and that Pitt had nothing to offer a nobleman of his eminence that could compensate him for the loss of Fox's friendship. But though the Duke would make no official statement of the party position, others were not so reticent, and at the New Year of 1793 the followers of Grey and Fox were amalgamated under Fox's leadership as the only Opposition party. The Portland Whigs were henceforth unequivocal supporters of Pitt, in whose Cabinet Portland finally consented to take office in July 1794.[1]

It was indeed no longer possible to halt between two opinions, though truth were hid in the centre. Men alive must choose their parts, and leave posterity to be wiser—if it can. To the question of Reform or repression at home was added the question of foreign war. Fox and Grey were opposed to the war policy. They pleaded in the House that we should acknowledge the French Republic and send a Minister to Paris to treat with the *de facto* Government. They allowed that it would be necessary to protect Holland if the Dutch were attacked, but they complained when Pitt and Grenville threatened France before Holland herself

---

[1] *Elliot*, ii. 84–98. *Malmesbury*, ii. 440–78. Russell's *Fox*, ii. 320–3.

had felt alarm or had asked for our protection. They thought that the opening of the Scheldt to navigation was an insufficient reason for England to go to war with France, when acts of spoliation more extensive and more wicked were being perpetrated in Poland without our challenge.

When Poland [Grey told the House] was beginning to recover from the long calamities of anarchy, combined with oppression ; after she had established an hereditary and limited monarchy like our own, His Majesty's Ministers, with apparent indifference and unconcern, have seen her become the victim of the most unprovoked and unprincipled invasion. Then [continued Grey] His Majesty's Ministers beheld with supine indifference or secret approbation the armies of other Powers [Prussia and Austria] in evident concert with the oppressor of Poland [Russia], advancing to the invasion and subjugation of France [and threatening its destruction in the Brunswick Manifesto]. But no sooner, by an ever-memorable reverse of fortune, had France repulsed her invaders and carried her arms into their territory, than His Majesty's Ministers began to express alarms for the general security of Europe, which it appears to us might have been expressed with greater justice on the previous successes of her powerful adversaries.

The statements of fact here contained are correct so far as they go. Both Jacobin France and the despotisms of Eastern Europe were out for plunder, each side intending to overset what England rightly valued—'the balance of power in Europe.' But in entering the Netherlands and threatening Holland, France was stepping on to ground which England has never been willing to see pass under the authority of any power that might threaten her island security. In 1831 Grey, as Reform Premier, whose policy depended on maintaining good relations with Liberal France, was compelled to threaten her with war if she tampered with the real independence of Belgium. In 1793 England was certain in any case to choose her side according to her own political sympathies. And therefore, in the existing anti-Jacobin temper of her governing and middle classes, it was certain that she would sooner or later join in the crusade against the French Republic. Incidentally, whether she wished it or not, she would then be fighting to rivet the chains of the military despotisms of the East on Poland, Italy, Hungary, and Germany. After great varieties of fortune, this was accomplished in 1815, and the nineteenth century was spent by England in wishing it undone, in sympathising with all the causes and nationalities she had helped to overthrow, and in ever-increasing jealousy of the Teutonic and Slavonic powers which she had spent so many millions to inflate. But all this should not be laid at the single door of Pitt, as Grey was inclined to lay it. It was the fault of Burke and the Girondin and Jacobin military adventurers, of Russia, Prussia, and Austria, and, in a lesser degree, of the English people. The political sympathies of the English in 1792-3 rendered war with France inevitable, because the French were then incapable of remaining at peace with a neighbour unsympathetic to their cause. In that hour of their dæmonic exaltation, he who was not with them was against them. France would not have retired out of Belgium or kept her hands off Holland, whatever Pitt had done, unless like the Corresponding Society he had sent messages of congratulation to the Convention. And if he had done that, the English would have removed him from being their governor.

Fox and Grey themselves could have made nothing of the situation at Christmas 1792. Europe was already rushing down the inclined slope of its evil passions to the fate that befell it. The red star, not of Pitt, but of Burke, was in the ascendant. But the curious may be allowed to speculate what would have happened if, from 1789 onwards, England had adopted the sympathetic attitude of Fox and Grey towards the French Revolution. If England had interposed her veto against any attack on France by Prussia and Austria in the summer of 1792, would the French then have been saved from Jacobinism, the Terror, and the policy of military adventure that grew out of those domestic horrors ? If England had been her friend, would France have listened at all to English wishes, and could the two Liberal Powers of Western Europe have stood together for peace and liberty ? That was the ideal of Fox and Grey, but the English had been in no mood to try the experiment, and now in any case it was too late.

All that Fox and Grey could now do was to record their protest against what they knew to be a tragedy, and less justly attributed to Pitt as a crime. But a tragedy it certainly was, and must have been, whatever course the war had run. If the allied armies had got to Paris in 1793, as might well have happened if they had acted in August with concert and vigour,[1] Pitt, whatever his own fluctuating intentions towards France might have been, would have had no alternative but to allow the *émigrés* to re-establish the *ancien régime*. The threats of Brunswick's manifesto would have become facts. We should have extinguished freedom on the Continent. Fox and Grey could not bring themselves to wish for this consummation, and who that loves either France or liberty shall blame them ? The conquest of England, which they dreaded most of all, was not a possibility in the early years of the war. The worst results, that must have followed on the complete success by either party, were happily avoided. England was never conquered, and France was only conquered after twenty years, when the social results of the Revolution had taken such root that Wellington and Blucher could not restore the complete *ancien régime* on French soil.

What actually happened was bad enough. Europe was barbarised by twenty years of war ; and militarism

[1] Fortescue, *British Army*, 1906, iv. 116–18.   *Dropmore Papers*, iii. pp. xxi–xxii, 484–5.

became the type and standard of the modern world. In 1815 all Europe outside France was laid at the feet of the Teutonic and Slavonic military despotisms. In England herself the twenty years' war involved forty years' political reaction on the model of Burke's neo-Toryism. And it was during these years of war and reaction, when the poor were at a discount indeed, that our Industrial Revolution took place under the worst possible conditions. It was in time of war and repression that the millions in town and country acquired their new economic and social being. The physical and moral deterioration of the masses, in the early nineteenth century, was largely due to the war, both to its economic effects and to the political and social reaction in ideas that an anti-Jacobin war so unduly prolonged.

If it was still possible at Christmas for onlookers to hope for peace, the execution of Louis XVI in January 1793 dispelled the last illusions. The French did not want peace with England, or they would have listened to Deputy Paine's earnest appeal to them to spare the man from whose head the crown had fallen. They preferred the stormy eloquence of Danton : ' The coalised kings threaten us ; we hurl at their feet, as gage of battle, the head of a king.' Brave words of a brave man; but no less bloody than brave, they fell cold on the ears of Fox and Grey. To them the news of the King's execution came as a sentence fatal to their hopes for peace between France and England, and for liberty in either land. ' An account is come that the King of France was executed on Monday morning,' wrote Grey to a friend. ' Bad as I am thought, I cannot express the horror I feel at this atrocity. War is certain— God grant we may not all lament the consequences of it.' The horror of the ' French cannibals ' which had been generated in England by the September massacres was redoubled by the slaughter of the kindly King. On that royal theme every chord in the English nature vibrated with pity and indignation. In a few days war broke out between the two peoples, each blinded by the frenzy of its own self-righteousness.

Since the above was written another great war has been fought and won. It has been fought on behalf of the principles of Fox and Grey, in alliance with Republican France and America and free Italy, against the despotic principle represented by Prussia and Austria, the powers of darkness whom the posthumous victory of Burke and Pitt made masters of the Continent for a hundred years. The fact that all parties in our country should in our own day have united to overthrow the system of despotism in Europe, and thereby ' make the world safe for democracy,' throws back the light of a new era on the history of British politics in 1792–4. Even if we regard the war against Republican France as having been forced upon us by the French Jacobins, we must at least feel that it has indeed proved the tragedy that Fox, Grey, and Wordsworth then believed it to be.

And whatever may be thought of the war itself, it is impossible for the present generation to maintain the distinction that used sometimes to be made between the alleged impropriety of Grey's Reform proposals in the last decade of the eighteenth century and the acknowledged propriety of his Reform Bill in 1831 ; for it is no longer possible to argue that engagement in a great war renders Parliamentary Reform unsafe. This theory has now been refuted in practice. We have seen Conservative Ministers, in the midst of a struggle with a foe more formidable than the French Jacobins, take part in passing as a war measure a Bill tantamount to manhood suffrage, coupled with the emancipation of women. On that day Fox and Grey were pleasantly revenged on Burke and Pitt.

CHAPTER IV

THE GREAT REPRESSION—HARDY'S TRIAL—GREY'S REFORM MOTIONS—1793–1797

' I began attacking abuses thirty or forty years ago when it was almost safer to be a felon than a Reformer.'—SYDNEY SMITH TO LORD J. RUSSELL, 1835.

' I think this enlightened age, as it is called, is as much given to persecution as the most barbarous. The transportation of the Deputies and Directors [by Bonaparte] is not perhaps quite so bad as that of Muir and Palmer, because there is the pretence at least of danger from their stay ; but such pretences are seldom wanting to persecutors, and are always false. *Men persecute because they love persecution*, and so far am I from believing fear to be the true cause of persecution, that I begin to think that fear is the only motive that ever can persuade men to suffer those who differ in opinion from them to breathe the same atmosphere with them.'—FOX TO GREY, Oct. 5, 1801.

ONCE war had begun, all proposals for Reform were but marking out ground for the future, under conditions sufficiently disagreeable for the present, but the few Reformers now left were prepared to take the fortune of their faith. In February 1793, while the country was resounding with preparations for the war in Flanders, the Friends of the People brought out their promised Report on the State of Parliamentary Representation.[1] Its accuracy was not challenged,

---

[1] See p. 60, above. The Report is printed at the end of *Wyvill*, iii., and can be compared to the contemporary and yet more complete *History of the Boroughs of Great Britain*, in two volumes, which placed the number of proprietary Members for England and Wales higher— at 358.

though it contained a printed list of the 'proprietors' of all the rotten boroughs of Great Britain ; and Hardy tells us that it ' gave the people more information about the partial and corrupt state of the representation than any other publication at that time.'[1] The tables showed that more than 300 out of the 513 representatives for England and Wales owed their return to individual 'proprietors' : half a dozen were put in by the Lords of the Treasury ; 88 were absolutely nominated by Peers, and 72 had their election secured by the influence of Peers ; 82 were absolutely nominated by individuals below the rank of the peerage, and 57 had their election secured by the influence of such individuals. The proprietors themselves numbered 71 Lords and 91 Commoners. The meagre number of 11,075 voters returned a clear majority of the Members for England and Wales ; 51 constituencies had less than fifty voters each. The Scottish Report, equally detailed, is summed up in the following words :

The inhabitants of Scotland are supposed to be near two millions ; their representatives are chosen by 2643 ; Scotland sends 45 Members ; a single county in England, namely Cornwall, sends 44.

Seats were openly advertised for sale in newspapers ; if the proprietor became bankrupt, his borough influence was set down as a saleable asset. ' The price of a seat in Parliament,' it was said, ' was better known than the price of a horse.' When at this period the Borough of Gatton came under the hammer, the auctioneer referred to the advantage and glory of nominating two Members of Parliament as ' *an elegant contingency*,' on which he expatiated as ' the only infallible source of fortune, titles, and honours in this happy country.'[2] The professional gentleman was not far wrong.

[1] Add. MSS., B.M., 27814, f. 24.
[2] Holcroft, *Memoirs*, ii. 191. See Veitch, *Genesis of Parliamentary Reform*, chap. i., on the whole subject.

CHARLES GREY, M.P.

From the picture by Sir Thomas Lawrence (1793) at Howick.

On the basis of their Report, the Friends of the People drew up a petition to the House of Commons. It sets out the anomalies of representation : how Cornwall outweighs Yorkshire and Middlesex together ; how ' no less than one hundred and fifty of your Honourable Members owe their elections entirely to the interference of Peers,' in spite of the law forbidding Peers to interfere in elections ; how, although the Lower House was meant to represent the people and act as a check on Crown and Peers, it had in fact become the instrument of Peers and Crown. 'Private Parliamentary patronage' is complained of as the great evil ; 154 patrons ' return a decided majority of your Honourable House.' In place of the multitudinous borough franchises of the day—motley relics of mediæval custom and of more recent local chicanery—they pray the House ' to regulate the right of voting upon a uniform and equitable principle.' It is not suggested what the ' principle' should be, except that it should be ' uniform '—a startling proposal for a great change, realised in 1832.

On May 6, 1793, Grey rose to make the Reform Motion of which he had given notice more than a year before.[1] He moved that the petition of the Friends of the People should be ' referred to the consideration of a committee.' In 1780 Universal Suffrage had been advocated by the Duke of Richmond, since turned alarmist.

I do not [said Grey] approve the Duke of Richmond's plan of Reform, though I think it better than the present system ; any plan would be better which would secure the sending of such Members to the House as would vote independently. I could [he said] mention a plan which appears to me much better,

but since he was only moving for an enquiry into the state of the representation, he would not now divulge

[1] See p. 47, above.

his own ideas on the way to amend it. The debate that followed was confined to the question whether or not an enquiry should be held into the alleged abuses. The well-known arguments in favour of rotten boroughs were produced to the general satisfaction by Jenkinson. That gentleman, who afterwards governed England for many years as Lord Liverpool, told the House that :

We ought not to begin first by considering who ought to be electors, and then who ought to be elected ; but we ought to begin by considering who ought to be elected, and then constitute such persons electors as would be likely to produce the best elected.

By this logic, the worthy Jenkinson made it clear to the saviours of their country that the electors who had elected them must be the best possible of all electors. ' By their fruits shall ye know them.' No wonder it took Grey forty years to get the better of this particularly alluring and practical form of the *argumentum ad hominem.* Fox wound up the debate with a fine speech for Reform, and then the Honourable Members very prudently decided by 282 to 41 that it was best not to enquire how they had got into the Honourable House.

In the last months of 1792 the democratic movement had been in most places suppressed, and everywhere dominated, by very practical demonstrations of aristocratic and popular displeasure.[1] It was, therefore, not from any arguable necessity, but either out of panic, or, as Fox thought, from the love of persecution inherent in man, that Ministers from 1793 onwards conducted a system of governmental repression that soon shocked even the strongly anti-Jacobin opinion of the man in the street. During the next generation the freedom of the Press in England existed only in name,

---

[1] See pp. 62–63, above.

owing to the frequency of Government prosecutions, while the right of public meeting and association was by law abolished. Nothing was beneath the notice of Ministers. Some unwary expression in a sermon or a newspaper article, some angry retort rapped out in political controversy heated by drink, was enough to ruin a man for life. Prosecutions of Reformers, dissenting ministers, and editors lend a sinister interest to several volumes of our 'State Trials.' In Scotland there was neither justice nor mercy. In England one man here and another there escaped by Erskine's wit and eloquence, but the greater number of those accused were ruined.

Daniel Holt was sentenced to four years' imprisonment, of which he died, first for republishing a Constitutional Reform tract of Major Cartwright's, which had been held perfectly innocent when it first saw light in 1783 ; and secondly for publishing another address in favour of Parliamentary Reform of which the judge in passing sentence said, ' The second of these libels most grossly and impudently asperses the Parliament of this Kingdom, and brands them with the imputation of venality and corruption, and calls for a Parliamentary Reform.' [1] The editor of the *Courier* was imprisoned for calling the Czar of Russia a tyrant. The system was so widespread that for fear of the Attorney-General no publisher could any longer be induced to print the Reform pamphlets of so respectable a citizen as the veteran Major Cartwright, or even of the old Yorkshire Reformer Wyvill, an avowed opponent of Paine.[2] So abject was the terror that protests against the worst acts of governmental tyranny could not be inserted in newspapers.[3] Finally, in 1798, Pitt got tired of formulating accusations against his political enemies,

[1] *State Trials*, xxii. and *Life of Cartwright*, i. 199-200.
[2] Cartwright's *Mock Reform*, etc., p. 47. *Wyvill*, iv. pp. xiv, 559.
[3] *E.g.* Add. MSS., B.M., 27808, f. 111.

and kept batches of them in prison for months and even years together without trial.

It is strange that Fox and Grey should ever have been regarded as ' un-English ' for opposing a system which took away the freedom of utterance so long the special pride of Englishmen, and subjected our ancestors to the perpetual and daily fear of the spy and the political tribunal. Fox and Grey had a much truer conception of the British character, of the spirit of our constitution, and of those things for which England stands in the comity of nations, than had the men who, while they claimed to be monopolists of patriotism and sole defenders of the national traditions, completely changed the spirit of our laws, substituted Burke's terror of the ' swinish multitude ' for Chatham's trust in ' loyal Britons,' and attempted to reduce the inhabitants of this island to the level of the tame nations who obeyed the King of Prussia and the Jacobin tyrants of France.

The historian of the revolution of 1688 has remarked that the oppression in Scotland under Charles and James II was worse than the oppression in England, and that the passions let loose by the revolution when it came were proportionately more violent to the north of the Tweed. The same is true of the long years of tryanny that preceded and caused the more peaceful revolution of 1832. ' _Thairty-twa_ ' was an even greater deliverance, a more complete reversal of men and things in Scotland than in England. In England under the old _régime_ there were some popular electoral contests ; in Scotland none, even in the counties. In England there was municipal life in some boroughs ; in Scotland every burgh was a close oligarchy. At the worst period of reaction, one English member out of five voting usually voted with the Reformers, but all the Scottish members, save one or two, were votes procurable by Government for value received—Dundas knew how. ' The Lord Advocate should always be a

tall man,' one of them said. ' We Scotch members
always vote with him, and we need therefore to be able
to see him in a division.'[1] ' Politically,' wrote Cockburn,
who was through it all, ' Scotland was dead. It was not
unlike a village at a great man's gate. Without a single
free institution or habit, opposition was rebellion, submission probable success.'

When therefore the spirit of the new age, which
Burns lived to breathe, puffed out the Scottish Democrats
so that they began to hold meetings in favour of popular
representation in Parliament, and to form associations
to spread the demand, such unofficial action by unprivi-
leged persons was a thing entirely novel, and, in the eye
of authority, monstrous. They were regarded as rebels
and treated as such. The trials of Muir and Palmer
at Edinburgh are the chief events in the domestic annals
of our island for the year 1793. Their cases were
watched from London with tense anxiety, and when it
was known that the two high-minded gentlemen who
had advocated Democratic Reform were to be transported to Botany Bay for ' leasemaking,' the horror of
the English Opposition and the satisfaction of the
English Ministerialists were loudly expressed. Lord
Braxfield,[2] ' the Jeffreys of Scotland,' had in Muir's
case pronounced from the bench that to agitate for a
popular franchise was, in the circumstances, of itself
sedition, and that ' the landed interest alone had a right
to representation.' It was in vain that Fox and Grey
appealed for mitigation of the sentence. Like Bomba's
prisoners in later times, these refined and educated men

[1] Pellew, *Life of Sidmouth,* i. 153.
[2] The Judge in *Weir of Hermistoun.* See Cockburn's *Memorials,*
33, 113–117. Braxfield is known in anecdotal history for his apology to
a lady whom he had cursed in peculiarly foul language for a mistake at
whist—' Your pardon's begged, Madam. I took ye for my ain wife.'
Also for his reply to the reformer Gerald, who pleaded that Jesus Christ
was an ' innovator '—' Muckle he made o' that ; he was hanget.' See
Cockburn's *Examination of the Trials for Sedition in Scotland,* 1888, for
the Muir and Palmer cases, besides the *State Trials* report.

were loaded with irons and herded with the basest criminals in the hulks. Neither Pitt nor his supporters were shaken by the numerous public and private appeals on their behalf. It was not from ignorance of their sufferings but from a deliberate wish that they should suffer, that Ministers left Muir and Palmer to their fate. They suffered, but they were not forgotten. Forty years on their names were seen by Lord Grey on the banners that welcomed him in the Reform Bill celebrations at Edinburgh; while Ebenezer Elliot wrote, in his ' Triumph of Reform ' :

> O could the wise, the brave, the just,
> Who suffered, died, to break our chains ;
> Could Muir, could Palmer, from the dust,
> Could murdered Gerald hear our strains. . . .

But until the coming of the new age, Scotland was silenced even more completely than England. For she had no Parliament of her own and no real representatives even in the English capital. There was no free Press. ' As a body to be appealed to, no public existed.' From 1794 to 1816 there was no political agitation of any kind ; when in 1814 an anti-slavery meeting was held in Edinburgh, it was remarked that ' this was the first assembling of the people for a public object that had occurred here for about twenty years.' [1] The lawyers of the capital were the only men in Scotland who were privileged occasionally to open their mouths on politics ; from their courageous school of intelligence and public spirit issued Brougham, Jeffrey, and the *Edinburgh Review.*

Grey, who was destined to deliver Scotland in the end, was not backward with his protest at the beginning. He wound up the debate in the House, and ' told ' in the division, when the motion for papers on Muir's trial was voted down by 171 to 32.

[1] Cockburn, *Memorials*, 83–96, 282.

The Duke of Richmond [he said] had gone greater lengths than either Mr. Muir or Mr. Palmer, in recommending Universal Suffrage, and telling the people that they must depend on their own exertions in procuring a Parliamentary reform. The efforts of the noble Duke and Mr. Pitt in 1782 on that subject may be regarded as having produced the exertions of these unfortunate gentlemen in Scotland. But what is the result? The noble Duke and Mr. Pitt sit in His Majesty's Cabinet, and give their sanction for carrying into execution the sentences passed on Mr. Palmer and Mr. Muir, that they should be banished for fourteen years and doomed to live with the outcasts of society. I entirely agree with my Right Honourable friend [Mr. Fox] that if the criminal law of Scotland is extended to England, it will no longer be the country where a freeman could live.

Ministers, however, thought that something might yet be done even with the inadequate laws of South Britain. They determined to take not only the liberties but the lives of their political enemies in England. In May 1794 they raised another cry of conspiracy and insurrection as baseless as that of December 1792. They suspended Habeas Corpus, instituted a Parliamentary ' Committee of Secrecy ' to unravel the hellish design, and, with all the solemnity of a Cecil discovering Gunpowder Plot, arrested on a charge of high treason the shoemaker Hardy ; Holcroft, the play-writer, one of the simplest of souls, who walked into Court to give himself up ; the lecturer Thelwall, the friend of Coleridge and Wordsworth ; [1] and Horne Tooke, the eccentric

[1] ' We were once sitting in a beautiful recess in the Quantocks,' wrote Coleridge, ' when I said to Thelwall, " Citizen John, this is a fine place to talk treason in." " Nay, Citizen Samuel," replied he, " it is rather a place to make a man forget that there is any necessity for treason." ' The habit of the Democrats of this period, of addressing each other as ' Citizen,' was unwise, as it had a French flavour. But the terms ' Convention ' and ' Delegate ' for their meetings and those who attended them from a distance, though objected to as treasonable and made a principal ground of accusation in these trials, were names and ideas customary among British Reformers in the 'eighties, and Pitt himself attended a ' Convention ' in 1782.—*State Trials*, xxv. 383–388; *Wyvill*, iii. 24.

and humorous parson-lawyer and philologist, who had diverted himself so well at Purley, and who was now to divert the nation at Pitt's expense. The spies and law officers of the Crown and all the weight of Government influence was directed to getting these and eight other Reformers hanged.

Wordsworth, in that middle period of his genius that gave us the ' patriotic sonnets,' when his judgment was ripe but not rotten, and his political views for awhile partook of the poised balance of the rest of his nature, wrote in the ' Prelude,' looking back on these proceedings of Pitt in the year of Robespierre's catastrophe :

> Our Shepherds, this say merely, at that time
> Acted, or seemed at least to act, like men
> Thirsting to make the guardian crook of law
> A tool for murder ; they who ruled the State—
> Though with such awful proof before their eyes
> That he, who would sow death, reaps death, or worse,
> And can reap nothing better—child-like longed
> To imitate, not wise enough to avoid ;
> Or left (by mere timidity betrayed)
> The plain, straight road, for one no better chosen
> Than if their wish had been to undermine
> Justice, and make an end of Liberty.

The events of the summer might indeed have calmed the nerves of Ministers. ' The glorious First of June ' which ratified our acknowledged supremacy at sea, the fall of Robespierre, and the accession of the Portland Whigs to the Cabinet, might have made them feel safe from the poor prisoners whom they had locked up in May. But persecution had become with them a policy or a habit ; at the end of October the great treason trials began, and lasted through the following month.

Grey and his friends knew that their own liberties, if not their lives, hung upon the verdict. If Hardy could be hanged for founding the Corresponding Society to advocate ' representative government,' on

MARY ELIZABETH (Ponsonby), LADY GREY, 1776-1861.

From the picture by Sir Thomas Lawrence at Howick.

the ground that it was the 'direct opposite of the government which is established here'; if he was to be found guilty of treason because he had summoned a 'Convention of Delegates,' as the Reformers patronised by Pitt had done twelve years before; if Horne Tooke, who had publicly denounced not only Paine's doctrines but universal suffrage, was to be hanged for associating with the members of the Society for Constitutional Information—if in short Pitt succeeded in this as he had succeeded hitherto in all his other alarmist moves, then the Friends of the People might expect to be the next victims. As late as 1798 Pitt confessed to Wilberforce that he lacked only the means, not the will, to imprison Fox;[1] and if he had not now in 1794 received a check from the juries, the Parliamentary Whigs would have been in very real danger. This was Lord Holland's life-long opinion. And Erskine, the great advocate who now saved England from a reign of terror, said to Thelwall, while they were waiting for the decisive verdict of the first trial, that if Hardy was found guilty on such evidence, he himself and the rest of the Whigs 'must all fly to America without delay.'[2]

Grey believed that if Hardy swung his own neck would be in danger. The autumn of 1794 was a memorable season in his life. He had just become engaged to be married to Miss Ponsonby, a love match if ever there was one, and the prelude to fifty years' unbroken happiness. Before him was the full prospect of the best things life can give, which he of all men knew how to value—but across it, on the threshold, lay the shadow of the prison and the gallows. Under such conflicting emotions he wrote his first extant letter to his future wife :

[1] *Life of Wilberforce*, ii. 422–3. Pitt's letter, May 5, 1798. Fox had said that the House of Hanover owed its throne to the people.

[2] Add. MSS., B.M., 35154, f. 28. Holland, *Further Memoirs*, p. 296.

The first trial, which will be Hardy's, comes on on Thursday. I believe I shall attend it, in order to learn how to conduct myself when it comes to my turn.   You see by these new constructions of treason they have found a much better way of disposing of obnoxious persons than by sending them to Botany Bay, and one which will save both you and me a great deal of trouble.   I am not, however, very ambitious of being classed even with Algernon Sydney.

His next letter to Miss Ponsonby is dated from the bench of the Old Bailey, where he had been accommodated with a seat beside the judge, with Major Cartwright at his elbow.   Below, in the presence of a great political audience, two future Lord Chancellors, Erskine and Scott [Eldon], were contending, not without mutual discourtesy, for the sympathies of the Tory jurymen, and no less was at stake than the potential life and liberty of every English Reformer.   It was a scene more fraught with real issues and more truly dramatic than the expense of spirit in Westminster Hall, where Burke and Grey were still obliged to meet in the manager's box—one shudders to think on what terms ! —as joint prosecutors of the great Proconsul.   Here it needed no splendours of imagination and rhetoric to hold the interest of the auditors, half of whom felt themselves to be on trial beside the accused.   On the third day of the proceedings Grey tells the lady who was to share his fortunes :

I am writing from the Bench, with a Judge at my elbows, who I am not quite sure does not think I ought to be in Mr. Hardy's place at the bar ; and I cannot write more than a single line.   They are now examining one of the Government spies who has been employed to frequent a meeting at Sheffield, and who is exhibiting a shocking scene of infamy.

On this day Erskine scored his first great point by reducing Alexander, a paltry successor of the great Titus Oates, to the state in which all such wretches deserve to be reduced in the witness-box.

' Look at the jury, do not look at me, Sir ; I have had enough of you. I wish you would look at those gentlemen ; they are very good-looking men ' ; and then, as the wretch writhed and stammered, ' I am entitled to have the benefit of this gentleman's deportment.' *Lord Chief Justice :* ' Give him fair play.' *Erskine :* ' He has certainly had fair play ; I wish we had as fair play—but that is not addressed to the court.' *Mr. Attorney-General* [*Eldon*] : But whom do you mean ? ' *Erskine :* ' I am not to be called to order by the bar.'

Another witness he addressed as ' good Mr. Spy,' until the Court interfered. It was partly by such simple arts and such honest indignation that Erskine won over the twelve ' good-looking ' men on whose puzzled consciences so much of English history depended. It was no easy task, for he was striving against a mass of prejudice and influence. Day after day the sword of justice still hung doubtful over the head of Hardy and the heads of the host behind him. Grey's undated notes to his future wife follow one another thick :

Of this trial I will say nothing. I have no power to express my abhorrence of the whole proceeding. If this man is hanged there is no safety for any man. Innocence no longer affords protection to a person obnoxious to those in Power, and I do not know how soon it may come to my turn.

So horrible a scene of perjury as was exhibited last night, makes one blush for the depravity of nature. But what shall we say of those who can employ such instruments, to whose means of seduction, which poor men often cannot resist, these horrors are owing, and who are neither more nor less than conspirators against the lives of their fellow men.

After the breakdown of all evidence about arming for insurrection and communications with the French,[1] after Erskine's great speech to prove that propaganda is not treason, and after a neutral summing up by Lord Chief Justice Eyre very different from Lord Braxfield's

---

[1] In November 1792 the democratic societies had rashly communicated with the French; but never once since war broke out.

on Muir, the jury retired for three anxious hours. One thing, probably, weighed with them, though it should not. Everyone by this time knew that public opinion in the capital, though strongly anti-Jacobin, was in this case as strongly against the Government. And when they had brought in Hardy *Not guilty*, the rejoicings that night were such as to be long remembered among the historic outbursts of London's joy.

By so much had Pitt outstripped the panic of his own partisans. If he had tried Hardy for sedition, instead of on the capital charge, he would, in the then state of opinion in the street, in the jury box, and on the bench, have probably got an honest but unjust verdict of ' Guilty.' The check he had now received in court, enthusiastically endorsed by a public opinion that was politically favourable to him, showed that the mass of our countrymen were not bloody-minded, and that their dislike of the French political methods of the day was not hypocrisy. Erskine the Whig, and the twelve jurors believed to be Tories, had between them saved our common English civilisation, which the man in the street valued more highly than did the politicians to whose charge it had been specially trusted.

If it had been anxious work for Grey and Miss Ponsonby, it was tragic for poor Hardy, as honest a fellow as ever sewed shoe-leather. Months before he came up for trial he had learnt from the gaoler that his wife was dead. Far gone with child, she succumbed to the shocks she had received, first when the Bow Street runners seized her husband and ransacked their house, and again when a Government mob attacked it to celebrate the victory of the First of June. Hardy's own life was saved, but he lost most of his business, for respectable people would not deal with the men whom Windham and the Ministerialists chivalrously described as ' acquitted felons.' But Hardy was made of stuff as stout as any of the working-class leaders who have succeeded him. He lived to an honoured old age and

held his head high.   At length, when the young statesman who had watched his trial had become the Reform
Premier, Hardy wrote to Hobhouse, in April 1831:

> You perhaps will smile when I say that I am now for the
> *first time* a Ministerial Man.   I rejoice greatly to see the great
> cause of civil liberty prospering, and that I have lived so long to
> witness it.   Having now entered the eightieth year of my journey
> of life, I am now thirty-seven years older than it was decreed in the
> Privy Council of erring mortals that I should be.   It is really
> an extraordinary change or *revolution* that has taken place in
> this country.   *The King* and *his Ministers turned Parliamentary
> Reformers!* They are committing the very same crime, if
> crime it be, that the Pitt and Dundas infamous Government
> charged the Reformers in 1794 with, the highest crime known
> in our laws—High Treason![1]

In comparison with the tension and tragedy of
Hardy's trial, the case of Horne Tooke that followed
was almost a comedy, and the gallant ex-parson did his
best to make it seem so.   While he was returning one
cold night from Old Bailey to Newgate, a lady admirer
pressed forward and put a handkerchief round his neck.
'Pray, madam,' he said, 'be careful, for I am rather
ticklish at present about that particular place.'   While
in prison, he sang every night at dinner an old Whig
song against the House of Stuart that he had learned
from his grandmother :

> Here's a health to our old constitution,
> Let the trumpets sound
> And the hautboys play.
> Huzza ! huzza !
> To the downfall of all tyranny ;
> I long to see the day.
> Huzza !

Grey, Sheridan, and Erskine went to Newgate to witness
one of these jovial evenings.   'I always disliked him,'
writes Grey, 'and never met him before but in contest.

[1] Add. MSS., B.M., 36466, f. 309.

But the oppression and persecution of which he is the victim made me forget all that is past. Our going seemed to be a real comfort to him. He is in very good spirits, and whether the issue be life or death, I think he will conduct himself like a man.'

Horne Tooke worthily revenged himself on the statesman whom he had so often supported politically, and who was now angling for his life : he haled Pitt into the witness-box and made him look foolish. It turned out that Pitt had sat with Horne Tooke as a ' delegate ' at a ' convention ' for Reform in 1782. The ' delegates ' then had been gentlemen, and now they were working men ; that, no doubt, made all the difference, but it was difficult to draw a legal distinction. The element of the incongruous that struck everyone outside ministerial circles, in the notion of Pitt hanging his old supporter, is reflected in Brooks's betting book, where we read, in Grey's handwriting, October 11, 1794 :

General Fitzpatrick bets Mr. Grey 5 guineas to 1 that Mr. Horne Tooke is hanged before Mr. Pitt.

Yet for all this grim jesting, Tooke's chances of survival were not estimated very high, for while his trial was going on Lord Townshend and Grey had an even guinea on his being hanged, Grey taking the optimistic view.[1]

Horne Tooke was acquitted, and said that he hoped it would make the Attorney-General more cautious in future. After Thelwall, the lecturer, had in his turn

---

[1] There had been some speculation at Brooks's about Grey's and the Duke of Bedford's matrimonial prospects in the summer, at a time when Grey must have been pressing his suit for Miss Ponsonby's hand. On July 27, 1794, we read : ' Col. Tarleton bets Mr. Grey 5 guineas that he [Grey] is married before the Duke of Bedford.' And again on July 30, 1794, ' The D. of Bedford bets Lord Lauderdale ten guineas that neither his grace or Mr. Grey are married on or before 30 July, 1795.' The Duke died a bachelor in 1802.

been tried and found ' Not guilty,' the remaining nine
were discharged.

A few days before this happy conclusion the joy-
bells rang for the marriage of Mr. and Mrs. Charles
Grey (Nov. 18, 1794). We shall often have occasion
to dwell on the homely delights and ever-increasing
preoccupations of a patriarchal state, which made Grey
one of the happiest of men and the least active of politicians, during the long years when he was content to
be prime minister of populous Howick. But during
the first two years after his marriage (1795-6) he was
still hard at work in Parliament, speaking again and
again for the liberty of the subject, opposing the
perpetually renewed suspension of Habeas Corpus, and
attacking Pitt in good set terms for persecuting his old
Reform associates ' with the real bitterness of an apostate.'
Grey told the House that he would ' rather live under
Nero or Caligula ' than in contemporary France, but
that ' those who were most violent in their declamations
against the proceedings in France, were the most servile
in their imitation of them.'

It is agreeable to see that Grey now put himself
forward against an unduly large grant to the Prince of
Wales out of the public money. During the rest of
his life he was ill seen at Carlton House, save on some
rare occasions of princely expansion which he never
strove to turn to account. Indeed, in his thoroughbred aristocratic pride, he was as little suited for a
courtier's life as the noisiest democrat of the Corresponding Society.

He warmly supported a motion for altering the
game laws of that period,[1] which confined the pleasures
of shooting to a small and arbitrarily chosen section of the

---

[1] Grey shot well, but he was not an ardent sportsman. In Nov.
1804 he writes to Fox from Howick : ' There were a good many wood-
cocks here when they first came over, but the weather continuing mild
and open, they are gone further into the country. But I seldom shoot
now.'

landed gentry, for whose benefit the harsh and inquisi-torial game code was enforced against all other classes in the kingdom.   The motion was lost, after Jenkinson, who always said the *juste mot*, had remarked that it was ' a time when every deviation from *legal custom* ought scrupulously to be guarded against.'   Such was the avowed principle of those who were supposed to make our laws, during the advent of the Industrial Revolution; tragically enough, social and economic changes could not be induced to wait till ' legal custom ' was on the move again.   England was hurried on, while her laws stood still.

But indeed the laws did not stand still ; they went back.   In the winter of 1795 began the period of repressive legislation, as if there had not been enough repression already under the old laws.

Since the acquittal of Hardy on the high treason charge, the numbers of his Corresponding Society had gone up, in spite of public disapproval.   In 1795 as many as 2000 members were regularly attending their divisional meetings in London.[1]   The Society thus continued the work it had begun of educating the work-ing men to read and to think, and to associate for political objects.   But the Ministers were still determined to crush it, and since the old laws had failed them, they were ready to make new ones.

They found their opportunity in the rough demonstra-tion against the King's coach in October 1795, which they attributed to the Corresponding Society and to a monster meeting recently held under its auspices in Copenhagen Fields.   When the King went to open Parliament on October 29 a starving mob had hissed the state coach, and followed it crying out, ' No Pitt ! No war ! Bread, bread ! Peace, peace ! ' It was an established custom for discontented mobs in the eighteenth century to hiss the

[1] Add. MSS., B.M., 35143, ff. 8-11.

coach, without any republican or other theoretic implication ; and the mob in 1795 was not a republican but a peace-and-bread mob. The glass of the state coach was broken by a missile that was certainly not a bullet or aimed with any murderous intent.[1]

The broken glass of the King's coach supplied Ministers with material for a panic, a little better perhaps than that out of which they had worked up the trial of Hardy. But this year they took care to succeed by appealing not to a court of justice but to the High Court of Parliament. The Christmas session thus opened was occupied in the passage of two Bills, known as the ' Gagging Acts,' against Seditious Meetings and Treasonable Practices. The first of these made it illegal for more than fifty persons to assemble for any purpose not approved by the magistrates, and visited with the penalty of death those who refused to disperse when ordered. The magistrates of that time were such violent partisans that this meant the end of public meetings to criticise government. With an eye on Thelwall, lectures were subjected to kindred resrtictions. The Treasonable Practices Bill made it high treason, punishable by transportation, to speak or write against the Constitution ; as Fox said, a man was now to be sent to Botany Bay if he argued that Manchester ought to have as many members as Old Sarum. Pitt's father would have cut off his right hand rather than introduce such a Bill.

Grey wrote to his mother-in-law, Mrs. Ponsonby :

You will have heard a great deal of the attack made on the King the first day of the session. That there was a most violent

---

[1] Add. MSS., B.M., 35143, ff. 15–19, 37–50, where Place gives a very amusing inside account of the whole affair, and shows the absence of connection between the demonstration and the Corresponding Society. All the same, one of the most ruffianly of the leaders of the mob round the coach was a member of the Corresponding Society (J. Binns' *Recollections*, 54–6).

and furious mob is certain, expressing, in a tone which it would be well for him to attend to, their discontent and impatience under the grievances which they suffer. But that there was any serious attempt made or attempted to be made on his person, I do not believe. The idea of a ball having been shot at him is completely done away by positive proof, from a person who saw it, that the window of his coach was broken by a stone. This, tho' an outrage much to be lamented, differs materially from an attempt on his life. Ministers, however, do all they can to propagate the alarm, and last night a new Treason Bill in consequence of it was introduced by Lord Grenville into the Lords. We shall oppose it, but I have no doubt of its being carried by acclamation through both Houses of Parliament.

The most celebrated speech in the debates on Pitt's ' Two Acts ' was made by Horsley, Bishop of Rochester, who said that ' he did not know what the mass of the people in any country had to do with the laws but to obey them.' It was one of those phrases that attract attention because they blurt out the real issue on which parties are contending.

A furious agitation, for and against the two Bills, arose, the last stir of political life before the ' Euthanasia,' as Fox called it, settled on the country for twenty years. Throughout November loyal addresses and petitions for the Bills were handed about, accompanied by every kind of intimidation and calumny against those who refused to sign. Even so the signatures against the Bills were said to be over 130,000 and the signatures for them only 29,000. Yet Place, who gives us these figures, afterwards wrote :

Infamous as these laws were, they were popular measures. The people—ay, the mass of the shopkeepers and working people —may be said to have approved them without understanding them. Such was their terror of the French regicides and demo- crats, such the fear that ' the throne and the altar ' would be destroyed.[1]

[1] Add. MSS., B.M., 35143, f. 52 ; 27810, f. 91.

This no doubt was the prevalent feeling in London, which Place knew so well. But in the North a somewhat different atmosphere seems to have prevailed. The feeling in Northumberland was so hot against Pitt's two Bills, that while Grey opposed them at Westminster his constituents held a county meeting at Morpeth with Sir John Swinburne in the chair, and sent up to their member a petition against the Bills from the ' Noblemen, Gentlemen, Clergy, Freeholders and Inhabitants of the County of Northumberland.' In London Grey took it round to the Duke, who signed it, and then carried the document to the King at St. James's Palace, where it ' was very graciously received,' he writes, ' though perhaps the prayer of it will not be much approved, and I fear certainly not granted.' No other county except Derby petitioned as a corporate body. Even the county meeting at York was divided.[1]

The Bills passed, and political life died out in England. The new laws destroyed the usefulness of the Corresponding Society and the other democratic clubs, which dwindled and disappeared, the last of them being abolished a few years later by an *ad hoc* statute. In February 1796 Fox wrote : ' The whole country seems dead, and yet they certainly showed some spirit while the Bills were pending.'

Since it was now by law criminal to agitate the main questions of politics anywhere outside the walls of Parliament, it behoved the opposition members to be more than ever vigilant and active in the one place where free speech was still permitted. Major Cartwright wrote to Fox that the Bills were ' intended for silencing for ever the voice of complaint, especially on the grand subject of Parliamentary Reform ' ; and that when they were passed it would rest ' almost wholly with the friends of freedom in Parliament to nourish the cause of freedom.'

[1] Grey's letters to his Northumbrian supporter, Mr. Thomas Bigge, August to December 1795, and *Wyvill*, v. pp. xxiv-xl and 314-16.

Unfortunately, by the great dereliction of duty known as 'the Secession,' the Reformers in the House took a precisely contrary course. But before they indulged in the selfish ease of ' Secession,' they salved their consciences by one last great demonstration in force on May 26, 1797, when Grey made his second motion for a reform in Parliament. That debate and division is the last milestone in the Parliamentary history of the question until after Peterloo.

Grey was at this time in favour of household suffrage. On March 8, 1794, he had written to Major Cartwright explaining why he would not go as far as the Major's logical scheme for universal manhood suffrage :

A considerable part of the dispute seems to me to turn upon a misapplication or a misrepresentation of the rights of men. Nobody holds those rights, which it is now so much the fashion to speak of in mockery or reproach, higher than I do ; but they do not consist in universal representation or in any particular form of government. Government being formed for the protection and security of rights, whatever mode is best calculated to produce that end, whether it be universal or a more limited system of Representation, is that to which people have a *right*. It is from such a conviction that in the formation of a new system I should wish to stop short of Universal Representation. If a right of voting, so extensive as to comprehend *all the householders* of the Kingdom, were established, the present system of corruption would be completely defeated, and all the advantages that can be expected from a system of Universal Representation, without many of its mischiefs, would be obtained.

In May 1795 the Friends of the People met once more after an interval of a year, during which they had ' agreed to suspend their proceedings ' owing to the war and the general discouragement of Reformers. At this meeting, which proved to be their last, they adopted an elaborate scheme of reform, including a redistribution which would destroy the rotten boroughs, and a household rate-paying franchise, uniform for the whole country.[1] Two years later Grey based his scheme on these proposals of the Friends of the People, except that he confined the rate-paying franchise to boroughs. His motion in the House on May 26, 1797, was more definite than in 1793.[2] He now rose to ask ' leave to bring in a Bill,' and the Bill was outlined in his speech. He proposed that Parliaments should be limited to three years ; that the poll should be taken on one day throughout the whole island ; that ' if possible, one person should not be permitted to vote for more than one member of Parliament.' He proposed to raise the English and Welsh county representation from 92 to 113 and to extend the right of voting in counties now confined to freeholders to certain classes of copyholders and leaseholders.

For the boroughs he proposed much greater changes, beginning with a complete system of redistribution, which would have abolished rotten boroughs and given the great towns a considerable though not quite a numerically proportionate representation. He would have the 400 members for these newly formed borough divisions elected ' by one description of persons, which were householders, paying taxes ' (viz. rates).[3] Fox, speaking later in the evening, explained that this meant householders paying scot and lot, that is Church rate and poor rate, and that this would give an electorate of 600,000 for all the boroughs, which 'would give to

---

[1] *Wyvill*, v. pp. xiii–xxiv. 'That every householder in Great Britain, paying parish taxes, except Peers, should have a vote in the elections of one member of Parliament.'

[2] P. 75, above.

[3] The Parliamentary Report omits the words ' paying taxes,' which are found in the report in the *St. James' Chronicle*. Both reports are very poor. In his letter to Cartwright in 1794, quoted above, Grey had spoken of ' householders ' without qualification, but Fox's speech on May 26, 1797, explains Grey's plan on the assumption of its meaning householders paying ' scot and lot.'

every member about 1500 constituents.'[1] Fox thought
this was restoring our old constitution, not going forward on any French system ; he declared that ' the
common law right of paying scot and lot was the right
of election in the land ' in old days, and quoted ' the
celebrated Glanville ' as his authority. He objected,
he said, to universal suffrage, not because it would
lead to a wild democracy, but for the opposite reason
that it would enfranchise servile and dependent classes.
' Housekeepers ' suffrage would give the largest possible number of ' independent ' voters.

These proposals of Fox and Grey for a household
or rate-paying franchise were, in principle at least,
nearer the Act of 1867 than to the Act of 1832 ; on
the other hand, Fox's figures, if correct, do not seem
very large. But the ' nicely calculated less or more '
did not trouble either side in 1797. The arguments
used against Grey's motion were arguments against any
and all reform as ' Jacobinical ' in the circumstances
of the time, rather than against any particular scheme
as being too extensive. Neither were the Foxite
Whigs frightened by the boldness of the measure,
which was a flag of battle rather than a practical proposal. As many as 91 members voted for Grey's
motion, against 256.

At the end of his speech Grey had foreshadowed
the secession of the Foxites from Parliament, by the
singular announcement that if his motion was not
carried, he would not in future speak in the House,
but only vote on important measures. And Fox himself, in winding up the debate, declared that he would
henceforth devote more of his time to his private

---

[1] The Friends of the People, in May 1795, had calculated that the
scheme would give about 1,200,000 voters, or about 2400 constituents
to each member (*Wyvill*, v. p. xxii). But this was based on the calculation of applying the rate-paying franchise to counties as well as to
boroughs.

pursuits, 'and the leisure that I love.' It is a pity that so fine a public service as these two had just rendered was marred by so impotent a conclusion.[1]

[1] The working-class movement for Parliamentary Reform and its suppression by Pitt, described in these chapters on account of its important relation to Grey's contemporary action and subsequent career, has held too little place in the political histories of this period. Indeed, it is only of recent years that such indispensable sources of information in *Add. MSS.*, *Place Papers*, British Museum, were first brought into the light by Mr. Graham Wallas in his biography of Place. Now, fortunately, this grave lacuna in our historical knowledge is being made good, for example, in the study of the question by Pitt's latest biographer, Professor Holland Rose; and, from a different point of view and in more detail, in Mr. Veitch's *Genesis of Parliamentary Reform*, 1913, and in *The French Revolution in English History*, published in 1918, after its brilliant and well-loved author, Mr. P. A. Brown, had been killed in action. But even so the *Place Papers* have only been skimmed. Large selections from them ought to be published, so that the question between Pitt and the working-class Reformers could be judged by the world on fuller knowledge.

CHAPTER V

THE SECESSION—THE FOXITE WHIGS AT HOME—HOWICK— IRELAND—1797-1801

' If our reliquiae could be kept together, if it were only Russells and Cavendishes and a few more, with you at the head of them, not only would it give me great satisfaction, but it might be a foundation for better things at some future period.'—FOX TO GREY, March 12, 1803.

' How I do long to return to Tacitus and our own comfortable fire ! '—GREY TO HIS WIFE, Dec. 29, 1799.

THE Secession of the Foxites from the House of Commons lasted intermittently from the winter of 1797 for about three years, when it gradually came to an end as Whig after Whig stole back to his place. At no time was it complete. Tierney attended regularly, Sheridan occasionally, and on the question of the Irish Terror the whole party under Fox came up to vote. But there was no consistent opposition for three years.

Lord Lansdowne, fully reconciled to the Whigs in their adversity, tried to save them from committing this mistake. ' Secession,' he said, ' means rebellion, or it is nonsense.' In this case it was nonsense. Fox and Grey were not riding off with pistols and broadswords in their belts to proclaim a Republic from St. Anne's Hill, or to call out the train-bands of Northumberland. They left Westminster, not to make history, but to read and write it ; to learn Homer by heart, and to dispute together about Chaucer and the Faery Queen. They could find only the feeblest political excuses for a defection that was in fact personal. They said it was a protest against Government tyranny, but the floor of the House was the one place in England where that tyranny was not exercised to silence debate. Attacks made on the Government in the House could be reported in the newspapers without fear of prosecution. The debates were in those days the chief means of political education, and newspapers gave two, three, and sometimes all four sides of their single sheet to very full reports. During the years when Pitt's repressive legislation had given a monopoly of free speech to Members of Parliament, the Liberal party there refused to exercise it. And the country suffered accordingly.

Pitt is said to have been vexed by the cessation of his enemies' fire from the front, because it encouraged his great supporter to attack him from the rear. When the King turned recalcitrant, he could now no longer threaten him with Fox. It is possible that in this way the denial of Catholic Emancipation as an accompaniment of the Union, the well-head of Irish troubles in the nineteenth century, was indirectly the outcome of the Secession. It was certainly the triumph of George III and the more reactionary Cabinet Ministers over Pitt.

In matters where he did not differ from the King, Pitt was left absolute master of the field. It was during the Secession that Pitt systematically imprisoned large numbers of Reformers for years together without trial, treating them like convicts and feeding them on bread and water.[1] While England was adopting the system of *lettres de cachet* of old France, scarcely a voice was raised against the scandal : the Press was gagged by fear of prosecution, and those Liberals who might have spoken in Parliament so as to be heard had deserted their post. Now also (1799–1800) the infamous and disastrous Combination Acts suppressing Trades Unions were passed, opposed by Lord Holland alone in the

[1] Add. MSS., B.M., 27808 ff. 110–12, 27809 ff. 203–61; Oxlade's narrative, 1798–1801.

Lords, and by Sheridan almost alone in the Commons. The rest of the Opposition were 'in secession,' enjoying the leisure of their country homes while the Government was perverting the whole growth of the new industrial society.[1]

During the same period when he had no criticism to fear, Pitt determined to alter the Toleration Act in a way that would soon have filled the prisons with Dissenting ministers, whom he had come to regard as a species of black Jacobins. His Cabinet approved the plan, and in 1800 he was only dissuaded from carrying it into effect by the strong remonstrance of his friend, Wilberforce. That excellent man found much in Pitt's conduct to lament. It was the hour of Dundas and the powers of darkness. The slave trade, once threatened and hard pressed, now throve exceedingly ; to descant upon its horrors was the sign of a 'Jacobin,' and Dundas could raise in the House 'a roar that has seldom been equalled' by a sneer at Wilberforce and his 'straggling humanity.' It was a sorry ending for a great century, which had ushered in far other hopes for mankind.[2]

A portion of the responsibility for the evils that befell the British islands between 1797 and 1801 must be assigned to Fox and Grey, who preferred domestic joys and the cultivation of the Muses to the work of an unpopular Opposition, that always seems but never is quite useless. Grey, supported by Bedford, Lauderdale, and Whitbread, was the chief mover for secession in 1797 ; in twelve months he had repented and wished the step retraced. Fox, more slow to consent on public grounds, though yet more anxious for personal retirement, warned the 'young ones' that if once they persuaded the old man to come away it would be harder

---

[1] Hammond, *Town Labourer*, chap. vii.; Graham Wallas' *Place*, chap. viii.

[2] Wilberforce, *Life*, ii. 17–19, 336, 360–6, 397. In 1805 Dundas had reason to be sorry that he had provoked a saint.

still to make him come back.   When it was proposed
to draw up a public statement of the reasons for secession, it was found that ' every individual differed as to
principles and motives.'   Those of Fox and Grey were,
in truth, nothing more subtle than disgust with the
course of politics, and a simple human preference for
books and gardens, family and friends.[1]

Married life was new and delightful both to the young
man and the old.   Grey's family was just beginning
its long increase.   Fox, who had given up gambling
when the party paid his debts in 1793, two years later
secretly married Mrs. Armitstead,[2] and became thenceforth as truly domesticated a character as Farmer George
could have wished any of his subjects to be.   He who
in youth had left a princely fortune on the gaming
table, now found his happiness in shopping with his
wife, buying ' *cheap* china, for they were great econo-
mists ' ; in lying still for hours on a green bank, in the
very spirit of Andrew Marvell, until he taught the
jays of St. Anne's Hill not to fear his motionless form,
but to continue their depredations on the old fruit-wall
opposite ; in reading for his history of James II ; and
in writing to Grey on such topics as this :

In defence of my opinion about the nightingales, I find
Chaucer—who of all poets seems to have been the fondest of the
singing of birds—calls it a *merry note*, and though Theocritus
mentions nightingales six or seven times, he never mentions
their note as plaintive or melancholy.   Sophocles is against us.[3]
I am afraid I like these researches as much better than those
that relate to Shaftesbury, Sunderland, etc., as I do those than
attending the House of Commons.

[1] *Lady Holland*, i. 148, 180, 215.   Holland, *Memoirs*, i. 84–94.   Fox,
Memoirs, iii. 136–7.

[2] The marriage was made public in 1802.   In 1803 Grey writes
to Mrs. Grey : ' Fox seems in the highest spirits and is in the best looks.
He is like a young man in the prime of life who has just married a girl
of sixteen.   Is it not a fine thing to grow young at fifty ? '

[3] Wordsworth thought as Chaucer and Fox.   See ' O Nightingale,
thou surely art.'

Burke used to harangue his friends for an hour on end about the ' *ambition* ' of Fox, declaring that he sought to overturn the constitution, ' because a Government like ours was not a proper one for great talents to display themselves in ' ; while Gillray week by week depicted him inviting over the French or striking a treaty with the Devil. How very different was the real Fox, and how different his real crime—to have yielded when his followers pressed him to join their retirement from the public arena ! ' At no time,' so those who really knew him have reported, ' did the warmth of his heart, the sweetness of his temper, and the refinement of his taste give such tranquillity to his home. The trees and the flowers, the birds and the fresh breezes gave him an intense enjoyment, which those who knew his former life of politics and pleasure could hardly have imagined.' [1] Other friends of liberty suffered much in these bad years, and Fox felt for them deeply, but of his own happy life these years were the happiest. When he was in politics he liked to win, but he could well afford to lose. ' *Ambition* should be made of sterner stuff.'

Fox was a mighty worker and a mighty idler. In his second capacity he was no good example for Grey, whose worst political fault was inactivity. But his precept at least was good enough. When Grey wrote to him : ' What am I doing ? you will ask. Literally nothing. If it be true, as Burke said, that Idleness is the best gift of God to man, there never was anybody so highly favoured of heaven,' Fox replied : ' I love idleness so much and so dearly that I have hardly the heart to say a word against it, but something is due to one's station in life, something to friendship, something to one's country.'

Fox at least idled no further off from the scene of action than St. Anne's Hill ; but Howick was three, four, and sometimes even five days' posting from

---

[1] Fox, *Memoirs*, iii. 35 ; *Malmesbury*, ii. 448.

London, according to the luck of weather, wheels, and horseflesh. In the Parliamentary recesses of 1795, 6, and 7, Grey and his wife lived at Howick as his uncle Henry's guests and prospective heirs. His extreme unwillingness to leave Mrs. Grey and Howick, which became the plague of successive generations of his colleagues, was already a pleasing absurdity. But the querulous tone of his letters in absence is the measure of his extreme happiness when at home—a happiness which diffused itself through all the family at Howick. In November 1799 he writes to his wife :

Look at all your rich acquaintance, and tell me whether the situation of any of them is really and intrinsically as happy as ours. I will answer the question for myself, and in doing so I think I may answer it for you too, that there is no creature upon earth with whom I would change : no, not even with Bonaparte.

He was never a rich man—a man with fifteen children seldom is—and at this time, when his family was as yet small, his means were smaller still. In a series of letters to the most active and friendly of his constituents, Mr. Thomas Bigge, in which he tries to excuse himself for being at Howick during the autumn session of 1797, one of the reasons that he gives for his own truancy is that—owing, of course, to Mr. Pitt's ' infamous impositions '—he cannot afford to keep an establishment in London or move his family so far in the winter. He offers to resign his seat if, as Sir John Trevelyan of Wallington warns him may occur, there is a county meeting held to consider the ' secession ' of their member. Meanwhile he will thank Bigge to send him ' Southey's and Coleridge's poems,' those gentlemen being interesting young enthusiasts in the Democratic cause.

A year later, at Christmas 1798, he roundly confesses to Bigge that the Secession was a mistake, and that he has put himself into a most difficult corner.

When one takes a single wrong step, there is no line to be pursued which does not lead into some kind of embarrassment. A total secession without resigning my seat, I must acknowledge to be wrong, and so long as it is out of my power (on account of private reasons which have not escaped you) to resign my seat, and still less in my inclination to take any active part while Fox abstains from doing so, there is no mode of conduct I can adopt which in my own opinion would be perfectly right.

The difficulty was that if he returned to Parliament, as he now wished to do, it would be said that he had decoyed Fox into secession in order himself to return and step into the vacant leadership. The course which he actually adopted of a graduated return to his Parliamentary duties, accompanied at each stage by strong appeals to Fox to come back too, in the end freed him from the snare in which he had entangled himself. Even the hypercritical Lady Holland wrote on the subject : ' Unless I knew Grey to be of an honest, open, warm-hearted character, I should myself suspect a little fraud, but I fully acquit him.' From January 1799 onwards Grey attended on Irish nights only, to oppose the Union ; from November 1800 onwards he took part in all the debates and made some effective speeches about national burdens, imprisonment without trial, and other grievances ; in March 1801 Fox put in his first appearance, and very gradually and unwillingly resumed the leadership. During all these nice operations the personal friendship of Fox and Grey was never once overshadowed, but went on ripening until, excepting always Lord Holland, Grey stood decidedly first in Fox's political affection.[1]

[1] In 1799 Grey writes to Holland : ' I have had a letter from your Uncle [Fox] which deprives me of all hope of his attending even one discussion upon the Union, and to say the truth makes me feel a little uncomfortable about my own attendance, though I am sure he did not mean that it should have that effect.' The letters from Fox to Grey are preserved from 1800 onwards, those from Grey to Fox from December 1802 onwards. See also *Lady Holland*, i. 215 ; ii. 139–40.

The social life of the Whig Opposition at this period is almost as important a subject for study as its political activities, if we would learn how in that age a Parliamentary party attached to the principles of Reform managed to survive the long reaction. The secret lies in a paradox. Fox's scanty followers were more democratic politically and more aristocratic socially than the Whigs of any time before or after. The party chiefly consisted of the Dukes of Bedford and Norfolk, Lords Holland and Thanet, Lansdowne and Stanhope, the Cavendishes and a few score of other gentlemen of fashion, some of them sitting for rotten boroughs belonging to members of this circle. Such was the party that had in May 1797, at the bidding of Fox and Grey, voted 91 strong for Household Suffrage. On Fox's birthday in the following January, the Duke of Norfolk gave the toast ' Our Sovereign, the People.' He was at once dismissed from his lord lieutenancy and his colonelcy of militia. Fox, in a fit of generosity, repeated the toast, and was cut off the Privy Council. Pitt wrote to his intimates that he would like to put Fox in prison, but could not trust a jury. Fox's letter to the Duke of Norfolk expresses the sense in which the toast had been given :

My dear Lord,—The toast relating to the sovereignty of the people will be universally and I believe truly considered as the cause of your removal, and thus you will be looked up to as the marked champion of that Sovereignty, under which alone King William and the Brunswick Kings have held their throne. The Ministers call for unanimity, for suspension of party disputes, for the purpose of repelling a foreign enemy, and then they dismiss Your Grace from not only a Lieutenancy, but a Regiment, for an opinion certainly of a theoretical nature at any rate, but an opinion which to have controverted in the times of the first two Georges would have been deemed a symptom of disaffection.[1]

These genuinely democratic aristocrats attracted to

[1] Unpublished.

themselves a considerable number of the old Whig connection who cared little for democracy, but who found Tory society insupportably tedious. The Foxites had captured Brooks's, and many who regarded dining and talking there as the chief privilege of life, were in that way gradually won back through personal channels to political connections they would otherwise have repudiated. In this way the Cavendishes now,[1] and some years later the Spencers and Lord Fitzwilliam, drifted back into the party. 'The Duke of Devonshire,' writes Lord Holland, 'a man of little popular feeling and still less exertion, but of great probity, honour, and good sense, and fond of the society of Mr. Fox and of his immediate friends, had been with great difficulty brought to vote once or twice with the Administration.' In June 1794 we find him betting at Brooks's with Lord Thanet that the Duke of Portland will not take office under Pitt. And when Portland immediately proceeded to disappoint his expectation, Devonshire for his part went back to the Fox connection. 'In this,' says Lord Holland, 'the Duchess of Devonshire was not a little instrumental. In a very short time after the feverish and unnatural separation of 1793 she had the satisfaction to see most of that society, of which she was the ornament and soul, reunited in the support of Mr. Fox.'

It was now a very small and a very select society. They were men of fashion in an age when to be fashionable was neither easy nor vulgar. They were men of culture, with a knowledge of Greek, Latin, French, Italian,[2] and English literature very uncommon in later times. The Tories called them Jacobins and ' outcasts,' but they in turn looked down upon the Tories as somewhat unfashionable and decidedly illiterate people,

[1] Lord Frederick Cavendish was brother to Mrs. Grey's grandmother, Lady Betty Ponsonby. The Greys often stayed at his seat, Twickenham Park, during the 'nineties.

[2] See note at end of this chapter.

although Pitt had nine-tenths of the upper classes and the writers of the *Anti-Jacobin* on his side. ' If Pitt had any learning,' wrote Fox, ' or if those of his friends who have, had any genius,' they would quote Demosthenes, ' who is better adapted to their side of the question.'[1]

Politics and seats in Parliament went by privilege in those days, and if all the privileged classes had been reactionary, Reform would never have come without civil war. It is easy to sneer at the Whigs for being aristocrats, but it is lucky that in an aristocratic age a few aristocrats were Liberals. Whig fashion and culture had their effect on our political history, for they strengthened the minds of these few men to hold out in favour of Reform, against the frown of power and against the opinion of their fellow-countrymen, and to wait in the cold of opposition for forty years. Literature consoled them for loss of power, and aristocratic pride made them indifferent to the censure of society. If they had not been such aristocrats, they would not then have dared to side with democracy.

A gathering at one of their great country houses, like Holkham or Woburn, where they stayed together for weeks at a time, shooting, riding, reading, and above all talking and listening to Fox talk, was the one thing which could partially compensate Grey for absence from Howick—itself such another place, but smaller and more homely. He often writes to his wife from Woburn, the Duke of Bedford's place, as on July 23, 1800 :

I did not find as large a party as I expected. It at present consists of Fox, Lord Robert [Spencer], Fitzpatrick, Lord John Townshend, [Philip] Francis, Dudley North, Richardson, and

---

[1] I suppose the dangers of the Macedonian power, denounced by Demosthenes, would correspond to the dangers from French aggression. Did Fox mean they were to quote Greek in the House ? Members would, I suspect, have understood it almost as little as their successors would now understand Latin.

myself. Sheridan and Adair are expected to-day, and Hare to-morrow. Fox is in the highest spirits. It is quite delightful to see such a man in the midst of a society which he appears to like, so unassuming, good humoured, and cheerful. Everything seems to be a source of enjoyment to him, and I hardly know which to envy most—his amiable disposition or his unrivalled talents. When I descend from admiring him to think of myself, how I sicken at the contrast ! He is enthusiastic about poetry, and admires Spenser as much as we do. You may remember how cheap Francis appeared to hold us for this taste at Woolbeding.[1] He is not stout enough to disparage Spenser as much as he did then, before Fox, but I assure you his opinions upon this subject, as far as he has ventured to express them, have gained him no applause.

The room we inhabit is the Library, where we lounge over books or join in conversation as suits our inclination. In this manner the morning, or the greater part of it, passes, with perhaps a sauntering walk in the pleasure ground, or the Tennis Court, where Fox and Lord Robert generally play for an hour or two. We dine at four, and generally walk out after coffee, after which there is a Party of the good players, from which I am excluded, at Whist, in a room which opens into the Library, where the rest of the party amuse themselves as in the morning. Supper is served in another adjoining room about eleven, after which we generally sit up pretty late.

In June 1801 his benevolent uncle offered Howick to him as his own residence.

I have news to tell you [he writes to his wife] such as will, I think, be equally surprising and pleasing to you. Sir Harry has in the handsomest way possible consented to our going to Howick, and to our living there on our own bottoms in future. You must begin soon to make your preparations, and above all prepare yourself to become a very notable Farmer's wife, for we shall be very poor, but I hope, too, very comfortable.

So on July 17, 1801, they entered Howick as its master and mistress, and on the anniversary of that day, forty-four years later, he there died. Sir Harry, whose kind

---

[1] Lord Robert Spencer's house, near Midhurst in Sussex.

CHARLES	HENRY,	BALAAM	GEORGE	LOUISA	WILLIAM
(General)	LD. HOWICK	(the donkey)	(Admiral)	(Lady Durham)	(died 1815)

HENRY, LD. HOWICK (3rd Earl)

ELIZABETH (Lady Elizabeth Bulteel)

FREDERICK (Admiral)

Some of the Grey children on the sea-shore near Howick, 1813.

From the picture by Henry Thomson, R.A., at Howick.

act almost amounted to an inspiration, lived bachelor-wise in London and elsewhere till his death in 1808. The house which they entered in that first summer of the new century was the same dignified but comfortable mansion of good Northumbrian stone that now conceals itself homelike among the tall trees.[1] But those trees are, with a few older exceptions, of Grey's own planting. And it was he who made and planted the mile-long track down the bottom of the burn's cleft to the sea—a favourite haunt of the tribe of children and the invariable Sunday walk of young and old together. When the rocky coast is reached by this pleasant path, the quarry can still be seen whence Sir Harry in 1780 hewed out the grey stones that now are Howick. There, too, is Howick Bay, a sandy cove encircled by rocks, where the supplies from London were sometimes landed.[2] And there is the lonely sandstone cottage that was abandoned to the children for a seaside study and playhouse, as soon as they were old enough to look after themselves among the rocks. Public schools were not part of the family plan. Indeed the Grey boys and girls—the girls, fortunately, the elder—were numerous enough to be a school in themselves under governesses and tutors at Howick (*see* Genealogical Tree, end of book). Grey's second son, Charles, writes :

When I speak of a childhood and youth of more than common happiness, I do not speak too strongly. Rarely indeed, if ever, has the grown man or woman had reason to look back upon that early period of life with such fond recollection.

And he adds :

[1] The outer hall, containing the entrance vestibule, was added by Grey about 1812, together with some of the stables and outhouses.

[2] They would come by boat from Alnmouth, having come to Alnmouth by ship. Such sentences as ' a great cargo of books is gone by an Alnmouth ship ' are common in Grey's family letters. The servants went to and from London by ship at the yearly move.

Considering the nature of the rocks forming the coast of Howick, over which we clambered at will, it does seem almost like a special protection of Providence that averted any serious accident.

Three miles north along this secluded coast, on the other side of the fishing village of Craster, stood the ruins of Dunstanborough, grandly alone on their promontory. There, under the castle walls, was the wild and dangerous landing-place where Queen Margaret of Anjou had stepped ashore on one of her desperate enterprises. The place was regarded as haunted at night, and Lord Grey told his visitors that ' the fishermen often see lights moving among the ruins.' The legend of the Castle ghost, ' Sir Guy the Seeker,' was thrown into the ballad of that name by ' Monk ' Lewis, when he was stopping on a visit at Howick.

The country between the hills and the sea consisted of rolling grass lands, mostly open moor when Grey settled at Howick in 1801, but enclosed in large fields in the course of the next thirty years.[1]   It was perfect for a gallop across, were it not for those sudden little precipices so common in Northumberland ; one of these near Howick was called ' the Heugh,' along the top of which was a favourite ride.   On one of his journeys up to Parliament, in January 1808, Grey writes from the inn at Grantham :

When the sun was shining with a fine mild air, I figured to myself you and my two sweet girls on the Heugh.   I saw Ida [the mare] going beautifully ; and the light on the house and craig behind, with a calm blue sea, were delightful to my imagination.   Oh that I could see them in reality !   Yet I am very confident that my stay in the place I hate most will be short.

Grey seldom lacked an excuse for delaying his

---

[1] It is pleasant to remember that wages and conditions were far better in Northumberland for the agricultural labourer all through this period than in the south or in the country generally. See O. J. Dunlop, *The Farm Labourer*, pp. 87–90.

loathed return to 'the place I hate most,' for it was odds but either one of his numerous progeny was ill, or another one expected. On one such interesting occasion, in the last days of December 1810, when the arrival of a small new Grey at Howick happened to coincide with an incipient Cabinet crisis connected with the Regent's *velléités* towards the Whig aspirants to office, the happy father writes to Whitbread from Howick : ' I would not have been absent to be myself Regent or King.' Fox, and Holland after him, often smiled over these excuses, which annoyed less good-natured colleagues. And in the days when the nurserymaids at Howick and elsewhere threatened their recalcitrant charges with ' Boney,' he had the further excuse, pleaded to Fox in October 1803, that ' to leave my family in so exposed a situation, under the possibility of the enemy's landing, I hold to be impossible, and I am sure you will admit it.' In the following February, still safe at Howick, he writes to his benignant chief : ' I am not afraid of any serious landing here, but even an alarm might be unpleasant, and we had one, owing to a mistake in firing the beacons in Berwickshire, only yesterday.' This was none other than that famous night alarm when, on the other side of the border, Mr. Oldbuck girt on his old sword, and Lovel and Hector were reconciled in their country's defence.[1]

The comedy of these excuses for staying at Howick and lamentations at leaving it, lasts a good thirty years. In October 1809 Tierney writes to him :

Which of your ancestors it was who purchased or seized an estate in Northumberland I do not know, but I wish with all my heart he had been knocked on the head for selecting such an out-of-the-way spot for the residence of his descendants. There are a thousand things which it would be most desirable to talk over. No good can be done unless you come to town.

[1] The end of Scott's *Antiquary*.

In 1821 it is still the same story ; Grey writes to his wife :

> To describe my melancholy at having left you all is impossible. Oh how I wish I was now going on with 'Kenilworth Castle' to the same audience that I had last night ! [1]

At length, in 1830, he seems to have felt satisfied of the necessity of occupying Downing Street awhile ; but after his retirement from office and public life in 1834 he could stay at Howick all the year, and there was no man to make him afraid.

The trouble was by no means over when he had been fairly got to London. In January 1805 Fox writes to him at Howick :

> And now as you have addressed yourself to Mrs. Fox, let me do so to Mrs. Grey, and beg her not to think of letting you come alone, or that at least she will follow very soon after. God knows when you are in town without her you are unfit for anything, with all your thoughts at Howick, and as the time for which your stay may be necessary must be uncertain, you will both be in a constant fidget and misery.

He was never really well in London. He is always complaining of what he calls his ' London feels.' Holland House, in Kensington, then well out in the country, was often a refuge to him. He was there more and more often as the years went by, the lord becoming ever dearer to him and the lady less formidable.

> I came here yesterday to dinner [he writes in 1808], and

---

[1] Not Scott's *Kenilworth,* but a poor imitation of Scott, if we may judge by the rest of the letter. Scott wrote fast enough in all conscience, but not fast enough to supply his devotees at Howick and elsewhere. Some of them were even then capable of criticism. ' We are in the middle of the *Pirate,*' writes Lady Georgiana Grey ; ' I like it, but Papa does not—he says it bores him.' In December 1815 Lady Holland writes to Grey : ' This new novel of Mrs. [*sic*] Austen's is very inferior to her former writings. It is called *Emma.* It is really very flat and without any interest, else I would send it you.'

having been most kindly pressed to do so, stay till to-morrow, when the Hollands themselves go to town. I always like Lord Holland's company, and the least breath of country air makes me feel so much better than I do in London.

Grey was on intimate terms with his wife's relations, the Ponsonbys, the famous Liberal family of Ireland, answering to the Tory Beresfords who were identified with the existing system. From the time of his marriage in 1794 he took a deep interest in the tragedy enacting over there. During the last years of the century he corresponded across the Channel with his wife's father, William, afterwards (1806) first Lord, Ponsonby ; with her uncle George, leader of Opposition in the Irish, as afterwards in the English, House of Commons ; and with her mother, who also was a shrewd adviser on her country's affairs.

It is a satisfaction to record that one day, in the middle of their ' secession,' the Whigs appeared in the House of Commons, led by Fox, and took part, over sixty strong, in a debate and division on the horrors that had provoked the rebellion then raging in Ireland. Burke, who had died the year before, had with rare insight called the Protestant ascendancy of that day ' Jacobinism,' and indeed it would take a casuist to choose between the wickedness of systematised torture in Ireland and of systematised massacre in France. On June 22, 1798, the day after the rebellion thus provoked had been crushed at Vinegar Hill, Lord George Cavendish and Lord John Russell,[1] in the English House of Commons, moved a vote of censure on the Irish Government for its harsh treatment of the Catholics and their claims, and after that had been defeated by 212 to 66, Fox moved a motion condemning ' scourges and other tortures employed for the purpose of extorting confession ' ; but a motion that ' the House

[1] Afterwards 6th Duke of Bedford ; father of the great ' Lord John,' then a child of five.

do now adjourn' was carried by 204 to 62. Grey spoke on the first motion. The Tories had cleared the galleries, so that this damaging debate might not be reported in the newspapers or in the Parliamentary reports.[1] But some account of this inquisition held *in camera* is given in Grey's letter to his mother-in-law, Mrs. Ponsonby:

Bad as the public accounts [from Ireland] are, they are not worse than I expected, or than I shall continue to expect, so long as that horrible system, to which I for one shall for ever ascribe the present revolt, continues to be acted upon. We made all the efforts we could to give some check to it, and I really thought that by the last debate in the House of Commons we had made at least such an impression with respect to the conduct and language of my Lord Clare, as would probably have occasioned his removal from office. Indeed, the whole *Irish* Government in the House of Commons was, in a great measure, given up. Our animadversions upon them were not answered. In the attack upon the [Irish] Chancellor [Fitzgibbon, Lord Clare] persons even on the other side, Wilberforce for instance, joined us, and there seemed to be a very general disposition to shift the blame from our Ministers here to the Government there, which I thought might lead to some changes.

In the House of Lords, however, a very different tone was assumed, and put an end to all these speculations.

To me, who think that the use of the scourge and the bayonet will only create fresh provocations, and that, though we may gain victories, victories will not gain the people, the accounts published every day in the Government papers furnish only fresh matter of despondency and dismay.

Then followed the Union, which, being unaccompanied by Catholic Emancipation, perpetuated for generations to come the race hatred engendered by these events. Throughout 1799 and the following year Grey made a point of attending Parliament on Irish nights, although until November 1800 he still 'seceded' from the House on English questions. ' I

[1] *Parl. Hist.*, xxxiii. pp. 1511–1517.

feel,' he writes to his wife, ' as eager to defeat the Union as if I were myself an Irishman.' But neither his efforts in England nor those of his kinsmen in Ireland could avail, and in 1801 the brothers William and George Ponsonby were sitting as Foxite Members of the Parliament of Great Britain and Ireland.

Note to p. 106. Fox, in his letter to Lord Holland of February 18, 1796, has a long passage, written in very choice Italian, discussing the merits of various Italian poets and authors. The passage is omitted as irrelevant in Fox, *Memoirs*, iii. 130-131. I here append a translation of ' By the Banks of Allan Water,' by Grey, from a copy in his own handwriting, now in possession of Lord Halifax.

Dell' Adige sul lido
Isaura m' incontró,
Dei fiori di Primavera
Ornata e bella andó.
La cercó un cavaliero
Giurando eterno amor,
Sull' Adige non era
Donna piú lieta allor.

Quando d'autunno i frutti
Cogliea la giovenù,
Isaura vidi ancora
Ma non sorrise piú.
Pria che passó la State
Lasciolla il Traditor,
Sull' Adige non era
Donna piú maesta ancor.

Con nimbi intanto e gelo
L'Inverno ritornó,
Ma il rigor del cielo
Isaura non curó ;
Non pianse piú l'infido
Piú non la strinse amor,
Dell' Adige sul lido
Morta giacea allor.

BOOK II

THE STAGNATION OF PARTIES
1801–1830

INTRODUCTORY

Milton ! thou should'st be living at this hour :
England hath need of thee : she is a fen
Of stagnant waters : altar, sword, and pen,
Fireside, the heroic wealth of hall and bower
Have forfeited their ancient English dower
Of inward happiness. We are selfish men.

So wrote Wordsworth, when the century ended in
misery and gloom ; nor did the severe language of the
poet do more than give an English voice to what all
Europe then thought of us. Burke, Pitt, and Fox were
great men, but each had his own terrible shortcomings,
and under the malign presiding influence of King George
the net outcome of their dealings with the country they
all loved so well was little better than the poet has said.
Even Milton, one fears, would scarcely have helped,
for Pitt would have sent him to Botany Bay. And so
we had, when the reforming century opened, a Press
and platform silenced ; an Opposition sulking out of
Parliament ; suspicion of the ' lower orders ' as the
potential enemies of the State, instead of that frank
trust of the people that has belonged to all the great
periods of English history ; the poor in town and
country sinking to the lowest depth of dependence and

of want ; Ireland an epitome of the evils that mis-government can inflict on mankind ; our military fame diminished ; our one triumph and safety the ' storm-beaten ships ' that have never failed England in her need. But the next thirty years that lie between the Treaty of Amiens and Grey's Reform Ministry saw the most astonishing revival of ' sword and pen,' and raised our country's reputation in the world to a point that it had scarcely touched under Queen Anne or Queen Elizabeth. Nelson and Wellington adorned their country with honours won in fair fight from the greatest fighting man and fighting nation that the world had ever seen. Scott made the study of British antiquities, manners, and history the concern of all educated men and women in both hemispheres, counteracting the Napoleonic roar, that filled the highways of Europe, with something quiet and old and British ; Byron mocked the Holy Alliance, and both of them together made the Romantic Movement ; while Wordsworth and Coleridge, Turner and Constable, Shelley and Keats, Lamb and Jane Austen made England even greater than foreigners knew.[1] And besides so much genius of the first order, the little island was full of remarkable men—Cobbett and Brougham, Cochrane and the Napiers, Porson and Bewick, Eldon and Sydney Smith, Coke of Norfolk, and dozens more of that time whose names or faces crowd upon the memory; all stand self-planted like forest oaks, deep-rooted and growing, each after his own singular pattern. We have become more civilised, more social, more subtle than that race of men, but decidedly less interesting. No wonder the country that could boast such children was proud and strong, first defeating Napoleon, and then under Canning turning round to defy the priests and despots whom we had exalted

---

[1] It is true that several of these had done much of their best work prior to 1800, in the period stigmatised as sterile in the lines of Words-worth quoted above.

in his place. In comparison with other countries of contemporary Europe we had, as the poet had prayed,

> Manners, virtue, freedom, power.

But these thirty years, so great in the breed of men and in the noblest trophies of letters and of arms, were fatally sterile in politics. England could organise herself for no social purpose, and allowed her millions to become the economic prey of the blind forces of war and of the unguided industrial revolution. It was the period of the stagnation of parties. We have seen how, during the French Revolution, three parties had been formed— the anti-Jacobin Tory, the Reforming Whig, and the Paineite, later called the Radical. From 1800 to 1830 they all three remained as they had begun in the 'nineties, without any change in their respective principles, or in the distribution of power between them. The Tories governed as they pleased ; the Whigs waited, content to preserve their own identity ; the Radicals, after Waterloo, gained some influence over the public opinion of the masses, but none on the action of Government. The omnipotent Tories adopted Burke's later creed that the laws of the eighteenth century must apply for all ages to come, and that demands for change in Church or State must be answered by 'criminal justice.' A doctrine of such extreme conservatism would have done less harm in mid-eighteenth century, when England was in a condition of stationary welfare ; but when rigidly applied by Eldon and Castlereagh to England in the vortex of economic and social change, it was utterly disastrous. The state to which it reduced Ireland became evident even to the Duke of Wellington when he surrendered to O'Connell in 1829. The state to which it reduced England when Grey took office in 1830 was such that the dissolution of society seemed only too probable, and was in fact only averted by the commencement of an age of rapid reform.

Grey, as we have seen, had been active and effectual

during the formation of parties. But during the stagnation of parties he slumbered. Throughout this period of waiting his main duty was to sit still. In fact he sat too still. He refused either to ally himself with the Radicals or to enter upon a reform agitation in rivalry with theirs. But at least he had the merit of keeping the Reforming Whig party opposed to the existing system of repression in Church and State. In the new century he did nothing to create a stream of reform opinion, but he kept the Parliamentary channels open and the Whig party machine ready to act as the popular instrument, against the day when the flood should come ; and when it came the mill worked and ground the corn of a new and happier age.

CHAPTER I

THE 'EUTHANASIA' AND THE CONFUSION OF PARTIES— PEACE AND WAR—1801-1805

'If the country has, as I think it has, though tacitly, changed the nature of its government, it would be exceedingly absurd to say that the small Minority who lament that change, after having used their efforts to prevent it, should exclude themselves from any participation in the new system.'—UNPUBLISHED LETTER of FOX TO WILLIAM SMITH, Nov. 15, 1801.

IN these words the Whig leader defined the attitude of his followers, when on their return from the Secession they found the political life of the country dead, the popular societies abolished by law, the Press gagged, and the thought of the people preoccupied wholly with the monstrous power of Buonaparte. The 'euthanasia of politics' that Fox had so long dreaded had in fact set in. He and Grey gradually ceased to agitate for Reform,[1] since the question could no longer find a response outside Parliament. Accepting the fact that the Liberal elements in the constitution had been suppressed, they had yet to decide whether they would take an active, and if necessary an official, part in working the new system which they disapproved but could not alter. This question, which remained to plague the Whigs many years after Fox had been taken from them,

---

[1] At the general election of July 1802 Grey made a strong pronouncement at Alnwick for reform of Parliament as being 'indispensable' (*Creevey*, Nov. 4, 1834). This opinion he never once in his life abandoned, but he ceased to urge it frequently.

arose out of the situation created by the events of 1801. In that year, although Tory principles remained unchallenged in all departments of national life, the Tory party began to break up on personal issues into so many hostile sections that Whig help would clearly be required to unite with one or other of these, if a Government was to be formed of experience and ability on a level with the dangers of the State.

Although the quarrels of the Tory leaders were mainly personal, especially in their later developments, they arose in the first instance from the semblance of dispute on a public question. Pitt had aspired to make the Act of Union an act of reconciliation, by permitting Roman Catholics to sit in the Parliament of Great Britain, from which, as also from the late Dublin Parliament, they had hitherto been excluded. Irish Roman Catholics had acquiesced in the Union only because this prospect had been held out to them. They were now to find themselves deceived. George III developed conscientious objections to Catholic emancipation, as a measure contrary to the principles of his coronation oath. Pitt therefore resigned, and Addington took his place as Prime Minister in February 1801. Pitt had resigned, not in order to coerce George into submission, but to salve his own conscience, and possibly also to enable a new Minister to make peace with France on terms which he himself would have found it mortifying to accept. For any good it could do to Ireland, his resignation was rendered worse than useless by his promise that he would not again bring forward the Catholic question in the lifetime of George III. This act of submission to the Royal will was made on the ground that George III would otherwise go mad for good and all. Periodic fits of lunacy had recently returned, and the astute patient, in his lucid intervals of sanity, had made use of his privileges as an invalid to extort from Pitt this surrender of principles on the top of his resignation of office. Mr. Lecky has remarked that Pitt

would have deserved more credit for his delicacy if it had not coincided so perfectly with his interest, and if it had not involved him in what may be not unfairly called a gross breach of faith with the Catholics.

Pitt's promise never again to disturb the King's mind with the grievances of his Irish subjects enabled the Tory party to become, in its popular appeal, the No-Popery party. All effective championship of Roman Catholic grievances was henceforth left to the Whigs, and made them more unpopular than ever, both with the country and the Court. Grey felt bitter resentment against Pitt, and against Canning after him, because, while holding Liberal views on the Irish question, they consented to leave it in abeyance, and to reap all the advantages of favour with Crown and people as heads of the No-Popery party. This state of things continued after the final madness and the death of George III, for the Prince of Wales had become almost as anti-Catholic as his father before he was called on to succeed him. When, after Waterloo, the Tories became the unpopular party, they still retained a last hold on the sympathy of the masses through the No-Popery cry.[1] Much that was strongest, both good and bad, in the English nature was at that time expressed in a hatred of the Church of Rome. The religious revival of the day took the form of Evangelical Protestantism, alike in Church and Chapel ; the Marian persecution and the massacre of St. Bartholomew were household words,

As late as 1831 young Gladstone, canvassing for the Tories, wrote : ' You would be astonished how unanimous and how strong is the feeling among the freeholders *against* the Catholic question. Reformers and Anti-reformers were alike sensitive on that point and perfectly agreed. One man said to me, " What ! Vote for Lord Norreys ? Why, he voted against the country *both* times—*for* the Catholic Bill (1829) and against Reform " ' (Morley's *Gladstone*, bk. i. chap. iii.).

alike in cottage and in hall ; the easy-going and often sceptical toleration, characteristic of the age of Gibbon, had given place to a stern and bitter temper against ' infidelity ' on one side and ' Popery ' on the other. In these circumstances, the unselfish conduct of the Whig leaders in their championship of this hated cause for thirty years, on behalf of people with whom they had nothing in common in religious, political, or social environment, and who could not lend them a single vote in either House of Parliament, goes far to ennoble the annals of English statecraft between 1800 and 1829.

While the Addington Ministry was in process of construction, Grey thought it would prove at least as bad as its predecessor.

It is formed [he wrote to Wyvill on February 11, 1801] avowedly on the same principles in every respect but one [the denial of Catholic emancipation], in which it differs from the old administration only in carrying to a greater length than they did the principle of Intolerance and Persecution. Such an appointment, destitute as it is of character, of property, of talents and of principles, ought not to create any relaxation [in the business of opposition].

Yet the very weakness of Addington's Cabinet in talents and prestige led to a less rigid enforcement of the system of persecution begun by Pitt. The new Prime Minister was to some extent afraid of opposition, and since he had so few friends among his fellow-statesmen, he could the less afford to be bitterly hated by the people. The Reformers who had been kept in prison for several years without trial were released in March 1801,[1] and in the following year, after the Peace of Amiens, a certain increased freedom of the Press was perceptible. Moderate Reformers like Wyvill dared again to publish their pamphlets.[2] There was some respite in the activity of the persecutors, but there was no real freedom, for

---

[1] Add. MS., B.M., 27808, ff. 112–113.
[2] *Wyvill*, iv. p. xv.

repression had become a permanent system and the
spirit of resistance was dead.

The talent of the Tory party had gone into
opposition or retirement. Grenville and Canning, the
heavy troops and the light, were alike contemptuous
of the unfortunate ' Doctor,' who had nothing but the
courteous bedside manner of his father's profession to
recommend him as a physician of State.

> Pitt is to Addington
> What London is to Paddington

summed up their view of the situation. Nor can it be
doubted that a Cabinet which excluded Pitt and Fox,
Canning and Sheridan, Grenville and Grey, and was the
butt of the satires and cartoons of all parties in the State,
aroused the easily moved scorn of Buonaparte at the most
critical stage of our relations with France, when only a
very strong Government over here had any chance at all
of rendering peace permanent. Buonaparte, after ex-
tracting excellent terms from Addington at the Treaty
of Amiens, proceeded to push on his encroachments in
Central Europe as if there were no more need to reckon
with England. It is very possible that not even Pitt and
Fox together could have preserved peace with Napoleon,
but it is certain that it was far beyond the Doctor's skill.

Addington had soon to look round for ' talents '
to strengthen his Ministry, and since Pitt's followers
were so hostile, he began to court the Whigs.

There were personal divisions in the Whig as well
as in the Tory camp. Fox, Grey, Holland, and their
friend the Duke of Bedford, who died in 1802, formed
the core of the party, while Sheridan and Tierney and
to a less degree Erskine were severally detached from
this central group.

Sheridan and Grey had been mutually antipathetic
ever since the days of the Regency debates, and fresh
grounds of offence were always occurring. Fox and
Grey regarded Sheridan's influence at Carlton House,

and the use to which he put it, with constant
suspicion.

It is quite impossible to place any dependence on the Prince
[wrote Grey to Fox in August 1803], and the similarity of
their characters in some respects is, I believe, one cause of
Sheridan's influence over him.

In January 1802, at a Whig Club banquet, Sheridan
had spoken of

those persons who, thrown by accident in the outset of life into
situations for which they are not fitted, become Friends of the
People for a time, and afterwards, finding their mistake, desert
the popular cause. (*Reiterated plaudits and laughter.*)

It was a most gratuitous attack on a colleague. Grey had
in no sense ' deserted the popular cause.' Grey's comment
to his brother-in-law Whitbread is scarcely too harsh :

My dear Sam, I do not think Sheridan can have the excuse
of being drunk for what he said, or if he had it is but a poor
compensation for me, whilst an attack is circulated in all the
newspapers so obviously directed that nobody who knows that I
was chiefly concerned in the institution of the Friends of the
People and at that time ' *in the outset of my political life*,' can
misunderstand it. The applauses of the Club were if possible
more disgusting than Sheridan's attack. As to being drunk, I
know that Sheridan has the peculiar faculty of making a beast
of himself where nobody else would, yet immediately after the
cloth was removed, upon one of the first toasts after dinner,
industrious and active as he is in this respect, I think he
could hardly so soon have completed his daily work. But this
is not the first time I have been attacked by him in a similar
way.

Meanwhile Tierney was writing to Grey a series of
embittered tirades against Fox, which appear to have
been dictated rather by a sense of personal neglect than
by any political disagreement to which the writer could
put a name. Tierney's attacks on Fox put an end to

---

[1] *Morning Post,* January 20, 1802.

his correspondence with Grey, and injured the cordial relations of the two men which had begun in their common efforts as Friends of the People. In 1806 the correspondence was resumed, and lasted on terms of friendship, political and personal, for more than twenty years.

Tierney and Sheridan, thus alienated from the chiefs of their own party, willingly listened to the overtures of Addington. Tierney, in May 1803, became Addington's Treasurer of the Navy, and Sheridan, while refusing office, lent his support to the Government. Erskine also supported Ministers. Rational politics were dead, and party connections were on all sides dissolving so fast that at the end of 1801 Addington actually attempted to induce Grey and the Duke of Bedford to take office under him without Fox. Grey afterwards wrote to Fox, ' My escape from the scheme of last year I think one of the happiest of my life '—as indeed it was if there was ever any danger of his taking office without his friend and leader.[1] And in April 1803 he writes to his wife, referring to this earlier transaction:

I have no reason to believe the Ministers would offer better terms than they did a year and a half ago, and I should feel myself compelled to insist upon a great deal more. In short, I would not negociate on any ground but that of having a majority in the Cabinet, Fox being one.

Fox, meanwhile, was drifting towards an alliance not with Addington but with Addington's enemies the Grenvilles, and he finally carried over Grey and the Whig party into that connection. But so long as peace and war were hanging in the balance during the

---

[1] In February 1802 Fox wrote to Grey, ' My reason for asking you the question I did [whether all negotiations with Addington were broken off] was not indeed anything like a *suspicion*—my dear Grey, how could such a word come from your pen ?—but because I believed some persons understood the thing differently.' One of these persons was Lady Holland—see her *Journal*, ii. 147. See also Fox, *Memoirs*, iii. 352–3.

brief respite of the Peace of Amiens, union was impossible, because the Grenvilles and Windham led the war party, and Fox the peace party, while Pitt kept silence, and Addington as Minister occupied a middle position on the question of the inevitableness of a renewed breach with France. In the winter of 1802 Fox wrote to Grey:

> With respect to men, you know my inclination would rather be to the Grenvilles, as men of spirit, but the line they have taken with respect to war and their professed desire of reinstating Pitt make any junction with them impracticable for the present.

To which Grey replied :

> I have not considered the possibility of joining the Grenvilles. I agree with you in preferring the men, but the line they have taken up puts it quite out of the question.

' The line ' taken up by the Grenvilles and their friends led straight to war. They denounced Buonaparte in season and out, and attacked Addington for his efforts to preserve the Peace of Amiens. Fox, meanwhile, had been to Paris with Mrs. Fox and the Hollands, had seen the First Consul, and had come back enraptured with the man so much dreaded by the Grenvilles. Indeed we find that Grey, in the very letter of December 5, 1802, in which he objects to the Grenville party as too warlike, warns Fox in his turn against taking too roseate a view of the pacific character of Buonaparte.

> Nothing [writes Grey] lately has given me more pleasure than to find, after the opportunities of information which you have had, that you think peace may be preserved with honour. I confess everything I have learnt seems to me to evince a disposition in the Chief Consul very unfavourable to such an opinion. I do not mean to contend that by any of those acts of open and undisguised ambition by which he has annexed new dominions to France, either the letter of the Treaty of Amiens is violated, or that the Power of that country is, in point of fact, extended. Italy, Switzerland, Spain and Holland, and Germany too, were

all left at his mercy. But there may be a way of using power so threatening and so insulting as, at last, even under the most disadvantageous circumstances, to force resistance. And he appears to me to be determined to make us drink the cup of our disgrace to the very dregs ; to omit no opportunity of studied aggravation and insult, and to push us point by point till at last we shall be compelled to take some measure which may give him a pretence for the hostilities which he meditates.

In the event of war, to which I look as too certain, which will then indeed be a war of destruction, what choice have we left but to support it ?

I rather envy you having seen all the wonders of Paris, though my hatred to the Government would, I believe, even if I were at liberty, prevent my going there. Perhaps you will think this very foolish, but I certainly never felt a stronger indig-nation against the principles of the Coalition against France, than I do against those of the Consular Government.

One sentence in Fox's reply can hardly be read without a smile :

As to France, I am obstinate in my opinion that Buonaparte's wish is peace—nay that he is afraid of war to the last degree.

But he then continues with more insight :

The present object is to avoid war ; and though you agree with me in that, I do not know that you see the misery of war now quite in so strong a light as I do. Only reflect upon Ireland and Finance on one side, and the impossibility of hurting France (or to speak more properly, of diminishing her power) on the other.

Indeed, if Windham and the Grenvilles had known that ' to diminish the power ' of France we should have first to lead her in triumph to Vienna, Berlin and Moscow, they might have called for war with less eagerness.

When the final breach with France came, Grey, in spite of his intense distrust of Buonaparte, considered, as Wilberforce did then and as some of the best informed historians have done since,[1] that Addington had mismanaged the final negotiations about Malta in a way that went far to put us apparently in the wrong when we were essentially in the right. In a series of letters to his wife he describes the great debates that ushered in the Napoleonic war, when the finest speeches ever made by Pitt and Fox, the one rousing the nation as only Pitt could rouse it, the other in protest against the crime of provoking war, were hurled across the House over the heads of the shuddering and incompetent Ministers.

London, May 17, 1803.

We are now actually at war, and we can only say God send us a safe deliverance ! which under such Ministers can hardly be hoped. Hawkesbury,[2] in moving to have the king's message taken into consideration on Monday next, was absolutely convulsed with fear and could hardly articulate from the violence of his agitation ; and to make the thing quite ridiculous Addington appeared in the full dress of the Windsor Uniform, and strutted up the House in the midst of a burst of laughter just as the Speaker was reading the *Medicine Act* a second time!

May 24.

Pitt made one of the most inflammatory speeches that ever was heard, and has plunged the country into another war of ten years. I answered him, and under all the disadvantage of speaking to a House pre-occupied and inflamed by one of the most magnificent pieces of declamation that ever was made. I got through it, however, *tant bien que mal*, and ended by moving an amendment merely to say that we would support the war in which we are engaged, and holding out the hope and desire of Peace. My reason for moving an amendment was that I could not consent to the original address, which implied an approbation of the endeavours of Ministers to preserve Peace and asserted the War to be unavoidable, without sufficient information. Fox is in reserve for to-day.

---

[1] *Dropmore Papers*, vii. pp. xxxii-xxxiii.
[2] Lord Hawkesbury (formerly Mr. Jenkinson, afterwards Lord Liverpool) was Addington's Foreign Secretary.

House of Commons, May 25.

Here I am again in this odious place, where I now pass my life. Fox's speech was the most wonderful display of wisdom and genius that ever was exhibited. It makes everything else shrink into dust.

A few days later Fox wrote to Holland :

Grey and I are, if possible, still more *one* than ever ; indeed, the good humour with which he bore staying in town so long against his will, and his kindness in shewing his agreement with me upon all occasions, have made me love him more than ever.

We were thus, without allies, at war with Napoleon. It was the era of the camp at Boulogne and of Nelson's watch off Toulon.

In Britain is one breath ;
We all are with you now from shore to shore,

wrote the poet who had eyed askance the opening of the war of 1793. So far as the people were concerned there was no thought save of union against the foe. There were some who held with Fox that war might have been avoided, but all were determined to conquer now that war had come. We were no longer banded with kings to suppress a democracy, but defending our own island against a tyrant. The people were at one ; but the great politicians and the King still had small-minded quarrels, so that no man abler than Addington could be set up to lead the country in the hour of its worst peril and most heartfelt union.

Lord Grenville was in many ways a narrow man ; he had little sympathy and no imagination for anything outside the governing class of his own country. But his patriotism, though confined and cold, was pure. He was not, like his brother the Marquis of Buckingham, for ever scheming to serve himself and his relations. Grenville now eagerly sought to unite Pitt and Fox and all the political talent of the day in a Cabinet of national defence. If Pitt and George III had consented, the thing could have been done, and it would have had a noble air. The politicians would have reflected the unity of their fellow-countrymen. But Pitt loved supreme power and had no wish to share it. Only on one occasion did he offer to share, and then, when the King refused to have Fox, made no serious effort to overcome his resistance, which gave way the moment Pitt was dead. It was this that brought about the strange political combination of the Tory Grenvilles with the Reforming Whigs.[1] Grenville, impressed by the danger of the country, tried to act as a connecting link between his old colleague Pitt and Fox himself. Pitt played with and then rejected the idea, and Grenville, indignant with Pitt, and bound in honour to the Foxites, cast in his lot with the group of politicians from whom in principle he most differed. It was an unnatural alliance due to chance, and was for many years inimical to the healthy development of parties, but unlike the coalition with North it did no injury to the reputation of the statesmen who formed it. It was done 'all in honour, ultra-honourably.'

The only great public question on which Grenville and the Foxite Whigs agreed was Catholic Emancipation, although until 1805 they do not seem to have realised the importance of this link. But another strong influence was drawing the parties together. Lord Grenville commanded not only the Parliamentary retainers of his brother Buckingham, but a number of the Whig connection who had seceded with Burke and Portland. Burke was dead, and Portland, for all that he had been so unwilling to break with Fox in 1792, had since found complete salvation as a Tory. But Windham, Lord Spencer, and others still thought of themselves as Whigs, and now that the heat of the anti-Jacobin

---

[1] Grenville's character in all these dealings has, I think, been amply established by the *Dropmore Papers*, vol. vii.

panic was over, remembered old days and felt once more the attraction of Fox's circle of friends. The chief agent in bringing about the reunion was the Hon. Thomas Grenville, younger brother of Lord Grenville and the Marquis of Buckingham, who, unlike the rest of his family, had been a Whig before the split of 1793, and had never ceased to be a denizen of Brooks's Club. He was a man of many friends, and was naturally in a position to act as mediator between his brothers and the two sections of the Whig party, with one of whom he had of recent years acted in politics, while socially he had never broken with the other. Thomas Grenville was, in particular, a friend of Lord Spencer, who had done Pitt yeoman's service as First Lord of the Admiralty ; if the alliance of the Grenville party with Fox and Grey did nothing else, at least it brought back the House of Althorp to the ranks of Reform.

The first definite proposal for united action was made to Fox by the Grenvilles and their Whig friends under pressure, as we may say, from Napoleon. In the winter of 1803-4 the British nation became aware that a flotilla of 3000 craft had been collected near the camp of the Grand Army at Boulogne. Since the days of the Spanish Armada there had been no such fear in our island. Lord Grenville would wait no longer, but on the last day of the year 1803 broached to Pitt his scheme for ' an understanding between the considerable persons in the country, forgetting past differences and uniting to rescue us from the fearful danger ' of invasion. Pitt declined to move, and Grenville thereupon applied to Fox. Fox at once consulted Grey, who was of course at Howick :

St. Anne's Hill. Jan. 29, 1804.

Dear Grey,—I have had a direct communication (wholly unsought by me) from that part of the Opposition which sits at the Bar end of the House to the following effect : that it is their wish to join with us in a systematic opposition for the purpose of removing the [Addington] Ministry, and substituting one on the broadest possible basis. Stowe [1] and all its appendages, Lord Spencer and Windham are the *proposers*. Of Carlisle and others we have no doubt, and FitzWilliam, as you know, is eager for such a plan. There was an openness and appearance of cordiality in the manner of making the proposal that much pleases me.

Upon the subject of Pitt there was no reserve. It was stated that he, for himself, peremptorily refused entering into anything that could be called Opposition, and that a full explanation had taken place between Lord Grenville and him upon that point. The result of this explanation was, that all political connection between them was off.

To this Grey replied from Howick on February 2, 1804 :

My dear Fox,—When I have considered that alone we can do little good, and have examined the different Parties with which it might be possible to form a junction, I have always thought that of the Grenvilles the most eligible. Yet now that the proposal comes directly from them, and it is necessary to say Aye or No, I doubt and fear.

They certainly are able men : their conduct is direct and open ; we agree with them in opinion both as to the character and the measures of the present Administration ; and the overture which they have made, appears, from what you say, well calculated to inspire confidence.

But, on the other hand, their Opposition has appeared to proceed rather from personal disappointment than from public principle : they are extremely unpopular, and it is not till they have failed, first, in their endeavours to set up Pitt as the only man who can govern the Country, and next to gain the Country and inflame it in support of a War which they hoped to conduct, that they have recourse to us.

I should rather approve of your second answer, expressing a general inclination to support ; promising it on certain occasions, but declining, for the reasons you give, a regular and systematic attendance.

---

[1] Stowe, the famous seat of the Marquis of Buckingham, means politically the Grenville family.

Fox accordingly replied to the Grenvilles, in the sense agreed to by Grey. On March 12 Fox wrote to Mr. William Smith, ' I will not conceal from you that if I had followed my own opinion entirely, I should have gone further.'[1]

Owing to Grey's objections, the alliance was still informal. But Fox's energy made it serve as well as the most complete fusion. Throughout April he and Grenville pressed Addington close in Parliament on national defence, Pitt aiding from his lofty isolation. All this while Grey stayed at Howick, reading with mingled feelings Fox's joyous despatches from the scene of action :

> Our division last night was 107 to 128. If Pitt plays fair we shall probably give Addington his death blow unless he runs away. What I have seen of Lord Grenville confirms me in my opinion that he is a very direct man.

Grey replies :

> I am glad you are so well satisfied with the conduct of the Grenvilles. Have you ever had any explanation with them on the subject of peace ? I wish the event may not exemplify the old fable of the Log and the Stork—

the stork being ' Pitt's crest,' as Fox is amused to remember. Near the end of the month Addington tottered to his fall, and Fox compelled Grey to come to town. On the way up he writes from a wayside posting-house to his wife : ' " Alone, unfriended, melancholy, slow." Not very slow either, for I have come about 100 miles to-day, but as melancholy as heart can be. The contest does not animate me, and I hardly wish for success.' When he arrived in London

---

[1] Unpublished letter. The best and fullest account of the transactions of January–May 1804 will be found in the *Dropmore Papers*, vol. vii. pp. xxxviii–xli and letters in text. But the Grenville-Fox alliance was not ' successfully concluded ' as early as January 31, as might be supposed from an expression used on p. xxxviii.

he heard that Addington had resigned. The King sent for Pitt to form a Ministry ; and the famous transactions that then took place are nowhere better told than in Grey's letters home :

May 7, 1804.

I write from Fox's, whilst I am waiting for the result of Pitt's interview with the King. Lord Grenville is now with Fox in the room below, having come from Pitt. Perhaps it is very foolish to enter into any speculation when there is only a partition between me and certainty, and probably I shall in ten minutes know what has passed. But I must talk with you as if you were here waiting with me, and tell you my opinion that it will end in Pitt's coming in without any of us.

Well! Fox is just come in, and my speculation is confirmed. Pitt, after pressing very strongly the necessity of a junction with Fox, finds the King so obstinate in refusing to admit him, that he is obliged to give it up. Fox is the only person objected to, and Pitt is now gone to Lord Grenville.

If, by stating Fox to be the only person objected to, they mean that the King would accept of me or any other of Fox's friends, and that they have hopes of gaining us, they are, as far as relates to me at least, completely mistaken. No earthly consideration should make me accept Office without Fox. How unceasing the persecution of him is ! How honourable to himself, how disgraceful in all those who submit to it ! As far as concerns myself, I am sorry for this, for I had really and unaffectedly something like a horror of Office.

May 8. The objection being personal to him, Fox expressed a wish that his friends should accept, if they could be admitted as a party to their full share of influence and power, and rather more [influence and power] than if he himself formed a part of the arrangement. Pitt seemed inclined to discuss this proposition in a personal interview with Fox, but I put an absolute veto on it, and we are all excluded. The Grenvilles have also refused, and have indeed behaved in the most honourable way ; so that Pitt must make up his Ministry out of the rump of the old Administration and his own immediate friends. In short, I believe the list I made out at Howick will be pretty near the thing.

I saw Pitt in the House of Lords, and I think he looked very miserable. We have no right to impute any unfairness to him, for he always avowed that he would do as he has done, but I would rather be any man in England than him.   How much more exalted the situation Fox occupies !

These events achieved for Fox the fusion he desired of his own followers with the Grenvilles and their Whig adherents.   The gallant refusal of those statesmen to take office with their former chief Pitt so long as Fox was left out, silenced all objectors against them in Fox's circle, and Grey, who of all things admired personal loyalty in political dealings, ceased to be a critic of the Grenvilles.

The new alliance for awhile had as its journalistic fugleman no less a person than Cobbett, a rising power in the land, now in the passage between his former Tory and his later Radical position.   Equally unstable, but more important so long as it lasted, was the patronage of the party by the Prince of Wales, which rendered it liable to come into power any day, if the physicians pronounced the King mad.   Stories, some true and some false, of the eccentric behaviour of the monarch who had ostracised Fox were current coin at Brooks's.   In May 1804, the week after Pitt had formed his last Ministry out of those who were ready to submit to the Royal caprice, Grey writes to his wife : ' One story is that, upon being stopped by some embarras in Bond Street, the King put his head out of the chaise window, and cried: " Hot Buns ! " ' And a few days later he writes :

I don't know how Pitt feels, but I should be miserable in his place.   The uncertainty of the King's remaining even as he is, and the embarrassment to which Pitt must be daily exposed by his extravagance, must make the task of government a dreadful one.   He looks pale and ill.

Pitt had indeed too many reasons to look ' pale and ill.'   The King's periodic fits of lunacy, which it was impossible entirely to deny even in public, were one part of his trouble.   Then there was the gout of which

Pitt himself was dying. The awful burden of public care, with the Grand Army on the cliff thirty miles away, pressed to the ground an invalid who had to bear it all alone ; the only real colleague in his cabinet, Dundas, was removed for awhile from public life on a charge of financial impropriety, driven home by Wilberforce himself. Pitt was reduced so low that even the resignation of the Addingtonians out of the Ministry was a serious matter for him. The Opposition were strong in divisions and far superior to Government in debating talent.

God knows [wrote Grey to his wife] Pitt has as many things to embarrass him as his worst enemies could wish. Before the debate began last night his countenance exhibited strong marks of care and vexation and afterwards of rage and disappointment. Fox spoke admirably.

In May 1805 the cause of Catholic Emancipation was brought up in both Houses by the Opposition, when Grattan's exiled eloquence first enthralled the British Parliament.

The Irish delegates [wrote Fox to Lauderdale] have been peremptorily refused by Pitt, and now come to us. I like this very much, and cannot help thinking that Lord Grenville and myself bringing the thing forward is the best possible thing both for the country and ourselves.

Fox's notion of the ' best thing ' for a party would not have appealed to Taper and Tadpole, for the espousal of the Catholic cause, now deserted by Pitt, was a sure road away from popularity and from office. It was significant that the Prince of Wales' members voted against the Catholics ; the body of the Whig party had doubted the wisdom of taking up so thankless a task, but were overborne by the generous firmness of Fox, Grenville, and Grey.

The curtain was now ringing up on the great middle

act of the Napoleonic drama—the first scene being a cantata of picturesque Chouan brigands. The vendetta between the Bourbons and the Corsican who reigned in their stead culminated in the Chouan plot against his life, responded to by his fierce vengeance wreaked on the innocent Duc d'Enghien. These events roused a passion of devotion to him in the people of France, and of loathing for him in the Courts of Europe. And his own nature seemed to have drunk the poison. Forgetful of his earlier ideals, as armed defender of the benefits of the revolution in Western Europe, as legislator and healer of ruined France, he gave himself up wholly to the lust of power and conquest, the rattle of artillery along all the roads of Europe, and the glitter of the Byzantine ceremonies of a Court.

> Thou mightest have built thy throne
> Where it had stood even now ; thou didst prefer
> A frail and bloody pomp which Time hath swept
> In fragments towards oblivion.

He crowned himself Emperor in Notre Dame, the Pope attending. But with what new trophies should he celebrate his Empire, as he had celebrated his Consulship with Marengo ? As if to give him the opportunity he desired, the Third Coalition rose up against him to be destroyed.

Nelson, hot on the traces of trembling Villeneuve in and out of the West Indian Archipelago, and Calder waiting for him in the fog, had rendered the camp at Boulogne an idle spectacle, a sword nailed fast in its sheath. The Third Coalition saved Napoleon from acknowledging failure. In September 1805 he rushed across Europe with the Grand Army, lately ' of England,' now ' of the Danube.'

Pitt had agreed to pay £12 10s. a year for every man put into the field by Austria, by Russia, and by Prussia if she too would join. How far the Coalition was the outcome of these subsidies, how far of Napoleon's deliberate provocations, how far of the Czar Alexander's ambitions—and whether Pitt was wise or foolish to call in the great military powers to help Nelson—are subjects on which historians differ still, as politicians differed then.[1] Pitt's policy was certainly a failure, but whether any other course would have turned out any better is a matter of mere speculation.

Fox at any rate maintained, before the event proved him right, that Pitt's proceedings would lay eastern Europe at the feet of Napoleon. The Grenvilles, on the other hand, believed in the old policy of their former chief, and looked for victory from the subsidies and the Coalition. On September 22 Grey wrote to Fox :

> The best use that can be made of the Alliance would be to *negociate*, but this, I suppose, our Ministers are not likely to do, and we shall have to regret again, perhaps, when its strength is broken, that we did not take advantage of it when in a situation to inspire some fear.

At that moment it would have been as easy to ' negociate ' with a cannon-ball flying towards its mark. The Grand Army was half-way between Boulogne and the Danube.

In October Mack surrendered at Ulm, but Nelson triumphed at Trafalgar. In December Austria and Russia were laid low at Austerlitz. Napoleon was master not merely of western but of central and south-eastern Europe.

On January 3, 1806, Fox wrote to Thomas Grenville :

> Perhaps you are now convinced that there might be something worse than even a rickety peace. However, I will not triumph too much on my foresight. The more a man feels the desirableness of lowering the power of France, the more indignation ought he to feel against those who have so enormously aggrandized her.

---

[1] Mr. Holland Rose gives the case for Pitt; Mr. Fitzpatrick (in the *Dropmore Papers*, vii. pp. lv-lxxiii) the case against him, both writing dispassionately and on fullest knowledge.

Fox, however, was able to come to an agreement with the Grenvilles, Windham, and Spencer on the understanding that, much as he condemned the origin and the conduct of the war, England must now pursue it with vigour, and keep all engagements with her allies. On January 14, 1806, he wrote to Grey, ' Tom Grenville came yesterday and I think things look well for an agreement. Pitt is, I believe, still very ill, and I doubt much whether he will appear the first day.' There was therefore the prospect that when Parliament met the followers of Fox, Grenville, and Addington, now Lord Sidmouth, would together fall upon Pitt on the ground of his proved failure to conduct the affairs of the country in the political isolation which he loved and to which the King's prejudices against Fox had consigned him.

If Pitt had returned from Bath to meet these charges, it would have taxed his genius to answer them with Napoleon in Vienna. He took the best way of defending his reputation. He died, and left those who blamed him for Austerlitz to lead the country on to Jena.

CHAPTER II

' And many thousands now are sad—
Wait the fulfilment of their fear ;
For he must die who is their stay,
Their glory disappear.'
WORDSWORTH ON THE DEATH OF FOX.

ON the death of Pitt the King was helpless in Lord
Grenville's honest hands, and was therefore compelled
to employ Fox. So there came into being the Ministry
of All the Talents—to give it the less homely of its
nicknames. It was composed of two sorts of Tories
and two sorts of Whigs : the Foxite Whigs ; the
Grenvillites, Whig and Tory ; and the Addingtonian
Tories. The last-named could scarcely claim to add
to the talents of the Ministry, but they served to give
it a broader bottom, and so left its enemy the King
no immediate chance of sending for a different set of
servants. They ' stopped up all the earths,' as Fox
laughing said, referring not to himself as the fox.

There was no question of passing Parliamentary
Reform, to which not only the King and the Opposition
but all sections of Ministerialists except the Foxites
were alike opposed. Catholic Emancipation was
eschewed by the ministerial followers of Addington,
now Lord Sidmouth, not to mention the King and
the majority of both Houses. Although Parliamentary
emancipation was thus rendered impossible, Fox,
Grenville, and Grey were determined, short of that, to

do something for the Irish Catholics, but they made the error of not coming to an understanding on the subject with their Royal captive before consenting to take office.

There was, however, one great reform, hated by George III like all other great reforms, which they found themselves able to accomplish. Since the new Ministers were 'very direct men,' they passed the Abolition of the Slave Trade which Pitt had for so many years alternately supported and betrayed. They could not even attempt to reform England ; they tried to give peace to Europe, and failed ; they fell the moment they touched Ireland ; but they stayed the plague in Africa. That one Act renders All the Talents a bright spot in a dark period. In the middle of the greatest reaction in our history, when only retrograde measures were added to the Statute Book, these men, who held office for but one year, secured a measure which would have been a noble year's harvest for any Ministry in a reforming age.

They passed one other reform, Windham's Army Act, an attempt, by substituting limited for life service, to scramble out of the existing chaos of military organisation. The King and his son, the Duke of York, the Commander-in-Chief, opposed it bitterly, it was not popular in the country, and Windham himself was generally disliked. But, as over the slave trade, Fox insisted that the Bill should be passed. Unlike Pitt, he showed himself ready to risk the fall of the Government rather than leave undone that which he thought right and was pledged in honour to perform.

The Cabinet had been patched together out of parties recently at deadly feud, yet nothing is more remarkable in its inner history than the good behaviour of these parties to one another. For example, Windham, who was brought in as a Grenvillite, was far better treated by Fox and Grey than by the Grenvilles themselves. It was Fox who insisted that the Cabinet should stand by him over the Army Bill ; and after

Fox's death it was Grey who successfully protested against Windham being superseded at the War Office to make room for Thomas Grenville, in accordance with the Marquis of Buckingham's ideas of what was due to his family. Grey even offered to resign his own office to smooth out the difficulty. Both at the first formation of the Ministry in February 1806, and again at the reshuffling in September after Fox's death, nothing but loyalty and generosity between the various sections could have enabled a Government to be formed at all. In a Ministry of All the Talents there are, in the nature of the case, more men with good claims on office than there are places to satisfy them. In February Whitbread, Tierney, Lauderdale, and Philip Francis were not given office at all, while even Sheridan and Thomas Grenville were not in the Cabinet.[1] It has been recorded by Holland that Grey

---

[1] The chief offices were filled as follows :

	February 1806.	September 1806.
First Lord of Treasury .	Lord Grenville	Lord Grenville.
Admiralty . . .	Grey	Thomas Grenville.
Chancellor of Exchequer	Lord Henry Petty (afterwards 3rd Marquis Lansdowne)	Lord Henry Petty.
Sec. of Foreign Affairs .	Fox	Lord Howick (Grey).
War and Colonies . .	Windham	Windham.
Home Dept. . .	Lord Spencer	Lord Spencer.
Lord Chancellor .	Lord Erskine	Lord Erskine.
Lord Chief Justice .	Lord Ellenborough	Lord Ellenborough.
Lord Privy Seal . .	Lord Sidmouth (Addington)	Lord Holland.
President of the Council	Lord Fitzwilliam	Lord Sidmouth.
President of Board of Trade . . .	Lord Auckland	Lord Auckland.
Master of the Ordnance	Lord Moira	Lord Moira.

The above formed the Cabinet.

Lord-Lieut. of Ireland .	Duke of Bedford	Duke of Bedford.
Board of Control . .	Thomas Grenville	Tierney.
Treasurer of Navy .	Sheridan	Sheridan.
Secretary at War .	Gen. Fitzpatrick	Gen. Fitzpatrick.
Chancellor of Ireland .	Geo. Ponsonby	Geo. Ponsonby.

did a bad turn to his old school and college friend and brother-in-law, Samuel Whitbread, by too hastily misinforming Fox and Grenville that Sam did not want office. If Grey ever said so, at least he had some excuse. On February 7 he writes to Whitbread : ' I certainly had remained ever since our last conversation on this subject under the impression that you felt a great unwillingness to any office.' But if Grey made this original error, he afterwards did all he properly could to retrieve it. His long letters to Whitbread show that he behaved all through this affair with affection and consideration, though he did not, like the Duke of Buckingham, hold a pistol to his colleagues' heads if his family was not catered for to his satisfaction. Nevertheless, Whitbread's discontent with his party dates from this period. He was angry with his friends on personal grounds for their not giving him office, and on public grounds for their failure to make peace with Napoleon. After they had gone back to opposition he was justly indignant at their neglect to support strongly his demands for popular education and social reform. In the last ten years of his life, which ended so tragically in 1815, Whitbread was often a cause of grief to Grey, who loved his brother-in-law better perhaps than he understood him.

Grey himself was First Lord of the Admiralty, a position which he filled without reproach from February to September 1806. The work of the department, reckoned in time of war the hardest of any Cabinet post, kept him somewhat aloof from general politics until Fox's death ; his labours at the Admiralty were sweetened for him by close official connection with the famous sailor, Lord St. Vincent, who happened to be a personal and political friend.[1]

From April 1806 till November 1807 Grey was known to the world by the title of Lord Howick. In

[1] In July 1806 Lord St. Vincent writes to Grey : ' I hope that among you a Black Eye will be given at the ensuing General Election to some of the pitiful opposers.'

1801 Addington had conferred a peerage on his father, General Sir Charles Grey. It was no more than the General's due for good service, formerly in the war of the American Revolution and latterly in the West Indies against the French Republicans. Indeed, his father's elevation had been hanging over Grey's head for many years before the blow fell.[1] He regarded it as a grave misfortune that set a term to his own career in the Commons, and destined him at the height of his powers and authority to pine in the limbo of the Lords. Indeed, it proved the chief misfortune of his life, and a heavy handicap to the party after Fox's death. Fox and his friends had commiserated Grey on his father's peerage in 1801, but since the mischief was done, and nothing could now save him from sitting among the Lords in nature's unswerving course, they raised his father from Baron to Earl in April 1806, on the principle that one may as well be hung for a sheep as for a lamb. Grey thereby became Lord Howick, though still a commoner, until his father's death.

The life of the administration was derived from Fox's popularity and his power of genial management, exerted in the Cabinet equally over old friends and old foes, and not unfelt even in the highest and most hostile quarter. The bane of the administration was Fox's ill-health, which showed itself almost at once.

Lord Howick (Grey) [writes Holland] came to him with a proposal which included a Peerage, if he liked it, to save him from the yet more laborious duty of the House of Commons. Mrs. Fox was in the room when this suggestion was made. At the mention of the Peerage, he looked at her significantly, with a reference to his secret but early determination never to be created a Peer ; and after a short pause he said, 'No, not yet, I think,

[1] In Brooks's betting-book, June 5, 1794, we read : ' Col. Tarleton bets Mr. Grey five gs. that Sir Chas. Grey is created an English peer on or before the 4th June next.'

General SIR CHARLES GREY, of Fallodon, afterwards first
Earl Grey; 1729-1807; father of the Prime Minister.

From the picture by Sir Thomas Lawrence (1795) at Howick.

not yet.' On the same evening, as I sat by his bedside, he said to me, ' The Slave Trade and Peace are two such glorious things. I can't give them up, even to you. If I can manage *them*, I will then retire.'

One of these ' glorious things ' he did achieve, leaving the Slave Trade Abolition Bill in such train when he died that Grey and Grenville put it through both Houses just before the King could dismiss the Ministry. But he was less fortunate about peace, not through any fault of his own. His tenure of the Foriegn Office has been singularly little attacked, and the more it is studied in detail the more admirable it appears. In principle and in method he shows himself a ' Briton ' indeed, as Scott said, but a Briton tactful and sympathetic with foreign Courts and peoples, as well as firm for the interests of his own country and loyal to her allies.

If half as much could have been said of the ruler of France we should then and there have had peace. Napoleon at first offered to negociate with Fox on the basis of restoring Hanover to King George, leaving the Cape and Malta to us, and Sicily to our Bourbon ally. In other words, he suggested the principle of *uti possidetis*, each side to keep what it then held, except only that Hanover was to be restored. Negociations began on this basis, but then Napoleon changed his mind, inveighed against *uti possidetis* as *des formules latines*, and laid claim to Sicily for his brother Joseph, then King of Naples. It was a terrible disillusionment for Fox, who had clung so long to the roseate view of Napoleon ; but he was man enough to read on the page of facts that he had been mistaken, and at once to accept the consequences. Nothing could be better than his words to Lord Holland :

Bad as the [Bourbon] Queen and Court of Naples are, we can, in honour, do nothing without their full and *bona fide* consent ; but even exclusive of that consideration, and of the great importance of Sicily, which you, young one, very much underrate, it is not so much the value of the point in dispute as the manner in which the French fly from their word, that disheartens me.

The revival of the claim on Sicily was specially preposterous because, after the negociations had been begun, we had further secured our position there and defeated the French preparations to invade the island from Reggio, by the victory of Maida on the Calabrian coast. That brilliant little action, on July 4, 1806, heralded the victories of the Peninsula by demonstrating the superiority of the English line over the French column. To use a language familiar to the statesmen of that time, Maida was to our land warfare the lucky day *qui primus almâ risit adoreâ*, putting an end to the unjust contempt in which our army had long been held.

In September 1806, at the height of the crisis that should decide whether Napoleon would after all choose peace or war, and whether Prussia would join Russia and England or continue as the vassal of France, Charles Fox was taken from those who loved him. His last words were that he 'died happy.' And, in spite of all, he had lived happy and spread happiness around him like a wind blowing from the hills. He had loved life too well to be a perfect statesman, but he had brought human life and love with him into the political world, and since he passed out of it, though it has been dignified by equal genius and higher virtue, it has never again been made Shakespearian by such a kind, grand, human creature. The last fifteen years of his life, though apparently the most complete in their failure, were in fact the best, the greatest, and in the end the most useful : he stood up for liberty in evil days, when without such a Titan to bestride them the friends of liberty would have ceased to exist in Parliament, and in the country would have lost all hope for the future. His death, as Wordsworth felt upon ' the lonely road ' above Grasmere, was the last blow to ' many thousands ' of humble men, now left without his shield to the mercy of intolerant enemies. They had indeed a hard, long time before them. But Fox had left his disciples in high places as well as low, and Holland, whose proud epitaph on himself was that he was ' nephew of Fox and friend of Grey,' lived to see his friend reform the Government of Britain according to the maxims of his uncle.

Grey stepped into the three positions vacated by the death of Fox : the Foreign Office, the leadership of the House of Commons, and the leadership of the Whig party. The first two of these posts he held for six months, and never again ; but the less official leadership of the party, not dependent on the breath of kings, he held until his retirement in 1834. There were indeed occasions on which he wrote in private letters that he regarded himself as having retired, but nobody marked him, and, except perhaps for the few months of Canning's Ministry in 1827, he was always held, to use Byron's phrase, as ' the Capo Politico of the remaining Whigs.' [1]

In the Cabinet Lord Grenville was officially his chief, but politically they were on equal terms, the two Consuls of the Coalition. In order that Grey should have time to lead the House of Commons, he was moved from the Admiralty to the Foreign Office, where the work, if yet more responsible, was in those days lighter. Since Grenville had for so long been Pitt's Foreign Minister, he naturally exercised great influence over Grey during his first and only six months at that Office. The somewhat lofty and unsympathetic tone towards Foreign Powers that we catch in Grey's despatches has in it more of Grenville than of Fox. If, on the one hand, Grey can be accused of no complaisance to Napoleon, on the other he showed a certain stiffness towards Prussia and Russia. In this he was

---

[1] Byron's *Journal*, Jan. 15, 1821.

encouraged by the King, whose fixed idea seems to have been to get Hanover guaranteed to him, while Europe was burning. In the important matter of subsidies the Grenville-Grey policy was the very opposite of the old Pitt-Grenville methods. Instead of lavishing the British tax-payers' millions on foreign armies, the new Government even refused to help Russia in the matter of a city loan.[1] Pitt's subsidy system, always denounced by the Whigs as extravagant, had come to such dire mishap at Austerlitz that the reaction against it was for a time carried perhaps too far, Grenville himself leading.

During Grey's first fortnight at the Foreign Office, the negotiations with France, which had come to grief before Fox died, were officially broken off, in spite of Talleyrand's efforts to keep our envoy, Lord Lauderdale, in Paris until Napoleon's plans with regard to Prussia were matured. In a letter to Whitbread, who thought that peace should have been made, Grey writes :

I do not see how it was possible for Lauderdale to show a greater disposition for Peace. It was necessary to bring back the French to the offer [of Sicily] by which they had induced us to enter into the negociation, and the whole time he was at Paris he was engaged in an ineffectual struggle for that purpose. You know poor Fox's anxiety for Peace—an anxiety certainly not lessened by the situation in which he was during the negociation. He certainly approved of Lauderdale's conduct, and thought that the French Government had left him no choice. The last time he spoke of the negociation was on the Sunday before he died. He then said the great points for this country to adhere to were : (1) Sicily ; (2) The Russian connection, and on these the negociations broke off.

Grey's first despatch as Foreign Secretary, written on September 24, 1806, gave instructions to Lord

[1] *Dropmore Papers,* viii. p. xlv. The views here expressed of Grenville's and Grey's foreign policy, 1806-1807, are largely those of Mr. Walter Fitzpatrick, confirmed by my own study of the *F.O. Papers* in the Record Office.

occupied by Napoleon. On the other hand, we accommodated Russia by sending our fleet up the Dardanelles to prevent the Turks from moving against her at the instigation of France. The Admiral mismanaged the operation, and the expedition failed to overawe the Porte.

We were at war with Spain and Holland, vassals of Napoleon. A few weeks before Pitt died, Admiral Sir Home Popham and General Sir David Baird had captured the Cape of Good Hope from the Dutch. Popham borrowed a battalion from Baird, sailed across the Atlantic without instructions from home, and in June 1806 captured Buenos Ayres from the Spaniards, as a little present to the Empire on his own behalf. The news touched the covetous imagination of our merchants, who clamoured for the reversion of the Spanish colonies, their trade and wealth. The Government yielded to this foolish cry, having yet to learn, like Napoleon, that Spaniards, whether pure blood or half breed, are stubborn to defend their country against the invasion of more progressive races. Grey, almost alone among his colleagues, had the good sense to oppose these projects of South American and Mexican conquest. In a minute addressed to the Cabinet he protests against reinforcing Buenos Ayres, or any further undertakings across the Atlantic. He argues that our European allies will think us indifferent to the common cause and bent only on the private plunder of the globe ; that such distant expeditions will dissipate our small forces, which should be kept in hand, ready to defend Ireland or to be thrust into any casual opening in the barrier of Napoleon's Continental power. Events proved Grey right. General Whitelock, sent with an expeditionary force to Buenos Ayres, was defeated by the inhabitants risen to defend their country ; and the army that was fitted out for Mexico under Sir Arthur Wellesley was happily stopped in time, in order to be sent first to Copenhagen and afterwards to the Peninsula, where the Spanish rising against Napoleon gave it better use in the Old World than it could possibly have found in the New.

The last thing of which All the Talents could be accused was servility towards the Prince of Wales. For years past Fox had been somewhat, and Grey altogether, estranged from the Prince, with whom they had once been familiar friends. And the proud Grenville was at no time either a courtier or a boon companion. Indeed, Holland himself, a man most loath to 'crook the pregnant hinges of the knee,' complained that the party interests were compromised by the personal neglect of the Heir Apparent practised by his father's Ministers. On Fox's death Holland managed to persuade Grey to write to the Prince a friendly but dignified letter, expressing a hope that the Prince would still 'support those honourable principles which united so many friends around Mr. Fox.' The Prince replied on September 18, in his flamboyant and protesting style, sincere enough it may be at the moment of writing :

As to ourselves, my Friend, the old and steady adherents and Friends of Fox, we have but one line to pursue, one course to steer ; to stick together, to remain united, and to prove by our conduct, in our steady adherence to those principles which we imbibed from Fox when living, that we are not unworthy of him, and that his Memory will forever live in our Hearts.

It is a little difficult to know what 'principles' are referred to by the Prince, who had already abandoned Catholic Emancipation and Parliamentary Reform. Grey remained undeceived, and drew no nearer to Carlton House. In that establishment the influence now prevailing was that of Lady Hertford and her son, Lord Yarmouth, a nobleman of infamous character, who achieved dual immortality as the original of Lord Monmouth in 'Coningsby' and of Lord Steyne in 'Vanity Fair.' Representations were made to Grey by many of his supporters that he should court the Prince, with an eye on favours to come. But he writes to George Ponsonby on April 24, 1807 :

> If the Prince could be kept steady by any reasonable sacrifices I should concur in the propriety of making them. But the truth is he is completely influenced by Lady Hertford and Lord Yarmouth, and is also ready to do anything to obtain such an arrangement as he wants respecting the Princess [viz., to divorce his second wife, Caroline of Brunswick]. These are the true causes of his conduct towards us, which he must seek to justify in some way or other, and his complaint of our inattention is merely a pretence.

So Grey deliberately kept aloof from Carlton House, both during and after the Ministry of All the Talents, and thereby contributed greatly to the Whig exclusion from office when the Prince actually became Regent. In May 1808 Grey writes to Holland :

> I am much obliged to the Prince for his expressions of civility about me, but it is impossible that I should ever be in favor with him. I do not mean that this is impossible from anything that has formerly passed between us, for I believe he has in a very great degree the good quality of forgetting resentments which most Princes would cherish. But I am in every way unsuited to him, and still more unsuited to those who are always about him, and by whom it is his misfortune to be influenced. I wish the Prince had a little more feeling of what is due to the dignity of his own situation, for it must be confessed that the persons who surround him very materially contribute to diminish the respect of the public for him now, and afford a very melancholy prospect of the influence under which the Government is hereafter to be conducted.

It was during the Ministry of All the Talents that the Prince began to demand a divorce from one of his two wives, Caroline of Brunswick. A committee of the Cabinet, not including Grey, held the 'Delicate Investigation' into the charges against her. They drew up a report censuring her for levity, but acquitting her of the serious charge. They certainly cannot be accused of truckling to the Prince in this matter, as the Tories did in 1820. As yet the Tories posed for popular champions of the Princess ; but when her husband became King and they his too obsequious servants, they themselves persecuted Caroline in a way the Whigs had refused to do. Grey never altered his attitude about the Princess : both in 1806 and in 1820 he held that she was a light and vulgar woman, not to be made into a heroine, and that the charges against her were matters of evidence not to be approached in a party spirit. The Delicate Investigation, he wrote to Holland, ' is without any comparison the most disagreeable of any in which any Government was ever engaged. It cannot end well for us in any way.'

The Ministry of All the Talents might have continued in office, not indeed to pass reforms, but to carry on the war, had there not been one question, the pacification of Ireland, which partook of the character of forbidden reform, and yet in the Whig view was essential as a war measure. ' The advantage of carrying this great question,' wrote Grey to Holland, ' depends very much on its being carried in time ; and I cannot help fearing that the overwhelming torrent of Buonaparte's power will come upon us before we have raised the dams and mounds that are necessary to risk it.' Grey is here writing of the full measure of Catholic Emancipation, but since that was known to be impossible for a Government that included Sidmouth and his followers, they had to consider what smaller concession would on the one hand be granted by the Houses and by the King, and on the other suffice to stave off awhile the growing impatience of the Irish. Unless the Ministry proposed something at once, the Catholics threatened to bring up in Parliament their demand for full emancipation, which would split the Ministry and cause its downfall. Grey therefore, on January 10, 1807, wrote to George Ponsonby, now Lord Chancellor of Ireland :

If anything can be done for the Catholics, would it not be better to open the Army to them, by giving them the same privilege of serving and advancing in rank in every part of the King's dominions that they now have in Ireland. The strange anomaly of a person being enabled to rise to all except the highest ranks in the profession in Ireland, and being subject, if the Regiment in which he serves should be removed to England, to severe penalties, cannot be defended in argument.

It could, however, be defended in practice. George III treated it as if it was the Palladium of the Constitution. When this infinitesimal reform was proposed by his Ministers they understood him to consent to its introduction ; but after they had introduced it he turned round upon them and said he would have none of it. The Cabinet, in great distress, decided by a majority to withdraw the Bill. But the new Duke of Bedford, their Lord-Lieutenant, wrote from Ireland on March 16, 1807, to tell Grey that he disagreed with the withdrawal of the Bill 'to which the honour and good faith of the Government was unquestionably pledged.' Grey replied on the 19th :

My feelings and opinions were the same as your's, and I never was called upon to make so painful a sacrifice of both, as in agreeing to withdraw the Bill which I had introduced. This sacrifice, however, I had brought myself to make in deference to the opinion of my Colleagues, of a great majority of our friends in Parliament and, as I believed, of the Public in general. The consideration, however, which weighed most with me was the state of Ireland, and the danger of adding to all the bad effects of so severe a disappointment of the Catholics, the calamity of establishing a government there founded on principles of exclusion. The evil of this was strongly urged by Grattan, and his opinion against our resignation was earnestly pressed.

But King George was not to be cheated of their resignations. As they consented to withdraw the Bill, he demanded a promise similar to that which he had extracted from Pitt about Catholic Emancipation, that they would never trouble him in the matter again. The Ministry, unable to endure the humiliating bondage of such a pledge, resigned.

You may imagine [continues Grey in the same letter] the relief I have found in the conclusion of the business by the King's requiring us to withdraw the reserve we had made of entire freedom in the advice we might hereafter find it necessary to give respecting Ireland. This left us no alternative. The Government is at an end. The assurance we have been required to give was never before required of any Ministers, and could not be honestly complied with. I confess that I still think that our case would have been plainer and clearer, if we had stood on our first ground. Lord Spencer was determined to resign even if the King had not clogged our concession with any further condition, and this determination must have prevented our continuance in office.

So fell All the Talents. Holland has depicted an amusing scene in one of these last Cabinets, between Grey and Lord Chancellor Erskine, the hero of the treason trials of 1794, who rivalled his successor Brougham in eccentricity and untrustworthiness as well as in genius and public service:

Our Chancellor, Lord Erskine, shone least upon this trying occasion. He talked much nonsense and false religion, and declaimed against Papists. When the moment of decision approached, he played with pencils and pens, took up books, and pretended even to sleep with the hope of not being committed in any resolution we might adopt. Lord Howick [Grey] or myself jogged his elbow and drew his attention to the matter in discussion. He confessed afterwards with a droll simplicity that he had been strangely affected by the book he had looked into. It happened to be the ' Life of Egerton Lord Ellesmere,' who had received the seals at the same age as himself (fifty-seven), and had held them no less than twenty-seven years. The contrast of his own prospects and the fate of his more fortunate predecessor had overwhelmed him ; and no Papist ever called down the vengeance of heaven on an heretick with more fervour and fury than Lord Erskine at that moment damned the Holy

Catholic Church and all who maintained its tenets. Lord Howick was indignant at conduct so uncongenial with his own generous temper and elevated mind. The chagrin which Lord Erskine would manifestly feel at the loss of office seemed to reconcile Lord Howick to the event ; and every hint dropped by the other on the propriety of a temporizing policy, made him spurn more contemptuously at everything like compliance or submission.

The Ministry had lived just long enough to perform its most important service to the Empire and to mankind. Fox had been determined to abolish the slave trade, and had been finely supported by Grenville and Grey. The Bill could not be a Government measure officially, because Windham was opposed to it, but it had in effect the full support of Government. Fox, on his death-bed, had urged his colleagues to finish the work he had set in train. On the decisive evening in the Commons, February 23, 1807, Grey made the principal speech, declaring that the measure was more near his heart than any that had been brought forward since he entered Parliament, and expressing a hope that the abolition of the slave trade would lead to the gradual emancipation of all slaves. Owing to the strong support of the Ministers, and to the sudden revival of abolitionist agitation in the country which their action encouraged, the Bill was carried that night by 283 to 16. Two years before, owing to Pitt's failure to give it real support, it had been defeated by seven. Grenville wrote to Grey :

I most heartily congratulate you on the glorious event of last night. Come what will, we may now feel the sentiment which Fox so often expressed, that we may not have been called in vain to the stations that we occupy. How much it is to be regretted that he did not live to feel the pleasure of such an event.

But they were not yet out of the wood. The sudden development of the quarrel with the King in March threatened the life of the Ministry, and if Portland superseded Grenville and Grey before the Bill had received the Royal Assent, Africa would be plunged back into the horrors of the slave trade for perhaps another generation. It was an awful crisis, and Clarkson's words recall the agony of that last struggle on to the top of the ' obstinate hill ' :

It was reported that the new Ministry [Lord Portland's] was formed ; among them were several who had shown a hostile disposition to the cause. On March 23 the House of Lords met. Such extraordinary diligence had been used in printing the Bill, that it was then ready. Lord Grenville immediately brought it forward. But here an omission of three words was discovered which, if not rectified, might defeat the purposes of the Bill. An amendment was immediately proposed and carried. Thus the Bill received the last sanction of the Peers. But the amendment occasioned the Bill to be sent back to the Commons. On the 24th, on the motion of Lord Howick [Grey], it was immediately taken into consideration there, and agreed to ; and it was carried back to the Lords, as approved of, on the same day.

But though the Bill had now passed both Houses, there was an awful fear throughout the Kingdom lest it should not receive the Royal Assent before the Ministry was dissolved. This event took place the next day. But a commission for the Royal Assent to this Bill among others had been obtained. As the clock struck 12, just when the sun was in its Meridian splendour to witness this august Act, this establishment of a Magna Charta for Africa, it was completed. The ceremony being over, the seals of the different offices were delivered up, so that the execution of this commission was the last act of the administration of Lord Grenville—an administration which, on account of its virtuous exertions in behalf of the oppressed African race, will pass to posterity, living through successive generations in the love and gratitude of the most virtuous of mankind.[1]

[1] Clarkson, *History of the Abolition of the Slave Trade*, 1808.

CHAPTER III

' I cannot say how much I like Earl Grey—a fine nature, a just and vigorous understanding, a sensitive disposition, and infirm health. These are his leading traits. His excellencies are courage, discretion, and practical sense ; his deficiency, a want of executive coarseness.'—SYDNEY SMITH, 1810.

THE King had reinstated the ultra-Tories, under the Premiership of the ex-Whig the Duke of Portland. Their first step was to dissolve Parliament, in May 1807, although there had been a General Election in the previous October. The electoral influence of the Crown, which had been withheld from their predecessors in office at the last election, and a loud ' No-Popery ' cry, enabled them to improve their Parliamentary position against the outgoing Whigs and Grenvillites. And inside the walls of the House they could now once more count on that large body of members who always supported the Government of the day. The ' No-Popery ' election cost Grey his county seat, which he had held without difficulty in spite of his ' Jacobinism ' ever since his entry into Parliament. The blow was dealt by the Duke of Northumberland, whom he had every reason to regard as his political ally. Indeed, on September 10, 1806, ' when the dissolution of Mr. Fox was hourly expected,' Grey had written on his own initiative to the Duke, suggesting that if his son, Lord Percy, wished to succeed the great Tribune as member for Westminster, ' not a moment should be lost in his appearing in person !'[1] The proposal, which was acted upon, is a good proof of Grey's loyal alliance with the Percys.

What then was he to think when, at the General Election eight months afterwards, without the excuse of any new issue arisen in politics, the Duke put up this same Lord Percy to run with T. R. Beaumont against Grey for the representation of Northumberland ? It was done without any warning, so that Grey's friends had no time to organise their campaign or to collect money. Even his staunch supporter, Sir John Swinburne, could ' only give £500,' and on the eve of the poll they had but £4,000 in hand. In those days a contest for a county of vast acreage, if fought *à outrance* between two great families, cost at least tens of thousands. The freeholders had to be brought from their distant homes to the scene of the election at York or Alnwick, and kept there for days together at the expense of the candidate who hoped for their votes. Stately palaces and princely estates had been sunk in Yorkshire and Northumbrian elections, of which the fame was handed down from father to son among the grateful freeholders. Grey wisely determined that, rather than fight such a contest against the lord of Alnwick, he would husband his slender means for his numerous progeny, and *solutus omni foenore* leave them Howick with its beeches, its broad green fields, and pleasant stone farms intact. He retired just before the poll, although he was the popular candidate. Even at Alnwick, he writes, ' nothing was heard but my name in the streets, and those who had got drunk with Lord Percy's and Beaumont's ale, did nothing but cry *Howick for ever !* '

Grey's feelings towards the Duke are expressed in the following letter to Holland :

[1] Add. MS., B.M., 31, 158, ff. 199–200. For the history of the Westminster elections of this period see Wallas' *Life of Place*.

It is provoking to have lost a sure seat in such a manner. As to the Duke, I will only say that good comes out of evil, and that what he has done will relieve me from the necessity of listening to his lies and small talk on Saturday, and his damned dinner at Alnwick Castle, for the rest of my life. Tierney [acting as Whig 'Whip'] may certainly take the Duke's members, as least such as will pay due obedience to him, out of our list. But after all, our numbers will be very strong, and we shall have the satisfaction of making what are called 'good divisions,' when the more important business of Fox-hunting, etc., does not prevent.

We are told that the two great Northumbrian families were 'reconciled in 1829.' But the following story, from the memoirs of a grandson of Lord Grey's, dates from a later year !

Lord Grey was very kind to his grandchildren. His son, Uncle Francis, asked him to let the boys come to Alnwick. They were given ten shillings, which they spent on a hatchet each, and as they walked home they cut notches in all the Duke of Northumberland's gates. They were dragged up to Grandpapa by Uncle Francis, and he told him that they had spoilt all the Duke of Northumberland's gates. 'No, boys, did you really ?' answered Lord Grey. 'Here is ten shillings more, and if there are any gates that are not notched, go and cut them.'

But to return to 1807, before Grey had yet passed the Reform Bill : the ex-member for Northumberland was accommodated by Lord Thanet 'in the handsomest manner' with his borough of Appleby—famous for its pigstyes to which votes were attached. In July he resigned Appleby in favour of the Duke of Bedford's Tavistock. But he was not long in need of pocket boroughs. In November 1807 that fine soldier, the first Earl Grey, died at Fallodon, whereupon his son ceased to be the commoner, Lord Howick, and sat among the peers of the realm as the second Earl Grey. This enforced promotion proved, as had been long anticipated, a disaster to his party and to his own career. 'We lost our best qualified leader in the House of Commons. His place has never been adequately supplied,' wrote Lord Holland in 1817 ; and the words remained true until Althorp took the lead of the Whig Commoners in 1830. In the same year, 1817, the greatest of Earl Grey's opponents, the Duke of Wellington himself, said in his blunt fashion to gossip Creevey : ' As leader of the House of Commons, Grey's manner and speaking were quite perfect. But he is lost by being in the Lords. Nobody cares a damn for the House of Lords; the House of Commons is everything in England, and the House of Lords nothing,' a truth which the Duke had one day to re-learn under the tutoring of Grey himself.

Grey was a fine orator, and had risen to precocious eminence by his mastery of that art in its most high and palmy days. But oratory requires an audience, and when the House of Commons was closed to him he could find none other. The electoral hustings were forbidden ground to a peer. After Waterloo, democrats of the new era, like Hunt and Cobbett, figured sometimes at a ' public meeting,' though not without danger and disrepute. But it was not among the duties of a respectable party leader, least of all in Grey's estimation, to address assembled multitudes of his supporters. He eschewed even the decorous eloquence of Fox dinners and Whig club banquets.[1] Henceforth his voice was scarcely ever raised in public except only in the House of Lords, and their lordships, though many of them were great and distinguished men, formed an execrable audience. His own description of the matter to his wife in January 1808 may be repeated :

You will see by the papers that I made my debut in the House of Lords last night. What a place to speak in ! With just light enough to make darkness visible, it was like speaking

---

[1] ' I cannot tell you how this Fox dinner annoys me, and the idea of being set up there as a sort of show, to bring people to hear me speak.'—Grey to his wife, December 25, 1818.

in a vault by the glimmering of a sepulchral lamp to the dead. It is impossible I should ever do anything there worth thinking of.

If we remember that the peers who assembled to cheer him, or rather to murmur faint applause when he sat down, could generally be counted on the fingers of one hand, it will not seem unnatural that a man, sensitive and easily depressed, should have yielded more and more to the promptings of his natural indolence and to the call of his domestic affections. The close companionship of Lord Holland, the soul of friendship incarnate, just enabled him to survive the few annual weeks of his London life.

As the years rolled by, Earl Grey became less and less active as a party leader—often offering to retire, sometimes declaring that he had retired, but never in effect allowed to depart. In September 1808 Tierney wrote to him with the freedom of an old acquaintance:

> Have you a reason which you can publicly assign for staying away? The death of your uncle [1] has removed the old one, a scanty income. What new one have you got which you can state? You must show yourself in the field as the leader of a party, or you must cease to be so. Do not flatter yourself that a residence in Northumberland is compatible with the station you at present hold in public estimation, or that you can put greatness off as may be most agreeable to you.

And so the comedy went on.

For a score of years to come the conditions of Grey's public career were most unfortunate. Had he been able to remain as leader of the Opposition in the Commons, he and his party would have been in closer touch, and united action would have engendered some degree of warmth. In the chill and silence of the hostile House of Lords he heard and felt little of the stir of new forces, until his youth returned to him in the miraculous year of the French barricades.

---

[1] Sir Harry died in 1808, leaving Earl Grey as his heir.

The history of the Whig party in the same period is a weary tale of personal and sectional quarrels, from which Grey kept loftily apart. Their divisions were made worse for want of some acknowledged chief of high repute, sharing their daily life in the Commons. Grey's peerage had left vacant the post of leader of Opposition in the Lower House. George Ponsonby was chosen, on the principle of taking not the ablest but the least objectionable person, with the result that all the more able men felt aggrieved, though several of them would have been yet more aggrieved if one of themselves had been chosen. Ponsonby remained official leader in the Lower House until his death in 1817, but his influence was small, and moral unity was never obtained among his flock. Thus in February 1808 Grey writes to his wife :

Whitbread's manner, of which I find the complaints universal, has offended Tierney very much, and Tierney on his part is very wrong-headed. Whitbread says Tierney wants victory over George Ponsonby, and objects, therefore, to everything that is not proposed by himself. Tierney complains that Whitbread is almost intolerable from the irritation occasioned by disappointment at not being the avowed leader. Though I have the character of a hot, intemperate fellow, I begin to think I am the most reasonable person amongst them. In the House of Lords we are all harmony and good humour. Between Lords Grenville, Holland, Lauderdale, and myself there is not a shadow of difference or uneasiness.

Whitbread's chief offence was his habit of introducing motions for peace, with which the bulk of the Whigs and Grenvillites disagreed. When Napoleon's Treaty of Tilsit with Russia had put the seal on his domination over Europe, neither Grey nor Grenville thought that England could make peace ; such a peace, acknowledging Europe to be a province of France, must lead to our own speedy destruction. And Whitbread's more excellent schemes for popular education and social reform, being regarded by Lord Grenville as 'Jacobinism,' only made the situation inside the party worse. Here is one scene out of a hundred, recorded in Grey's letters to his wife:

Jan. 19, 1808.

Whitbread came yesterday and dined with us at Lord Grenville's. He began upon the subject of peace in so hot and, I must say, so wrong-headed a manner, that the impression produced must have been most unfavourable to him. Old Grenville seemed dumbfounded, and hardly spoke a word. You may guess I was on thorns, as the vehemence of his manner was more particularly applied to me. I saw him at Brooks's this morning, and he seemed to have recovered. It is true I avoided everything that might again irritate him.

In these circumstances even the hospitality of Holland House was not always as gay as in the years gone by, when the spirit of Fox pervaded its halls. Two days later Grey writes:

Our dinner at Holland House was for the purpose of talking over Parliamentary business, but hardly anything passed on the subject. I felt low and out of spirits, and after what passed at our former dinner I was afraid of beginning. Old Grenville, who is the awkwardest of all human beings on occasions of this sort, sat with his usual silence, and there was in short no conversation of any consequence except what passed in little knots after dinner in the drawing-room. It is Whitbread's *manner* rather than *opinions* that are to be complained of.

In 1809 the party was split in two on the sordid question of the hour—the case of Mrs. Clarke, which absorbed England while Napoleon was laying Austria low for the last time in the Wagram campaign. The Duke of York, so long commander-in-chief, had a mistress, Mrs. Clarke, who quarrelled with him and sought revenge. Under the patronage of a Tory member of low character named Wardle, who had been guilty of great cruelties during the Irish Rebellion, she brought forward her charges. She was able to prove that she had received money from officers to use her influence on their behalf with her royal lover. All England was ablaze. Half the Whigs, including such highly honourable men as Whitbread, Romilly, and young Althorp, took up the case with a righteous anger which was perfectly sincere, whether or not it was entirely justified. If the whole party had followed suit, a great effect might have been produced. But Grey, as in the Queen's trial of 1820, refused to make party capital, and, looking closely at the facts, saw much against Mrs. Clarke, but no proof of corruption in the Duke of York. Grey's refusal to move in the matter was deeply resented by half the party, for it was remarked that the agitation, though not officially supported, had done more to stir up popular feeling against the Tory Government, the Royal Family, and the whole oligarchic system than anything else—except, perhaps, the similar case of Dundas—since Pitt's gagging Acts had put an end to political life in the country. This was only too true ; one evil result of stopping up the stream of legitimate democracy is that discontent, denied its proper channels, will find its way out by the sewers. This law of political hydrostatics was further illustrated by the excitement over the Queen's trial in 1820, and by the prevalent but utterly false belief that another of George III's sons, the Duke of Cumberland, murdered his valet Sellis in 1810.[1]

Grey at any rate refused to head the cry about Mrs. Clarke. ' It is not by such means,' he wrote to Holland, ' that I wish to see the influence of the Crown reduced.' His views on Mrs. Clarke and her patron are expressed in a letter to his wife of May 8, 1809 :

[1] It was the courageous honesty of the Radical Place at the inquest that cleared the Duke's character. See Wallas' *Place*, chap. ii. Yet I possess a ' coloured cartoon,' dating some fifteen years after Sellis' death, representing his ghost appearing to the Duke of Cumberland to reproach him for the murder !

I was very glad to see that one member spoke of Wardle as I think he deserves, and said he would as soon vote thanks to Mrs. Clarke for her virtue, as to him for his patriotism. I really think they stand on pretty much the same ground. An informer, however useful his information may prove, is generally shunned as an infamous character ; and I do not see that Mr. Wardle, who by his own acknowledgment, formed an intimacy with a vile prostitute to get into her secrets, induced her to betray the man whose confidence she had before abused, and who stole her letters for the purpose of supporting his charges, deserves to be viewed in a much better light.

May 10. The violent party in the House of Commons are going on worse than ever, and still continue to receive, I am sorry to say, too much encouragement and support from Whitbread. A new code of political morality and honour has been adopted, and everything seems to be greedily taken up that can tend to throw discredit on the general system of Government. Lord Grenville seems very uneasy on this point. It is difficult, however, to find a remedy for evils which have been brought on by the manner in which the present Ministers came into office.

Indeed the savage hatred of the Royal Family which characterises this period in our history, was due not merely to the assailable private character of its younger members, but yet more to the political intransigeance of its venerable patriarch, who from the threshold of the madhouse still made and unmade Ministries, and vetoed measures of reform.

However right he may have been in the case of Wardle and Mrs. Clarke, Grey was too nice in his choice of associates to be an effective leader of Opposition. His dislike of the Radicals, being shared by the great majority of his parliamentary followers, condemned the Whigs to impotence as a popular party, until they introduced the Reform Bill. In 1792 and the following years Grey had felt much attraction as well as much antagonism to working-class democracy, but in 1810 he seemed only to remember his antagonism to Paine, not his sympathy with Hardy. In January of that year, when Sir Francis Burdett was the Radical leader, Grey writes to Holland :

The persons whom you designate Burdettites and Jacobins are in truth the best friends of the Court. By diverting the public attention from all useful and practical objects, they provide the best means of escape for the Ministers from those difficulties in which their folly and wickedness have involved them. They aim at nothing but the degradation of all public character, their watchword being that all Ministers are alike, and that no advantage is to be derived from any change, thus co-operating most effectually with the Court in withdrawing all public confidence from its opponents. With this class of patriots I was at war in 1792, I am so now, and there is in my opinion a degree of meanness in appearing to court them in the slightest degree to which I never can submit.

The Radical literature of the time shows that the democratic distrust of the Whigs had been increased by the Ministry of All the Talents, because Grey had introduced no Reform Bill during his year of office. The Radicals did not stop to reflect that half his colleagues had been Grenvillites and Addingtonians, bitterly opposed to reform. They regarded him as a traitor because he had not attempted the utterly impossible and so broken up the Ministry the moment it was formed. He would, in fact, at any moment of his career have been only too glad to pass 'a moderate measure of Reform,' but, as he told the House of Lords in his speech of June 13, 1810 :

I doubt much whether there exists a very general disposition in favour of Reform. Whenever this great question shall be taken up by the people of this country seriously and affectionately, there will then be a fair prospect of accomplishing it. But until the country shall have expressed its opinion upon this subject, the examples of the other nations of Europe should deter us from any precipitate attempt to hurry on to premature or violent operation a measure on which the best interests of the nation so essentially depend.

This utterance may be regarded as the low-water mark of Grey's reforming enthusiasm, the result of the prolonged war and the unnatural alliance with Grenville. During the last years of the Napoleonic struggle he was thinking more about Catholic Emancipation than about Parliamentary Reform. He was much occupied by the arguments which his reverend friend, Sydney Smith, had recently laid before the public in the serious drollery of the 'Plymley Letters'; he too believed that the non-fulfilment of Pitt's undertakings to the Irish Catholics was a present danger to the Empire at war with Napoleon, in whose service Catholic and Protestant, Atheist and Jew, were equally welcome and equally privileged. After his experience in the Ministry of All the Talents, Grey had made up his mind never to take office except with power to alleviate Irish unrest by admitting Catholics to sit in Parliament. In January 1810 he writes to Holland that 'the immediate settlement of it by a legislative measure, including the enforcement of the veto,[1] is the *sine quâ non* of my accepting office.' And again : 'It is a cause in which you have both the King and the people against you. . . . I have been and am ready to make all the necessary sacrifices, being, as you know, quite determined not to accept of office without the power of immediately settling the question.' It was at this time and on this subject that his dislike of Canning took the hard form that it ever after retained. He never could forgive a statesman who was in favour of Catholic Emancipation, for consenting to take office under the Duke of Portland at the expense of the Ministry of All the Talents, which had fallen because its members attempted to do some

---

[1] Viz., the veto of the Crown on the appointment of Roman Catholic Bishops, a proposition not then regarded among Roman Catholics with such horror as it would now arouse, although it did in fact cause great difficulties as between the Whig statesmen who thought it essential to the passage of the Bill, and the Irish Catholics who naturally disliked it.

small thing for the Catholics. In October 1809 he wrote to Holland :

> I am not at all inclined to political proscriptions, and you must remember how ready I was, even before our administration appeared to be in danger, to enter into terms with Canning himself. But what passed then, his immediate acceptance of office upon the principle of the late [1] administration, his conduct towards us the moment he was in power, and all that has happened since, has made so deep an impression on my mind that I could not bring myself, either in or out of office, to act with him.

This ' deep impression ' was never effaced, but only augmented by subsequent happenings.

In 1808 the revolt of the Spaniards against Napoleon's act of dynastic brigandage aroused the romantic enthusiasm of the Whigs, who saw in a people betrayed by their princes but true to themselves another chapter of the book of freedom, to be added to the tales of Wallace, Tell, and Kosciusko. Lord Holland, who had travelled much in Spain, was the best informed and therefore the least optimistic, but the most steadily determined of all, upon this issue. On June 19, 1808, Grey writes to him :

> I cannot sufficiently thank you for your very interesting account of the state of Spain. I wish I could add that your account had raised my hopes of the success of the Insurgents. But though in this, which I am inclined to think the most atrocious of all his villainies, Bonaparte's measures appear to have been too well taken, and though the poor Spaniards are deprived of all the advantages which timely preparations and a good Government might have afforded them, still we must not despair. I hope they will persevere. If I was a Spaniard I should urge

---

[1] Viz., the Duke of Portland's administration, March 1807 to September 1809, in which Canning was at first Foreign Secretary. Perceval had succeeded Portland as Premier just before this letter of Grey's was written. Grey and Grenville had been asked to join Perceval's administration and had refused.

them to do so, even with less hope than they may have of success, nay, with the certainty of ultimate destruction. From hence I trust they will have every assistance that can be afforded in men, ships, and money, to the utmost possible extent. I almost wish we were in office at this moment, for the sake of sending Lord St. Vincent with the fleet, and you to the Insurgents.

Lord Grenville, however, objected to the sending of troops to Spain, which for a time led to a serious difference between himself and Grey. Grey was right, but unfortunately he did not stand by his opinion to the end, but allowed himself to be shaken by the reconquest of Spain by the French in the following winter. On January 26, 1809, he writes to Grenville :

I have just got the account of Moore's death, and of all the disasters that preceded it. It deprives me of all power of expression and almost of thought. I must confess that, as things have been managed, it is much to be regretted that your opinions against sending troops to Spain at all did not prevail.

From this time forward Grey sided with Grenville rather than with Holland as to the possibilities of effective co-operation with the Spaniards. The *Edinburgh Review* and the bulk of the Whig party made the same great mistake.

In June 1809 Grey writes to Holland :

The total want of support to our army, the miserable resistance in every attack except at Saragossa, certainly do lead one to view the national character of the Spaniards and their prospects of future success in a very different light from that in which you see them. Nor have I the smallest hope, if Buonaparte should be able soon to terminate his Austrian war, that he will find any great difficulty in settling the business of the Peninsula.

In this state of mind Grey could not believe that Wellington's earlier victories, such as Talavera, were doing any real good, since they were generally followed by retreats. But as the course of events happily proved him wrong, he became gradually silent on the subject, both in public and private, as the Duke carried the war nearer and nearer to the Pyrenees. This error on Grey's part, which he shared with a man so fiercely anti-French as Grenville, was an error of calculation, not of sympathy, and did not arise from any wish to make peace with Napoleon so long as he was overlord of Europe. It was only in the winter of 1813 that Grey began to wish for peace on the terms of leaving a shrunken Napoleon as monarch of France. At that stage of affairs his foreign policy again began to differ from that of Grenville, who was more anxious to fight the war to a finish than were the Ministers themselves.

Grey's motives for dreading the attempt to conquer France, which he deprecated alike in 1813 and 1814 and again in 1815, were first his natural 'pessimism,' as we should now call it, about the outcome of any military operation, and his unwillingness to take risks in war. Secondly, his dislike and fear of imposing the Bourbon Government on an unwilling France, though he admitted that a restoration carried out by the French themselves would be desirable as being Britain's best guarantee of safety. Thirdly, a thorough distrust of the character of our Allies, the despots of Russia, Prussia, and Austria, whom he held to be a set of scoundrels, out to increase their own territories at the expense of the smaller states of Europe, and capable of leaving us in the lurch at any check or for any bribe, as they had so often before done in the last twenty years. For these reasons he thought that, although no course was safe, the least dangerous policy for England would be to bring all the belligerents into a moderate peace, if such was to be obtained, rather than to undertake the risks of trying to conquer France with such unreliable allies. The event proved him wrong.

On October 24, 1813, four days after the end of the battle of Leipsig, but before the news of it had reached England, Grey wrote to Holland :

With respect to peace, I don't know what you had written, but I conclude that it could not have been that we should give the *signal of sauve qui peut*, or that we should indicate any disposition to be ' mere benevolent spectators,' much less to desert the Allies in the promotion of a *necessary* contest. What I wish is that we should *with the Allies* offer a joint negotiation on moderate principles. Buonaparte would not accept this. Probably not. Both his disposition and his interest might, as Grenville says, prevent him. But I am obstinate in this opinion—that whether successful or not there would be great advantage in making the proposal. A *sincere* proposal, mind, and with a real anxious wish for its success. For this, I believe, so far from weakening the Alliance, would, if properly managed, strengthen it more than any other measure, and Grenville, I am afraid, is sadly mistaken if he thinks the Allies actuated by no other motive than that of their common danger, or that they have no jealousy of the designs of each other, or that the lesser German Princes do not fear them all.

In this letter Grey cannot be said to have differed in policy from the Ministers, who did not even repudiate the extraordinary action of Metternich and Lord Aberdeen in suggesting to Napoleon in November—such was their dread of him even after Leipsig—a frontier along the left bank of the Rhine. Napoleon, most unwisely, failed to accept at once this advantageous basis of negotiations, and the offer was withdrawn.[1] The Allies crossed the Rhine and invaded France in the early months of 1814. It was then that Grey's timidity about military operations appeared almost fantastic :

Howick, Feby. 6, 1814.

My dear Holland,—I think with you that a moderate check to the Allies would be best for peace, in all views ; but if they are checked at all, is it likely to be moderate ? They have imposed upon Buonaparte the necessity of driving them back, before he can treat, or rather conclude a peace with credit, or indeed with safety. The means he has collected are I am per-

[1] Ernouf's *Maret*, 605-9; Gordon's *Aberdeen*, 36-9 ; Rose's *Napoleon*, chap. xxxvi.

suaded most formidable ; for the nonsense in the papers about his inability to assemble an Army is only to be laughed at ; and if he should defeat them in an advanced position, without having one fortress to cover them, I doubt very much whether they will get back to the Rhine as well as he did. It certainly would be best of all that they should be forced to repass the Rhine without a defeat in the field. It would be sufficient to restore people to their senses here, and not enough to enable Buonaparte to withstand the very strong and universal desire for peace that now prevails in France.

But he seems to have changed his attitude somewhat in the following letter to Lady Holland a month later, partly no doubt because the Allies' invasion had fared better than he expected, also because he felt it necessary to repudiate the tenderness for Napoleon now prevalent at Holland House.

Howick, March ye 12, 1814.

Dear Lady Holland,—I am afraid I cannot quite submit to your politics. I very much doubt whether anything will diminish Buonaparte's desire to revenge himself on this country, and I very much fear, even if his dispositions were more pacific than I believe, that our embarrassments, after a peace has been concluded, will afford such temptations for attacking us as it will be hardly possible for flesh and blood to resist. The more the power of France can be reduced, therefore, the better for us. Upon this principle the restoration of the Bourbons, as it would probably disable France for the next 20 years at least, would be best of all. Do not imagine, however, that this would lead me to promote war for such an object.

After the return from Elba, Grey, like the Marquess of Wellesley, deprecated a war waged for the express purpose of dethroning Napoleon. Fortunately, Wellesley's brother settled the question at Waterloo before Grey had done more than deliver one speech in the House of Lords, protesting against a war 'undertaken on the principle of personally proscribing the present ruler of France.' He prepared another oration which he never delivered, but which exists in manuscript. The two together indicate fully the views he held. He believed that the people of France were predominantly for Napoleon as the bearer of the tricolor, and against the Bourbons, but determined now to have their constitutional rights, and unanimously in favour of peace. He feared that if our arms were not instantly successful, Russia, Austria, and Prussia, who had almost gone to war with each other over the division of the spoils, might desert us in pursuit of their private interests. We should then be left as in 1803, alone against France, and committed to wage war till we had dethroned Buonaparte, that is till the Greek Calends, —negotiations on any ordinary basis between the two Governments being precluded by our outlawry of the French Emperor.

Grey's arguments are so far persuasive as to make us more than ever grateful to the Duke for Waterloo ; for they conjure up a very reasonable picture of the condition we should all have been in if the war, having been begun, had not been won and finished out of hand. But if, in accordance with Grey's policy, Napoleon had been left peacefully on the throne of France, Britain could scarcely have indulged in that very complete measure of disarmament and that breach with the despotic Governments of Austria, Prussia, and Russia which marked the fortunate turn of our policy after Waterloo.

It was indeed lucky that Grey, for reasons wholly unconnected with the war, so often refused office in the latter part of the war. He was by nature a pessimist about the chances of battle, and could never have developed either the enterprise or the tenacity requisite for a good War Minister. His bold conduct of affairs in 1830–32, when he guided the country into and through her great revolutionary crisis, showed that as a domestic statesman he had more ' nerve,' tenacity, and phlegm than any of his colleagues, more even than Holland and Althorp. But in war he would authorise

no such startlingly bold adventures as Schedule A of
the Reform Bill ; he would take no such risks as that
famous second reading division in the Lords.   In war
he was always expecting the worst, often over-estimat-
ing the foe, periodically subject to cold fits.   It is true
that these tendencies sometimes led him right, as when in
1807 he protested against the South American adventure
that was supported by the rest of the Cabinet.   But
his timid views on the Peninsular and Waterloo cam-
paigns show that he was fortunate in his determination
to remain out of office during all that period, although
the reasons for his repeated refusals were concerned
only with domestic politics and personal issues.

On three several occasions between 1809 and 1812
Grey with his party might have taken office in a Coalition Ministry, but fortunately each time he refused.
His refusal in September 1809 to coalesce with
Perceval in order to strengthen a High Tory Ministry
on the retirement of the Duke of Portland, was obviously
right and was little questioned even at the time, although
some dismay was caused in Brooks's by his characteristic
rejection of the proposal by return of post from Howick.
But the issue was more complicated both for him and
Grenville in the negotiations of 1811 and 1812, when
the Prince of Wales, on becoming Prince Regent, felt
constrained to make advances to ' the old and tried
friends of Mr. Fox,' as to the formation by them and
Lord Wellesley of a Ministry dependent on the support
of Carlton House and on the influence of the Crown.
But Grey was right in supposing that there could be no
substance of power in a tenure of office on such terms,
least of all for any good purpose such as the passage of
Catholic Emancipation.   What chance would there have
been of Grey and Grenville forcing that measure through
the Lords in 1812, seeing that it was all that Wellington
himself, driven by O'Connell, could accomplish in 1829 !
Grey thoroughly distrusted the Prince Regent as ' the

worst anchoring ground in Europe.' Yet the Ministers would have to depend on his support against a Parliament hostile to everything Grey cared for, and against a country hostile on the Catholic question. Such a dependence on Royalty would ' unwhig ' them indeed ! Grey was a wiser and nobler man than he had been in the Regency debates of 1788.

Furthermore the Prince Regent had for some years past been turning Tory by political conviction on the Catholic and other questions, and passing at the same time under the personal influence of the infamous Lord Yarmouth, whom Grey would not consent to court or even to tolerate. For old times' sake the Prince thought it necessary to make a show of negotiating with the Foxites, but Grey shrewdly suspected that he did not really wish the negotiations to succeed. Sheridan, now in his decline, was still intimate at Carlton House, where he used his influence with the Prince to revenge himself on Grey for the cold shoulder that had so long been shown him. The net outcome of the tiresome negotiations of 1811 and 1812 was to widen the breach between the Prince Regent and the Whigs and to render George the bitter enemy of Grey, so much so that when he became King he decreed a personal taboo of the Whig chief as Minister, similar to that which his father had so long maintained against Fox.

The right of the Crown to choose its own Ministers, provided that they could, with the help of the Court votes, piece together a majority in the House of Commons, was a recognised practice of the Constitution up to the reign of William IV. Hence the personal relations of George, Regent and King, to each of the political leaders were of no small importance. By refusing to court the Prince, Grey wittingly debarred himself from all chance of power during the life-time of a man practically the same age as himself. In an era of sycophancy in high places the two following letters are refreshing. The first is written to his wife on June 25, 1813 :

I do not think there is now much chance of our being asked to the Prince's *fête*, but in case a sudden movement of caprice should induce him to send us a card, I wish you to answer it without delay, and to say that we *cannot* come. Don't make any excuse that can carry any meaning but a direct refusal to go.

On June 18, 1814, he writes to Lord Holland about the Regent's unhappy daughter :

I cannot express the indignation I have felt at the treatment of the Princess Charlotte. Cruelty to a Daughter is not an unnatural accompaniment of base and unmanly conduct to a wife. I know how wrong it would be to oppose a doubt to the unimpeached veracity of Carlton House, but nothing less than so sacred an authority could induce me to believe that she can be contented in her present situation. I should otherwise say it was altogether incredible and impossible. I really believe her life to be in danger ; if it is possible, something should be done in Parliament for her protection.

These two letters do much to explain why so many people still respected and trusted Lord Grey, in spite of his too frequent ' statesmanlike ' utterances to the effect that nothing could be done, and that least of all could he himself be called on to do anything. A fire still burnt within him which should one day break out and consume the world of Old Corruption.

CHAPTER IV

WHIGS, RADICALS AND REFORM——PETERLOO AND THE
SECOND REPRESSION——HOME LIFE ; LAMBTON AND
BROUGHAM——THE QUEEN'S TRIAL——CANNING AND
THE WHIG SPLIT——1816-1827

'You may be assured that any nibbling at Reform will not now
do.'—GREY TO LORD HOLLAND, *Feb.* 9, 1822.

IT was now to be proved whether the method of political
and social change in Great Britain would be by violence
and revolution or by peaceful progress through Parliamentary channels. Under the *régime* established by
Pitt and perfected by Perceval and Castlereagh, it was
by no means clear that England would not in the coming
era be forced to proceed to a war of classes. This would
inevitably happen some day, unless the British Parliament could be brought to reform its own method of
election. Self-appointed bodies can seldom be induced
to make themselves elective ; and Burke's doctrine, that
the existing Constitution was sacrosanct and that the
laws of England must never be changed, had now the
sanction of twenty years' acceptance and practice, culminating in the glories of Waterloo. The men who had
beaten Napoleon were less than ever inclined to abdicate
to the mob. Hope of change without violence lay only
in one quarter : the small party of Fox and Grey had
refused to acquiesce in Pitt's acts of repression or to accept
the theory that Parliament might never be reformed.
If the Whigs had merged themselves in Pitt's reactionary

bloc, Reform would have been impossible without revolution, and the history of England would have
approximated more and more to the histories of France,
Spain, Russia, Austria, and Germany. That we kept
our Anglo-Saxon moorings was due to the men whom
it was the custom of their enemies to represent as bad
patriots.

After the end of the Napoleonic war the issue clearly
emerged. The terrible sufferings of the mass of the
people, unequalled at any other known period of our
history, were due to the industrial revolution taking
place at a time of fierce social and political reaction, when
the wage earners in town and country had no political
rights, and under Pitt's Combination Acts hardly any civil
rights against their task-masters. This state of things
produced a Radical agitation from 1817 to 1819, more
popular and more lasting in its effects than the Paineite
movement which Pitt had suppressed.

The attitude adopted towards this new agitation
by the Tories and by the Whigs respectively would
show what chance there was of Reform in the long
run coming without revolution. The first response
of the Tories was clear and simple—suspension of the
Habeas Corpus Act in 1817, the Peterloo atrocity, and
the Six Acts in 1819. Spies and *agents provocateurs* were
let loose among the Radicals. Pitt's armoury of panics
and repression was refurbished without the excuse of
a foreign war. Social war of the Haves against the
Have-nots was Castlereagh's programme for the nineteenth century.[1]

---

[1] Recent historical research has done much for Castlereagh's reputation as a Foreign Minister, but less than nothing to justify the domestic
policy for which he made himself personally responsible by introducing
the Six Acts into the House of Commons. Indeed, the study of the
H.O. and other papers by Mr. and Mrs. Hammond, embodied in their
Town Labourer and *Skilled Labourer*, 1760–1832 (Longmans, 1917
and 1919), has shown the system of coercion and spying to have been
even worse than was known.

On the other hand, the attitude of the Whigs in the crisis of 1817–9 had a dual aspect, leaving it still uncertain whether they would or would not ever come to the rescue of the country as they ultimately did in 1831. On the one hand, they opposed in both Houses of Parliament the repressive legislation of the Government, they exposed and thereby in the end killed the spy system,[1] they denounced Peterloo, and maintained the right of free speech as the Palladium of the Constitution. In so doing they rid themselves of the Grenville alliance, a dead-weight upon their future advance. On the other hand, they felt and expressed so much aristocratic aversion to the Radicals, even while they were defending their liberties, that union of action between the Whigs and the mass of the people was rendered impossible. The position of the unpopular Government was secured by this cleavage among its opponents. The violence of the recrimination between Whigs and Radicals in 1817–9 was enough to make some acute observers despair of a Liberal party ever arising out of their union.

As to Reform of Parliament, the Whigs still inscribed it on their banner, but not as their chief and most immediate object. They were so deeply divided as to the extent to which a Reform Bill should go, that the question was left to be agitated by individuals among them like Lambton and Russell, not by the party as a whole. A political body that dare not give a lead on the prime question of the day is of very little use to anyone. During the next decade the Whigs were singularly futile and powerless, and were at one time outbidden by Canning in the affections of the people. But at least they continued to exist as the only party with seats in Parliament that could ever possibly take up the question of Reform, and save the country

---

[1] See the last chapter of Mr. and Mrs. Hammond's *Skilled Labourer*, entitled ' The Adventures of Oliver the Spy.'

from the catastrophe of civil war towards which it was moving.

For all that was good and for all that was inadequate in the policy of the Whigs at this period, Grey was largely responsible. It was he who, as acknowledged leader, broke with Grenville ;[1] resisted the repressive legislation and the spirit of Peterloo, yet denounced the Radicals ; urged the need of Parliamentary Reform, yet declined to lead an agitation for it as an immediate measure. All this has long been known, but one important fact about Grey has hitherto remained secret : in 1820 he had already made up his mind that when Reform was brought forward it must be no half measure, but that at least a hundred seats must be taken from the rotten boroughs. It is highly characteristic of him that he confided this great decision to Lord Holland in private, but never publicly proclaimed it, until, more than ten years later, he surprised the world with Schedules A and B of the Reform Bill. He feared in 1820 that if he came out, while in opposition, for the full measure which he secretly favoured, he would break up the party ; and that if he came out for a smaller measure, the party would be lost at the bar of public opinion. And so he let the Reform question drift.[2]

He was honourably determined not to make promises in opposition which he was not sure of being able to fulfil in office. Galled by the Radicals' taunt that he had failed to keep his pledges in the Ministry of 1806-7, he laid it down to his intimates as a principle that an opposition should promise less than it hopes to perform when in power.[3] As regards Parliamentary Reform

---

[1] Grenville's farewell letter to Grey, ending their regular political correspondence, is dated Feb. 23, 1817.

[2] See Appendix A, below, letter to Holland, Dec. 6, 1820.

[3] ' The lesson that I have learnt is to pledge myself to as little as possible while in opposition, and when in Government, if ever it should be my lot to be again in that station, to do as much as I can ' (Grey to Lord Holland, March 19, 1811).

he certainly acted up to this unusual precept in a way that puzzled contemporaries and still puzzles historians. It was difficult to believe that a statesman had always intended when he came into power to do more for the people than he had ever promised to them. Yet such was the case with Grey. He was too scrupulous for a leader of opposition, as well as too inactive and dignified to suit an era that was fast becoming democratic. As Sir Francis Burdett said of him, ' Grey should not have been a *patriot* ' (viz. in opposition) ; ' he should have been a Minister, that was his line.'

His fixed idea during this long period of inertia was to preserve the identity of the Foxite Whigs as a *via media* between Tory and Radical, in the belief that their day would come. But he would make no effort to bring that day nearer, and was perpetually damping the more ardent spirits of his children and infuriating his son-in-law Lambton, by telling them that it would never come ' during my life or even yours ! '

In all that Grey said and did, and still more in all that he failed to say and do, at this period, his bad health was an important factor. He was subject to recurrent fits of depression. Lady Grey, too, was often very unwell between 1816 and 1826.[1] On account of his own health and his wife's, Grey was more than ever anxious to get his standing resignation of the Whig leadership accepted by his colleagues. But Holland, into whose hands he wished to resign the succession, was firm in insisting that Grey's departure would dissolve the Foxite ' remnant ' into its component parts of quasi-Tory and quasi-Radical. This argument and the strong entreaties of his wife alone kept Grey at his post. Even so he writes to Holland in January 1822 :

---

[1] On account of her health they left beloved Howick for three successive winters, 1823–5, and lived at Government House, Devonport, kindly offered them by the Duke of Wellington, to whom it belonged as Governor of Plymouth.

HOWICK, 1832.

' I can now consider myself as little more than a by-stander.'[1]

It would be a mistake, however, to imagine that Howick was ever a gloomy house. Pessimism about politics is compatible with a great deal of happiness at home. It was impossible for Grey not to be happy, with a wife whom he adored, amid a swarm of fifteen children growing up in singular harmony ; never sent away to school ; galloping over the broad grass acres ; climbing the sea-worn rocks ; talking endlessly about politics and literature, about themselves and their acquaintances ; listening to their father read aloud by the hour in the well-furnished library ; and, regard-less of the age of formality in which they lived, calling their parents by pet forms of their Christian names. Grey was ' Car,' and the letters of his wife and daughters show that his occasional fits of impatience or depression were cheerfully absorbed into the prevailing atmosphere of fun and good humour.[2] Lady Grey, writing to their eldest boy, Lord Howick, to apologise for the few-ness of her letters during her illness, says :

Car is the person to blame, for he makes such a fuss about my being quiet, and comes with such a grave face to feel my pulse after the least exertion, that for a quiet life I submit to make none.

And again, when Howick had taken his seat in the Commons in 1826, she writes :

[1] Grey's letter to Lady Holland, Jan. 12, 1816, is the starting-point of many letters on the subject between Grey and the Hollands. In May 1824 Lady Grey writes to her husband : ' I really cannot express how much I regret the determination you seem to have taken entirely to give up all interference in politics. My dearest Charles, this subject is become a very sore one with me, and adds very much to the depression for which you scold me so unmercifully.'

[2] ' Think of Grey telling me that yesterday morning he made his first appearance in a new " Wellington " coat, which was no sooner seen by Lady Grey and her daughters than it was instantly stormed and carried fairly and by main force from his back, never to see the light again ' (Creevey, *Papers*, March 17, 1828).

Dearest Henry,—A thousand thanks for writing to me. You were quite right in supposing that I should be very anxious about your father's speech, and your account of it delights me. He tells me it was but indifferent, but I am too well accustomed to his disparagement of himself to be alarmed at it, and if he is not bouncing about the room, and making exclamations and groans, I may be certain that he said nothing of which the recollection makes him hot.

His wife's life-long devotion to him is expressed in many beautiful love-letters of this late period of their married life. But the gracious power of laughing at those whom you love, without loving them less, helped the ladies of a family that embraced Grey, Howick, and Lambton. The relation of the dignified Whig patrician to his eager son and heir with the Free Trade heresy, and to the hot-tempered Radical of ancient lineage whom his daughter Louisa had married, form a political and domestic comedy of many acts and scenes. Grey and his son-in-law were made to love and plague one another. And if Lambton was Grey's gadfly, the need was apparent.

John George Lambton is better known in the history of the Reform Bill and of Canada by his later title of Lord Durham. His father was that William Lambton, Grey's Eton, Cambridge, and Parliamentary friend, and one of the original ' Friends of the People,' whose death in 1797 had left his son at five years of age the inheritor of his unfulfilled renown. John Lambton's position as the head of the oldest and most prominent family in the mining county of Durham, where the new industrial democracy was growing up, became one of national importance as soon as it appeared that he had great talents, that he was a Radical in his opinions, yet a Whig in his party allegiance.

His first marriage in 1812, before he had come of age, was characteristically celebrated at Gretna Green ; but the lady died in the year of Waterloo. In December 1816 he married Grey's eldest daughter Louisa. The nearness to Northumberland of Lambton Castle, Durham, the happy intimacy that sprang up between the Howick swarm and their vivacious brother-in-law, and the real affection that at once bound Lambton to Lord Grey,[1] brought modern democracy into the heart of the Whig counsels. Lambton was 'Radical Jack' to the Durham miners, but he was genuinely loyal to the Whig party and to its chief. Grey's intense indignation at the repressive measures of the Government, at the employment of spies like the famous Oliver to provoke disturbances among the starving operatives, at the official approval accorded to the Peterloo magistrates before any enquiry had been made, and the closely argued speeches in the Lords in which he defended the liberty of the subject in these matters, seemed to Lambton much more genuinely Liberal than the words and attitude of a good many other Whigs.[2] On George Ponsonby's death in 1817, Tierney for a short time succeeded him as nominal leader of opposition in the Commons, but his lead was spiritless and aimed at attracting moderate votes rather than at maintaining Liberal principles. 'I felt a good deal dissatisfied with the tameness of the debates, or the repressive system of the Government,' wrote Grey to Lambton on March 15, 1818, 'but your speech and those of Romilly and Brougham in the last debate have quite removed that feeling. Tierney ought to have spoken.'

[1] 'I have never felt the blessing of a Father's care or advice, and I fear I have suffered from it. It is therefore more gratifying to me than I can express to be able to look upon you in that sacred light ; upon you whom I have always venerated as the first of men in public life, and since I have been admitted in your society as the most exemplary in private life' (Lambton to Grey, December 11, 1816).

[2] On June 10, 1817, Grey wrote to the Marquess Wellesley, an occasional ally of the Whigs, asking his attendance to oppose the renewal of the suspension of Habeas Corpus. He asks 'whether we shall allow a practice to be established of suspending the rights of the people of England, like the cash payments of the bank.'

Lambton replies :

I am ready to support anyone whom you think best adapted
to the situation. But I trust you will not think of giving up
your own superior control over the whole. There are many
who only co-operate because they have confidence in you personally, and there is a very strong party who have serious objections to Tierney's wavering and indecisive system, in whose
hands, were you to withdraw, the whole thing would be placed.
I do not say that it is necessary for you to take any active part,
but do not vacate the situation you now hold of being Fox's
representative.

The chivalrous warmth of Lambton's political and
personal loyalty to his father-in-law in these early years of
their connection carried him to unexpected lengths. In
February 1819, at the Westminster by-election caused
by the tragic death of Sir Samuel Romilly, Lambton
flung all his energies with great effect on to the side of
the Whig candidate George Lamb, against the Radical
candidate Hobhouse, solely because the local Radicals,
guided by Francis Place, had made severe attacks on
Lord Grey which Hobhouse had not been in a position
to repudiate. Grey, knowing that Lambton really
agreed much more with Hobhouse than with Lamb on
general politics, was deeply touched by his son-in-law's
impetuous action in his defence.

It is not perhaps surprising that the Radicals attacked
Grey, seeing how he on his side thought and spoke
of them. In October 1819 he wrote to Sir Robert
Wilson about Hunt and the Radical leaders :

Is there one among them with whom you would trust yourself in the dark ? Can you have, I will not say any confidence
in their opinions and principles, but any doubt of the wickedness of their intentions ? Look at the Men, at their characters,
at their conduct. What is there more base, more detestable,
more at variance with all taste and decency, as well as all morality,
truth, and honour ? A cause so supported cannot be a good
cause. They may use Burdett for their instrument for a time,

and you also if you place yourself in their trammels, but depend upon it, if a convulsion follows, I shall not precede you many months on the scaffold, which you will have assisted in preparing for us both.

When Sir Robert Wilson opposed the Reform Bill in 1831 he used to cite this letter to his friends as proof that not he, but Grey, had deserted his principles. Yet in fact Grey, as we now know, was in favour of abolishing the rotten boroughs wholesale, even at the time when he used such violent language against the Radicals. And while he wrote thus to Wilson, he was engaged in defending these very men, whom he so much feared and disliked, from unjust and extraordinary coercion.

From 1816 onwards Grey was in much closer personal relations with the advanced than with the conservative Whigs. Besides Lord Howick and Lambton and those of his own household, Sir Robert Wilson and Henry Brougham were at this time among the most frequent and favourite visitors at Howick. To Sir Robert, Grey was drawn by his strong interest in Liberalism on the Continent, with which Wilson was closely associated in spite of the great part he had played as a soldier in the downfall of Napoleon. In 1816 Grey writes to him :

I have no expectation that in my time at least the cause of rational liberty will triumph. In France it seems to me less likely than anywhere else ; and the severest charge that can be made against Buonaparte is that by the power he exercised, and the use he made of it, he prepared the French for irredeemable submission to that degrading despotism which now seems to be their lot.

On the news of Napoleon's death, Grey writes to his wife :

I perhaps ought to feel more strongly almost than anybody all the harm he has done to the cause for which I have been contending all my life.

The most remarkable and entertaining of all the visitors to Howick at this period was Henry Brougham. The antithesis of Grey in almost every respect, Brougham was the embodiment of plebeian self-confidence, self-assertion, and vitality. He was a born leader of opposition, an unrivalled agitator. Only office and Cabinet counsel, destined to show Grey's strength, would reveal Brougham's limitations. During the Napoleonic war the Whigs had unduly neglected his great talents, and had not even regularly supplied him with a seat in Parliament. But whenever he was in the House he led the opposition in fact though not in name. His fierce attacks in Parliament, supported by organised agitation in the country, had caused the withdrawal of the Orders in Council in 1812, and the more doubtful boon of the defeat of the income-tax in 1816. The movement for the abolition of slavery was becoming more and more popular, not a little because Brougham had become its loudest champion. Scottish in all save descent, he believed in popular education, and did much to make a hostile world believe in it too. That 'the march of mind' in the new generation should be associated in common parlance with the astonishing energies of this one man was in reality a compliment, though it was sometimes meant as a sarcasm.[1] The Queen's trial of 1820 showed him to the world at the height of his powers.

In September 1809 Grey told Creevey that Brougham was 'the first man this country has seen since Burke's time.' A dozen years later he still immensely admired and had not yet begun to suspect him. 'On you must depend,' Grey wrote to him in 1822, 'in the first degree, the efficiency of any administration that can be formed !' It is a curious speculation what Brougham's career in office would have been like, if the Whigs had

[1] *E.g.* in Peacock's *Crotchet Castle*, where 'the learned friend' is Brougham. His great public service in initiating the movement for law reform dates from February 1828. See the excellent life of him in Atlay's *Victorian Chancellors*.

come into power at the beginning of the reign of George IV. The jealousy of his disposition, the eccentricity of his actions, and the instability of his mind, though already recognised as defects, were not yet heightened by that touch of the insane which turned his later years into a long comedy, a contrast in likeness to the tragic close of Burke's overburdened intellect.

There is near Alnmouth a ford on the Aln which can be crossed when the tide is not too high. One day Grey, who had Brougham staying with him at Howick, began to cross the ford, when the marks by the river side indicated that it was rather doubtful whether the passage were safe. Half way over Grey turned in his saddle, and shouted back, ' Brougham, can you swim ? ' ' I never have swum,' was the self-confident answer, ' *but I have no doubt I could if I tried.*'

The action of the Whigs in the Ministry of All the Talents in their ' delicate investigation ' into the conduct of Caroline, Princess of Wales, has been alluded to in a previous chapter.[1] Since then, Caroline's manner of life abroad had been so eccentric and coarse as to arouse very natural suspicions. Whether she was guilty or not no man at this hour can with certainty say. On the other hand, it is certain that her marriage had been a legalised bigamy, since her husband had previously been married to Mrs. Fitzherbert, who was still alive;[2] it is certain that George cast off his second wife almost at once, before he could even pretend to have any ground against her, and that he had lived ever since in open relations with a number of other women ; and that while so living he had set spies of most doubtful character on Caroline's conduct abroad. That was all our

---

[1] See p. 155, above.

[2] See p. 18, above. In the Grey family correspondence of 1820 we find : ' The Queen says, " I never did commit adultery but once, and I have repented it ever since. It was with the husband of Mrs. Fitzherbert ! " '

ancestors knew, and all they needed to know in order to form a passionate determination that this woman, innocent or guilty, should not be divorced by such a man on such conditions.

That man, by the death of George III, had now become King ; and his wife, early in June 1820, returned to claim her position as Queen. The Ministers, to propitiate George IV, introduced a Bill of Pains and Penalties against her into the House of Lords. This divorce bill would have to pass both Houses like any other law, but evidence would be taken before the Lords as in a Court of Justice. Outside the walls of the House the feeling in all classes was as strong for the Queen as it was for the Reform Bill a dozen years later.

As the Queen's trial dragged its foul length along day after day for four months, an utter contempt for their rulers, Royal and other, sank deep into the hearts of the people. Though the Queen was in a sense the heroine, her low vulgarity was in itself a powerful argument for levellers and republicans. The whole system of political corruption and oppression, rooted in the throne, which Pitt had fostered and his successors had rendered so triumphant, everything for which the old Toryism stood, was industriously rolled over and over in the mud before the eyes of the whole nation, with Brougham, the Queen's Attorney-General, for showman of the spectacle. The Radical cartoonists, strong in the rising genius of Cruikshank, had already fared sumptuously on Peterloo, and now battened on the shapeless figure of George IV.[1] In these bad years two images stood familiarly to the starving workmen of England for the two aspects of government as they knew it : a mounted yeoman, shako on head and sabre in hand, riding over the bodies of shrieking women and children ;

[1] George was often represented as a Chinese Mandarin because the Pavilion at Brighton, which he had built in the Chinese style, was his favourite residence.

and a fat 'Chinese' voluptuary lolling on a couch, surrounded by obsequious Ministers catering for his whims and vices.

The temptation to the Whigs was immense to take up Queen Caroline's cause as a party cry. But Grey, though he loathed the husband and despised the obsequiousness and folly of the Ministers in bringing in the Divorce Bill, disliked the wife and was in two minds as to her guilt or innocence. Above all he remembered that he had now, much against his will, been called on to act with his brother peers as jury in her case, and that, if the Bill passed the Lords, the Commons would in their turn be called on to pronounce by their votes a quasi-judicial verdict. As early as August 1819, when coming events were already casting their shadows before, he had written to Brougham : 'We as a party have nothing to do but to observe the most perfect neutrality, and to decide upon the evidence as we should do in any other case.' To that principle he steadily adhered to the end, much to the disgust of more eager politicians.

In this spirit he sat out the Queen's trial before the Lords through the summer and autumn of 1820, following the evidence with the utmost impartiality and altering his balanced opinion more than once as the case proceeded. His daily letters to his wife at Howick describe the scenes and give us his inmost thoughts.

On June 23 he mentions the preliminary attempts at a compromise on the floor of the House of Commons :

All that I heard of Brougham's speech was very bad : a very inadequate defence of the Queen if he felt her to be innocent, and betraying in every word of it, as indeed he appears to me to have done in every part of his conduct, a consciousness that he was charged with the management of a bad cause.[1]

---

[1] Mrs. Brougham did not call on the Queen, an omission that she bitterly resented. The Queen disliked and distrusted Brougham, but could not dispense with him.

[July 3.] Lauderdale assured me that the evidence against the Queen is complete and to the last degree disgusting. I have always believed that if the case came to a public hearing she must be ruined, but those who maintain her cause will have ample opportunity of still more inflaming the public mind, already in a state of such fearful irritation, and worked upon by the other cause of discontent, distress. This is her only game, which she will play desperately and fearlessly, but I hope unskilfully. Otherwise I should feel by no means confident that it might not succeed, and that she may not resemble the Empress Catherine in more features of her character and fortunes than one.

[July 4.] The Ministers ought to be hanged for the situation into which they have brought this unfortunate business, and I am by no means sure that this will not happen before its conclusion.

It will be seen therefore that Grey began to listen to the evidence with no predisposition in favour of the Queen. The bad character of the Italian witnesses against her evidently surprised him, and he was much relieved to find that at the end of all he was able honestly to pronounce that no case had been made out against her.

[August 21.] The witnesses are obviously of the lowest class, and exposed to strong suspicion, and certainly far inferior in respectability and credit to those whom most Ministers declared to be unworthy of belief in 1807. We have not finished the first witness. His name is Theodore Majocchi. He has already, if he cannot be contradicted or discredited, proved a complete case. When he came to the bar the Queen stood up close opposite to him, fixed her arms akimbo, looked him full in the face, cried out or rather shrieked out, 'Theodore!' and ran out of the House. She did not appear again.

The mob outside is as good-humoured as possible. My white hat meets with great applause from them. 'Ah! you're a Radical—the Queen for ever!' are the salutes with which I am greeted as I pass.[1] The Duke of Wellington, on the con-

---

[1] Orator Hunt, the famous Radical whose arrest at the Reform meeting, Manchester, the year before, was the occasion of Peterloo, wore a white top-hat, which became the symbol of Radical opinions for years to come. Many respectable people abandoned wearing white top-hats for this reason.

COPLEY   MAJOCCHI   BROUGHAM   THE QUEEN   EARL GREY   LORD HOLLAND
(Lyndhurst) (standing straight)   (standing,   (speaking)   (standing,
and INTERPRETER   with paper)   with hand
(bowing over table)   in pocket)

From the engraving by J. Bromley
and J. Porter, after the painting by
George Hayter.

trary, is hissed and hooted with a degree of violence which once or twice has appeared rather alarming.[1]

[August 22.] Brougham is not, I think, a good cross-examiner, and indeed it is very difficult through an interpreter, but he has damaged the witness Majocchi a good deal. Majocchi answers, nine cases out of ten, ' *non mi ricordo*,' [2] and often in cases in which, if he had told the truth in the first instance, not to recollect is impossible.

It will be a most singular event if with such strong presumption of her guilt as can leave little doubt of it, the nature of the evidence should allow the Queen to escape. Flahaut stood very near the Queen (her back was to me), and could see her face perfectly when she made that strange exhibition on Majocchi's first appearance. He says her countenance was that of a fury.

[August 24.] I dined at Brooks's with Thanet and Brougham. The latter is in great spirits and high good humour.

[October 2.] I hear of nothing but processions with addresses to the Queen. Tegart told me that in one which passed this morning, there were counted 160 carriages and four. What disgusting folly ! if it does not deserve a worse name. I have not made up my mind. Whenever I do so, to whatever obloquy I may expose myself you at least will, I am sure, do me justice.

Now began the defence :

[Oct. 4.] Brougham has just concluded a most powerful and effective speech. I think he has many faults, but he also has powers which perhaps no other man possesses. He has made a great impression on the House, and if his evidence comes at all up to his statements, the Bill will not pass the Lords.

[Oct. 12.] Lieutenant Hownam gave upon the whole a very good evidence, and has left the fact of the Queen's sleeping

---

[1] The Duke supported the Bill, not from servility to the King, but from contempt of the mob. He particularly disliked George IV ; when warned by Portland that if the Bill passed the Lords there would be reprisals to expose the King's past life, he replied : ' The King is degraded as low as he can be already ' (*Greville*, Oct. 15, 1820).

[2] ' I do not remember.' After this, the most famous incident in the most famous trial of the century, our ancestors used ' *non mi ricordo* ' as a proverbial expression implying mendacity.

under the same tent with Bergami in such circumstances that I do not think it possible to infer guilt from that circumstance alone, in such a manner as to justify a vote of the House in favour of the Bill.[1] Every other fact of the case is decidedly damaged.

[Oct. 14.] My hopes revive of throwing out this Bill, against which I think I may now say certainly that I shall vote. The impression made against it yesterday was very great.

[Nov. 3.] I have just finished a speech of three hours, if I may believe my friends very successfully, and to say the truth I am not dissatisfied with myself. Jenky [2] is now roaring in answer to me, and I feel myself quite unable to listen to him.

Grey's speech, which was printed in full and circulated through the country, was an admirable summing up of the more important evidence, to demonstrate that there was no proof of guilt. His closely argued verdict had a much greater effect on the Queen's behalf than if he had been her partisan from the first, as so many of his friends had wished him to be. When a few days later the Ministers withdrew the Bill, which they could scarcely hope to force through the closely divided Lords, and would certainly lose in the Commons, Grey enjoyed on his return to Northumberland a popular triumph that he had deserved all the more because he had not gone out of his way to court it. At Alnwick the whole population of the town, and the farmers from twenty miles around, had gathered to welcome him, thereby ' giving great offence to the Duke of Northumberland, on whom so many are dependent.' They had arranged to take out the horses and draw Grey's carriage the whole seven miles to Howick, and only desisted when he made it clear that in that case he would get out and walk. They could not, however, be prevented from seeing him home by moonlight. ' Every tradesman of Alnwick and multitudes of the most respectable farmers, all well

---

[1] The Lieutenant's evidence impressed some of the Lords very differently, in a sense damaging to the Queen.

[2] ' Jenky ' = Jenkinson, viz., Lord Liverpool, the Prime Minister.

mounted, their hats and horses' heads covered with blue ribbons,[1] and rending the air with shouts, accompanied him to his hall door.'

Whatever popularity he had gained by his speech and vote in the Queen's trial, Grey had thereby forfeited what small chance he ever had of holding office in the new reign. George IV regarded him as George III regarded Fox—as a personal enemy whom he would never receive as Minister. For his part, Grey was ready to give all men, including kings, their due, but no more. In January 1822, in one of the many affectionate and carefully paternal letters that he wrote to Lord Howick at Trinity, Cambridge, he sums up in a sentence his views on 'Princes.' The Duke of Sussex was the Whig member of the Royal Family, and a man of really liberal views. ' I am very sorry,' writes Grey, ' that you declined Mr. Brown's invitation to meet the Duke of Sussex. I have no reason to recommend any extraordinary pains to conciliate the favour of princes, but a proper respect is due to them, for which they have an additional claim *when they behave well, which they rarely do.*'

The Tory Cabinet survived the measureless shame and unpopularity of the Queen's trial, because the King, much as he hated the Ministers for bungling the Bill, hated the Whigs still more for voting against it, and for their association with his arch-enemy Brougham. Now the choice of the Prime Minister effectually rested with the King. The Whigs only mustered some 170 votes in opposition, and they would do nothing on the one hand to court the King for office, and for the large number of votes in the House which was the perquisite

---

[1] In Northumberland blue was the Whig, and is still the Liberal, colour. At the time of these demonstrations Lady Grey wrote, ' It is a pity Henry [Lord Howick] is not of age, as I believe he could at this moment carry the county with ease.' He failed six years later, when the Tories, thanks to Canning, Peel, and Huskisson, had justly become less unpopular.

of Ministers favoured by the Crown ; nor on the other hand would they lead the Radicals in an agitation for a really extensive reform of Parliament. In 1830-1 the Whigs, under altered circumstances, were able to do both these things at once, and only thus managed to maintain themselves in office until they had remodelled the Constitution that was so heavily weighted in the interest of their rivals.

But though the Tories for the present continued in office, the darkest hour of our domestic history was already over. Some measure of trade prosperity came to alleviate the worst pangs of economic distress. And in 1822 changes began to take place in the personnel and spirit of the Government.

In January of that year Peel succeeded to the Home Office. He stopped the whole system of coercion and espionage in England, without any ill effects on public order. His life's work of transforming the old Tory party into the Victorian Conservative party was begun, not as some think with the Tamworth manifesto of 1834, but when he cleared out the mystery of iniquity in the Home Office, a dozen years before. It was then that Pitt's system received its first real blow. The fact that Peel still swore by Pitt, and was still an anti-Catholic and anti-Reformer, gave him that secure place in the Tory citadel which he employed gradually to transform the whole spirit and method of the party. The Reform Bill, though he opposed it, enabled him to complete his work.

In August of the same year, 1822, the death of Castlereagh [Lord Londonderry] made Canning the leader of the Commons and the head of the Foreign Office. Canning had in April reaffirmed his objection, based on the principles of Burke, to all reform of Parliament ; he never descended from this position, but he proceeded as Foreign Minister to put unreformed England at the head of the Liberal movement in Europe and America. The repeal of Pitt's Combination Acts

against workmen's Trade Unions,[1] and the beginning
of penal law reform, showed the spirit of the new age
working on the Tory Parliament. At the General Election of 1826 Grey put up his
son and heir to stand for his own old county seat of
Northumberland. By the time the fifteen days of
open polling were ended, the contest had cost the family
£14,000, which it could ill afford, chiefly in transport
and tavern bills for the Whig freeholders. It was one
of the most famous elections in North-country annals ;
volumes of record and recrimination were published
about its details. Lambton, whose own election for
Durham was a walk-over, threw his magnificent energies into Lord Howick's campaign. His invasion of
Northumberland was bitterly resented by some, for
although Lambton chanced to be a Northumbrian
freeholder he was pre-eminently a Durham magnate ;
nor were his politics popular with the Whig or Tory
gentry. Grey indignantly defended his son-in-law's
civic rights on the north of Tyne and welcomed his
aid. This quarrel and the personal hostility between
the Grey family and Thomas Wentworth Beaumont,
the Whig-Radical candidate,[2] lent zest to the election.
And since the two Tory candidates, Liddell and Bell,
disliked each other as much as the two Liberals, Howick
and Beaumont, the consequent recriminations about
' secret coalitions ' and ' splitting votes ' with the enemy
wore every one's temper to the edge, especially as the
campaign was conducted in the hottest summer on
record.

On one of the last days of the polling, while the rival
parties and their brass bands were conducting themselves

---

[1] See pp. 99–100, above.

[2] Son of the T. R. Beaumont who, with Lord Percy, had defeated
Grey in 1807 (see pp. 160–1, above). The Beaumont of the third generation long afterwards told my father, Sir George Trevelyan, that the
election of 1826 cost his father, T. W. Beaumont, £80,000, after he had
disallowed £10,000 of the original bills sent in.

at the Alnwick hustings for all the world like the men
of Eatanswill in the 'Pickwick Papers,' an altercation
arose on the platform, which ended in Beaumont calling
Lambton a liar. The gentlemen adjourned to the
neighbouring inns to arrange preliminaries. It was
the last night of June. News reached Howick Hall,
and before dawn of July 1 Earl Grey in dreadful
anxiety had galloped into Alnwick, 'unattended by
a single groom,' as was noted by local reporters, now
all agog. 'In all the wide border' there was 'racing
and chasing' of the authorities to stop the duel. But
the law was dodged and the meeting took place with
pistols on Bamborough sands, to the safety and satisfaction of both parties. 'Radical Jack' went back to
Durham thrice a hero of ballad, and the ties were drawn
closer than ever between him and the household at
Howick, out of zeal for whose cause he had risked his
life.[1]

Lord Howick and Beaumont were both beaten,
each to the joy of the other. But Howick was provided
with the rotten borough of Winchelsea, and the day
when he should sit as a Northumberland county member
was not long postponed. In Parliament he soon made
his mark, greatly to the delight of his father, who was
ambitious now only for his son. But Grey was less
pleased that Howick's enthusiasm was chiefly devoted
to the cause of Free Trade.

On the question of corn [Grey writes to his son Charles in
1827], Henry's opinions are quite at variance with mine, and if
carried into effect would prove most injurious to the country, and
would at once ruin him and me. But however I may differ from
him, I never can find fault with his acting boldly in support of
an honest opinion.

In February 1827 the sudden illness and retirement of Lord Liverpool caused the progressive and

[1] *Poll-Book of the Election*, printed Alnwick 1827; MS. letters of
the Grey and Lambton families; Reid's *Durham*, i. 170–2.

reactionary wings of the Tory party to fall asunder. For some years past, only the Premier's moderating influence had held them together in one Cabinet, where many a battle had been fought over Canning's foreign policy and Huskisson's Free Trade. The Tory cleavage was one of principle and became permanent, but it had the temporary effect of splitting the Whig party also, on a question not of principle but of persons and tactics.

In April 1827 Canning and Huskisson, having quarrelled with Wellington and Eldon, appealed to the Whigs to enable them to carry on a Government that should prolong the recent Liverpool policy, essentially liberal on foreign and commercial questions. The main body of the Whigs, including Holland and Lansdowne, Lambton and Brougham, consented to the alliance. Canning formed a Ministry out of his own Tory supporters, henceforth known as Canningites,[1] with Lansdowne and Tierney almost alone to represent the Whig interest in the Ministry.

It cannot be said that the Whigs drove a hard bargain, and Grey complained that they had driven no bargain at all. The new Cabinet announced that it would maintain the Test Act against Dissenters, and refuse Parliamentary Reform on principle ; Catholic Emancipation was to be left an ' open question ' as it had been for thirty years past in every Tory administration, that is to say the Catholics were not to be emancipated. It may well be asked what the Whigs got in return for breaking up their own party. The answer made by Holland and Brougham was that they had taken the only means to prevent power falling back into the hands of Wellington, Eldon, and the Tories of the old school. They claimed also that their action made a lasting division in the Tory ranks, and so prepared great things for the future.

---

[1] The chief Canningites, besides Huskisson (*ob.* Sept. 1830), were Palmerston, William Lamb (Lord Melbourne), Charles Grant, and Lord Goderich, all of whom joined Lord Grey's Reform Cabinet, Nov. 1830.

There was indeed much to be said on both sides of the contention that now divided Brooks's. The action of the Whigs who followed Holland into Canning's camp did render permanent Tory reunion impossible, and led to the inclusion of the Canningites in Grey's Reform Ministry three years later. But it was a perilous game, and its first effect was to divide the Whigs themselves and put an end to the separate existence of their party. If Canning had not chanced to die when he did, there could have been no Whig reunion and no Reform Bill. For Canning was one of the most determined and by far the most popular and powerful of the opponents of Parliamentary Reform.[1] If he had lived, his genius, so justly attractive to young Liberals, would have continued to lead the progressive politicians of the country, by the path of a liberal foreign policy, further and further away from Parliamentary Reform. Grey's distrust of the Canning-worship of the other Whigs was therefore a sound and useful instinct on the whole, though some of it was due to personal prejudice.

It is impossible not to feel that both Grey and the Whigs from whom he differed in 1827 had made their difficulties for themselves, by their timidity in not giving the country a lead on Reform during the previous decade. They had stopped so long in the water that Canning at last had stolen their clothes. He had become England's Liberal hero, because his foreign policy at least meant something that people could understand and follow, at a time when they were given no other lead. The Whig divisions in 1827 were the just punishment of a party that would not take an active line of its own. It looked like the end of the Whigs, but Canning's death enabled them to survive and reunite. They got one more chance, and took it.

---

[1] 'The Reform Bill frightened me in 1831,' wrote Mr. Gladstone; 'Burke and Canning misled many on that subject, and they misled me' (*Life*, bk. i. chap. iii.). The worst of great thinkers, said John Bright, is that they so often think wrong.

There was nothing inevitable about the Reform Bill ; the way for it was cleared by a series of extraordinary accidents, of which Canning's death in August 1827 was the first and most important.

The reasons why Grey refused his support to Canning in 1827 are clearly set out in his famous speech in the House of Lords on May 7 against the new administration, and in his private letters to Lord Holland and to his own family.[1]

First and foremost, he thought that for the Foxites to become unconditional supporters of a Tory Ministry, without obtaining any influence over its policy, was tantamount to 'the dissolution of the Whig Party and the total destruction of its consequence and character.'

So much for underlying principle. Descending to details, he declined to support a Government that was not only opposed to Parliamentary Reform but had taken its stand against the relief of the Protestant Dissenters in the matter of the Test Act, and would do nothing for Catholic Emancipation. Grey despised Pitt and Canning because, although they were as much in favour of Catholic Emancipation as he was himself, they were ready to hold office without emancipating the Catholics. To a Ministry formed on that basis he would give no help. If Catholic Emancipation had been part of the programme of the new Administration, he would have advised his friends to join it, and would have lent it his 'fair support,' though he would not himself have taken office under a statesman he distrusted.[2]

His 'rooted distrust of Canning' was the legacy of early years. Long before Waterloo Canning had managed to arouse against himself the suspicion and disapproval of statesmen of all parties, who regarded him rather as Disraeli was regarded in the early part of his career. These old-world impressions lingered in

[1] See Appendix B, below: 'Grey's views of Canning's Policy, 1822–27.'

[2] See letters, Feb. 9, March 13, April 14, 1827, Appendix B, below.

Grey's mind, though they were quite unknown to the men of the younger generation. If Canning had ever been an ' adventurer of genius ' he was now a sober and careworn statesman.

Lastly, Grey, though he was no less a ' Liberal ' in foreign affairs than Canning, regarded his rival's proceedings in the two hemispheres with a critical eye. He thought that if England had taken a stronger line at the Congress at Verona, reactionary France would never have dared to invade Spain in 1823, and to suppress the Liberal movement in the Peninsula ; and that even after Verona Canning should have threatened war to prevent the French from crossing the Pyrenees. He regarded Canning's recognition in 1825 of the already accomplished independence of the Spanish colonies in America as too belated to have merit ; England seemed to him merely to have followed the lead of President Monroe. The famous speech in which Canning had said : ' I called the New World into existence to redress the balance of the Old,' was in Grey's eyes a piece of egoistic claptrap, intended to cover up the fact that he had failed to save the Liberals of Spain from the French Reactionaries. He even refused to believe that Canning had differed seriously from his colleagues in the Cabinet, forcing his foreign policy through against their will. Posterity has not endorsed this criticism of the Foreign Minister who initiated a trend in British policy which Grey himself revived and continued a few years later.[1]

During the brief Premiership of Canning from April to August 1827, Grey was almost completely isolated. Except Althorp and some of the Russells, all his old and new political colleagues had deserted him to follow the statesman whom he most disliked. Even his lifelong correspondence with Holland House was suspended. ' I am left nearly alone,' he wrote to his

[1] See letters, Appendix B, below. For the defence of Canning, see Stapleton's *Canning*, vol. iii. pp. 403–25, and Temperley's *Canning*, *passim*.

son Charles on July 2nd, ' being separated from almost all my old friends, including Lambton. But do not believe any reports you may hear of my having formed any new connections. I stand aloof from all parties, acting upon my own principles.'[1] The party that it had been the work of his life to foster at every sacrifice of his own popularity and ambition had for the moment ceased to exist. If he, instead of Canning, had died in 1827, he would have appeared in history as a pathetic figure, an honourable man indeed, but one of the least successful of British statesmen. But the fatality that had for forty years dogged his fortunes and those of Parliamentary Reform was now, at this hour of discouragement, about to give way to an amazing run of luck. A series of unexpected events, personal and political, foreign and domestic, led England swiftly on to the crisis, like many paths hastening to one end.

[1] He had been falsely accused of combining with Wellington to turn out Canning, because he had voted in June for a Corn Law Amendment of the Duke's with which he agreed. See his letter to Lord John Russell, *Early Correspondence of Lord John Russell*, i. 262–5.

CHAPTER V

THE TIDE SETS IN—1828-1830

'What is passing is a renewal of a more frightful kind than the prospects of 1791, 2, 3, 4, and 5. The occurrences of those days, involving the Crown as well as the Houses of Parliament, by express mention, in revolutionary projects—the language "No King"—gave a treasonable character to the proceedings of that era which enabled Government to deal with it by law. That is now carefully avoided, and the proceedings of this day are therefore the more difficult to be dealt with. They are, of course, more dangerous. The sacrifice, too, of the Test Act and the passing of the Roman Catholic Emancipation Bill have established a precedent so encouraging to the present attempts at revolution under name of Reform, that he must be a very bold fool who does not tremble at what seems to be fast approaching.'—LORD ELDON TO LORD STOWELL, *April* 1830.

THE death of Canning (August 1827) cleared the ground for the reunion of all the Whigs under Grey ; for the absorption in the Whig party of the ' Canningite ' statesmen, including Palmerston and Melbourne ; and for the passing of the great Reform Bill by these combined forces. But the first effect of Canning's death was exactly the opposite. After an attempt to carry on a ' Canningite ' Ministry without Canning had speedily been wrecked by the proverbial inability of ' goody Goderich ' as Prime Minister, George IV sent for Wellington, who in January 1828 formed a Cabinet of Tory reunion. The Duke and Peel were from the first the two pillars of the new structure, and were all that remained of it at the end ; but the original Wellington Ministry contained also the Canningites under the leadership of Huskisson.

The Whigs were dished indeed. Grey and Althorp had the mournful satisfaction of pointing out to their erring friends that 'the insurrection at Brooks's and Lord Lansdowne's weakness' in joining Canning had discredited and broken up the Whig party, merely to reinstate the Tories under Wellington.[1] The bitterness of the personal divisions between the Whig leaders in 1827, though the subject of their difference was removed, could not at once be forgotten. Grey's friendship with Brougham never recovered, and even his far deeper confidence in Holland was not restored to its former perfection until the rapid movement of events in 1830 compelled the two veterans to resume their old, loving and intimate consultations for the public weal.[2] The Whig party, in fact, had to endure a period of convalescence before it was fit to take the field for the greatest and most glorious campaign in the hundred and fifty years of its history. But while the Whigs were slowly reuniting, the Duke was busy breaking up the Tory party into three hostile factions. At length in 1830 the breaches that he had made in his own rampart gaped so wide that the long-hesitating Whigs were tempted to close their ranks once for all and lead the

[1] Althorp to John Russell, Jan. 13, 1828.

In young Macaulay's *Political Georgics* (dated March 1828) we read :

'How Cabinets are form'd and how destroyed,
How Tories are confirmed, and Whigs decoy'd.'

And further on :

'Though scowls apart the lonely pride of Grey,
Though Devonshire proudly flings his staff away,
Though Lansdowne, trampling on his broken chain,
Shine forth the Lansdowne of our hearts again.'

Devonshire had held the Lord Chamberlain's staff, and Lansdowne had sat in the Cabinet in the Canning and Goderich Ministries.

[2] The political correspondence between Grey and Holland is rare in 1828. As might be expected, Lady Grey was more unforgiving towards Grey's old friends for their 'desertion' of him in 1827 than was Grey himself, *e.g.* Lady Grey's letters in Appendix C below.

eager nation to storm the citadel of privilege. If any statesman did as much to pass the Reform Bill as Lord Grey, it was the Duke of Wellington.

Grey's refusal to prefer one section of Tories to another was justified by events to this extent, that more Liberal [1] legislation was passed under Wellington than under the Canningite Ministry which Lansdowne and Brougham had supported. Canning's Cabinet had been pledged to prevent the Repeal of the Test and Corporation Acts, and to shelve Catholic Emancipation ; fifteen months after the Duke took office both relieving Bills had become law !

The Test and Corporation Acts excluded all Dissenters from holding public office, great or small, municipal or national, though in practice a yearly Indemnity Bill was passed to pardon those who had broken the law. In February–March 1828 a private member's Bill to repeal the disabling statutes, introduced by Lord John Russell, was carried through both Houses. The majority in the Commons had been so great that the Government thought it wise to negotiate its passage through the Peers, their Lordships only adding a rider to exclude Jews from the benefits of the Act. ' Peel is a very pretty hand at hauling down his colours,' wrote Lord John in answering congratulations. A year later a still more magnificent flag, guided by the same skilful hand, came fluttering down on to the deck.

[1] The word ' Liberal ' begins in these years to appear in common parlance, not to describe a party, but to express the general tendency of progressive views on various subjects, whether held by Canningites, Whigs, or others. Thus, on January 21, 1828, Campbell writes of the Duke's new Ministry : ' The Whigs are all out and Canning's friends remain in. That is exactly the combination of circumstances that I dreaded. A pure Protestant and ultra-Tory administration I should have been very well pleased to see. This would have led to a combination among all the Liberals, who would ere long have been again in office, with power to carry their measures into effect.' ' Liberal ' was already a party term in France.

But before Peel and the Duke emancipated the Catholics, they first rid their Cabinet of the men who believed in Catholic Emancipation. There had been from the first constant friction with the Canningites in the Cabinet on economic and foreign policy, but the final breach came very significantly on a question of Parliamentary Reform. The Lords had swallowed the Repeal of the Test Act, but they drew the line at Lord John Russell's next Bill, which proposed to give the two members of Penryn, a borough that had to be disfranchised for gross corruption, to the wholly unrepresented city of Manchester. In rejecting this infinitesimal measure of middle-class enfranchisement the Peers did much to provoke in the country the feelings that soon afterwards carried the Reform Bill. Even prudent anti-Reformers like Croker deeply regretted the action of the Lords. Now the Canningites, since the death of their great leader, were rapidly becoming moderate Reformers, and the defiant action of the Upper House was more than they could tolerate. Huskisson quarrelled with Wellington about Penryn and the similar case of East Retford, and resigned from the Cabinet, followed by Palmerston, Grant, and Lamb (Melbourne), none of whom ever rejoined the Tories.

The Duke could have kept the Canningites if he had wished, for Huskisson regretted his letter of resignation and wished to recall it. But Wellington, annoyed no doubt by the constant bickerings in his Cabinet, seized the opportunity to weed out every element of Liberalism. Since the Duke chose thus to take his stand on the old Toryism alone, he should have done everything to keep together the old Tories, in face of a ring of enemies, who in Parliament immeasurably surpassed the Government rump in debating power, and in the fast moving world outside already outnumbered the faithful by ten to one. But after getting rid of the Canningites the Duke next proceeded to pass Catholic Emancipation ! (March–April 1829). He thus split up what was left of the Tories, bitterly alienating from his person and government the very elements on which he could have most firmly relied to hold the fort against the coming Liberal assault. Old Lord Eldon, the Duke of Cumberland, the Oxford dons, the country parsons, and the more old-fashioned squires raged against the King's Government and the victor of Waterloo with the fury of men betrayed. The personal attacks on the Duke were so fierce that he thought it his duty to silence the clamour by calling out Lord Winchilsea to exchange shots in Battersea Fields. Not till they had pulled down Wellington, and put Lord Grey into Downing Street, did the High Tories feel that they had been avenged.

To have forced on a quarrel with the Canningites just before he found himself obliged to surrender to O'Connell, shows how strictly unpolitical were the qualities of this great soldier and public servant. Administration he understood ; when aided by the peculiar genius of Peel he could administer the laws better perhaps than the Whigs themselves. Legislation as a part of administration he understood ; when to preserve the peace of Ireland he saw that it was necessary to emancipate the Catholics, he could sweep down all Royal and aristocratic opposition as powerfully as when he ordered ' everything to go in ' on the evening of Waterloo. But politics, the free play of organised opinion in a civil community, were always a mystery to him. In 1829 he showed as much contempt for the Protestant indignation of the squires and parsons as he showed in 1830 for the demand of the ' middle and industrious classes ' for Parliamentary Reform. From the time of the Convention of Cintra onwards, he had on every occasion been finely indifferent to what any portion of the public would think or say of his action ; this soldier's virtue was the ruin of his statesmanship in all that he did between 1828 and 1832.

It would have been not unnatural if the Duke had

fallen from power directly he had passed Catholic
Emancipation, as Peel fell directly he had repealed the
Corn Laws in 1846. The circumstances were not
dissimilar. But in 1829 George IV was determined
not to have Grey, and the Whigs had not yet completely recovered from their internal divisions. Neither
was Grey the man to combine with Canningites and
ultra-Tories to overthrow a Minister whom he respected
as much as he respected the Duke, because a measure
had been passed which he regarded as thirty years over-
due. He would give no signal of attack until a year
later, when the Duke had defied the Liberals as out-
rageously as he was now defying the Tories.

In the constant shifting and obliterating of party
landmarks and connections during the three years that
preceded the Reform Bill, one of the permutations and
combinations most often discussed at Brooks's was
whether the Duke would ask Grey to enter his Cabinet,
and if so whether Grey would accept. Even if such
an union had been made to carry Catholic Emancipation
—and on no other terms would Grey have looked twice
at any proposal for office—it would not have lasted
long, because the difference on foreign policy between
the two men was fundamental. But if a coalition had
taken place at all, even for a short while only, it would
have ruined the fair picture of Grey imprinted on the
public eye, as the man who had for principle's sake
rejected office for twenty years past. It was well,
therefore, that he never joined Wellington ; his high
personal reputation for disinterested Liberalism was all
of it needed to save the ship of state amid the breakers
of popular impatience and rage, during the long crisis
of the Reform Bill.

The Duke, when he formed his Government in
January 1828, and again in January 1829 when he
was contemplating Emancipation, would have liked to
ask Grey to join his Cabinet, but on both occasions the
hostility of George IV prevented the offer from being

made. Grey was then neither supporting nor opposing Government, and his leadership of the distracted Whig party was cold and shadowy. The passing of Catholic Emancipation in April 1829 made him feel more friendly to Wellington than ever before or after ; provided the Catholics were emancipated, he who had borne the burden and heat of that long day was devoid of jealousy at seeing a rival enter into his labours at eventide. But during the course of the next twelve months the Duke's reactionary policy abroad, the rising question of Parliamentary Reform, and the gradual reintegration of the Whig party made the union of Wellington and Grey daily more impossible. There had never at any time been political correspondence or conversation between them, or any negotiations direct or indirect. When at length the death of George IV (June 1830) removed the Royal obstacle to Grey's attainment of office, the Duke had ceased to consider Grey eligible, and Grey was in open opposition.[1]

When the year 1830 began, it seemed that ' party was destroyed in this country,' that the group system had become the method of British Parliamentary government, and that administrative opportunism had replaced political principle as the guiding star of modern Cabinets. But before the year had ended the lists were fairly set for the struggle between the two great parties, whose rivalry supplied the method of British progress for the remainder of the century. This sudden hark-back to the party system was caused by the honest intransigeance of the Duke on Foreign Policy and Parliamentary Reform ; the two issues were forced to the front over here by the second French Revolution, and they were the two subjects on which Grey was best fitted to give a liberal lead to the Whig party and to the nation at large.

[1] See Appendix C, below : ' The question of Grey taking office under Wellington, 1828-1830.'

The first step in the new direction was taken in March, when some members of the Whig party in the Commons, long leaderless,[1] chose for themselves a spokesman in Lord Althorp. The quiet gathering of forty or fifty members who met in his rooms in the Albany to induce him to take the lead, was the starting-point of Whig-Liberal reunion. Grey had taken no part in bringing about the Albany election, which was announced to him as a *fait accompli* by a letter of Althorp's; but he had for many years past liked and trusted the man now selected as his lieutenant; they had both been opposed to the Whig union with Canning, and Grey soon came to regard Althorp as the one absolutely indispensable colleague. The coming together of the two men was indeed the most happy chance, the sort of chance for want of which parties have gone to pieces in 1782 and on other occasions since. Between them they commanded the political and personal devotion of all the Whigs, and fortunately for the world they were both advanced Parliamentary Reformers. In thought, feeling, and manner they had so much in common that they understood each other completely. Yet Althorp supplied all Grey's deficiencies, and filled the gap between the somewhat lofty isolation of the veteran nobleman and the younger generation of Russells and Whitbreads, Macaulays and Bullers, now thronging the floor of the House. Everyone could unbosom himself to Althorp. And even Brougham dared not challenge the position of a man so much his inferior in talents that Campbell wrote 'there is a better speaker than Althorp in every vestry in England.' Althorp excelled his fellowmen in character as Brougham excelled them in talents, and in the close quarters of the House character carried the day, though in the country at large it was Brougham

[1] Tierney did not die till January 1830, but his leadership had been a failure in 1818 (see p. 187, above), and had lapsed without his being replaced by anyone else.

who did most to raise the great winds of public agitation.

Althorp is one of the most attractive and characteristic figures in all our long Parliamentary annals. If a foreigner or a present-day Englishman can penetrate the secret of Althorp's power, he has the historic gift of understanding the old English character and the political system of a bygone age. An aristocrat of the bluest Whig blood,[1] he was in physical build, in thought and taste, akin rather to great squire commoners like Coke of Norfolk, too close down to the soil and its tillers to be truly described by the word 'aristocrat.' He declared with obvious truth that he 'detested the life of a grandee.' He was always trying to escape from London, Parliament, office, everything that could keep him from his country home. This was a great bond of sympathy with Grey. The Master of the Pytchley at the zenith of its glory, Althorp had given up fox-hunting once and for ever on his wife's death in 1818, because it seemed to him wrong to be as happy as he always must be following the hounds over hill and dale, while she was lying cold in the grave. Her death, though it prevented him from being the happiest man in England, made him one of the most useful, checking the strain of manly self-indulgence in the sportsman, and giving his best energies to the public.[2]

But it was among his farmers and their turnips, not at Westminster, that he would have greatly preferred to serve his country, if God had let him. He read the Bible constantly, in simple-hearted search to find his duty and the strength to do it. His mind worked so

---

[1] He died Third Earl Spencer. For the political history of the Spencers in the Foxite period, see pp. 106, 133, 144, above. Le Marchant's *Memoir of Lord Althorp* (1876) is a delightful magazine of the Whig tradition, as also is the Life of his compeer, *Coke of Norfolk*.

[2] The squires of Northamptonshire thought that the Master of the Pytchley was the greatest of all public servants, and when he gave up the hounds prophesied that he would never again be so famous.

slowly that the constant demands of political leadership for rapid decisions put upon him a strain almost physically painful, and his conscientiousness added the tortures of responsibility keenly felt. Yet far cleverer men admitted that he excelled them all in coming to the right practical conclusion at last, and the very pains that his decisions had obviously cost him commended such dearly bought treasures of wisdom to his colleagues and followers, and sometimes even to his opponents. These qualities, set off by a modesty and kindness that never once gave way to petulance, reconstituted the Whig party in 1830, and in the following year carried the Reform Bill through the Lower House.

As long ago as 1810 Grey had announced that he would not waste time in promoting Parliamentary Reform against the King and the estates of the realm entrenched for the defence of the old system, until the people of England would ' seriously and affectionately ' take up the question for themselves. Then and then only, he said, he would act. He had not regarded the Radical agitation of 1817-19 as supplying the needed impulse, because it was almost entirely a working-class movement, a demand for universal suffrage which would have turned the middle classes against it the moment it became serious. It had died down under the combined influence of repression and better times. The middle classes had not taken up Reform ' seriously and affectionately,' though they had for the most part ceased to be Tory. They would unite with the lower classes to right the wrongs of Queen Caroline, but not their own. Throughout the 'twenties, reforming Whig gentry complained that county meetings and other organs of ' respectable ' opinion were still lukewarm about Reform. It was in the year 1830 that the change began, for which Grey, all too patiently perhaps but very faithfully, had been waiting as the signal for his own action.

The distress of the country, of which all classes were again complaining after a period of prosperity, suggested various remedies, to some Currency, to others Corn Law repeal ; the most universally agreed upon was to relieve taxation by retrenchment and the abolition of corrupt pensions and sinecures. But it occurred to people who differed more or less widely as to economic remedies, that they could all agree on Parliamentary Reform as the indispensable prelude to any effective change. In January 1830 Thomas Attwood, who had Currency fads of his own, had the good sense and boldness to form the Birmingham Political Union, ' to obtain by every just and legal means such a reform in the Commons' House of Parliament as may ensure a real and effectual representation of the lower and middle classes of the people in that House.' The Birmingham example was discussed all over the country, and was imitated during the spring in a number of other towns great and small. The formula of these Political Unions was to unite the ' middle and lower classes ' to obtain an undefined measure of Parliamentary Reform.

During these same spring months of 1830 Cobbett was riding round the cities and market towns of England, preaching Parliamentary Reform as the way to relieve the distress of which all classes were complaining. He found with delight that at farmers' ordinaries and in commercial rooms where he had previously been looked at askance, the solid middle class paid him the greatest respect and thronged to hear his advice.

England owes Cobbett a great debt. He had obtained a hold on his countrymen at this critical moment greater than that of any man or any newspaper, because for more than twenty years past, in season and out, in spite of persecution and calumny, he had championed the wrongs then suffered by the poor at the hands of omnipotent privilege. In his ' Register ' and other publications he had devised and conducted, single-handed, a system of political education for the masses, at a time

Sir F. Burdett   Cobbett   Althorp   Stanley
(standing)

On the first day of the Reformed Parliament, 1833, Cobbett
seated himself on the ministerial bench, to the surprise of
some of its occupants.

From " H.B." Political Sketches.

when they had no serious political writing within their reach. Having now attained to the height of his influence at the moment when the national discontent was also at its height, he used his authority to preach Parliamentary Reform as the preliminary to all other redress. He was called a ' firebrand ' by both Whigs and Tories, but the advice coming from him in 1830 to reform Parliament did more to prevent conflagration in this country than all the ' repressive measures ' that ever were passed.

Such was the state of public feeling when the death of George IV on June 26, 1830, and the accession of his brother the Duke of Clarence as William IV, opened out a new prospect. The Royal veto on a Whig Cabinet and Liberal laws, under which that generation had grown up, had vanished in the night, not because the constitution had been altered, but because a King had ascended the throne who thought it his duty to hold the balance evenly between Whigs and Tories. A little *gauche*, a little eccentric, a little stupid, but thoroughly honest, simple, and kind, and with no exaggerated ideas of his prerogative, the ' Sailor King ' was a great improvement on his two predecessors. Hitherto neglected by his fellow-subjects as a man of no account, he took a childish pleasure in his sudden popularity during the first weeks of his reign. An undignified *bonhomie* led him to walk the streets of London unattended, courting the rough enthusiasm of the mob ; the people, all agog for signs of political change, took it that a ' skipping king ' who ' ambled up and down ' must be a democrat at heart. The delusion thus engendered led to the very general mis-understanding of Grey's slowness about peer-making in the later stages of the Reform Bill ; few guessed at the difficulties he had with the King, because a wrong estimate had been popularly formed of William's political views at the moment of his accession. We, who know how undemocratic the King really was, can see that he treated the Whigs and their Bill as well as he did only out of an honourable sense of constitutional duty to his Ministers, which George III had never felt. He had no personal preference for the Whigs as a party or for Grey as a man, and liked Wellington much better than George IV had done.[1]

On the second day of the new reign Grey said to his son Howick, 'that the Duke of Wellington has made the best use of the opportunity afforded him by the protracted illness of the late King to gain the confidence of the present one, and that there is no probability of a change of government unless it should be occasioned by its extreme weakness in Parliament.' In the same conversation Grey told Howick that he had 'a short time ago' received an offer from Huskisson on behalf of the Canningites of an alliance with the Whigs to turn out the Duke and form a joint Cabinet under Grey as Premier ; to this Grey had replied that although the time was not yet come for an alliance in form, ' he had no indisposition towards Huskisson and his friends, but that on the contrary he was quite ready to act with them when the occasion should offer.' [2] On June 30 Grey made in the House of Lords a declaration of war against the Government.

Such was the state of parties, when the general election necessitated by the new reign took place at the end of July and the beginning of August 1830. Two out of three sections of the Tory party were hostile to

---

[1] See Ellenborough's *Diary*, ii. 283, 286, 438 : ' I consider the death of the King one of the fortunate events which have often saved the Duke of Wellington ; I really do not know how we [the Wellington Ministry] could have gone on had he lived two months ' (June 27, 1830). But George would never have sent for Grey, or allowed the Reform Bill to be introduced as a Government measure.

[2] Lord Howick's *Journal*, June 27, 1830. Grey had in the past disliked Huskisson, and had once, under provocation, written of him, in January 1828, as ' that rogue Huskisson.' But Howick's journal makes it clear that Huskisson would in all probability have been in Grey's Cabinet if he had lived till November.

the Government, the Canningites in almost open league with the Whigs, and the High Tories sulking in their tents to revenge themselves on the Duke for Catholic Emancipation. But for the fact that borough-owners had more to say to the returns than the public at large, an immense Whig majority would have been secured. The ' open ' seats in town and country were almost all carried by the Opposition. Reform was the popular cry, and on that and the abolition of negro slavery Brougham was, by the help of Wilberforce's friends, returned for the greatest of English constituencies, although he had no local connections with Yorkshire. The event was regarded by all England as a herald of coming change.[1]

While the elections were still only beginning, news came from France which more than doubled the popular enthusiasm for Reform. In the ' days of July ' (28–30) the mob of Paris had defeated the soldiers and overthrown the reactionary monarchy of the Bourbons. The tricolour once more floated over France and the keystone of the arch of the Holy Alliance had been removed.

Charles X and his minister Polignac had provoked their own downfall by illegally suspending the Constitution. Even Lord Eldon and Sir Walter Scott had disapproved of their action, which placed Charles X in the moral position of our James II, and led him straight to the same fate. The Revolution, though the fighting had been done by workmen, was not permitted to turn ' red,' but solidified round Lafayette, the National Guard, and the *bourgeois* King Louis Philippe. It could not therefore be denounced, however much it

---

[1] The enormous expenses of a Yorkshire election, that had been the undoing of many great landowners who had fought for the blue ribbon of English electioneering, were, of course, defrayed by Brougham's supporters, not by himself. As the Duke of Wellington said about it, ' No gentleman could bear the expense. The middle classes had it all to themselves ' (*Ellenborough*, ii. 329).

might be regretted, by English Tories. It could not, like the Revolutions of 1789 and 1848, be used to conjure up 'old panic' over here ; 1830 still stands as the one occasion in all the ages when the French set a political example that influenced us otherwise than by repulsion. Its first and smallest effect was to increase the number of seats carried by the Opposition in the General Election of August.

Its real importance was that it gave Englishmen the sense of living in a new era, when great changes could safely be effected. To act boldly on behalf of the people, it was seen, did not produce anarchy as the Tories had argued ever since 1789 ; it was half measures that were dangerous, and resistance to the people that was fatal. Our middle-classes saw the *bourgeoisie* safely governing France, and blushed that in England they themselves were still subject to the aristocracy. The working men saw that the *ouvriers* had defeated the army in fair fight, and the word went round that what Frenchmen had done Englishmen could do. At every crisis in the next two years, at Wellington's fall in November, at the various stages of conflict over the Reform Bill culminating in 'the days of May,' a resort to arms was at the back of all men's minds on account of this new French Revolution, and formed an integral part of the plans of popular leaders like Place and Attwood, as the last remedy to be applied if Grey should fail to win the nation's rights by constitutional means. The knowledge that Englishmen were so thinking and that Frenchmen had so acted gravely affected the politics of the propertied class as a whole, and of not a few of the borough owners themselves. The recollection of Paris, and the knowledge that everyone else was recollecting Paris, drove them to make concessions they would never have dreamt of two years before.

It was under the influence of the joyful news from France and of the Whig victories at the General Election, that Grey in the late summer of 1830 entered into closer political correspondence with Holland, with Lambton (recently become Viscount Durham by creation of the Goderich Ministry), and with his other old political friends. Only Brougham kept half apart, and was suspected at Howick, rightly or wrongly, of intriguing with the Canningites and others to get the lead of the Opposition parties for himself. The Greys all declared that the Yorkshire election had turned his head. Durham did his best to act as peacemaker, and to prevent a complete breach between his father-in-law and Brougham.[1] The subjects privately discussed between the Whig leaders in August, September, and October were, as their letters show, alliance with the Canningites, absorption of Stanley and Sir James Graham in the party, the overthrow of the Duke's Ministry, the reversal of his foreign policy and the preparation of a Reform Bill— in fact all that actually took place when Parliament met in November.

When Huskisson, who was negotiating on behalf of the Canningites, was killed in the famous railway accident, Grey wrote to Holland (September 19, 1830), ' I never was more shocked than at the account of poor Huskisson's death and at the dreadful manner of it. I had not a good opinion of his political integrity, nor could I have trusted him without securities ; but he might have been most useful at this moment, and I feel that the public has sustained a great loss.' Palmerston,

---

[1] Durham's letters to Grey, Aug., Sept., Oct. 1830. On Oct. 4 he writes : ' I do not believe Brougham's activity originates in a desire to make himself leader, but in extreme anxiety to overthrow the present Government.' Durham adds that Stanley and Graham have joined the Whigs on the express understanding that Grey is ' at the head.' ' I know your ladies [Lady Grey and daughters] are no friends of Brougham's. I wish to keep everything as smooth as possible ; he is am extraordinary man, difficult to manage as an ally from the wild eccentricities of his genius, and dangerous to an almost fatal degree as an enemy.' On October 28, 1830, Grey's brother-in-law, Edward Ellice, wrote to him : ' I see on all sides great jealousy of Brougham's assumption of the office of leader, great distrust of his prudence and intentions.'

Melbourne, and Grant, having twice in three years lost a renowned leader of their small party by premature death, were less than ever willing to stultify themselves by joining Wellington, though he kept making offers to them to come into his tottering Ministry.[1] Under the influence of the new era, they as well as Graham and Stanley were steadily moving towards union with the Whigs, on the basis of a moderate Reform.

Meanwhile Grey and his family were seeing to it that the coming Reform should not be too ' moderate.' The account in the *Memoirs* of the 3rd Earl of Malmesbury of his visit as a very young man to Howick in the late summer of 1830, throws a vivid light on things public and private :

My father-in-law, Lord Tankerville, was an old Whig, and a friend of Lord Grey, and he took me on a visit to Howick, where the old Earl lived in patriarchal retirement amidst his numerous family. Two of the latter, Lord Durham and Mr. Ellice (commonly called ' Bear Ellice '),[2] both clever and ambitious men, had great influence with Lord Grey, and used it without mercy. He was one of the most striking figures I ever saw, the very type of a *grand seigneur* and of an intellectual man. Whilst I was at Howick I was struck with two peculiarities of the family, one of which was that all the sons and daughters called their parents by their Christian names, ' Charles ' and ' Mary,' which had a strange effect ; the other was the taste of the whole family for argument. They were always in a state of discussion, even as to the distance between Howick and Alnwick, and the shortest road to and from each, which one would suppose they had verified long ago. Lady Georgiana was very agreeable, and played beautifully on the harp—an instrument then much appreciated. As I suppose I was then looked upon as a mere boy by the party, politics and future

---

[1] In July, and again at the end of September, and again near the end of October ; see Palmerston, *Life*, i. 381-3.

[2] He became Whig Whip on the formation of Grey's Government in November ; had married Grey's sister Hannah in 1809 ; was called ' Bear Ellice ' on account of his connection with the North-West fur trade ; himself, he was very unlike a bear. See Appendix G, below, ' Bear Ellice.'

onslaughts on the Tory Government were freely spoken of without gêne in my presence ; and I remember one day Lord Grey breaking out and declaring that the greatest rascals in the world were Lord Castlereagh (then dead), Brougham, and Talleyrand, and I recollect this explosion the more because when he formed his Government three months later he was obliged to make Brougham his Chancellor, and to receive Talleyrand as Ambassador of France.[1]

Ellice and Lord Durham were often at Chillingham [Lord Tankerville's seat, a dozen miles from Howick], and their talk, of course, was chiefly as to the coming change, and of the re-arrangement of the boroughs and franchise, their great object being to ' cook ' them (as they themselves called it), so as to expel as much as possible all local interests belonging to Tories.

The young man had clearly overheard fragments of talk as to the scope and principle of the Reform Bill that Grey, Durham, and Ellice hoped soon to bring in, and his recollections are evidence that the course of England's political history was to no small extent mapped out at Howick two or three months before the Duke fell. But it is pertinent to remark, as regards the charge of ' cooking,' that the disfranchisement clauses of the Bill actually introduced were not arbitrary but went on the principle of taking away members from all boroughs, whether Whig or Tory owned, of less than a specific number of inhabitants ; the Tories indeed suffered most, because they held most rotten boroughs.[2]

---

[1] See, however, p. 374, below, Appendix B, for a more favourable dictum on Castlereagh ; Grey got on very well with Talleyrand, and liked dealing with him, though he always declared he had no ' confidence ' in him.

[2] *E.g.* Lady Grey's letter to her daughter Caroline, on March 4, 1831 : ' The Tories are furious, and naturally people dislike losing their boroughs. The D. of Devonshire loses five, yet most handsomely supports the bill. Lord Fitzwilliam loses Malton and Higham Ferrers —the latter place deprives Henry [Lord Howick] of his seat.'

In 1827 Croker wrote to Canning that there were 203 seats in the Commons ' in the hands of what may be called the Tory aristocracy,' while ' the Whig seats are about 73.'

No doubt this made the principle doubly attractive to a shrewd Whig whip, but the extinction of the rotten boroughs was also the principle on which the British people had set its heart with fierce determination.

The French Revolution of July not only forced on the domestic crisis in England, but created a European crisis of which the English Reform Bill was the turning-point, just as the English Revolution of 1688 was the turning-point of the European resistance to Louis XIV. If Wellington had not fallen in November 1830, and if the High Tory party had not been for ever destroyed by the Reform Bill, it is probable that England would soon have been fighting side by side with her old allies of the Holy Alliance against revolutionary France, to the indefinite postponement of Constitutional Reform in our island. This danger was averted partly by resolute action of the British people, and partly by Grey's cool and steady liberalism in home and foreign affairs.

The danger was first made acute by the Belgian Revolution in the autumn of 1830. Imitating the mob of Paris, Brussels at the end of August drove out the Dutch garrison, and the other Belgian cities followed suit. Belgium forcibly asserted her independence of Holland, to whom after Napoleon's fall she had been unnaturally united by the Treaties of Vienna. For the second time in two months the Holy Alliance had been defied, and although Prussia, Austria, and Russia had shrunk from challenging the right of the French people to self-determination, they had no such scruples about Belgium. It was the desire of the Eastern powers to put down the Belgian Revolution in accordance with alleged obligations under the Treaties of Vienna. It was the equally clear intention of the new French Government to fight if necessary to protect Belgian independence, and how much of Belgian independence would be left when France had done fighting for it was a question which made even Grey and English Liberals anxious. Wellington's sympathies were all against the new France and against the revolt of the Belgian people. Though he and his Foreign Minister, Aberdeen, were desirous of keeping the peace, it is highly unlikely that he would have been able to do so, if he had continued in office, holding the views he did and surrounded by people who would have been only too glad ' to busy giddy minds with foreign quarrels.'[1] Even Grey and Palmerston, who were thoroughly ' Liberal ' in their attitude to France and Belgium, found it, when they came in, all they could do to reach a peaceful solution, for the French were none too reasonable. It is not possible to suppose that the Duke could have avoided war.

Grey's liberalism as regards the Belgian question was part of a general scheme of European polity inherited from Fox, always shared by Lord Holland and now endorsed by the whole Whig party and by the great majority of the British people. As early as September 3 he had stated fully the principles on which he afterwards acted as Minister, in a letter to his friend and would-be Egeria, the busy and agreeable Princess Lieven, wife of the Russian ambassador. She was an agent of the Czardom in Western Europe, and her views, highly

---

[1] ' Whether the Belgians intend to assert their independence, or whether they throw in their lot with France, in the one case as in the other, you will be forced to make war. At any rate such is the language held by the people about the Ministers, and they add that this will be the best means of rallying the old Tory party round the Government.'— Princess Lieven to Grey, September 6, 1830.

No one who reads the debate in the Lords on Jan. 26, 1832, in which Wellington and Aberdeen attacked the whole course of the Belgian Revolution and the whole of Grey's treatment of it in 1831, can doubt that if Wellington and Aberdeen had continued in power the question would in their hands have led to war. Aberdeen on that occasion said that the Belgian revolt was the most ' senseless ' and ' unintelligible ' in ' the history of the world.'

reactionary on all save Turkish questions, made no difference to Grey's friendship with her and none at all to his policy and action, as she discovered to her surprise and chagrin when he had fairly come into office.[1]

Dearest Princess [he wrote on September 3, when the first news of the Brussels revolution arrived], I have never yet known a popular revolution that might not be ascribed to provocation on the part of the Government, more or less remote. *Ce n'est jamais par envie d'attaquer, mais par impatience de souffrir, que le peuple se soulève,* is an observation as old as Sully, which all history will verify. That the example of France will give encouragement to the people in different countries, who suffer from the same oppression, to wish for a similar relief, cannot be doubted. But the security against this is not to be found in armies and Holy Alliances. The experiment of the fatal policy pursued in what is called the settlement of Europe at the general peace, if Governments ever could be taught wisdom, would afford a salutary lesson ; and instead of prompting them to measures for putting down public opinion by force, show them the necessity of setting to work to put their houses in order in time. You speak of a guarantee of the Netherlands ; I cannot

[1] The three volumes of correspondence between Lord Grey and the Princess (1890) must be studied alongside of the Princess's other letters, edited by Lionel Robinson (1902), which show her in a less amiable light behind the scenes. Her reactionary hatred of England as the home of freedom, carefully concealed in her letters to Grey, comes out in those to her brother (*e.g.* p. 350, *Robinson*, Sept. 1833). To Grey she does not seem to have been more treacherous than a woman of her diplomatic occupation must necessarily be, though she writes to her brother in November 1831 : ' If Grey should learn that I repeat to you what he tells me he will never again give me his confidence.' And after a tirade against England, in August 1833, ' Ah ! our good Russia, how much better is she governed ! Of the Ministers I have as yet only seen Lord Grey, and I am sending my report to my chief.' After thinking when Grey first took office that she could ' manage ' him, and finding she could not in the least, her final sad opinion of him (Jan. 1832) is that ' under the most haughty and aristocratic manners he is a thorough democrat.' For a letter of Lady Grey's about her, see p. 376, Appendix C, below.

find in any of my books of reference here the treaty which contains it.

A fortnight later he writes to her :

I think a case for interference, under the conditions of the Treaty [of Vienna] might be made out if it was our interest to interfere. But I see nothing to make that interference, as you seem to think, a matter of necessity.

On one subject only the Princess and Grey were in agreement—the Turkish question, wherein the Russian Court pursued a policy of liberation. On that subject Grey and Holland had been brought up in the ideas which Fox had first advocated in his opposition to Pitt's policy in 1791.[1] After thirty years' abeyance, the problem of Turkish misrule had been again brought to the front by the revolt of Greece in 1821. In November of that year Grey wrote to Holland :

My politics with respect to Greece and Turkey are line for line the same as yours ; they are the same that I learnt from your uncle in 1791, and all subsequent reflection has confirmed me in them. I quite agree with you that the danger arising from the extension of the Russian power and influence on that side [2] is so remote and contingent as to bear no degree of comparison with the certain evil of the existence of the Turkish Empire.

Again, on February 10, 1826, he writes to Holland :

It seems likely that a Turkish War will be resorted to by Russia as the most effectual diversion for a discontented army. In that case I shall strictly adhere to the lesson I learnt from your uncle : the expulsion of the Turks from Europe, *quocumque modo*, I shall think a great good. I am much less afraid of the extension of the Russian Empire on that side than towards

---

[1] See pp. 26–27, above.
[2] The *other* side would be towards Poland and Germany. Grey was strongly in sympathy with the Poles, as Princess Lieven was always bitterly complaining.

Germany, and any extension will in all likelihood only accelerate the division of that unwieldy and enormous mass. At all events the establishment of an independent Government in Greece may afford us a means of providing a barrier towards the Mediterranean.

It will be seen that this doctrine goes much further than the liberation of Greece ; it covers the total expulsion of the Turks from Europe. If this policy had been inherited by Palmerston, Russell, and the Whig leaders who succeeded Grey and Holland,[1] we should have been spared forty years of ' backing the wrong horse,' of maintaining Turkish rule in the Balkans and Armenia, and the costly expiation of Disraeli's ' peace with honour ' on the heights of Gallipoli.

In the 'twenties and early 'thirties, Liberal sentiment, whether led by Canning or by Grey, was solidly anti-Turk, because the classical sentiment for ancient Greece, sanctified by Byron's death, was stronger than fears of Russia. But when once Greece had been set free, and the issue had shifted to the fate of those ' barbarian ' Christians buried in the Balkan Peninsula and in Armenia, who could not boast the magic name of Hellas, the majority of British Liberals forgot the tradition of the elders and the doctrine of Fox and Grey, as to the monstrosity of Turkish rule.[2]

Grey, though strongly pro-Greek, had erred in feeling no enthusiasm for the destruction of the Turkish fleet in Navarino in November 1827, because he thought it would be followed by our desertion of the Greeks on land, and would only provoke worse Turkish reprisals at their expense. Fortunately, France and Russia con-

---

[1] Brougham, too, was in favour of the complete expulsion of the Turks from Europe. See his letter to Wilson on Navarino, B.M., Add. MSS., 30,115 : ' I am for seeing the Turk out of Europe.' Lord Holland, on Sept. 22, 1829, writes to Grey : ' You see the peace is all but made, and Constantinople has once more (I trust for the last time) escaped its inevitable fate. I rejoice at the first, and am sorry for the last event.'

[2] Grey somewhat modified his own views later, see p. 355, below.

tinued to protect the Greeks and this did not occur. Wellington, however, who came into office at this juncture (January 1828), reversed Canning's liberal policy in the Levant as elsewhere, and lent all the weight of England to protect Turkey and reduce the boundaries of the new Greek kingdom to the smallest possible limits. He wished to confine Greece to the Morea, and to leave Athens itself in Turkish hands ! Here he was opposed by France and Russia, who, though reactionary, never forgot that they were Christian Powers.

While this diplomatic contest over the limits of the new Greek kingdom, so discreditable to British statecraft, was going on in Paris, Grey wrote from Howick on September 9, 1829, to his own and Fox's old friend Adair, who was then in Paris ; in this letter Grey suggested a possible compromise between the generous Arta-Volo boundary desired by France and Russia, which Grey himself thought right, and the impossible Morea boundary urged by Wellington. Adair read Grey's letter to Pozzo di Borgo, the Russian Ambassador to France, who laid it before his disputing colleagues at the conference. They accepted ' Lord Grey's boundaries ' as a compromise, but one distinctly favourable to Greece.[1] ' I little thought,' Grey wrote to Holland, ' that living here at the bottom of Northumberland I should be marking out the limits of new Kingdoms.'

Grey made it clear to Adair [2] that he had only suggested

[1] The ' Grey boundaries ' ran from Zeitoum, at the mouth of the Sperchius, to the mouth of the Achelous, by a fairly straight line along the mountain tops. See F.O. 32 (*Greece*), vol. xvi., ' protocol No. 1 de la conférence au Foreign Office, le 3 fevrier, 1830.' This gave Greece command of Attica, Euboea, and the Straits of Lepanto, all of which Wellington had wished to take away from her. The *F.O. Papers* for 1829–30 entirely bear out the correspondence of Grey with Adair, Holland, and Princess Lieven as to the ' Grey boundaries.'

[2] Letters of Sept. 9, 1829, and Feb. 19, 1830. Grey's letter to Adair of September 9 is repeated almost word for word in the middle of his letter to Princess Lieven of Sept. 14 (*Lieven Letters*, i. 292–3).

this compromise in order to save Greece from being confined to the Morea as Wellington wished. He himself would have preferred the larger latitude of the Arta-Volo boundary. And indeed so slow are the ways of diplomacy that when he came into office at the end of 1830 he was still in time to bid Palmerston tear up 'the Grey boundaries,' and insist upon the Arta-Volo frontier which Wellington had opposed on behalf of England only a year before. Thanks to Grey's intelligent and active interest in the Greek question, the Arta-Volo line became the boundary of the new state until the addition of Thessaly in 1881.[1]

All these issues, foreign and domestic, were to be decided, after the good old English fashion, at the assembling of the newly elected Parliament. In the last days of October 1830 Grey came up to London for the session, and on this occasion Lady Grey came with him. The even tenor of their life at Howick, so little disturbed for a generation past, was at length cut short for a few eventful years. What thoughts were in his mind, as he posted up to London by the long North road he had so often traversed in the bitter days gone by, cheered only by the thought of Fox's welcome at the end ? That loved voice had long been silent, and the 'young ones' were white-haired Nestors among a new generation of men ; was it possible that at this eleventh hour he and Holland would be called upon to carry out their leader's whole political testament, on the strength of a prodigious national revulsion against all that had happened in England in the last forty years ?

[1] See F.O. 65 (*Russia*), vol. 184, Palmerston's letter to Lord Heytesbury, Dec. 31, 1830 :—'There has now been a change in the Governments of England and France ; changes of men have produced changes of opinion and of feeling in this matter' of the Greek boundaries ; so the Arta-Volo boundary is now desired by England. See also F.O. 65, vol. 191, letter of Lord Heytesbury, Jan. 19, 1831, and Palmerston to Heytesbury, Sept. 21, 1831, for the continuance of the negotiation.

If so, in the words of the quotation that was now often on his lips :

> Non adeo has exosa manus victoria fugit
> Ut quicquam tanta pro spe tentare recusam.[1]

For Tory and Radical, friend and foe, who thought, not without excuse, that the old man was a disillusioned valetudinarian who had left his reforming faith and his political activity far behind him on the road of life, a strange surprise was in store. When after little more than three years he returned to Howick, never again to be drawn from his ' private gardens,' he had by ' industrious valour ' realised the dream of his youth,

> And cast the Kingdoms old
> Into another mould.

---

[1] ' Grudging victory has not so much deserted these hands of mine, that I should refuse to try something for so great a hope ' (*Aen*. xi. 436–7). He several times in the 'twenties quotes this passage in letters to his sons and to Holland.

BOOK III

THE REFORM BILL

CHAPTER I

FALL OF WELLINGTON—FORMATION OF THE GREY
MINISTRY—DIFFICULTIES OF THE FIRST MONTHS
NOVEMBER 1830 TO FEBRUARY 1831

' What struggling confusion, as the issue slowly draws on ; and the
doubtful Hour, with pain and blind struggle, brings forth its Certainty,
never to be abolished ! '—CARLYLE, *Fr. Rev.* vi. 6.

WHEN, in the last days of October 1830, the Greys
arrived in town for the opening of the new Parliament,
they stepped into a scene of mere confusion. All was
in flux, nothing certain except that things could not go
on as before. There was no clear majority in the new
House against Wellington, still less in favour of Grey.
In pre-Reform Bill times many members came up to a
new Parliament unpledged, having been chosen to represent not principles or parties, but places and persons.
And even the action of the organised groups was still
uncertain. The High Tories sulked apart, scarcely
knowing their own secret, whether they would carry
their vengeance against the Duke to the length of the
fatal division lobby. As to the Canningites and unattached moderates, they had decided that there must
be a Reform Bill ; but that might mean much or little,

and if it meant little it was still thought that the Duke might supply them with what they demanded. In the first two days of November, before the King's speech, the unattached Stanley and Graham were taken into consultation by Althorp and Brougham, and were by them asked to consult the Canningites, as to the scope that should be given to Brougham's famous Reform motion, intended to unite the Liberal vote in the House.[1] But at the very same time (November 1), Littleton, purporting to speak on behalf of Stanley, Graham, and the Canningites, was telling the Government agents that if the Duke would reconstruct his Ministry and bring in a Reform Bill to enfranchise a few big towns, he should have the support of all moderate men.[2] It was for the Duke to choose ; if it had been for Peel to choose, history might have had another tale to tell.

Next morning, on that famous 2nd of November, when the King's speech would reveal the Duke's decision, the Greys still thought it possible that he might save himself by declaring for Reform.[3] After all, since he had yielded up his own convictions to the will of the Irish people, why should he hold the English at a cheaper rate ? And if he would but make the necessary show of concession, men like Palmerston and Melbourne

[1] Parker's *Graham*, i. 96–7.

[2] Parker's *Peel*, ii. 163–7.

[3] On Nov. 2 Lady Grey writes to her daughter Caroline : ' Car has had a dreadful cold, but he is so much better to-day he is going to the H. of Lords [where he drew the Duke's famous declaration against Reform that afternoon]. Yesterday I heard that the D. of W.'s friends were very low indeed. On the other hand there is a report, but mind it is but a report, that the Duke says that tho' he does not himself approve of Reform, he is ready to yield to the wish of the nation if it is proved to be in favour of it. That means that he will do anything rather than resign, and this has all along been my belief ! '

On Oct. 17, before leaving Howick, Grey had written to Holland : ' If Parliamentary Reform is proposed by Government, which I can hardly believe, tho' I have strong evidence, independently of yours, that it has been in contemplation, I must be found in the ranks of its supporters.'

would much prefer a sham Reform Bill to such a real one as Grey was nursing in his heart. The events in the House of Lords that afternoon (November 2) decided the question. The King's speech contained no allusion to Reform, and raised instead the Belgian question in these ominous words :

I have witnessed with deep regret the state of affairs in the Low Countries. I lament that the enlightened administration of the King should not have preserved his dominions from revolt. . . . I am endeavouring in concert with my allies to devise such means of restoring tranquillity as may be compatible with the welfare and good government of the Netherlands and with the future security of other States.

Grey had come into the House not knowing what he should hear ; but he at once challenged the Duke on both points. As to the Netherlands, he complained that by the words of the speech ' we are made to decide between the two parties and to pronounce a direct censure on the conduct of the people of the Low Countries towards their enlightened government. This is language directly opposed to the principle of non-interference ! ' As to domestic affairs, the dangers of the time, said Grey, could only be met by ' securing the affections of our fellow subjects, by redressing their grievances, and—my Lords, I will pronounce the word— by reforming Parliament.'

Then the Duke rose to reply. He attempted to explain away the language of the speech as regards Belgium, and declared himself desirous of co-operating with France in the settlement of the question. But the words of the King's speech rather than his explanation of them left their effect upon the nation, and during the fortnight that followed Attwood and Place concerted measures for a middle-class movement to refuse the payment of taxes, if the Government drifted any further towards war.[1]

[1] Wallas's *Place*, ed. 1898, pp. 247, 251, and note.

It was the last part of the Duke's speech that attracted the attention of all England. In answer to Grey's challenge on Reform, he declared :

The Legislature and the system of representation possessed the full and entire confidence of the country. I will go still further, and say that if at the present moment I had imposed upon me the duty of forming a legislature for a country like this in possession of great property of various descriptions, I do not mean to assert that I could form such a legislature as you possess now, for the nature of man is incapable of reaching such excellence at once ; but my great endeavour would be to form some description of legislature which would produce the same results.

He would therefore not bring forward any Reform Bill, and he would oppose any brought forward by others. On that word he sat down, amid a silence that surprised him. Turning to his nearest colleague, Lord Aberdeen, he asked, ' I have not said too much, have I ? ' ' You'll hear of it ! ' was the reply.

The Duke had thrown down his glove, and the country took up the challenge. Francis Place, who in his library at Charing Cross had for many years past kept a marvellously accurate barometer of political feeling among the different classes of the community, wrote to Hobhouse, on November 8, that ' the first step in the British Revolution ' was now being taken. The middle classes were furious with the Duke, and determined to obtain a sweeping reform. After forty years of flunkeyism they were tired of the aristocracy, and had come to consider political power to belong of right to their own class as the ' solid ' and ' intelligent ' part of the community ; and they further believed that Reform was the only alternative to a violent revolution in the present desperate temper of the working classes.

This *bourgeois* political philosophy was making converts rapidly among the visitors to Holland House and among the groups of excited country gentlemen now talking all day and night in Brooks's. An union of Whig borough-owners and statesmen with the shop-keepers and clerks of all England was bodying itself forth in many different minds as the only hope for a world in agony. It was to prove the stable basis of the early Victorian era ; but in 1830 the middle class, out for its rights against the Tory aristocracy, was molten lava, a revolutionary flood. And below that again roared the flames of a fiercer, deeper gulf of revolt, the desperation of starving peasants and operatives. What if that force of the unplumbed abyss, so potent for destruction, could be harnessed instead to work the engine of a middle-class revolution ? If it was a real revolution, however middle-class, the thing might be done—not otherwise. And therefore a really big Reform Bill might be the most conservative as well as the most liberal of all measures. Such had been Grey's private thought for ten years past, and now a great body of respectable opinion, under the influence of something like panic, was coming to the same view.[1]

There was indeed ground for alarm. 'The aristo-cracy rolls in wealth and luxury,' notes the Russian ambassadress, 'while the streets of London and the highways of the country swarm with miserable creatures covered with rags, barefooted, having neither food nor shelter.' Noble lords coming up to town from their estates report that labourers have been found lying four together under the hedges, dead of starvation. In

---

[1] See p. 183, above, and Appendix A, below. In the winter of 1830–1 Grey wrote to the Knight of Kerry : 'A great change has taken place in all parts of Europe since the end of the war in the distribution of property, and unless a corresponding change be made in the legal mode by which that property can act upon the governments, revolutions must necessarily follow. This change requires a greater influence to be yielded to the middle classes, who have made wonderful advances both in property and intelligence, and this influence may be beneficially exerted upon the Government by improvements in the representative system. Without some such concessions the change alluded to will lead rapidly to republicanism and the destruction of established institutions.'

Kent and Sussex the peasants, not wishing to lie dead under the hedges, have risen and are marching about the countryside unresisted, demanding a living wage of half-a-crown a day. Threshing machines are destroyed, and all over southern England ricks are fired nightly in the name of ' Captain Swing,' that dark abstraction of the people's despair and vengeance. In the industrial North the New Trades Unionism prevents spasmodic outbreaks, but prepares for an organised struggle with the troops on the French model. The armed force in the country is very small and no Ministry dare propose the expense of increasing it. Men who have aught to lose clamour to Government to save society, by concession, if there is yet time. Since the Duke will not, Grey must. All eyes are turned to him. So passes the first fortnight of November, the storm rising daily—who will ride it ?

On November 7, 1830, Wellington's Government, doomed since his declaration against Reform, took another step towards the brink. It had been arranged that the King was to visit the City in state on Lord Mayor's day. By ' the boldest act of cowardice,' the visit was countermanded because, though there was no fear of an attack on the King, the Duke himself was so unpopular that serious disorders would ensue when he showed himself beside his sovereign. Home Secretary Peel was forced to confess as much to a shouting House. Never was there such a theme for Parliamentary eloquence hunting an unpopular Government to its death. The image of a distressed King, longing to come down like a father among his people, but held aloof in his palace by hated viziers, was a pleasantly new motif for Whig indignation and for popular sentiment.

After the Duke's declaration against all reform, any thought of the Canningites and Moderates joining the Government had come to an end. Littleton, who the day before had made the proposal for a junction with Wellington, now became a Whig for life, and Palmerston

and Melbourne with him. Stanley and Graham, more
advanced and zealous reformers than these Canningites,
also became Whigs, though not for ever. It was determined to combine and throw the Government out ;
if nothing else turned up first, then let it be on Brougham's
motion for Reform, which had been drawn on ' moderate '
lines, to attract as many votes as possible in the House.
It was therefore less thorough than the Government
Reform Bill of the following year, which was drawn up
on the opposite principle of winning such support in the
country as to overawe ' moderate ' opinion in the House.
Brougham would only have proposed to disfranchise
the rotten boroughs to the extent of one out of two
seats apiece.[1] It was fortunate that he did not have a
chance of bringing forward his scheme, for he was then
regarded as the popular standard-bearer of the cause,
and if once he had come out for so limited a measure,
Grey could not have produced next year a Bill very much
more radical. But the stars in their courses were fighting for the complete destruction of the old order.
Brougham's motion was down for November 16, and
on November 15 the Government was defeated.

The *coup de grâce* came on a vote for further enquiry
into the Civil List proposals of the Ministry, carried
by 233 to 204. All sections of Liberals, now united as
a Whig party, voted together against the Government.
Some of the High Tories, to sate their revenge on the
Duke for Catholic Emancipation, had, like Wetherell,
abstained ; while others, like Knatchbull and Vyvyan,
actually voted against the Ministry, though they would
not have voted next day for Brougham's Reform proposals.[2] They were to repent at leisure.

[1] Parker's *Graham*, i. 96; Brougham, *Memoirs*, iii. 523.
[2] *Ellenborough*, ii. 439. It was presumably for this reason that
Brougham was so exceedingly anxious to defeat the Government on the
15th (see *Hansard*, November 1830, p. 548, note). There would be
less certainty of defeating the Government on Reform next evening, as
no Tories would vote for Reform.

Even so the majority was not great. But in the then state of the country it was enough. The Duke, fearing lest Brougham's motion should be 'carried by storm' on the following evening, resigned in the morning to forestall it, and to put the Reform question in the hands of 'responsible ministers' like Grey.[1] He little thought that he was thereby giving his rival the opportunity to introduce a Government measure far more extensive than Brougham's dreaded proposals. Such a nightmare as Schedules A and B of the Bill of the following March was not dreamt of in the Duke's philosophy. The subsequent Tory tradition that Grey was 'a traitor to his order' arose very naturally from this complete misconception as to his views. If his brother peers had known that even in 1820 he had wished to take a hundred seats from the rotten boroughs, they would have been less surprised by his 'new constitution' in 1831.

Early on Tuesday, November 16, 1830, the Duke resigned, and between three and four that afternoon the King sent for Lord Grey to come to him at St. James's Palace. Grey was already in close consultation with his old friends Lord Lansdowne and Lord Holland, the two traditional chiefs of the Whig party. He had that morning, before receiving the commission to form a Government, seen Brougham and offered him the Attorney-Generalship, and had met with an angry refusal. Grey's action in speaking to Brougham even before he had seen the King shows that the Whig chiefs understood from the first the importance of Brougham's position. If he were allowed, as he wished, to remain outside the Government, he would with his popularity and eloquence soon destroy it by flank attacks. On the other hand, the offer of the Attorney-

[1] Wellington, *Despatches*, vii. 361, 399. *Ellenborough*, ii. 435: On December 26 the Duke wrote: 'Lord Grey differs with Lord Althorp upon Parliamentary Reform,' meaning that Grey was not as advanced as Althorp; this was one of the Duke's great errors.

Generalship was far below his claims. But what else could they offer him ? He told them that he did not wish for office and that he would not leave the Commons, but that he would, if desired, accept the Mastership of the Rolls, soon falling vacant, a non-ministerial place held for life but compatible with a seat in the Lower House. This arrangement, from the point of view of Government, would be worse than leaving Brougham out altogether, as he would still be in the Commons a rival to Althorp's leadership, with a place and income held at no man's pleasure. Yet it appears that Grey, in his first interview with the King on the afternoon of November 16, proposed that Brougham should have the Rolls ; it was the King who refused, because Wellington's parting advice to his master had been the warning that the member for Yorkshire as Master of the Rolls ' would be too powerful for any Government.' The Duke had again done Grey an inestimable service.[1]

[1] Grey to Holland, dated ' Berkeley Square, Nov. 16, 1830 ':

' I have told Lansdowne everything that passed at my interview with the King, and desired him to communicate it to you. Nothing can be more satisfactory than everything the King said. I am to see Palmerston at nine, having determined to act as you advise. I am to see Richmond at twelve to-morrow ; he seems very cordial. I have also written to Anglesey, and am to see him in the morning ; what I wish is that he should go to Ireland, and in that I hope you will agree with me. But for all these things it is necessary that I should have the means of communicating with you, without the delay and difficulty of going to Holland House. Pray come, if it is not danger to your health ; but that must be the first consideration.' [Holland was said to be *hors de combat* from gout ' eleven months out of twelve.']

' Lansdowne will tell you my own feelings about my own place. *Brougham is the difficulty, and it really is the only one with the King.* Peace, Reform, and Economy the acknowledged principles of the new Government. *Carte Blanche as to all offices both in Government and the Household but Brougham.* You will have heard his speech to-night. *I saw him this morning and he positively refused the Attorney Generalship.* What is to be done with him ? You could do more than anybody.'

This letter, never before printed, confirms the story told by Brougham in *Memoirs*, iii. 77-8, to the effect that it was the King who refused

That evening a memorable scene took place in the Commons. After Peel had announced that, as a result of the division the night before, the old Ministry had resigned, Althorp rose, and turning round to Brougham asked him to postpone his Reform Motion, which was to have come on that evening. If the new Government was to have the least chance of obtaining agreement for its own Reform Bill, it was clear that Brougham must not raise the question prematurely, and so force people in Parliament and in the country to commit themselves beforehand for and against particular schemes. Brougham, not concealing his excited and angry state of mind, very grudgingly consented to wait 'till the 25th of this month and no longer. I will then,' he said, 'at no more distant period, bring forward the question of Parliamentary Reform, whatever may be the circumstances, and whosoever may be his Majesty's Ministers.' On the next evening (November 17) he again made occasion to declare ' I have nothing to do with Ministers, except in the respect I bear them and except as a member of this House. I state this for the information of those who may feel any interest in the matter.' It looked as if the new Whig Ministry would be ' wrecked at the bar.' Members asked each other at Brooks's that night, was this really the beginning of a new era, or only of a new disappointment, as in 1782, 1806, 1812 ?

> Nought's constant in the human race,
> Except the Whigs not getting into place.

Meanwhile Grey was steadily building up the rest of

him the Rolls, which has been often disbelieved. *Croker*, ii. 80, also tends to confirm Brougham's statement that the outgoing Ministers had warned the King against his having the Rolls. This is the more likely, as we have evidence in a letter of Ellice's to Grey of Oct. 28, 1830, to the effect that Brougham had been trying to get the Rolls before the fall of the late Ministry, and believed that Lyndhurst had promised it to him, though Lyndhurst denied this. The King a few days later did not object to Brougham having the Chancellorship, as that was not a life-appointment.

his Cabinet—Old Whigs and New Whigs, Canningites and unattached lords and gentry of reforming bent. The business was going unexpectedly well, without any final refusals to join the Government, or any quarrelling over places. Althorp indeed had shrunk from accepting the leadership of the Commons and Chancellorship of the Exchequer, till he discovered that unless he accepted them Grey would throw up the attempt to form a Government at all. With bitter misgivings, he yielded to this friendly *ultimatum*, but only on condition that the Rolls were not given to Brougham, who, if he were once irremovably entrenched in that post, would make the position of the nominal leader of the House impossible. It was therefore useless for Grey to try to induce the King to withdraw his veto on Brougham having the Rolls, since Althorp's veto was equally decisive. Over the rising edifice of Liberal government still hung the shadow of Brougham.

On Thursday, November 18, Lansdowne, after being pressed by Grey to accept the Foreign Office, refused on the ground that he would prefer to have leisure and health to give good counsel in the Cabinet, adding ' would not Palmerston suit the Foreign Office ? ' The post was offered and accepted that day, and so began Palmerston's first and best Foreign Ministry.[1]

At four o'clock that afternoon (November 18) Grey saw Brougham again, perhaps to implore him once more to take the Attorney-Generalship. What passed is obscure ; but Brougham seems to have been somewhat mollified by Grey's handling, and his passionate resentment at some incidents of the last day or two was assuaged ; but no arrangement was reached. Grey's cryptic account of the interview, in a note to Holland that evening, runs thus : ' Brougham has

---

[1] See letters of November 18, in Appendix D, below. These letters dispose of Princess Lieven's boast that she prevented Lansdowne having the F.O. (Robinson's *Lieven*, p. 275). She had in fact absolutely no political influence over Grey, sincere as was his friendship for her.

just left me *couleur de rose*. It was my unfortunate Note to you, delivered in his presence, that did all the mischief.'

That evening at nine there met in Lansdowne House [1] a fairly complete Cabinet, but without a Lord Chancellor and without Brougham. It was probably at this meeting that the desperate situation was retrieved at the eleventh hour by the resolve to offer the Great Seal to the member for Yorkshire. Very late that night Grey sent off a note to Brougham : ' It is necessary that I should see you as soon as possible to-morrow, that is as soon as possible after I am up, which, worn out as I am, cannot I fear be much before ten o'clock.' But Brougham had a case in the Lords at ten, so Grey had to get up earlier to see him as he passed down to Westminster (November 19). Grey asked him to become Lord Chancellor. He refused. He was right, if he was only thinking of his personal position, for to go to the Lords was, as events proved, to uncrown himself as popular leader and to disarm himself of his power to threaten and destroy Ministries. He would ' drop on the Woolsack as on his political deathbed.' But all that morning he was besieged by Whigs, now fairly on their knees to him. Finally Althorp, whose moral influence extended even over Brougham, told him that if he refused office, his act would bring the Tories in again, and make Liberal government and legislation impossible for another twenty-five years. At that he yielded, and there is no reason to think that he did not yield mainly on public grounds.

Perhaps no single appointment ever made so great a sensation.

At Brooks's [notes the aristocratic radical Hobhouse, on November 19] our friends were handing about a list of the new

---

[1] Grey's London house at this time was in Berkeley Square, only a minute's walk therefore from Lord Lansdowne's famous mansion—a convenient proximity for the work of Cabinet-making.

Administration. Brougham Lord Chancellor ! ! Reform of Parliament, Anti-Slavery, Law Reform, Useful Knowledge Society, *Edinburgh Review*, Sublime Society of Beef Stakes, hail and farewell ! ! But it is believed, and people seem glad to get rid of my learned friend from the House of Commons. He came. We set up a shout, and he soon went away.

The Whig ship was over the bar. Next day Campbell writes :

Such a day at Brooks's ! Who could have foreseen it ? This room presents at this moment a new and striking spectacle. It is filled with the new Ministers and their adherents, and great numbers are sitting round the tables writing lists of the new Ministers for their friends in the country.[1]

In four days Grey had accomplished what no other man in the country could have done. He had made out of scattered and divergent elements a Cabinet, and thereby a new Parliamentary party, at once sufficiently advanced in opinion to accept a sweeping Reform Bill, and yet sufficiently broad-bottomed to muster the votes to carry it.[2] In that age, with that King, with those nobles, a less imposing and aristocratic personality than Grey with his ' patrician thoroughbred look ' that Byron ' doted on,' would have failed to create and hold together a Government capable, under the existing Constitution, of peacefully handing over the power of the aristocracy to the middle class. People complained then and complain still that Grey's Government was very aristocratic in its personnel. It certainly was, but it passed the Reform Bill ; and the question is whether it would have been permitted to do so if it had not been so largely made up of aristocrats ; for the measure was,

---

[1] Campbell's *Autobiography*. Campbell, on November 17, wrote that Brougham had just told him ' the Great Seal is the only thing he could take, and it would then be thought his conduct was sordid.'

[2] Out of a Ministry of over forty persons, only one, Charles Wynn, resigned on the Bill. This argues great power of selection and knowledge of his men on Grey's part.

in effect, one by which the aristocracy, under the combined influence of persuasion, cajolery, and intimidation, laid down its monopoly of political power. It is almost impossible for people now living to realise the difficulties of the task Grey accomplished in 1830-2, the immensity of the chasm which he bridged, or his need for stressing the conservative elements of his Government in order to persuade the King and the aristocracy to surrender to the people. That he was at once intensely an aristocrat, yet a more advanced Reformer than Brougham, made him the man of the hour, and that hour was big with fate.

Grey's appointments have also been criticised for a tendency to nepotism. It was a proverbial fault of Whig Governments, alike in the eighteenth and nineteenth centuries. Yet if this list is examined it will be seen that the more important posts held by Grey's relatives and connections by marriage could not have been better filled. Durham and Ellice each played a great part of his own in passing the Reform Bill ; while Howick and Duncannon, if indeed the latter is to count as a connection of Grey's, fully merited their places. As to the fitness of George Barrington and George Ponsonby for their minor posts, I confess that I am uninformed.[1]

---

[1] See Appendix G, below, ' Bear Ellice.'

The Grey Ministry in November 1830 was as follows. Grey's relations and connections by marriage are in *italics*.

First Lord of the Treasury . Earl Grey.

Lord Chancellor . . Mr. Brougham, created Lord Brougham and Vaux.

Lord President of the Council Marquis of Lansdowne.

Privy Seal . . . *Lord Durham.*

Home Secretary. . . Viscount Melbourne (formerly Canningite).

Chancellor of the Exchequer and leader of House of Commons . . . Viscount Althorp.

Foreign Secretary . . Viscount Palmerston (formerly Canningite).

Colonial Secretary . . Viscount Goderich (formerly Canningite).

First Lord of the Admiralty Sir James Graham, Bart. (afterwards Peelite-Conservative).

President Board of Control (India). . . . Charles Grant, formerly Canningite, Baron Glenelg 1835.

Postmaster-General . . Duke of Richmond (formerly High Tory and later Protectionist Conservative).

Chancellor Duchy of Lancaster Lord Holland.

No office . . . . Earl of Carlisle (formerly a Tory, a Whig, and a Canningite).

The above formed the Cabinet.

Secretary at War . . Charles Wynn (formerly Grenvillite, resigned March 1831 on account of the Bill, succeeded by Sir Henry Parnell, who in January 1832 was succeeded by Hobhouse).

Master of the Mint and President of Board of Trade . Lord Auckland (always a Whig, afterwards Governor-General of India).

Lord Chamberlain . .	Duke of Devonshire.
Lord Steward . . .	Marquis Wellesley (attached to no party : Liberal leanings).
Master of the Horse . .	Earl of Albemarle.
Groom of the Stole . .	Marquis of Winchester.
Paymaster of the Forces .	Lord John Russell (entered Cabinet, June 1831).
First Commissioner of Land Revenue (Woods and Forests)	Hon. G. Agar Ellis (resigned from ill-health, and succeeded in Feb. 1831 by *Viscount Duncannon*, John Ponsonby, afterwards 4th Earl of Bessborough).
Treasurer of the Navy .	C. Poulett Thomson (later Ld. Sydenham, Gov. Gen. of Canada).
Attorney-General . .	Thomas Denman (knighted).
Solicitor-General . .	W. Horne (knighted).
Secretaries of Treasury = Government Whips	*Edward Ellice.* T. Spring Rice (afterwards First Lord Monteagle and Chancellor of Exchequer).
Under-Secretary, Colonies .	*Lord Howick.*
Treasury Board . .	Earl Grey, Viscount Althorp, Baron Nugent, Vernon Smith, Francis Baring, *Hon. George Ponsonby* (nephew of the other George Ponsonby, p. 165, above).
Admiralty Board . .	Sir J. Graham, Admiral Sir T. Hardy, Admiral Hon. G. Dundas, Capt. Sir Samuel Pechell, *Capt. Hon. George Barrington.*

Scotland.

Lord Advocate . .	Francis Jeffrey (of the *Edinburgh Review*, etc.).
Solicitor-General . .	Henry Cockburn (see his *Memorials* and *Life of Jeffrey*).

Ireland.

Lord Lieutenant.   .   . Marquis of Anglesey (formerly Canningite). Succeeded 1833 by Wellesley.

Chief Secretary .   .   . Hon. E. G. Stanley (afterwards 14th Earl of Derby and Conservative Premier. Entered Cabinet, June 1831).

Lord Chancellor (Ireland)   . Lord Plunkett.

NOTE.—The *Annual Register* for 1830 puts Lord Auckland in the Cabinet, and this error has been reproduced in other authorities. But see Walpole's *England*, iii. 193, note, ed. 1890; his name does not occur in the official lists of Cabinet meetings in the *Correspondence of William IV and Lord Grey.*

Grey's Government was first and foremost a coalition to carry Reform. As such it proved one of the most successful structures in our political history, setting its architect high in the rank of British statesmen. The whole was soundly planned, and many of Grey's individual appointments, above all the choice of Durham and Russell for the Committee to draw up the Bill, were happily inspired. But two appointments proved unfortunate, that of Stanley to Ireland and that of Melbourne to the Home Office.

It was essential to find a place for Stanley ; ' the Rupert of Debate ' proved one of the protagonists of Reform as afterwards of Protection, and the Derby interest stood for much in that aristocratic world which was being asked to make the great surrender. But the appointment to the Irish Secretaryship under Lord Anglesey of a young man like Stanley, at once so able, so vigorous, and at bottom so conservative, prepared the complete failure to pacify Ireland which darkened the Whig record in the coming era.

The circumstances of Stanley's re-election on taking office marked the little confidence that the people had in the Whigs in the winter of 1830, before the introduction of the Reform Bill changed the scene. Preston, though the seat of the Stanley influence, was also, like Westminster, one of a few boroughs which enjoyed under the old anomalous system a really democratic franchise, in striking contrast to the usual ' close ' borough. Orator Hunt's white hat rallied the Radical vote and defeated Stanley in Preston, to the huge delight of all Lancashire democrats, including the youthful John Bright, whose first interest in politics was aroused by the local rumours of this contest against privilege. Stanley took refuge in the close borough of Windsor, where he was returned by the interest of King William, who had already, under Grey's assuaging influence, quite grown out of his original shyness about his new

Ministers.[1] The Preston election proved to him that they had no understanding with the Radicals, who, he was convinced, intended to overset the throne. It was Grey's business to persuade him that only ' an extensive measure of Reform ' could prevent their fell designs. The fact that Grey believed it himself made his task the easier. The chief importance, perhaps, of public events from December to February lay in their effect on the mind of the King ; for such was then the custom of the Constitution that if William had not been brought to agree with the Reform Bill it could not have been introduced by his servants into either House of Parliament.

If Stanley was peculiarly unfitted to deal with manifestations of discontent in Ireland, Melbourne was equally unfitted to do so in England, though his lethargic temper was the very opposite of Stanley's. The fact that Melbourne had supported Castlereagh's repressive policy in Peterloo days, ought to have prevented Grey from appointing him to the Home Office. His administration there marked a retrogression from the Liberal policy of his predecessor. Peel had put an end to press prosecutions and savage repression, and had introduced an efficient civil police, endearingly called after his names, whose gradual extension prevented the constant and irritating use of the military to preserve order.[2]

Melbourne, the Canningite Tory, had served no apprenticeship in a party with popular sympathies ; and

[1] When other references are not given, statements in this book about the King's relation to Ministers are drawn from that invaluable source of information, the *Correspondence of King William and Earl Grey* (Murray, 1867). See below, end of Appendix C, p. 378, for the King's attitude when Wellington fell.

[2] During their early and quite unjust unpopularity, in the last days of the Wellington Ministry, the new police were less often called ' Peelers ' and ' Bobbies ' than ' raw lobsters,' ' Blue devils,' or ' Peel's bloody gang.' Twenty years later both they and their founder were thought of very differently.

in spite of his good nature as a ' man about town ' he lacked the broader and deeper humaneness of Grey, Holland, or Althorp. Unfortunately, they allowed him that winter to stain the reputation of the Whig party by cruelties which history, now that she knows the facts, can pardon as little as Peterloo.

In November 1830, throughout the southern counties, the starving peasants had rioted to obtain half-a-crown a day for wages ; the rioters had not killed or seriously wounded a single man ; their spirit was humane and not unreasonable, differing entirely from that of the Bristol rioters in the following autumn. Yet in the terrible assize of December three of the rioters were judicially murdered [1]—two of these being hanged by a refinement of cruelty in the enforced presence of a hundred of their weeping comrades—four hundred were imprisoned, and, worst of all, 457 men and boys were transported as convicts to Australia. In those days transportation commonly meant for the poor not only horrible physical sufferings but life-long separation from parents and friends, wife and child. ' The sentence of final separation on all these families and homes was received with a frenzy of consternation and grief. " Such a total prostration of the mental faculties by fear," wrote the *Times* correspondent, and " such a terrible exhibition of anguish and despair, I never before witnessed in a court of justice." ' ' The shadow of this vengeance,' we are told and can well believe, ' still darkens the minds of old men and women in the villages of Wiltshire, and eighty years have been too short a time to blot out its train of desolating memories.' [2]

If the pen of the already famous Edinburgh Reviewer,

[1] This is not counting the six men and boys more justifiably hanged for arson.

[2] Hammond, *The Village Labourer* (Longmans, 1911), chaps. xi., xii. The story both of the riots and the assize is there to be read, for the first time, in full detail. The remarks on Grey on pp. 312–14 are very just.

now Reform member for Calne, had been employed in contrasting the provocation given by these starving peasants to the punishment they received, the Winchester Assize of 1830 would stand in the national memory to-day by the side of Judge Jeffreys' Western Circuit. But the lives and sufferings of the agricultural labourer were a thing outside party tradition, hidden deeply from the knowledge of Tory and of Whig. In November all the propertied classes had been in panic ; in December they were calling for the punishment of those who had scared them. If Grey had shown in this matter the real statesmanship which our age would approve, he would have lost the confidence not only of the King and of all the aristocracy, but of the greater part of middle-class opinion to whom he was about to make his great appeal. If the Whigs had seemed to palter with ' anarchy ' and ' Jacobinism,' the ship of Reform could never have been launched. ' In the corrupted currents of the world ' it was as well for the cause of constitutional progress that in this matter Grey was blind to that which his generation could not see. Nevertheless it will always be a stain on a singularly pure reputation that he did not insist on a sweeping reduction of the sentences, which might have been effected without showing any dangerous belief in the cause of the labourers, or in the economic possibility of a living wage.[1]

Not content with the terrible Assize, Ministers proceeded to turn the law officers of the Crown on to

---

[1] On November 24, 1830, in the first days of office, while the riots were still going on, Grey wrote to Holland : ' Raising wages would no doubt have a good effect. But any resolution of this sort published by the Magistrates would evidently appear to be dictated by fear and would operate as a premium to violence, in quarters which this spirit has not yet reached. Besides, what authority have the Magistrates or can they have to direct any measures for that purpose ? They cannot prescribe to me what wages I am to pay my labourers, or what rents I am to receive from my tenants.' Then follows the individualist argument against fixing wages or rents, which at that time completely held the economic field.

prosecuting Carlile and Cobbett, the two leading journalists who had taken up the cause of the starving labourers, and had shown that the riots, which they deprecated, were provoked by a series of intolerable wrongs, for which there was no legal or peaceable redress. In January 1831 Carlile was condemned to two years' imprisonment. The renewal of press prosecution enraged the Radicals all over the country. Place saw, with more indignation than surprise, that Peel's generous policy had been reversed by the Whigs. He wrote to Joseph Hume about Carlile's case :

> Look at the words prosecuted, look at the barbarous sentence, and find, if you can, since the time when Castlereagh put an end to his own existence, any one who has been prosecuted and sentenced for such words ; scarcely, indeed, during his malignant sway were such words prosecuted.[1]

The prosecutions of Carlile and Cobbett weakened the Government in the country more than the sentences on the rioters, though both did them good with the King. In the northern industrial towns the working men were beginning to regard the new Government as no improvement on the old, and were abandoning all hope of an efficient Reform Bill. In January the population of Sheffield had a plan for disarming the soldiers if they entered the town, but they were wisely sent elsewhere.[2]

Cobbett was a harder nut to crack than poor Carlile. His trial at the Guildhall did not take place till July 1831. Denman, in prosecuting, had to speak of him with cautious respect as ' one of the greatest masters of the English language.' That mastery was very fully exercised in Court at the expense of the Whig Ministers, over whom Cobbett insulted and triumphed, like Horne Tooke and Hone over the Tories of old. But as the Reform Bill had then been introduced, the

---

[1] Add. MSS., B.M., 35,149, f. 24.
[2] Ibid. f. 24b.

Government was able to stand the shock of his acquittal, as the nation had something else to think about, and Grey was by then more popular than Cobbett himself. There were indeed limits to Melbourne's mismanagement of the Home Office. In spite of the frequent strikes and the disturbed and dangerous atmosphere of the years 1830–1832, he and Grey from the first resisted strong pressure to revive Castlereagh's coercion bills and espionage against the Trade Unions,[1] and a common interest in the fortunes of the Reform Bill soon induced Melbourne to consult the views of such a sound adviser as Francis Place on the best means of preserving order among the working classes.

Grey had come in on the threefold programme of Peace, Retrenchment, and Reform. Peace and Reform were to prove great realities, but Retrenchment was a *fiasco*. Although ' cheap government ' was the only economic panacea on which Reformers of all shades were agreed, they were all deceived in supposing that the services of a growing community in the nineteenth century could be cut down, or even prevented from increasing. National salvation did not lie along that path of mere negation. Only one branch of the tree of national expenditure was rotten wood with no sap in it—the scandalous pensions on which the political system of Pitt and his successors had largely rested. But King William and Grey were agreed that although they would prevent the repetition of such scandals, they could not in honour or justice withdraw grants for life that had been made, however wrongly, on the national faith. This decision caused acute disappointment to the country, fed for twenty years past on a literature of denunciation and exposure of the pension-holders. ' These damned pension lists,' wrote Creevey,

---

[1] *Melbourne Papers*, 122, 127–8. *Howick Papers, MS.*

'are a cursed millstone about the neck of the Government.'

For the rest, no large field of retrenchment could be found. The Tory country gentlemen had never been militarists, and their favourite ministers had wisely declined to keep up big armaments after Waterloo. The incoming Whig Government scraped and pared where they could ; and the King, whom they dared not seriously offend till their Reform Bill was launched, was not unreasonable over ' Household ' reductions. But the net outcome of Retrenchment proved very small, and the anger of the nation was proportionately great. The Whigs, who had headed the cry down this blind alley, and had turned out the Wellington Ministry on a Civil List vote, were denounced as deceivers and hypocrites.

In February 1831, Althorp's budget was a failure ; its chief proposals were rejected by opinion in the City and had to be withdrawn. The Cabinet discussed its own resignation, but Althorp, who was undoubtedly the most anxious of all its members to get back to private life, knew that they were bound in honour to remain till they had kept their word with the nation on Reform. This was also the fixed idea of Grey.

In February the Reform Bill was already drawn up and secretly agreed upon by King and Cabinet, but until it could be introduced there were bad times to weather through, testing the loyalty and temper of individual Ministers. Brougham, so at least his colleagues believed, dived into the underground regions of the Press, that ' fourth estate ' so mysterious to aristocratic statesmen, and set the *Times* attacking Grey and lauding the Chancellor to the skies. (February 1831.) Durham, whose fiery temper was seldom under good control, accused Brougham to his face in a violent scene, and the unappeasable feud between the two men began. But Grey, fundamentally loyal and generous, declared, contrary to the opinion of everyone else and perhaps contrary to his own, that he believed Brougham's assertions of innocence in the matter of the *Times* articles.[1] From the moment Brougham had taken office under him, he had resumed his former friendly relations, and doubtless understood that he must put up with a good deal of intrigue if he would live at peace with ' old wickedshifts,' as friend Creevey still called Baron Brougham and Vaux. The society in which these great men lived together while in office was neither formal nor dull. At a small dinner-party at Lord Sefton's, where Grey was present, the host marched out from the dining-room in mock procession before the new Lord Chancellor, carrying ' the fire shovel for a mace.'

Through the vexations and disgraces of these early months, as through the storms and dangers of the Reform struggle that followed, Grey was absolutely serene. Those who met him in private, again and again in their letters and diaries made note of his cheerful enjoyment of life. The ' peevish and wayward ' invalid of the long years of opposition had disappeared. Was it that a physical change in his health happened to coincide with his assumption of the Premiership ? Or had his famous ' low spirits ' in the past been all along moral and political, a kind of State valetudinarianism, curable only by office and responsibility for great public interests ? Certain it is, that from the moment of coming into power until the Reform Bill was on the Statute Book, he showed more ' nerve ' than any of his colleagues, and a sweeter temper than any except Althorp. From pessimist he had turned optimist. In the worst moments of February 1831 he was ' very cheerful,' relying on the coming Bill to burst like the sun through the clouds of present discontents.[2]

---

[1] *Butler*, 193–4 ; *Cre. vey*, ii. 219–20, Feb. 27, 1831.

[2] My authorities for this paragraph are too numerous for citation ; but here are three amusing pictures in the *Creevey Papers* of Grey during the Reform Bill time :

March 14, 1831. At Lord Grey's. ' Grey was all alive O ! quite

The one activity of Government, besides the Reform Bill, for the details of which Grey made himself personally responsible was foreign affairs. Ever since he had been Foreign Secretary in 1806 the affairs of Europe had a special attraction for him, and to maintain peace with the new Liberal France was one of the dearest objects of his life. He would have wished to take the Foreign Office himself, but since the duties of the Premiership prevented that, he became Palmerston's friend and tutor. There may be exaggerations in Creevey's statement that ' Palmerston never signed a dispatch that had not been seen and *altered* by Lord Grey,' but there is ample evidence that Grey took a leading part from 1830 to 1833 in every step of the perilous negotiations by which war was averted and Belgium settled. Under Grey's tutoring, Palmerston was more truly successful in his first period at the Foreign Office than in his more boisterous dealing with foreign countries in later years. Grey would have allowed none of those lectures to benighted foreigners from the island pulpit, those blustering irruptions and rapid retreats, those too frequent espousals of the wrong side in a foreign quarrel, which in later years made ' Palmerstonianism ' so dear to the British Philistine and so contemptible to wise observers. At once firm and pacific,

overflowing, never ceasing in his little civilities to myself, wanting me to eat this or drink that :—" Do, Creevey ; I assure you it's damned good ; I know you'll like it." Can't you see him ? It was not amiss for a Prime Minister to call out at dinner : " Do you think, Creevey, we shall carry our Reform Bill in the Lords ? " '

March 26. ' I wish you could have been with me when I entered the Premier's drawing-room last night. I was rather early, and he was standing alone with his back to a fire—the best dressed, the handsomest, and apparently the happiest man in all his royal master's domains.'

May 27. ' While I was riding in the Park yesterday I received rather a smartish pat on my shoulder from an unseen stick. When I turned round and saw my assailant in quite an ultra fit of laughing, who do you suppose it could be ? No other than our Prime Minister. When I praised his royal master [who had just given Grey the garter], he said : " He *is* a prime fellow, is he not ? " '

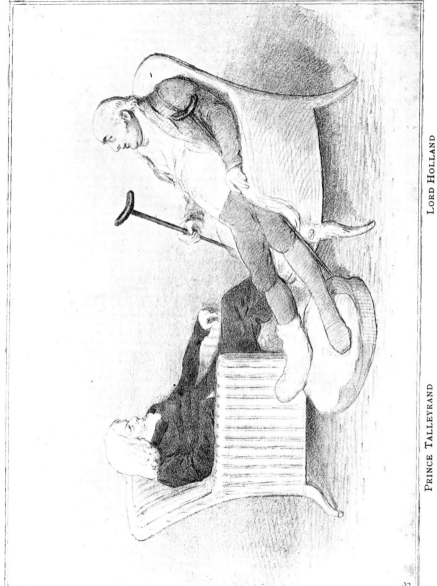

PRINCE TALLEYRAND   LORD HOLLAND

the foreign policy of Grey and Palmerston wrought with quiet dignity and won the confidence of all.

The Government of Louis Philippe, anxious to preserve peace with England, had sent over as its ambassador the *doyen* of the diplomatic world, the almost legendary Prince Talleyrand. Macaulay was not exaggerating when he pictured to his sisters the appearance in London drawing-rooms of this extraordinary patriarch :

His face is as pale as that of a corpse, and wrinkled to a frightful degree. His eyes have an odd glassy stare quite peculiar to them. His hair, thickly powdered and pomatumed, hangs down his shoulders on each side as straight as a pound of tallow candles.

Creevey adds that at table he used to make ' the cursedest nasty noises in his throat ' and was detested by Grey's ladies. But Grey's own dealings with Talleyrand were intimate and friendly, and greatly contributed to the peace of Europe.

On December 21, 1830, Grey was able to write to Lord Holland :

We go on admirably with foreign affairs. Yesterday a Protocol was signed by the five Powers, which amounts to a recognition of the independence of Belgium.[1] It is a great thing to have brought Austria and Russia to concur in such a measure.

The initial step thus taken, it remained to get the Belgians to select for themselves a monarch whom all the Powers of Europe could accept. The first serious crisis occurred in January–February 1831, when the majority of the Belgian Congress chose the Duc de Nemours, son of the King of the French. This England could only regard as ' union with France and nothing else.' Our business was to persuade the French Government to refuse the tempting offer ; the danger lay in

---

[1] See p. 225 above and p. 352 below.

the French Chauvinist party, more anxious for national self-assertion than for peace. In January 1831 Grey wrote to Lord Holland :

> There seems to be no hope but holding a strong language to France, whose Government, I think, would not like to run the risk of seeing her whole commerce swept from the sea. I wished and hoped better things, but whether from insincerity or weakness, things are taking a course in which we cannot acquiesce.

And again:

> I have had a very long interview with Talleyrand to-day. Both he and his Government profess fairly : and I am ready to give them credit for sincerity. But still things are taking a course which will lead too probably to war, and I am not quite satisfied with the measures they are taking to prevent it.

When once the French Government understood that the new régime in England was sincerely the friend of France, but that there were lengths of concession to which not even a Whig Government would go, they gave in and refused the crown for Nemours. So matters stood at the end of February 1831. A landing stage had been safely reached, but several more Belgian crises of an equally serious nature still lay ahead, which Grey and Palmerston staved off ; again and again saving Europe with noiseless and unobtrusive patience, and so keeping the ring clear at home for the more resonant battle of Reform.

CHAPTER II

THE PREPARATION OF THE BILL—NOVEMBER 1830 TO FEBRUARY 1831

'I was deeply impressed with the conviction of Lord Grey that none but a large measure would be a safe measure.'—LORD JOHN RUSSELL, *English Constitution*, p. xxxvi.

To the men on whom fell the task of enfranchising the working class in the following generation, to the Chartists and to John Bright after them, the most important aspect of the First Reform Bill was its limitations. But in the days of their fathers, to Radical and Tory alike, the miracle to be explained was why it went so far. And that is the question that presents itself to History. The answer is given by Mr. Butler, whose researches have provided for the first time a reliable and comprehensive history of the Bill and its passage :

> Lord Grey's statesmanlike conviction of the need and advantage of an extensive measure was the prime source of the Bill ; the wisdom of Russell and the will of Durham embodied this conviction in a bold and simple form ; and as regards the moderates in the Cabinet and the party generally, it was proved once again that a keen and determined minority will by their very momentum overbear a comparatively indifferent and undecided majority.[1]

It only needs to be added to this, that the conversion of the ' moderates in the party ' outside the Cabinet was effected by the persuasive and terrifying expression of the national will after the Bill had appeared in public.

[1] *The Passing of the Great Reform Bill*, J. R. M. Butler, 1914, p.183.

But until the measure had been drawn up in secret, and accepted by a conservative King and a mixed Cabinet, its makers had to work in the dark, uncheered by the popular approval, and guided solely by their own foresight of what the reception of particular proposals was likely to be. It was during these months of gestation before the Bill saw light, from the end of November 1830 to the end of February 1831, that Grey's tact and statecraft were put to their severest test, and won a triumph so smooth and perfect that the pitfalls and dangers he avoided with such skill have scarcely been noticed by posterity.

When, about a week after the completion of his Ministry, Grey asked Durham, as they came down the steps of the House of Lords, to 'assist him in drawing up a Reform Bill' and to take Lord John Russell into partnership in the enterprise, he deliberately gave the key of the position to the advanced section of Reformers in his Cabinet. When, a few days later, he consented to the proposal of Durham and Russell that the 'Committee of Four' to draw up the Bill should include besides themselves Sir James Graham and Lord Duncannon, the former closely confederate with Althorp, and the latter versed in the lore of Irish boroughs, deliberate exclusion had been made of all 'moderates' and adherents of 'bit by bit Reform.' [1]

---

[1] Three roads, of three different dates, qualities, and gradients, still lead from the west end of Rydal Water to Wordsworth's cottage at Grasmere. That sound supporter of the Bill, Dr. Arnold of Fox How and Rugby, used to call these roads respectively, 'Old Corruption,' 'Bit by Bit Reform,' and 'Radical Reform,' after the three rival policies of which every one was in those days talking. But the actual Reform Bill, according to its authors, was no one of the three, but came half way between 'Radical' and 'Bit by Bit.' Grey energetically repudiated both 'Radical Reform,' which he defined as Universal Suffrage, and 'Bit by Bit Reform,' which, he told the Lords, would have 'left the question in as unsettled a condition as before.' See his speech on the Bill, October 3, 1831, *Hansard*, pp. 934, 935. Also Parker's *Graham*, i. 121, where Graham writes : 'The plan was in unison with the instructions of Lord Grey ; it was no bit by bit Reform.'

No less marked was the exclusion of Brougham from these inner counsels. The Chancellor would have ruined all, for, while still regarded as the popular champion of Reform, he was wedded to the retention of half the rotten borough representation. And he would certainly have quarrelled on the Committee with Durham and Russell in particular, and in general with any colleague who tried to do business with him on equal terms. In the rivalry between Brougham and Russell for the leading place among Reformers, Grey had wisely sided with Russell. On October 8, a month before the Duke fell, Grey had written to Holland, referring to Brougham's coming motion in the Commons: ' He has taken the question of Reform into his own hands, which I do not think was quite handsome to John Russell.' In the Cabinet discussions of January 1831 Brougham tried in vain to have the introduction of the Bill in the Commons taken from Russell and assigned to Althorp.[1]

During December and January 1830-1, while the Bill was in the making, there was no shadow of ill-feeling between the men who were making it. The Committee of Four consulted deeply with Grey and Althorp.[2] ' My whole morning has been occupied with a long discussion on the plan of Reform with Lambton (Durham) and Lord John Russell,' writes Grey to his wife, on January 2, twelve days before the Committee sent in its report to the Cabinet.

Durham had not as yet conceived any grievance against his father-in-law's treatment of his claims, such as took possession of him in the ensuing summer.[3] His personal

[1] Appendix E, p. 381, below.

[2] For Althorp's scheme, very like Russell's, but not quite so sweeping, see his letter to Russell in December, *Butler*, 179. Graham's conduct in the Committee is said by Le Marchant to have been guided by Althorp.

[3] On November 2, 1830, immediately after his admission to the Cabinet as Privy Seal, he wrote to Lord Grey, ' I feel quite unable to put down on the paper the impression of those feelings which I entertain for all your kindness to me.' In the following August he had quite forgotten that he ever felt or wrote thus.

conduct as Chairman of the Committee in December and January seems to have been perfect. Since Russell was destined to introduce the Bill to the public in the House of Commons, Durham generously asked him to draw up the first 'plan.' Lord John's plan became the basis of the Committee's work, and remains the outline, with very little alteration in principle, of the Bill that passed into law. Lord John wrote that when he was drafting his plan, two considerations decided him in favour of a sweeping measure, 'the authority of Lord Grey,' and 'the dangerous excitement consequent on the Duke of Wellington's denial of all Reform.'[1] The most important principles of the Bill—destruction of the rotten boroughs *en masse* without money compensation, and an uniform middle-class franchise for all boroughs old and new—though they were first set down on paper in the solitude of Lord John's study, were the result of informal conversations, extending over a period of many months,[2] held between the Whig chiefs, especially Grey, Durham, Althorp, Ellice, and Lord John himself, the group whence emanated the Reform Bill. The time has now come to review the principles of the 'new constitution' which they gave to their country.

Anyone familiar with the political history of England from the Restoration of Charles II to the death of Queen Anne must be struck by the regular way in which successive general elections then gave effect to the variations of political opinion in the community. The alternation of Whig and Tory Parliaments in the reigns of the last Stuarts answered so happily and so accurately to the changing feelings of the public, that England was able to enforce her will in every big

---

[1] Russell, *Early Correspondence*, ii. 53. For the text of 'the plan' see his *English Constitution*, pp. xxxvi–xxxviii. See Appendix E, below, 'The Framing of the Reform Bill.'

[2] See p. 223, above.

question as it came up—in Marlborough's time, for instance, the country was able to use the Whigs to win the war, the Tories to make the peace, and afterwards the Whigs again to secure the Hanoverian succession.

But during the seventy years before the Reform Bill things were very different. Throughout that period, increasingly as time went on, the country failed to make its wishes felt, whenever they conflicted with those of the King and of the borough-owners. Public opinion had not the means to continue Chatham in power ; to stop the quarrel with America ; to punish the Peterloo Ministry for passing the Six Acts and for prosecuting Queen Caroline. The Tories, however unpopular they might be, had no longer anything to fear, nor the Whigs anything to hope, from a general election. Only when at last a King not unfavourable to the Whigs chanced to ascend the throne, at a moment when the Tories were split up into three mutually hostile factions, could Grey and his friends obtain a precarious hold on power, conceded to them with almost contemptuous indifference, as to caretakers who must soon hand back the government of England to the men who owned it as their private property.

The Constitution then had changed in a non-popular direction. The Whigs were right in their historical argument that the ' old constitution ' which the Tories identified with the rotten boroughs was only about a century old in its methods and spirit, however mediæval it might be in its form. It was the same, yet not the same. The reasons were clear. The population had gradually shifted from the old boroughs to new centres, and during the last forty years it had shifted with the increasing speed of great economic change. North England was insufficiently represented, and the new ' industrial North ' was hardly represented at all. That Old Sarum had two votes and Manchester none was important, not as a singularity, but as a symbol of the general state of the representation.

Indeed, although the names of the boroughs had been preserved without alteration since Stuart times, the position and character of the electorate had in many cases been changed, and changed for the worse. The process of bringing the borough elections under the control of small oligarchies in the borough, or of aristocratic influences outside, had been going on throughout the Tudor and Stuart periods ; but it was only in the eighteenth century that the process had been completed, and that the position of a single borough ' patron ' had been publicly recognised in the majority of cases.[1]

The variety of the franchise in the close boroughs was very great, but in effect each close borough belonged to one individual borough-owner, who was in a position to dictate or purchase the votes of the nominal electors. The borough-owner in his turn extracted from the Government of the day office, pensions, peerages, sinecures, and every form of advancement at the public expense for himself, his clients, and his relations. That is why the system was known as ' Old Corruption,' and why Pitt—as his good angel, Wilberforce, lamented —when once he had abandoned the idea of reforming Parliament, had to govern the country, not by ' principle ' but by ' influence.'[2]

The Friends of the People had drawn out a table in 1793, showing that over 300 out of 513 representatives of England and Wales owed their return to individual proprietors, 71 of whom were lords and 91 commoners.[3] The evils of the system were tempered, but not relieved by the fact that a few large boroughs

---

[1] Porritt, *Unreformed House of Commons*.

[2] *Private Papers of Wilberforce* (Unwin, 1897), pp. 72–4, a very remarkable passage that ought to be carefully studied. Wilberforce gave a moderate support to the Reform Bill of 1831 on these moral grounds (*idem*, p. 266).

[3] Pp. 73–4, above.

like Westminster and Preston had an almost manhood suffrage. But what were they among so many?

The men who drew up the Reform Bill determined to sweep away at one stroke all the 'nomination boroughs'—that is, to substitute the principle of election by the people for that of nomination by a boroughowner in a good many more than 200 seats. This revolution was to be achieved by two distinct processes—first, by disfranchising all boroughs where the population was below a certain number, so taking away some 160 seats that could be used to enfranchise new boroughs and to add to the insufficient county representation; [1] and secondly, by 'opening' to all £10 householders the franchise of those 'close boroughs' whose population justified their retaining one or more members.[2]

The Reform Bill, in the eyes of the sufferers, was first and foremost a confiscation of private property and of corporate and customary rights, as extensive as that which accompanied the destruction of the mediæval Church by the Tudors, and of the Monarchy by the victorious Roundheads. And this wholesale destruction of the property and influence of individuals was to be effected without compensation, though compensation had been part of the Reform schemes of Wyvill and Pitt half a century before, and of Russell himself in 1823. But in 1831 the country, already furious against the Whigs for their failure to retrench and for their refusal to abolish the life-pensions granted by the Tories,[3] would have lost all patience if asked to

---

[1] 'Schedule A' of the Bill was the list of boroughs that lost both their members; 'Schedule B,' those that lost one member out of two.

[2] *E.g.* Lord Lansdowne's Calne, or Great Marlow. The latter had been bought by a Welsh attorney, Williams, who, having speculated in coal-mines, invested the proceeds in buying the two Marlow seats; he paid the voters £15 a-piece at election time (Gunning's *Cambridge*, i. 103).

[3] See pp. 255–6, above.

buy out the 'borough-mongers,' the name by which the unfortunate borough-owners were execrated that year by nine Englishmen out of ten.[1]

It was this clean sweep of the 'borough-mongers' that gave the Bill the popularity which floated it over all rocks and shallows on its headlong course. Even Brougham, who had wanted half-measures, confessed as much after the event. In short the decision to destroy all the rotten boroughs was one of the most prudent acts of daring in history, and it is good to think that the motive was moral as well as political. Althorp told his colleagues that, after only a few weeks in office, his experience of the corrupt pressure of the borough-owners on the Government was such that he would no longer tolerate any vestige of a system which left seats in the Commons in the hands of individuals—no, not even to give 'able young lawyers' and budding Burkes, Cannings, and Macaulays a better chance of being put early and easily into the House by their patrons, nor even to find new Ministers a sure place of refuge on taking office under the Crown.

Although the total abolition of nomination boroughs was at once the most popular and the most fiercely contested part of the Bill, it is the part that has been least

---

[1] Four days after the Bill was brought in, Creevey (ii. 221) writes: 'To think of dear Ald(e)borough and Orford, both belonging to Lord Hertford, and purchased at a great price, being clearly bowled out, without a word of with your leave or by your leave. Aye, and such proprietors are treated as *criminals* by the whole country for making any fight on their behalf. To be sure, the poor devils who cling to the wreck will have mobbing enough out of doors before the business is over.' Lord Hertford, formerly the notorious Yarmouth, *alias* Lord Monmouth, *alias* Lord Steyne (see p. 153, above), had written at the time of the Duke's fall: 'They tell me Lord Grey is to resume the command of the Reformers. So probably some of the uninhabited Burgage boroughs will be bought up as in Ireland [viz., in 1800], either by public money or by the populous towns themselves to whom the elections will be transferred. I do not think Attwood and his Unionists will do anything beyond talking' (Add. MSS., B.M., 30,112). Imagine then this man's feelings when he heard of Schedule A!

questioned in the retrospect. The choice of the uniform £10 household franchise for all boroughs is open to more dispute ; yet I believe that the more closely the actual conditions of that day are studied, the harder it becomes to name any alternative which would not have led to disaster.

First, it is suggested that the working class should have been enfranchised by an uniform household suffrage. The answer to this is that such a Bill would never have passed, and indeed owing to William IV's insurmountable objection to Radical Reform could never even have been introduced. The King, the two Houses of Parliament,[1] and the middle classes would have been united against it. Right or wrong, it was then as unattainable as O'Connell's Repeal of the Union.

Secondly, it has been argued by more conservative temperaments like Peel, Disraeli, and Bagehot that there ought to have been no uniform suffrage at all, but a variety of different franchises. It was plausibly and honestly argued by Peel in 1831 that it was a grave evil to abolish the working-class electorate in Preston and Westminster in favour of the £10 householder ; that the new franchise should have been made to vary from place to place, democratic here, middle-class there, aristocratic or ' borough-mongering ' elsewhere. This doctrine still finds advocates. England, it is argued, should have been represented by her different classes, instead of being swamped first by a middle class, and thirty-five years later by a lower class electorate. If, it is argued, the working men had not felt themselves excluded from the new constitution in 1832 by an uniform middle-class franchise, they would never have been able in 1867 to obtain an uniform franchise for their own benefit.[2]

Now it is perfectly true that the uniform middle-

---

[1] The same House of Commons that passed the Reform Bill by 367 votes to 231 rejected Hunt's motion to enfranchise all householders paying rates and taxes by 123 votes to one vote.

[2] Bagehot, *Biographical Studies, Lord Althorp*, pp. 309-11, ed. 1889.

class franchise in 1832 led to the uniform household franchise in 1867. But democrats think that the uniform household franchise of 1867 was a good thing. Intelligent Radical leaders like Place, and the working-class electorate of Westminster whose sons were to have no votes under the First Reform Bill, welcomed the uniform middle-class franchise partly because they foresaw that it must lead in the end to an uniform working-class franchise.[1] These Radicals preached, not in vain, that it was the best tactics for the working class to get the Bill as it stood passed at once into law.

But even those who think that the uniform franchises of 1832, 1867, 1884, and 1917 have been a series of misfortunes, or at least of chances of perfection let slip owing to the original error of 1831, must answer the question which Grey and the Committee of Four had to ask themselves—how can the establishment of 'fancy' and 'variety' franchises be defended in the House and in the country? How, the Whig statesmen may well have thought, can we confiscate vast masses of property purchased or inherited, and then turn round and create at our own whim and fancy new private privileges, picking here and choosing there which rotten boroughs are to survive, which towns shall have household suffrage, which shall have a £10, a £20 or an educational franchise? Unless we have one rule to apply to all cases, the charge of 'cooking' in the Whig interest will be unanswerable. Our Bill will be hooted down if we propose to make a great revolution on any save an uniform basis. And Grey, whose object was to 'put the question at rest,' may well have thought that, even if it were possible to pass so arbitrary and whimsical a measure,

---

[1] Existing life-interests of voters were preserved under the Bill. 'Burdett and I thought our Westminster friends would oppose the £10 qualification clause ; but we were wrong, for we found all our supporters delighted with the Bill' (*Hobhouse,* iv. 88). Some of the most rotten boroughs had nominally a democratic franchise, as Gatton, where ' the right is popular, but there is nobody to exercise it.'

the question would be raised again in a year by every town that envied the franchise of its neighbour. Granted, then, that it was necéssary to fix an uniform franchise for all the boroughs, what was the standard to be ? The first decision of the Committee of Four was that which was finally adopted, in favour of householders rated at £10. But on second thoughts, at Durham's suggestion and against Russell's wish, they inserted the Radical panacea of election by ballot, and as a make-weight altered the more popular £10 franchise to the more exclusive £20. Durham, who was closely in touch with outside opinion, believed that the ballot was so generally demanded by Reformers, that it must be included at any price to ensure Radical support for the Bill. But the price he proposed was too high ; the £20 householders would have formed an oligarchy scarcely requiring the protection of the ballot. However, when the Committee's draft bill went up to the Cabinet in the middle of January, it contained the ballot and the £20 franchise. Grey and most of the Cabinet objected to the ballot, which was at once struck out. And after a month's uncertainty the more popular £10 franchise was restored. Russell, who was to introduce the Bill, produced at the last moment fresh calculations showing that the £20 franchise would yield a much more restricted electorate than the Cabinet ever intended to create ; it would make so many new ' rotten boroughs.' Durham, Althorp, and Brougham were also strong advocates of the broader franchise, which was re-adopted just in time. Ten pounds and no ballot was after all the best policy, for the King declared that he would never have agreed to the ballot, and the people would never have been content with the twenty pounds.[1]

---

[1] Appendix E, below. Durham and Brougham would both have liked household suffrage, but knew it to be impossible (*Brougham*, iii. 92, 523). Durham to Grey (MS.), October 11, 1831, ' In *my own* opinion *all* householders ought to vote, whether paying £10 or 10 shillings.'

Even the £10 franchise was none too generous ; it did not include the whole middle class. In the interest of democratic unity and progress this was, perhaps, a blessing in disguise, for if all the shopkeepers and clerks in the country had been given votes in 1832, it would have been impossible for Bright and Gladstone in days to come to get them to unite with the working class in support of household suffrage. It was as well, therefore, that the *bourgeoisie*, when they got over their first delirious delight, found that they still had grievances under the Bill. Only half of them had votes ; and the redistribution of seats, enormous as it had been, was yet far from being complete, or just to the middle class. Though ' nomination ' boroughs were all gone, there were many small, corrupt boroughs left over which the neighbouring gentry could exert great influence. The old borough-mongering oligarchy disappeared in 1832, but the landed gentry as a whole were the governing class until 1846, and even after the repeal of the Corn Laws they had immense power until the Reform Act of 1867. John Bright, in agitating for household suffrage in the 'sixties, thus summed up the electoral position :

The working men are almost universally excluded, roughly and insolently, from political power ; and the middle class, whilst they have the semblance of it, are defrauded of the reality.[1]

Bright used always to say of the First Reform Bill : ' It was not a good Bill, but it was a great Bill when it passed.' It was a great Bill because it passed—and by passing put an end to Burke's doctrine that the British constitution could not be altered with the changing years. A more perfect Bill, such as the experience of our later age could, doubtless, dictate, would have failed to pass in 1832, and its rejection would sooner or later have been followed by a civil war.

[1] Trevelyan's *Bright*, 365.

Such was the general character of the ' new constitution,' drawn up in three separate but similar Bills for England, Scotland, and Ireland. Duncannon, who was a Ponsonby and a friend of Dan O'Connell, advised about the details for Ireland ; the Reform Bills pleased O'Connell when they appeared, and in spite of the Whig Government in Ireland having begun a prosecution against him in January, he generously lent Reform the indispensable support of his Irish votes in the Commons.

If ever an Act of Parliament saved a country from revolution, Scotland was so saved by the Reform Bill. Although in temper, creed, and outlook on life the people were less submissive than the English, the civil institutions of the country contained in 1830 no single element of self-government. Scottish democracy had been nursed in the Kirk and in the Kirk alone ; and in the new age the Kirk no longer sufficed to contain so strong a spirit. There was not even local self-government : all town councils were self-elected, and the Scottish Burgh Act of 1833, which remedied this state of things, was regarded in Scotland as second in importance only to the Reform Bill itself. As to Parliamentary representation, whereas in England the elections for most of the counties and a few of the boroughs were real popular contests, the meagre handful of forty-five representatives that Scotland sent to Westminster were without exception chosen by small groups of privileged persons, generally sitting round a table. The total Scottish electorate was under 4000.[1] At the first

[1] Jeffrey to Grey, Sept. 27, 1831 : ' The total number of freeholders on the rolls for 33 counties of Scotland is 3255. But of these not less than 700 or so are enrolled in two or three or four different counties, so that the total number of individuals is not more than about 2500. Of these more than half are mere *Superiority* voters, with *no property* in the country. In the Burghs, 66 in number, the only electors are the magistrates, who annually re-elect each other without any control from the inhabitants. Their whole number is about 1440.' Whereas in

Edinburgh election after the Reform Act 'people stared at the very sight of the hustings, all from curiosity, many with delight, some with unaffected horror. This was the first time the people had ever exercised the elective franchise.'[1]

The man whom Grey had selected to preside over Scotland during the dangerous period of transition into the new era was the man who had done most to prepare the change in evil days gone by, Jeffrey, the editor of the *Edinburgh Review*. He was the new Lord Advocate, the post then roughly answering to that of Secretary for Scotland to-day. He drafted the Scottish Bill in February, after his colleague and future biographer Cockburn, the new Solicitor-General for Scotland, had spent much of December and January in London discussing the principles of the new Bill with Grey, Brougham, and the Committee of Four.[2]

In the last half of January 1831 the Cabinet discussed the proposals of the Committee of Four. Except for the ballot, there was singularly little opposition to the principles of the Bill, once Brougham's incipient rebellion against the total abolition of rotten boroughs

England each county and borough returned two members, in Scotland nearly all the shires returned one each, and burghs were grouped together to return one member for each group. For details of old Scottish representation, see *Political State of Scotland* in 1788, by C. A. Adam, 1887, and Porritt, *The Unreformed House of Commons*.

[1] Cockburn's *Jeffrey*, i, 318, 339.

[2] This is proved by the (MS.) correspondence of Jeffrey and Grey from December to February. We there learn that Jeffrey also went to see Brougham on the subject of the Scotch Bill, at Brougham Hall, in Cumberland, in the middle of January. Finally, on February 20, Jeffrey writes to Grey: 'I have now the honour of submitting to your Lordship a very rough draft of the Bill referring to the Parliamentary Representation of Scotland. The unseemly form in which it is sent can only be excused by the desertion of the only *amanuensis* in whom I could perfectly confide before I made my last additions.'

had been firmly suppressed by Grey.[1] Palmerston, Lansdowne, and Richmond, the chiefs of the ' moderate ' party, seem to have grumbled more against the Bill after it had been brought before the public, than during these preliminary counsels in the secrecy of the Cabinet. Like the King, they were persuaded by Grey, who had great influence over them all, to regard it as a conservative measure designed to save the threatened constitution and to put the question to rest. And like the King they were only gradually aroused to the enormity of what they were doing, by the unappeasable fury of the borough-mongers after the provisions of the Bill became known. At any rate it was only in April that Palmerston began appealing to Grey to modify the disfranchisement clauses.[2]

To prevent a premature outburst of Tory rage from frightening the King and the moderates in the Cabinet before they were irretrievably committed, was one of many grave reasons for secrecy during this critical period, and it is to the credit of all concerned how well the secret was kept to the very last day. Several of the ' Grey ladies ' were made partners in the secret as amanuenses, to prevent the employment of clerks. Durham's wife and eldest daughter had helped to

---

[1] On January 24 Grey writes to Durham, then too ill to attend Cabinets : ' I find from Althorp that there is likely to be more difficulty than I thought about Reform. Upon his saying to Brougham that he was glad to find there was so great a concurrence of opinion, he answered that he had great objection to the abolition of the close boroughs ; that they were by no means the worst parts of the representation ; that there would be no means for getting seats for persons in the Government, etc. ; he had hinted at this in the general discussion, but I thought had been satisfied by my answer, that whatever the inconveniences might be these boroughs could not be maintained. On this point I cannot give way. If he perseveres, he may throw us over with the King.'

[2] Correspondence (MS.) between Palmerston and Grey, April–May, 1831. Durham's letters to Grey, 1831–2, also show that Lansdowne and Richmond constantly exerted a similar pressure. But Grey was always adamant against modification.

make copies of the report of the Committee of Four.[1]

After the Bill had run the gauntlet of the Cabinet, Grey went down to Brighton on Sunday the 30th of January to unfold the measure to the King. It was potentially the most critical day in the whole history of Reform, for a refusal on the King's part to agree on some vital point must have led to a crisis, at a time when neither the Government nor their Bill had yet attained the consistency and popularity required if a crisis was to be faced. The resignation of the whole Cabinet, shaken by simultaneous failure on other questions, or a split between Brougham and the moderates on one side and Grey, Althorp, and Durham on the other, might easily have occurred if the King had exercised his admitted right of preliminary veto on the Bill. As it was, all went well. But he wrote to Grey four days later that if the ballot or universal suffrage had been in the Bill he would have refused permission to bring it in—a prohibition which Grey acknowledged as ' a command he was bound to obey.' [2] Such was then the custom of the constitution.

It is probable that Grey would have failed if it had been necessary for him to obtain the King's consent to the Bill in the previous November. William had been much attached to Wellington, and his first sentiments towards his new Ministers had been those of misgiving.[3] But in a few weeks he had been won round to an equally sincere confidence in Grey.[4] As their long correspondence shows, Grey was at infinite pains, without ever a touch of sycophancy, to conciliate his royal master by unfailing courtesy and attention, which, coming from so imposing a nobleman, notorious for his independence in relation to previous sovereigns of great fame, was

---

[1] *Althorp*, 296, note.
[2] *William's Correspondence*, i. 96–7, 106.
[3] See p. 378, below.
[4] *E.g.* letter of Jan. 12, 1831, *William's Correspondence*, i. 47.

flattering to one who was, by nature and experience of life, only a retired Admiral.

William was more easily courted, because his theory of constitutional propriety, the opposite of that of his father and brother before him, forbade him to listen to Tory advisers and favourites, so long as he had a Whig ministry. Even the Queen, who disliked the Whigs and was not over civil to the Grey ladies, was not at first permitted to talk politics to her husband. This new reading of the constitutional duty of the sovereign to his Ministers was fostered in the King's mind by his private secretary Sir Herbert Taylor, a man of no political prejudices and great political instinct, to whom the British constitution owes much of its development along the paths of peace.[1]

The King was prepared to hold the balance between Whigs and Tories, so long as each according to their rival methods helped him to defeat the ' extravagant and mischievous projects ' of the Radicals. His fixed idea that the Radicals wished to overset the throne, which made him suspect and dislike the uncompromising Durham in a manner only too apparent, was turned by Grey's more skilful management to the advantage of the Liberal cause. The Prime Minister persuaded the King that only a large measure of Reform could save the institutions of the country, especially the throne, from Radical assault. Ninety years have shown the substantial truth of this view, as contrasted with the Tory prophecy that if the Bill passed there would soon be ' No King, no Lords, no inequalities in the social system ; all will be levelled to the plane of petty shopkeepers and farmers; this not perhaps without bloodshed, but certainly by confiscations and persecutions.' [2] When the King called

---

[1] Taylor said to Denis Le Marchant : ' I should have opposed the Bill in every stage had I remained in the House of Commons.   But I see that it is for the King's interest that it should be carried, and I have done my best to assist the Ministers accordingly ' (*Althorp*, 434).

[2] *Croker* (ii. 113) to Sir Walter Scott, April 5, 1831.

the Bill ' an aristocratical measure,' [1] the Tories laughed bitterly and accused Grey of playing upon his simplicity. Yet in persuading the King that the Bill would save the throne and the aristocracy and prevent bloodshed, Grey spoke his own honest belief, which turned out to be correct.

There was, however, one aspect of the Bill which the King entirely misunderstood. He did not foresee that the ' aristocratical measure ' would be regarded as confiscation and revolution by the class and type of men with whom he himself had most natural affinity ; still less that it would lead to a conflict between the two Houses of Parliament in which the People, whose inter-ference he dreaded and deprecated, would finally thrust him aside from the post of umpire and act in that usurped authority with an extreme vigour. Yet even on this point Grey did not deceive him. The King was deceived by his own simplicity and did not raise the question until it was too late.

And so, on the anniversary of the execution of Charles I, his so different successor consented to ' the Bill, the whole Bill, and nothing but the Bill.' [2] Next day Grey wrote to his wife from Brighton :

Immediately after my arrival I had my interview with the King. Nothing could be more satisfactory than the result. He has approved of everything ; and we now can propose our Reform with the full concurrence both of the Cabinet and the King.

[1] Parker's *Peel*, ii. 178.
[2] Grey's letters printed in Brougham's *Memoirs*, iii. 93, and *William's Correspondence*, i. 91, prove that the long, decisive interview took place late on Sunday, January 30. But Grey apparently saw the King again on the subject of the Bill, handing in documents, on January 31, unless that date in *William's Correspondence*, i. 94, is an error for January 30. The King appears in these interviews to have given provisional assent to the substitution of the £10 for the £20 borough franchise, which Grey appears to have warned him might have to be done, and which was done more than a fortnight later. See p. 271, above, and *William's Correspondence*, i. 111.

The month of February had still to roll away, bringing with it every sort of failure in Parliament and the country, while the popularity and prestige of the Ministry decreased daily.[1] But Grey's spirits remained buoyant and serene, for he knew that he had a panacea for all these minor troubles. He had cut out, in front of his party's march, a clear path through that Reform jungle in which both friend and foe had expected to see him miserably entangled. Men who had known him too well as the hesitating and pessimistic leader of opposition, always trying to avoid responsibility and action, could not believe that he had stepped quietly forward and plucked the flower safety from the nettle danger. The Tories, wholly unconscious of their own impending doom, were almost sorry for 'poor Lord Grey.' Croker wrote to Lord Hertford that the Reform plan of the Cabinet was ' members to half a dozen great towns,' and to Wellington that ' our successors are at loggerheads, not on one, but on every measure. It is expected that we shall be sent for. Poor Lord Grey is, they say, harassed to death.' On February 20 the opposition leaders met at Peel's house, and decided to allow the not very terrible Reform Bill that they expected, ' to make its first appearance without serious resistance,' that is, not to divide on the First Reading, which Lord John Russell was to move on Tuesday, March the First.[2]

---

[1] See pp. 255–7, above.   [2] *Croker Papers*, ii. 97, 103, 108.

CHAPTER III

THE STRUGGLE FOR THE BILL—KING, COMMONS, AND
PEOPLE—MARCH TO OCTOBER 1831

' Never before were the Whigs bold, or the Reformers prudent.'—
HOBHOUSE, iv. 92.

BETWEEN the Strangers' Entrance to the present House
of Commons and the Central Lobby, men quicken
their pace to run the gauntlet of two opposing rows of
marble orators, who still gesticulate against each other
unappeased, across the floor of the passage. That passage represents in situation and dimensions St. Stephen's
Chapel, the old House of Commons and its lobby, on
the foundations of which it was rebuilt after the fire of
1834. Though not the very cradle, it has been the
nursery and schoolroom of Parliamentary government.
Pent in that narrow measure were the whole wisdom and
wrath of the Long Parliament. And there, as the last
great drama in the history of the Chamber before it
was destroyed by fire, the Reform Bill won its way,
through storms of passion which but for Grey's insight,
act, and courage might well have been the prelude to
a second Civil War.

Of the members who thronged to hear Russell
introduce the Bill on March 1, 1831, not more than
two in three could find seats by cunning or by force.
That ill-ventilated, ill-lighted, uncomfortable, sacred
room, affectionately compared by its victims to ' the
black hole of Calcutta,' had never witnessed a more
anxious and uncertain moment in history than when

Lord John's head was seen to emerge above the table, and his cool, small voice began to drop out bit by bit the fateful secret, so well kept to the very last hour. As he proceeded, the more advanced Whigs and the small Radical group known as ' the mountain,' of which Burdett and Hobhouse were the chiefs, cheered louder and louder in amazed delight. The Tories laughed and cheered in derision. The great mass of the Whigs sat rather quiet, not knowing yet what to think of such a sudden turn of affairs. Russell had announced in general terms that sixty English rotten boroughs were to lose their two members apiece ; and forty-seven more, one member each. Having finished with England, he was about to pass on to Wales, Scotland, and Ireland, when ' an honourable member called on him to name the disfranchised boroughs.' Thus challenged, he read the lists. And so, as an afterthought or chance of the debate, befell the most famous scene of all ; the particular is more poignant than the general, and it was only when the names of the doomed boroughs were read out that the meaning of the great change was felt by all. The members whose seats were marked for the sacrifice lay back and laughed in bitter contempt as ' a little fellow not weighing above eight stone '[1] swept away one by one the venerable legacies of 500 years.

It was thought by many, that night and ever after, that if Peel had risen when Lord John sat down, and had declared that the measure was a revolution and that he would at once divide the House against its being read for a first time, the Bill would have been defeated and the Ministers turned out, before the unpopularity which their various failures had won for them in the first three

---

[1] Two months later Sydney Smith wrote to Lady Holland : ' I met John Russell at Exeter. The people along the road were very much disappointed by his smallness. I told them he was much larger before the Bill was thrown out, but was reduced by excessive anxiety about the people. This brought tears to their eyes.'

months of office had been converted into the enormous popularity which the Bill brought them as soon as it was made known to the nation. But the Tory leaders, expecting to the last a very moderate measure, had come to the House agreed among themselves to allow the first reading.[1] Peel was by nature incapable of sudden decisions and lightning strokes. Neither was he, with his solemn manner and secretive temperament, in close personal touch with any section of the divided Tory party, which only gradually came together as the months went by under the compelling force of the Reform Bill.

As far as the wishes of that House of Commons were concerned, the life of the Ministry would not have been worth a week's purchase. But outside, the people took up the Bill with a shout. From Land's End to John o' Groat's, as fast as the coaches brought in the news of Lord John's speech, all was astonishment and rejoicing. Petitions from municipal bodies, and from the inhabitants of cities, parishes, and rural districts began to pour in to Westminster, in support of the Bill ; no member could walk the streets or receive letters from the country without reading clear proof of its amazing popularity. In the course of a week, many a Whig member like Campbell, who had been appalled as he listened to Lord John, saw that after all his chiefs had made a *coup*, and became himself inspired with the infectious breath of the popular enthusiasm.

The first full expression of the national purpose, with its threat scarcely veiled in the appeal to the conservative forces to avoid revolution by surrender, was uttered as early as the second day of the debate by an unofficial member, Macaulay of the *Edinburgh Review*,

---

[1] *Croker*, ii. 108, 110. Wellington wrote : ' We had previously determined not to oppose the first reading, and we could not alter our course after the measure was produced. But if we had known what the measure would be, we should have opposed it ; and our opposition would have been successful ' (*Despatches*, etc., viii. 293).

CROKER   PEEL   WETHERELL (speaking)
O'CONNELL, HUME (on third bench against the pillars)

The Bill in Committee.   Wetherell speaking in the
small hours of the morning.

From " H.B." Political Sketches.

whose oratory now first made its mark in the House.[1]

To divert the torrent of popular approval, it served little for Peel on the following night to enter a nice plea against abolishing the working-class representation at a few places like Preston and Westminster, while he stultified his argument by declaring against any increase of that representation, which alone could have made it effectual. Peel's whole later life showed that he should have been for the Bill. Unconsciously he was in a false position ; furious with the Ministers, but on ill terms with his party and with himself, he remained throughout the long struggle a respectable but not very effectual figure.

The men who best represented before the world the deep and genuine passions of the defence, were Wetherell in the Commons and Wellington in the Lords. Already, in the first week of the debate, Wetherell with his uncouth figure, wild gestures and grimaces, fierce, humorous invective, prolixity in obstructive tactics, legal astuteness in detail, and utter sincerity of belief that old England was being destroyed by fools and knaves, stood to friend and foe for the core of old oak in the Tory resistance. The famous gap between Wetherell's jacket and trousers became the oriflamme of war. But the silent Duke, with his House of Lords' vote held in reserve, was in fact a more formidable bulwark, for it was not in argument or even in passion, but in constitutional privilege that the opposition to the Bill was strong.

The fury of the Tories was directed against Grey. He had deceived them. They had confidently looked to ' poor Lord Grey ' to bring in a mild measure that would enrage the Radicals, divide his followers, and bring about his fall, or possibly, as some of them wished,

[1] So little known was he as a politician till the Reform Bill debates, that Hansard consistently spells his name wrong (Macauley) until August 1831.

his coalition with themselves. He had, instead, introduced a measure that was in effect an appeal to the people to strengthen his hand against both Houses of Parliament, and the appeal was proving successful. And this from the man who had a few years before declared in the House of Lords that he would ' stand by his order ' ! The words were now cast in his teeth. His idea of ' standing by his order ' was, indeed, not theirs. His plan was to save their estates in the country and their seats in the Upper Chamber, by wresting from them the irregular privilege of nominating members to the House of Commons. ' It seems,' he wrote of the Tory peers on March 20, ' as if God has deprived these men of their understanding. If they could succeed, they would ensure their destruction.'

A story became current that a headless man—some said one of Grey's own ancestors, beheaded for high treason, others said a Girondin victim of the guillotine—had appeared to the Prime Minister to warn him of the fate of those who stir up revolution. Caricaturists played on the theme, and it became the talk of the town. The substratum of fact lay in this, that, half a dozen years before, in a house he then inhabited in Hanover Square, Grey thought he saw ' a pale face look at him round a column,' and ' imagining it to be a person, he rushed to the place and then sought behind all the window curtains in that and the adjacent rooms without success.' The family appears to have rejected the supernatural hypothesis.[1]

When the first night's debate in the Commons had passed without catastrophe, Grey was well pleased

---

[1] Sir T. Dick Lauder's letter of Nov. 20, 1837 (*Howick Papers*), narrating what Grey had told him that day. Further details as to his daughter, Lady Georgiana Grey, having seen ' somebody in the room ' a few days before her father's adventure, are narrated on the same authority, and are confirmed by Lady Georgiana's own letter to the present Lord Halifax in 1894. Lady Georgiana in 1894 connects the incidents with a servant ' soon afterwards dismissed for stealing.'

with the reception of the Bill. ' I saw Lord Grey,' wrote Princess Lieven on March 2, ' when the first report of what had passed in the House was brought to him. He believed, or said he did, that it was a great triumph, and repeated with self-satisfaction : *" I have kept my word with the nation."* '

On March 4, only three days after Lord John's speech, he already saw that the Bill had had the effects that he intended. ' The public,' he wrote on that day to Lord Wellesley, ' is now completely with us, and the first effect of what we have done has been to set aside, at once, all the clamour for Universal Suffrage, annual Parliament and Ballot.'

Grey's belief that the cry for Universal Suffrage had been silenced by the Bill was true as regards the middle-class Radicals, but it was only partially true of the working men. They were divided between the instinct to support the Bill as the first ' great inroad in the accursed system,'[1] and the instinct to demand instead a measure that would enfranchise themselves and not the middle class alone. When in October the Lords threw out the Bill, their fury against aristocratic dictation brought them down effectively into the political arena. But in the first half-year of the controversy, many working men stood apart, viewing the Bill as a middle-class affair.

On the other hand, their ablest and most popular leaders and organisers were from the first moment active on behalf of the Bill, and succeeded in creating early an apparent, and ultimately a real, alliance of the middle and working classes. That alliance proved the most persuasive argument for the Bill with the higher powers, because it threatened revolution or radical reform as the alternative.

Cobbett was a Bill-man heart and soul. Though the Government still persisted in its vain and foolish

---

[1] Hunt, in the House of Commons, April 12, 1831 ; a speech well worth studying for some aspects of working-class feeling about the Bill.

resolution to prosecute him,[1] he wrote in his *Twopenny Trash* for April some generous words about Lord Grey as ' the real and sole author of this Reform, who has never had any hand in any of those measures which have caused our sufferings.' It was now indeed that Grey's long forty years at opposition gained him the popular confidence that nothing else could have given, and without which the State might well have suffered shipwreck.

Equally important with Cobbett's, though less in the public eye, were the influence and work of Francis Place, who from his library in Charing Cross had long directed the more reasonable part of the Radical propaganda throughout all England, and who was equally esteemed by middle and working class progressives. The unexpected events of March 1 had converted him in an hour from lifelong and bitter contempt for the ' gabbling Whigs,' to an ardent zeal for co-operation with his ancient enemies. He and Attwood of the Birmingham Political Union now placed the best Radical organisations of the country at the services of the Ministers and their measure. Hobhouse and Burdett, the ' gentlemen Radicals,' strong Government-men since March 1, formed the link between the plans of Ministers and the activities of Attwood and Place.

The avoidance of civil strife during the struggle for the Bill, and perhaps therefore the issue of the contest, depended much on the wisdom of the Home Secretary, Melbourne. Personally, he disliked the measure, but he thought the national demand for it would not be denied, and he supported it as a loyal member of a Government dependent on its success.[2] In the interests of the Bill and of public order he did not disdain to consult frequently with Place and Attwood through the medium of his secret agent, the mysterious Tom Young. Anti-democratic as he was at heart, and as he had shown himself in dealing with the rural labourers the last

---

[1] See p. 254, above.
[2] *Melbourne Papers*, 140; *Greville*, April 1, 1832.

winter,[1] Melbourne was shrewd enough, so long as the Reform Bill was the question of the day, to seek the advice of the men who led the democracy, to guide his administrative dealings with the Political Unions and with the Radical movement in general.[2]

The greatest vigour and active support for the Bill from beginning to end came from the middle class— a term that then covered all grades of society, from the humblest clerk or village shopkeeper up to the wealthiest monied magnate in the country. The master manufacturers were as yet seldom allied by matrimonial, social, or political ties with the aristocracy and the 'landed interest.' The law did not allow them to shoot game ; they were not invited to the country houses ; and very few of their class could obtain seats in Parliament. They regarded the 'landed interest' with something of the jealousy that the French capitalists in 1789 felt for the privileged *noblesse* ; and the distaste was mutual.

But most of all the multitudinous lower middle class, the world of Cruikshank and of Dickens, was stirred like the ocean by the attraction of the Bill, and by all that the ten-pound franchise seemed to offer. The agitation as conducted by Attwood, at once moral, orderly, and enthusiastic, brought the colour of romance and idealism into the drab surroundings of their lives. The fervour of their revivalist religion, and something more from sunnier skies, was heard in the Reform Bill song which they sang in their tens of thousands :

> See, see, we come ! no swords we draw,
> We kindle not war's battle-fires.
> By union, justice, reason, law,
> We'll gain the birthright of our sires.
> And thus we raise from sea to sea
> Our sacred watchword, Liberty !

Even the squires were perhaps half of them for the

[1] See pp. 252–3, above.
[2] Wallas' *Place*, chaps. ix.–xi. ; and *Place Papers*, B.M. ; Torrens' *Melbourne*, i. 368, 385–6.

Bill, though with less enthusiasm and with many misgivings. Not a few country gentlemen, Whigs by old allegiance, were ready to ' trust Lord Grey ' and hoped to beat their Tory neighbours at the next election ; others wisely dreaded revolution or radical reform as the only alternative to the Bill ; all were to some extent consoled by the increase in county representation, in place of rotten boroughs in which they had no personal interest. And when in August 1831 the Government was compelled by an adverse majority of squires in the Whig House of Commons to extend the county franchise to tenants-at-will at £50 a year,[1] it was felt that the gentry would always be able, by their influence with these tenants, to carry the rural seats. And in fact the ' landed interest ' conducted the Government until 1846, when the ten-pound householder revolted and repealed the Corn Laws.

And so we read of ' half the country gentry ' of Lincolnshire attending a meeting in favour of the Bill.[2] Peel himself wrote dolefully to Croker on the difficulty of ' bringing round the country gentlemen ' to see the dangers lurking in the measure ; [3] while in Grey's opinion ' a very large majority' of the gentry supported it in October.[4] Even the leaders of this class, the lay peers in the Upper House, were not so unevenly divided. There was indeed a large majority among the old nobility in favour of the Bill, and it was only the recent partisan creations by Pitt and his successors, many of them the price of rotten boroughs, which, added to the Bishops' vote, led the country to the brink of civil war.

---

[1] This was the famous ' Chandos clause.' Ministers were beaten in resisting it, by 84, at a time when they had a majority for the Bill as a whole at 136. So strong was the ' landed interest ' among the Whig members who passed the Reform Bill. Before the Reform Bill the county franchise had been confined to ' forty-shilling *freeholders*,' largely independent of the squires.

[2] Sir Robert Heron's *Notes*, p. 193.

[3] *Croker*, ii. 137 (Nov. 11, 1831).

[4] *William's Correspondence*, i. 376.

Upon the whole, the conduct of the country gentry, great and small, at this national crisis, when they supplied most of the leadership to both sides, was a credit to their patriotism, good sense, and power of vision.

The farmers, like the squires above them, were divided on the Bill. Tory broadsheets warned them that Reform would bring in its train Repeal of the Corn Laws,[1] but the appeal was only in part successful. Probably it was not very generally believed, for the Prime Minister and the majority of his Cabinet were against Repeal.

There was but one class opposed to the Bill with anything like unanimity—the clergy of the Church of England. On both sides of the Reform Bill controversy, sectarian zeal played almost as much part as social and political feeling. It was generally expected that Reform of Parliament would, if carried, lead to a revision of all ecclesiastical privileges—Church rates, the Church monopoly of Oxford and Cambridge, perhaps tithes, and possibly the establishment itself. In the anti-Jacobin days, when the upper and middle classes and most of the working men—pre-eminently the mobs of Birmingham and Manchester—had been violently against Reform, the Dissenters had fought and fallen under the banners of Fox and Grey.[2] And though in 1831 the issue seemed to many Englishmen to have

---

[1] E.g. *Reform and the Farmers*, 1831 :

'A farmer would Reforming go,
Whether he got any good or no.
The House was reformed, and it took a shy
At the price of corn, which it thought too high.
The very worst day since the farmer was born
Was the day they voted Free Trade in corn.'

Moral.

'A Reforming farmer, as sure as a gun,
Cannot care a pin for *Number One* ! '

[2] See pp. 33–7, above.

changed, the Church clergy thought, not unreasonably, that it was still exactly the same. The Church in those days leant heavily on the secular arm for the support which in our time she seeks in her own legitimate influence. She had, to a very large extent, left the population of the new industrial districts to dissent, to anti-clerical secularism, and to an ignorance more debased than any form of belief or unbelief. And even in the old country parishes, where the Church was then seen at her best, Miss Austen's charming clergy, though often scholars and always gentlemen, were only the squires' younger sons put into the family livings, in no marked way devoted either to their sacred calling or to their humbler parishioners. The Church had very largely lost her former hold on the masses. Men thought that she took too much and gave too little.

Conscious of their alienation from the multitude, the clergy sought to dig themselves in against the flood-tide of the coming era by perpetuating the old Tory régime. The 'parson magistrate' was often a fierce partisan, and his victims caricatured him savagely. The fact that it was a clergyman who read the Riot Act before the Yeomanry charged the Reformers' meeting at Peterloo had not been forgotten a dozen years later. Some of the priesthood had earned only too well their popular title of 'black dragoons.'[1] The distribution of the revenues of the Church among the clergy themselves, in those days notoriously unfair, was denounced by Radicals attacking 'Old Corruption,' and by farmers grumbling that their tithes went to feed idle mouths. The Dissenters, forced to contribute in the Church

---

[1] ' A parson magistrate wrote to the Home Office in 1817 to say that he had seized two men who were distributing Cobbett's pamphlets and had them well flogged. . . . A man caught taking a peepshow round the country containing a coloured print of Peterloo, who fell into the hands of the Vicar of Chudleigh, got off more lightly, being sent to the House of Correction as a vagrant till the Sessions' (Hammond, *Town Labourer*, 72; see also *id*. pp. 262, 268–9).

rates to the upkeep of fabrics where they and all their works were denounced, and excluded from Oxford and Cambridge, looked to Reform to remedy these inequalities, and more generally to give them a direct share in the councils of the nation. The part taken by Dissenting ministers in political agitation for the Bill aroused the scornful alarm of the class that had so long monopolised power. One of the Duke of Wellington's correspondents writes to him from Chelsea :

The address was voted to be presented to Lord Grey, for offering it to the King, by two *Dissenting, as they call them,* clergymen—one named Tracey, or Stacey, who afterwards exhibited from a cart to harangue the people, and who keeps, or is kept by, a small Anabaptist chapel in a shabby, mean street which runs out of Paradise Row.[1]

Nearly all Dissenters were now Reformers ; but, though Toryism was the rule among the Church clergy, it was no longer general with their congregations, who in some cases walked out of church rather than listen to a sermon against the Bill.

On March 22, 1831, the Second Reading of the Bill was carried in the Commons by one vote, amid scenes of excitement and enthusiasm best known to posterity from Macaulay's letter to his friend Ellis.[2]

Thirty members for rotten boroughs in Schedule A had voted for their own total disfranchisement, and eighty against it. The members for boroughs in Schedule B, to be half-disfranchised, had divided thirty-two for the Bill and fifty-two against. So numerous were the Whig rotten boroughs willingly sacrificed to their patrons' sense of what was patriotic and just.

Ireland had carried the Bill. Her members had voted fifty-eight for and thirty-eight against. While

[1] *Wellington Despatches,* viii. 47.
[2] Trevelyan's *Macaulay,* chap. iv.

the Ministry was prosecuting O'Connell in Ireland, O'Connell was saving the Ministry in England. The real sympathy and understanding which Grey had shown for Ireland in years gone by, when he had been powerless to help, had now become atrophied. He who had refused office again and again as a protest in favour of Catholic Emancipation, now stood in the way of any further step in the reconciling process. His Irish clock had stopped in 1829. In forming his administration in November 1830 he had not consulted O'Connell, directly or indirectly, about Ireland. He now took his views from Stanley rather than from Duncannon and Burdett, who were plying him with letters on the need of dropping the prosecution against O'Connell, and of a closer understanding with the Liberator for the sake both of Irish tranquillity and English Reform. To Burdett, Grey replied :

> I acknowledge that O'Connell has rendered good service on the Reform Bill ; but his measures to incite in the people of Ireland a spirit of the bitterest hostility, not only to the Government, but to the people of England, the Saxons, as he calls them, have always succeeded, as in a regular course, to his more moderate conduct in Parliament (April 3, 1831).

Yet in fact, O'Connell's whole influence in the ensuing months was used on the side of tranquillity in Ireland, as the Lord-Lieutenant himself acknowledged. Finally, all that the Government would do was just not to put in prison the man who could, with a word, have defeated their Bill and turned out their administration.

Grey depended on O'Connell not only for his majority, but for the peace of Ireland, with which the fortunes of the Bill were closely involved. In March and April the Prime Minister was working patiently, and at first unsuccessfully, to prepare the King's mind to dissolve Parliament. One of the chief reasons that induced the King for several weeks to refuse to have a General Election was the fear that it would lead to grave disorders in Ireland. ·And if O'Connell had, in fact, been playing the Whigs false, such fears would not have been groundless. Fortunately, the majority of one for the Second Reading weighed in the King's evenly balanced mind as an argument for appealing to the constituencies on the Bill, rather than change his Ministers. If the majority of one had been the other way, it is almost certain that he would have refused to dissolve ; Grey would then have resigned, and the crisis that finally came in May 1832 would have come a year earlier, under conditions even more dangerous for peace and progress, since the people would then have been confronted not only by King and Lords, but also by a small majority of the House of Commons, who might have enabled a Tory Ministry to be formed with at least some chance of continuance.[1]

For a month Grey kept on plying the King with conservative arguments for dissolution :

The excitement that now exists is directed to what I think a safe and legitimate object. In the event of dissolution, it would act in support of King and Government. If a contrary direction is given to it, you probably will see associations all over the country.

He also appealed to the King's sense of fair play, pointing out :

That this Government is now without its natural support, the Parliament having been chosen by the late Ministers, and all the seats usually at the command of the Ministers being now filled by their bitterest opponents.

Grey knew exactly how to treat William IV, and took infinite pains about it. It was fortunate that it fell to him, out of all the Cabinet, to conduct the correspondence and the interviews with their Royal Master.

[1] *William's Correspondence,* i. 176, 183, note.

On April 19, 1831, the crisis came. The Government was defeated by eight votes in a very full house, on General Gascoyne's plausible amendment that the number of members for England and Wales should not be reduced.[1] Grey's long preparation of the King's mind now bore better fruit than he had himself expected. He had thought to be out of office as a result of the King's refusal to dissolve,[2] but on April 21 William wrote to him that, to prevent the threatened resignation of his Ministers, ' he consented to dissolution ' as the lesser of two evils. This letter marked the real solution of the crisis. But it only took effect in a dramatic and spectacular secondary crisis on the following day, which to the world at large and in the memory of mankind will always represent the crisis itself.

The Tories, who knew that a General Election would be fatal to them, believed almost to the last moment that the King would never consent to dissolve. And when at last rumours got about that he was yielding to Grey, they determined to use their existing majority in both Houses to intimidate him. On the evening of April 21, the Commons carried against Althorp a vote which had the effect of preventing the Government obtaining the supplies already voted. In the Lords, Wharncliffe gave notice that he would next day move an address to the King against a dissolution. Next morning (April 22), at 11.30, Grey and Brougham waited on the King with a view to prevent these tactics from being further developed.

The King, who had already consented the day before to the principle of dissolution, was eager to meet his Ministers' wishes that he should prorogue the Houses in person that very afternoon. Only so could the Lords be prevented from carrying Wharncliffe's motion against

---

[1] The original Bill had proposed a considerable reduction in the total number of members in the House. Gascoyne's amendment was in principle incorporated in the final Bill that passed in 1832.

[2] See Appendix F, p. 382, below.

dissolution, which would indeed have no constitutional force, but 'might have had a bad effect in the country '; fortunately, William regarded it with indignation as an encroachment on his prerogative. If Commissioners were sent to prorogue the Houses for a dissolution, it was the privilege of their Lordships to keep the Commission waiting at the door till they had voted on any motion actually before the House. But if their Sovereign came in person, he could, of course, interrupt the debate, and if he then and there prorogued Parliament, Lord Wharncliffe's motion could never be passed. Such a demonstration of Royal support for the Bill and for the Ministers was certain to affect very favourably the result of the General Election.

With a sailor's readiness for action, William declared he would go at once. ' I'm always at single anchor,' he said. He swept aside the objections of flurried officials of the Palace that the horses' manes were not plaited and that the state-coachman and horseguards were not ready. ' My Lord,' he said to the apologetic Grey, ' I'll go, if I go in a hackney coach.' [1]

At two o'clock the Lords assembled in tumult, heated on one side with exultant triumph, on the other with baffled fury. Grey was absent, bringing along the King. Brougham kept rushing in and out of the Chamber over which he presided, bouncing up and down on the woolsack, and crying out that the Commons ' had refused supplies.' The Duke of Richmond, if more dignified, was even more provocative to his old Tory associates, whose tempers fairly boiled over. Londonderry shook his fist at Richmond, and was held back by his coat-tails. The Chancellor was hooted.

It is impossible [says the decorous page of *Hansard*] to describe the confusion, the noise, the impetuosity that prevailed

---

[1] Grey told this to Creevey next day (*Creevey*, April 23, 1831; *Hobhouse*, iv. 108). See Appendix F, below : ' The Dissolution of April 1831.'

from one end of the House to the other. The Peeresses present seemed alarmed. Some of the Peers were, as it appeared in the confusion, almost scuffling !

Through the uproar, the cannon could be heard booming out the approach of the King. A great swell of cheering marked the passage of his coach all the way from St. James's to Palace Yard. ' A loud voice,' says Hansard, ' was heard sounding out *God save the King.* At that instant the large doors were thrown open and His Majesty entered the House.' As he ascended the steps of the throne it was noticed that his crown, put on in haste, was precariously balanced on one side of his head. Behind him the tall figure of Lord Grey, carrying the great two-handed Sword of State like a mediæval headsman, seemed to the imagination of the Tories to be attending as the King's executioner and theirs.[1] The gentlemen of the House of Commons, no less angry and excited than the Peers, came thronging and shoving into the chamber at the summons of Black Rod.

' My lords and gentlemen,' said the King, ' I have come to meet you for the purpose of proroguing this Parliament, with a view to its immediate dissolution.' The great Tory party bowed beneath the weight of those words as helplessly as the Whigs just 150 years before, when merry King Charles had played them a like trick at Oxford. But King William added what no Stuart could have said : ' I have been induced to resort to this measure for the purpose of ascertaining the sense of my people.'

All through the dissolution crisis, now issuing so triumphantly, Grey had been calm and cheerful, in strong contrast to his fretfulness in former years, and to the recurring despondency of many of his present colleagues. ' I hear of nothing but Lady Holland's croaking ; others are as bad,' he wrote to Holland.

---

[1] *Greville*, April 24, 1831.

'Our friends do us the greatest mischief. If this measure is lost it will be by their cowardice.' Did Lord Holland show his wife this note, which only a Prime Minister would have ventured to write? Throughout the elections, Grey's letters show him in the highest spirits, and no wonder. If there is any occasion in British history since 1688, on which it is legitimate to speak of 'the People' as having been all on one side, the election of May 1831 is the case. Not only was a majority for the Bill of one wavering individual converted into a majority of 136 in pledged supporters, but the Tory members who survived represented little more than so many close boroughs, and stood nowhere for any mass of population. At Malmesbury, for instance, the successful candidates dared not put in an appearance for fear of the inhabitants of the place, who were engaged in burning them in effigy. The close borough system was indeed so water-tight at election time, that the Reformers made no further gains among the boroughs in Schedules A and B, beyond four seats that Ellice bought up from Lord Yarborough.[1]

But in the towns, great and small, where any real contests were possible, the anti-Reformers were annihilated. Newark showed the Duke of Newcastle that he could no longer 'do what he liked with his own,' though he had evicted thirty-seven tenants for voting against him at a recent election, and had boasted of the feat. Even Liverpool, the seat of a popular Orange and Tory tradition, for once returned two Reformers. Everywhere Whigs laid stress on the enthusiasm, and Tories on the violence, of the popular demonstrations.

But the Whig victory was most striking of all in the

---

[1] Compare the analysis of the Second Reading division on July 6, in *Hansard*, iv. 920, to the analysis of the division on March 22, in *Hansard*, iii. 818-24. The Tories accused Lord Yarborough of defrauding his niece, whose trustee he was, by hiring out her four seats for this Parliament to men pledged to vote away her property. A nice point in casuistry!

counties, where most of all under the old system of representation, ' the voice of England was heard through her freeholders.' In the late division on the Second Reading, fifty-three English county members had voted for, and twenty-seven against, the Bill; but after the elections only six Tories sat for English county seats. The Whig Ministers had themselves underestimated the popularity of their cause. Both Graham in Lord Lonsdale's Cumberland, and Althorp in Northamptonshire, were forced by the common people, against their own judgment as to the probabilities of success, to accept a second Reform candidate as colleague, and in both cases the pair of Reformers was triumphantly returned.

In Northumberland, where in 1826 Lord Howick and Beaumont had both been handsomely beaten,[1] and where in 1830 Beaumont had secured one seat and the Tory Bell the other, the Duke of Northumberland durst not in 1831 run a Tory candidate at all, though it was said that he had subscribed £100,000 to the central party funds out of pure zeal against the Bill. Howick and Beaumont made up their old family quarrel and were returned together unopposed. Howick's Committee were able to give back a considerable sum of money that had been subscribed by ' the working people out of their wages ' to meet the expenses of a contest.

Colonel Coulson [writes Howick, on May 2], who has so much influence in the west of the county, and who last time came down at the head of near three hundred freeholders on horseback to vote for Bell, endeavoured to secure the same votes for him now, and instead of succeeding was happy to escape without personal ill-usage, of which he, Colonel Coulson, was in great danger.

In Scotland, where the representation was even more of a farce than in England, the fury of the people was proportionately greater. Jeffrey, who was responsible for order in that land of fierce passions, wrote to Grey

[1] See pp. 199–200, above.

several times during the elections on the extreme danger caused on the one side by the violence of the people, and on the other by the love of the Tory burgh and county authorities for calling out the military. That tendency he repressed to the utmost extent of his powers, with the result that nothing very deeply to be regretted occurred, except that Sir Walter Scott's gallant and sorely tried spirit was hurt by the tempestuous hostility of his own ' brave lads of Jeddart.' The fact that nine Scotchmen out of ten were passionately for the Bill made no difference at all to the action of the close bodies with whom the elections rested. The county representation remained unchanged, and the Whigs gained seven seats in the burghs only because Ministerial influence was this time on their side.

In Ireland, in spite of the King's fears, the elections went off more quietly than in any other part of the three Kingdoms, and Anglesey, the Lord-Lieutenant, wrote to Brougham that ' nothing can be better than the behaviour of the agitators.'[1] Half a dozen more seats were gained there for Reform.

Grey's personal and constitutional position was profoundly affected by this amazing General Election. Mr. Butler has thus summed it up[2] :

Grey's position was in fact unique in the constitutional history of his time, and ranks him as in a sense the first of modern Prime Ministers. He was not the King's choice, like Pitt, whose triumph at the polls in 1784 the late election recalled, nor was he the choice of Parliament. He stood, after the election of 1831, directly on the support of the people. In this, as in so many points, the struggle for the Reform Bill looks forward, not to the decades which immediately followed its passing, but to the more democratic system of the twentieth century. But eighty years ago the organisation and exploitation of popular feeling were strange and exceptional. Lord Grey accepted them reluctantly enough, but they raised him for the

[1] *Campbell*, i. 513.
[2] *The Passing of the Great Reform Bill*, J. R. M. Butler, pp. 228–9.

moment to a pinnacle no Minister had reached since the days of Pitt, and which it is doubtful if Peel or Palmerston, or even Gladstone, ever attained after him!

All this is perfectly true. Grey understood it only in part, but he was by no means wholly blind to the change wrought by the election. The following letter of his wife's reveals his mind in the hour of electoral triumph, and his prognostications of the future of the Bill in the new Parliament.

Car seems pleased with the state of things, which he says is as good as possible. He adds, ' I do not dislike the violent opposition of the high Tories or that of the bishops, tho' it may create some trouble and excite strong feelings in the progress of the Bill. But with a decided majority in the House of Commons and the power of the Minister added to the strength we had before in the House of Lords, I do not fear the result.' For my part, I shall enjoy his attacking the bishops, who will no doubt afford him an opportunity of doing so.

Only in one quarter did the Prime Minister perceive a falling-off ; there were signs that the King was ' out of spirits,' and ' uneasy ' about the element of democracy that the elections had introduced into the solution of the Reform problem. The violence of the mobs shocked him. In that respect, if Ireland had been better, England had been worse than he feared. And he was beginning to scent the danger of strife between the two Houses, which he deprecated above all things. Nevertheless, Grey still found that towards himself his master's ' kindness and confidence do not appear at all diminished.' [1] It was indeed at this juncture that William insisted on the Prime Minister accepting the Order of the Garter, ' as a decisive proof of his unqualified confidence.' [2]

[1] Parker's *Graham*, i. 112; *William's Correspondence*, i. 260–76.

[2] Grey writes to Holland on May 25, 1831 : ' I need not say to you that this was totally unwished for by me, and quite unexpected, not a word having been said about a blue ribband, since I refused it when we first came into office. Coming in this way it was impossible, I thought, again to refuse it.'

From this time forward the King continued to urge him to modify the Bill, in order to avert a conflict with the Lords. But on this Grey was adamant from first to last. Palmerston, too, had written to him a fortnight before the dissolution, arguing for large concessions, so as to get the Bill through the old House of Commons; and during the election, when he unsuccessfully canvassed the dons at Cambridge, he wrote to Grey from that seat of wisdom, ' I have scarcely met six people who approve of our Bill ! ' [1] Above all Palmerston wished the £10 qualification raised. On May 15 Grey replied rather tartly :

I really do not quite understand what you mean by saying that we are hurrying on too fast. I am not conscious that we have altered our pace from the beginning. We brought in the Reform Bill, and are pledged to carry it through.

At the end of May came the first of a long series of Cabinet crises on the Bill, in which only Grey's firmness and good temper prevented a split. Palmerston and Lansdowne asked for a modification of the Bill ; Melbourne and Richmond at heart agreed with them ; while Durham's ' impracticability ' and ill-temper, when on the warpath against these backsliders, endangered the cohesion of the Ministry. [2] On May 29 the Cabinet met to consider a letter from the King, recommending alterations in the Bill to conciliate the Peers. Durham was fortunately away ill.

[1] Most dons in those days had to become clergymen of the Church of England. Grey wrote to Wellesley on May 5 (Add. MSS., 37311) : ' The elections continue to prosper everywhere, except at Cambridge. These Parsons, it seems, have fears for the property of the Church. Do you think the course they are pursuing the best calculated to preserve it ? '

[2] *Grey to Holland*, May 28, 1831. Other zealous reformers tried to impress on Durham the necessity of ministerial unity, and of carrying with them the less advanced section, which was Grey's special task. Thus Duncannon writes to Durham : ' You must consider Lord Grey's position. Necessity joined him to many whose opinions differed from his own, and who had a great *gulp* to make before they could agree to such a measure as the Reform Bill.'

Lord Grey [so Holland wrote to Durham that evening] spoke very decisively against making any alteration in the franchise. His expressions were so strong that they silenced Palmerston, and Lansdowne admitted that it was too late to make any change. I should say that, with the exception of Palmerston, all present agreed that a very probable consequence of attempting to conciliate the House of Lords by concession, would be to lose the House of Commons, and Lansdowne expressly said that this would be absurd to the highest degree.

Before the new Parliament met in the middle of June, Lord John Russell and Stanley had become members of the Cabinet. During the General Election, Lord John's father, the Duke of Bedford, that formidable buttress of the Whig Ministry and repository of Foxite tradition, had written to Grey : ' I think John ought to be in the Cabinet before Parliament meets again.' [1] The claim was just, though not specially on the ground put forward by the Duke, that if he was again in charge of the Bill in the Commons he should no longer have a mere ' half responsibility.' For in the new Parliament, Lord John, though he had been made a full Cabinet Minister, soon voluntarily relinquished the effective charge of the Bill in Committee to the most hardworking, tactful, and popular of all Parliamentary managers, Lord Althorp.

On July 6, 1831, the new Bill, materially the same as the old, passed its Second Reading in the Commons by a majority of 136. Then began the two hot summer months of battle in Committee, where every line in the Bill and every name in the schedules was fought by the

[1] Lord Grey, in his answer of May 22, says, with truth : ' I think you cannot doubt my sincere desire to put Lord John forward. I have given some proof of this by putting the conduct of the Reform Bill into his hands, upon the discussions of which he had generally attended the meetings of the Cabinet. The difficulty [of promoting him to the Cabinet] has been on account of the numbers, for I do not think he could be introduced without Stanley.' When the two were added, the numbers of the Cabinet rose to fifteen.

Tories, ably if somewhat extravagantly led by Sir Charles Wetherell. Under his legal guidance, the House of easy-going country gentlemen began to learn the meaning of obstruction and night sessions prolonged to broad daylight. The ill ventilation of that overcrowded chamber was not suited to such a change in Parliamentary methods. 'John Russell is ill,' wrote Greville on August 4, 'nearly done up with fatigue and exertion and the bad atmosphere he breathes for several hours every night.' A little later Macaulay wrote : ' I believe there are fifty members of the House of Commons who have done irreparable injury to their health by attendance in the discussions at this session. Wetherell's cursed lungs seem to be in as good condition as ever.' Cobbett, a tough bit of oak himself, afterwards declared that service in that most incommodious of houses required ' not only perfect health but great bodily strength.' It was well that the fox-hunting breed who then crowded the benches on both sides had the necessary stamina. Althorp's sweetness of temper was never ruffled, nor was his slow judgment ever at fault. Even that fierce opposition could seldom be angry with him.[1]

Meanwhile the people were in the mood to think that, after their verdict at the elections, the last word had been said. They were furious at the prolonged debate, clamouring for the business to be cut short and the Bill to be passed into law forthwith. Wetherell became the most unpopular man in the country. Large sections of society, particularly in the industrial north, seem hardly to have contemplated as a possibility that the Lords would, at the end of all this talk and delay, throw out

---

[1] On July 6, Jeffrey, previously accustomed to the society of Edinburgh rather than of London, writes : ' I have had two or three more Cabinet dinners. The most agreeable are Lord Grey's, where there are always ladies, and we were very gay there last Sunday. I am still as much in love with Althorp and most of his colleagues as ever, and feel proud and delighted with their frankness, cheerfulness, and sweet-blooded courage.'

the measure to which alone the nation looked for deliverance.[1]

As the Bill drew nearer to the Lords, Grey had much to trouble him. As early as June 2 he realised the strong probability that it would be thrown out there in spite of the General Election, and was already discussing with Holland the creation of half a dozen peers.[2] But, while he feared that that would be insufficient, he saw grave objections to the policy on a large scale. And the King was becoming every day more difficult to manage.

In August and September troubles came thick upon him. The dread anxiety of another European crisis, when first the Dutch and then the French troops entered Belgium, threatened his whole domestic structure of Peace, Retrenchment, and Reform with the terrible possibility of a war with France. But again his and Palmerston's friendly firmness prevailed to induce the French to withdraw across the frontier, after they had driven back the intruding Dutch. [3]

At the same time he was, in his own domestic circle,[4] distressed at the illness and misfortunes, and assailed by the resultant ill temper, of Durham, the son-in-law whom he loved both for his own sake and for Lady Durham's. When in November 1830 he had raised Durham to the Cabinet as Privy Seal—contrary to the wishes of some of his colleagues, but very wisely in the public interest—his son-in-law had written to him in terms

[1] Althorp actually wrote on October 10, three days after the Bill had been thrown out: ' It is quite wonderful, but I believe the people never had an idea that the Bill was in the slightest danger ' (*Althorp*, 355).

[2] Letter to Lord Holland, June 2, 1831.

[3] See p. 353.

[4] About midsummer in 1831 the Greys had moved into a suburban residence at East Sheen, between which and Downing Street the Premier's life was passed. Throughout the period of the Reform Bill, Grey's private secretary was his son-in-law, Charles Wood, afterwards first Viscount Halifax, well known in the Whig Ministries of the Victorian era as a man wise in counsel.

of warm gratitude.[1] Grey had then committed to him and to Russell the drawing up of the Reform Bill, and while that work was on foot, Durham's temper had remained good. But as the summer wore on, he suffered tortures from neuralgic pains in the head, while his beloved and noble child, Charles, known to posterity as the ' Master Lambton ' of Lawrence's most beautiful picture, was slowly dying of consumption. The unfortunate father's temper was soured by anxiety and pain. Forgetting what he had written to Grey at the time, he conceived a belated grievance because he had been given the Privy Seal instead of a great administrative office. Yet how could he have made his name immortal and his country safe by drawing up the right Reform Bill, if he had been all the last winter engaged in learning the mysteries of the Foreign Office or Admiralty ? Still more unworthy of the true greatness of his mind, was his constant pestering to be raised from a Baron to an Earl. On these grounds, according to Grey's children, he refused sometimes to speak to their father for days together. He seems to have felt no gratitude for having been put at the head of the Reform Bill Committee, and he came at length to speak to others of that appointment by which he and the world had profited so much, as if Grey had done it and everything else connected with the Bill in a fit of absence of mind ! [2] His letters to Grey of August 23 and 25, 1831, about the earldom and administrative office, are written in the style of a man unnerved by neuralgic pain and parental anxiety. There is evidence in his long correspondence with Grey from 1816 onwards, that his health and temper took a very decided turn for the worse in the course of 1831.

[1] P. 263, above, note ; and Appendix D, p. 379, below.

[2] *Hobhouse*, iv. 178, a passage that contains many inaccuracies and leaves a most unpleasant impression of the way he talked of his father-in-law and colleagues in 1832 ; Grey was most generously loyal to him, whatever some of his colleagues may have been.

On September 24 that year the long-expected blow fell : Charles Lambton died. The Bill was already in the Lords, and in ten days' time Grey would have to propose the Second Reading in a speech of the first importance. But neither his own grief nor his devotion to Louisa and her husband were stinted on that account. On the last day of September he wrote to Holland :

I see poor Louisa and Lambton [Durham] every day ; there is no mitigation of their suffering, and her affectionate, despairing look really breaks my heart.

And again to the Princess Lieven :

Why did the blow fall on this heavenly boy, whilst I and so many others who would be no loss to the world are spared ? I can think of nothing else, and am quite unnerved for the battle I have to fight.

But the great world moves on, regardless of what might have been, intent only on what shall be ; and the Prime Minister is only the first servant of the King and Kingdom. ' Whilst the funeral cortège of his favourite grandchild was slowly making its way to the north, Lord Grey, on October 3, moved the Second Reading of the Bill in one of the most memorable speeches ever delivered in the House of Lords.'[1]

Time past and time to come seemed to converge upon that debate : Grey began it by reminding the peers of his own youth, when he had made motions for Reform in the Lower House, in the presence of ' some of the greatest men this country has ever produced '—Fox, Burke, and Pitt ; his grave and ' beautiful ' eloquence of an older time enthralled an enthusiastic young Tory in love with all things grand and old, William Ewart Gladstone, who sat out that great debate of five nights

---

[1] Stuart Reid's *Durham*, i. 264.

for ' nine or ten hours every evening,' till ' compelled by exhaustion ' to retire.[1] Grey's speech was universally admired, but the Tories found it uncompromising. They objected to the threat of ' something infinitely stronger and more extensive ' as the alternative to the Bill, still more to the hint of possible ' civil war,' and the certainty of grave consequences, if it was rejected. In language however decorous, the Prime Minister proclaimed the rigid popular doctrine of ' the Bill, the whole Bill, and nothing but the Bill.' But otherwise he advanced the most palatable, conservative arguments for the measure upon which he insisted.[2] Grey spoke of himself as being ' more than any other man responsible ' for bringing forward the Reform question in general, and this measure in particular, nor did anyone dispute the claim.

In one of the closing passages of his speech he appealed directly to the Bishops not to render the Church odious to the mass of the people by taking a principal, possibly a decisive, part in throwing out the Bill. The words were courteous, and Grey declared himself ' sincerely attached to the maintenance of all the rights and privileges of the Church,' as well as to the ' purity of her doctrines and soundness of her discipline.' Referring to the Bill against Pluralities recently introduced by the Primate, he continued, in a passage of which a garbled version was soon to fly over the country like the fiery cross :

Those right reverend Prelates have shown that they were not indifferent or inattentive to the signs of the times. They have introduced, in the way in which I think all such measures

---

[1] Morley's *Gladstone*, Bk. i., chap. iii.

[2] The Bill, Grey said, ' would give to the nation contentment, and to all future Governments the support of the respectability, the wealth, and the intelligence of the country ; which is the surest ground of stability, and nothing short of which can enable a Government to make a stand upon the principles of the constitution.' ' A *bit-by-bit* amelioration would have left the question as unsettled as before.'

ought to be introduced, namely by the leading members of the Church itself, measures of amelioration. In this they have acted with a prudent forethought. They appear to have felt that the eyes of the country are upon them ; *that it is necessary for them to set their house in order*, and prepare to meet the coming storm. I implore them to follow, on the present occasion, the same prudent course.

Young Gladstone does not appear to have been shocked by this passage, and read at full it is entirely unobjectionable. But after the Bishops had voted for the rejection of the Bill by twenty-one votes to two, the word went round the country that Lord Grey had bidden the Bishops ' to set their house in order.' The popular campaign of mob outrage against the Bishops that autumn had for its watchword this one phrase, torn from its context amid the decorous periods of the Prime Minister.[1]

Though Lyndhurst spoke against the Bill, Brougham's oration was the only one in the debate that was matched by common consent with Grey's. Grey told Althorp that the Chancellor's speech ' united all the excellencies of the ancient with those of modern oratory.' It certainly was a fine speech, marred by the hyperbole of the climax, when, like Burke with his dagger, the Lord Chancellor exceeded the modesty of nature by kneeling down as he pronounced the final apostrophe :

' I warn you, I implore you, yea, on my bended knees, I supplicate you—Reject not this Bill ! '

The degree of genuflexion must ever remain a matter of historical dispute, or at least of individual conjecture. The friendly *Times* came to his rescue by reporting that ' here Lord Brougham slightly bent his knee on the Woolsack,' while the witty malice of his rival and biographer tells us that :

---

[1] ' He gravely told the bishops to *put their house in order*, and in one month from that time the palace of one bishop was in flames ! ' (Wetherell, in the House of Commons, December 17, 1831.)

He continued for some time as if in prayer ; but his friends, alarmed for him, lest he should be suffering from the effects of the mulled port, picked him up and placed him safely on the woolsack.[1]

The impartial Hansard is silent. At the end of the fifth and last night of the debate, October 7, 1831, or, rather, about five in the morning on October 8, Lord Grey rose to make his reply, which in its vigour and spirit recalled to veterans the days of his fiery youth. ' The group of young members of the House of Commons collected behind the throne were, in the warmth of their admiration, with difficulty restrained from cheering.'

His audience was moved by his answer to certain personal criticisms, both at the opening where he defended the consistency of his long career as a Reformer, from the days of the Friends of the People until that hour ; and at the close, when he declared :

I had no desire for place, and it was not sought after by me : it was offered to me under such circumstances that nothing but a sense of duty could have induced me to accept it. I have lived a life of exclusion from office—I had no official habits—I possessed not the advantages which those official habits confer—I am fond of retirement and domestic life, and I lived happy and content in the bosom of my family. I was surrounded by those to whom I am attached by the warmest ties of affection. What then but a sense of duty could have induced me to plunge into all the difficulties, not unforeseen, of my present situation ? What else, in my declining age,

' What else could tempt me on these stormy seas,
Bankrupt of life, yet prodigal of ease ? '

Then, after a final brush between Lyndhurst and Grey, on the vexed question of Lyndhurst's former views on Reform, they went to the fateful division.

---

[1] Campbell's *Lyndhurst and Brougham*, 398. Needless to say, that amusing volume is not a safe guide in either of its parts.

'I stood in a group with Grey and Holland,' wrote Campbell; 'the latter was a little excited, but Grey was tranquil and smiling, as if they had been dividing on a road Bill. There was no cheering, as with us in the Commons upon a great division, and no stranger would have imagined that a measure was decided that might occasion the land to be deluged in blood.'[1] 'There were some faint cheers,' wrote another spectator, 'at the announcement of the majority of forty-one against the Bill, but the general aspect along the Tory benches was rather of anxiety than exultation.'[2] It was past six o'clock, and the mob outside had fortunately melted away before dawn. As the tired statesmen trooped out into the streets on that sombre morning,

'the very houses seemed asleep,
And all that mighty heart was lying still!'

[1] Campbell's letters, written at the time (published in his *Autobiography*), are, of course, much better evidence of facts than many of his statements in the *Lives of the Chancellors*.

[2] *Althorp*, 350, 352.

CHAPTER IV

THE STRUGGLE FOR THE BILL—KING, PEERS, AND PEOPLE— OCTOBER 1831 TO APRIL 1832

'I know only two ways in which societies can permanently be governed—by public opinion and by the sword. I understand how the peace is kept at New York. It is by the assent and support of the people. I understand also how the peace is kept at Milan. It is by the bayonets of the Austrian soldiers. But how the peace is to be kept when you have neither the popular assent nor the military force—how the peace is to be kept in England by a Government acting on the principles of the present Opposition, I do not understand.'—MACAULAY IN THE HOUSE OF COMMONS, Oct. 10, 1831.

THE country was on the verge of anarchy, and one false step by the Ministers would have dragged it into the abyss. The whole social body was sick with many deep, internal maladies, little considered and less understood by the State physicians of that day. They had, however, produced a remedy which many of the people believed in as a panacea, and the great majority welcomed as the first step to improvement ; and now the cup had been dashed from the lip. The one feeling that the starving operatives shared with their employers, whom they regarded as their tyrants, was a passion for the Bill to destroy the aristocratic rule which they both detested. If that one hope of their despair, that one reconcilement of their deep divisions were now to be abandoned, chaos was come again.

In October 1831 the substitution of a Tory for a Whig Ministry would not have led, as it would in May 1832, to a systematic rebellion of the big towns, prepared and ready organised for the act, but to blind and unrelated paroxysms of the rage and vengeance of warring classes which must have been destructive in their course and would probably have been disastrous in their outcome.

The one real chance for the Tories of successfully resisting the Bill was to provoke a class war, which would end in rallying all the ' haves ' to close their ranks in self-defence against the ' have-nots.' The likelihood of such a disaster was greatest in the first three months after the throwing out of the Bill by the Lords on October 8, 1831. No one who has not studied the Home Office manuscripts for that terrible winter can quite realise how great the danger was. But Grey, little as he knew of that unplumbed abyss of misery and despair, knew that the danger lay below, and therefore made no false step on the heights above.

Before he left the House of Lords on the morning of October 8, the Prime Minister wrote a note to the King giving the numbers of the division that had just taken place. In a few hours he received an answer from William, declaring that the majority of forty-one was so great as to preclude the possibility of a creation of peers to carry the Bill, but earnestly desiring the Ministers to remain in office.

After a Cabinet held the same morning, Grey wrote a letter to Sir Herbert Taylor [1] accepting the veto on making peers, and foreshadowing his own continuance in office, but only on condition that the King would support his Ministers in ' carrying a measure *not less efficient*' than the lost Bill, ' though altered in its provisions ' ; this was ' absolutely necessary for the preservation of the public peace.'

---

[1] His letters to Sir Herbert, the King's secretary, were meant to be shown to the King. They were an informal way of addressing William.

And so, even before going to bed after the throwing out of the Bill, and long before the House of Commons or the people had had time to indicate their wishes, Grey had outlined the Fabian tactics which saved the country that winter. He would not resign, and he would not whittle down the Bill. But he would make immaterial changes in it, to save the face of peers wishing to drop resistance next time it came up to them. The useful formula of the ' no less efficient ' Bill saved the credit of the Government with the country. On one point, indeed, Grey was mistaken ; he did not yet perceive that in the long run his ' no less efficient ' Bill could only be carried by a creation of peers or by the imminent threat thereof. By the new year he had altered his opinion under the tutoring of events, and meanwhile his error had no serious consequences. The fatal mistake in October would have been to demand peers, and to go out on the King's then certain refusal.

The policy, peculiarly Grey's own, of the ' no less efficient ' Bill was opposed by Palmerston, who, on October 9, wrote Grey a letter protesting that the only way to pass the Bill through the Lords was to make it less ' extensive,' and this course, Palmerston added, would please ' the great bulk of the gentry of the country,' and many who had voted for the last Bill in the Commons.

Next day Grey replied to him :

My information leads me to believe that the middle classes who form the real and efficient mass of public opinion, and without whom the power of the gentry is nothing, are almost unanimous on this question, and animated by a settled resolution to press it forward. Of the gentry, too, I am persuaded that a very large majority are now impressed with corresponding sentiments. . . . [On] a suspicion that we are shrinking from the principle on which we have been hitherto acting, . . . public confidence would be at once withdrawn from us. We should be compelled to retire in disgrace. [Then either Wellington would come in and pass] a plan certainly not less extensive than ours [or] the more probable event would be that the people would take the matter into their own hands, and then God knows what might be the result.

On October 10, a few hours after Grey had written this letter, the House of Commons carried Lord Ebrington's vote of regret for the Bill and confidence in the Ministers by a majority of 198. Macaulay's fiery oration, including the passage quoted at the head of this chapter, reminded the House, with a bluntness that his eloquence saved from giving offence, of the questions of physical force that underlay and might at any moment overset the nice constitutional balancings of the King, Lords, and Commons.

Lord Althorp, whom Ministers agreed to put up as their sole spokesman in the Commons on this critical evening, made the famous announcement that he only remained in office in order to pass a measure *as efficient* as the late Bill. Palmerston and the moderates again stood committed against their will.

While the House of Commons approved by so great a majority of the resolution of the Ministers to remain in office on these terms, the country was calling to them in an agonised voice not to abandon their post. Fear of anarchy combined with fear of losing the Bill to make men dread Grey's resignation more than any other event. If the Duke took office, there were no plans for defeating him by revolutionary action, such as were ready in the following May. Attwood and the Birmingham Political Union, who on that latter occasion took the lead in organising resistance, confined themselves in October to holding a monster meeting of 100,000 men, then a marvel without precedent, and exhorting the great public, that already looked to Birmingham for guidance, under all circumstances to observe the law. Attwood himself told the council of the Union that unless they kept strictly within the letter of the law, the Duke, on accepting office, would break up their Union and arrest their leaders.[1]

---

[1] *H.O. Papers*, 44, 25.

Since the middle class as yet shrank from preparing an orderly resistance, it was all the more certain that if Lord Grey resigned there would be riot and outrage, and indeed insurrection, partly political and partly economic, on the part of the working men.

On October 10 Jeffrey wrote to Grey as regards Scotland :

There is the same concurrence and deep conviction on the part of *all* my informants, that the resignation of the Ministry or the abandonment of Reform would be instantly productive of the most frightful consequences in all the populous and manufacturing districts, an open defiance of authority, and most probably acts of lawless violence by combined and determined multitudes.

In England, the first week after the rejection of the Bill was sufficiently alarming. In London, Peel's ' new police ' saved the situation, though large mobs broke the windows of the Duke of Wellington and the other Tory peers. But in the rest of the country there were only the old, inefficient constables, little changed since the days of Dogberry and Verges ; lukewarm ' specials,' anxious ' not to do anything against the Bill ' ; and a few thousand soldiers who spent that terrible winter dashing about from place to place on their thankless, indispensable task, keeping down the spasmodic local outbreaks of the red terror—cursed, stoned, wearied out, but never failing in patience and duty.

At Nottingham, on October 10, the mob burnt the Castle because it was the property of the Duke of Newcastle, prominent against the Bill and famous for his political evictions. They also burnt several factories, as the symbols of capitalist tyranny. The magistrates on the 11th declared ' the town and vicinity are in a state of insurrection, and the whole force we have to oppose to the rioters is not above eighty men of the King's troops.' Yet such was the political passion against the borough-mongers felt by the respectable middle class of Nottingham, that even after this awful experience they petitioned the Government to dismiss the Duke of Newcastle from the Lord-Lieutenancy of the Shire.[1]

All over the country there were riots. Peers who had voted against the Bill went in fear for their property and even for their lives, though there was no actual case of murder. Their houses in town and country were not infrequently attacked. Noble lords, posting back to their country homes from Westminster, were hooted and hustled as they changed horses at the inn doors, where they were wont to be the objects of obsequious admiration. In Darlington, a lady driving beside Lord Tankerville was nearly killed by a paving-stone, as the family coach raced out of the town with its panels stove in and the floor covered with missiles of all sizes.[2]

But the rage against the Bishops was fiercest of all. In spite of Grey's warning, they had voted twenty-one to two against the Bill. The cry to exclude them from Parliament rose loudly not only from the working men but even in the middle-class *Times*, which was strongly opposed to the *ultra* Radicals. The anti-clerical violence of the mobs recalled the days of the Long Parliament. The Bishops of Durham and Exeter dared not go about their work in their dioceses. On the Fifth of November a mitred figure almost everywhere took the place of Guy Fawkes. Even in haunts of ancient peace, like Worcester, where as the Radicals complained ' there were so many Black Slugs living about the purlieus of the Cathedral,' that it was ' uphill work ' to form

---

[1] *H.O. Papers*, 52, 15, where the Duke of Newcastle, in his letters to Melbourne, accuses some of the magistrates of ' haranguing the mob ' about the Lords and the Bill, and ' indifferently suffering all these things to take place.' He himself could not (he said) ' venture personally into the manufacturing districts; I should either be murdered, or raise a riot by appearing.'

[2] *Malmesbury (Memoirs)*, p. 29. Lord Tankerville, though an old Whig, and a friend and neighbour of Grey, could not swallow the Bill.

JOHN BULL: "Come along, what are you afraid of? D—— it, let's have a row."

GREY (to King): "What can I do? You see he is forcing me along."

KING: "I tell you, my friends, I can't keep up with you if you go on at this rate. (Aside to Grey) I hope you haven't put any-thing bad in his drink. Certainly I never saw him so bent on mischief before."

"A Political Union": John Bull, Grey, William IV. *From "H.B." Political Sketches.*

a Union, they chalked 'Judas Iscariot, Bishop of Worcester,' on the Cathedral walls, and in moments of crisis partisans of the Bill paraded the streets of the town in noisy triumph.[1]

But there was one clergyman who had no share either in the unpopularity of his brethren or in the brutal feelings of many of his fellow Reformers. At a crowded meeting, held at Taunton on October 11, 1831, to call on the Ministers to remain in office, Sydney Smith did much to preserve the peace of the country, by relaxing its savage fear and rage into confident good-humour. The Duke of Wellington was likened unto Dame Partington, sweeping back the Atlantic with her mop:

The Atlantic was roused. Mrs. Partington's spirit was up. But I need not tell you that the contest was unequal. The Atlantic Ocean beat Mrs. Partington. She was excellent at a slop or a puddle, but she should not have meddled with a tempest. Gentlemen, be at your ease—be quiet and steady—you will beat Mrs. Partington.

As the reverend gentleman on the platform began, with dramatic force, 'trundling his imaginary mop with an air of resolute determination and an appearance of increasing temper,' a storm of laughter swept over that vast and highly-wrought assembly that had met in no pleasant mood. The Press and the cartoonists and the talk of men soon set people laughing over 'Dame Partington and her mop' under almost every roof in Britain. Such laughter was like light in a darkened landscape, bearing hope of a peaceful victory. There was no such kindly laughter heard in France in 1789.

Sydney Smith was a dear friend of the Grey family, and one of the acts of patronage which gave Grey the greatest pleasure had been conferring, in September, a Canonry of St. Paul's on this country parson of genius, who had waited as long and loyally for preferment as

---

[1] *Butler*, 297; *H.O. Papers*, 44, 25 (*Pol. Unions Secret*) Worc.

the Prime Minister himself. In that dignified age, it was generally held that so great a wit as 'poor Sydney' could never be made a Bishop. Grey's private correspondence has allusions to the subject. 'May I add,' writes Lord Milton, 'without being either impertinent or ill-natured, beware of making Sydney Smith a Bishop ; do anything else for him, but it will not do to give him a mitre.' The proposition appears to have been regarded as self-evident.

The only occasion on which Grey was brought into personal contact with his Radical supporters was not fortunate. Four days after the Bill was thrown out, not long before midnight, seventeen ' delegates ' from the London parishes, headed by Francis Place himself, appeared without warning or appointment at Downing Street to request the Prime Minister to reassemble Parliament in seven days, and pass the old Bill by a creation of peers. Hobhouse, the Radical member for Westminster, who knew Grey and Place equally well, thought the domiciliary visit a mistake and badly staged ; some of the deputation, he wrote, ' were such ill-looking fellows that my friend De Vear told me he had got before one of them that Lord Grey might not see him.' [1]

The Prime Minister, unpractised in the modern art of receiving democratic deputations, let them go away under the disastrous impression that he was about to introduce a watered-down Bill, though his real intentions were quite different. Place was very angry, but he never lost his head. After a few days he allowed his friends, Hobhouse, Burdett, and Grote the historian, to persuade him that even though Ministers would not precipitate a crisis at once, as he had wished them

[1] *Hobhouse,* iv. 148. Besides one major, the only delegate styled ' gentleman ' in the deputation was the ex-journeyman-tailor, Place. The rest were mostly small tradesmen ; see list in Add. MSS., B.M., 35149, f. 89.

to do, the only hope for the country was to trust them, and that confidence was in fact no more than their due.[1]

The conflict of mind that we read in Place's letters in these critical days was going on in the mind of the country at large, with the same happy outcome, a determination to trust Lord Grey, but to keep 'staring at the Government, staring at them firmly,' as someone aptly said at a Radical meeting. The country saved itself by this decision. It was here that Grey's character for upright dealing had its reward in gaining him this extension of confidence.

'Lord Grey's conduct has been the most open and manly of any Minister,' Place had written the day before his unfortunate deputation ; and even when he was most angry he confessed that he had 'unlimited confidence in Lord Grey's intention to serve his country,' and only doubted his judgment.[2]

Place had finally to be satisfied by a letter from Grey to Grote, in which the Prime Minister explained the need of a new Bill, as strong as the last, but with 'improvements' to afford the Peers 'an excuse for repairing the error of their last vote' ; or, as Grote put it, 'to afford a colour for the deserters from the enemy who may be fearful at resisting the people a second time.'[3] To recast the Bill on these lines, and also to rest Lord Grey and the other Ministers who were prostrate with fatigue, it was necessary to postpone the meeting of Parliament for some weeks. But the more the recess was prolonged, the greater the danger to the public peace, and it was fortunate that Grey, who feared that his own health would break down if they met before Christmas, was out-voted in the Cabinet on the subject, and that

---

[1] *Hansard*, viii. 850–1, Oct. 17, 1831, for Grey's account of the interview. Add. MSS., B.M., 35149, ff. 85–91 and 96–106, for Place's correspondence about it.

[2] Add. MSS., B.M., 35149, ff. 84*b* and 101.

[3] Ibid., ff. 109–10, 112.

an early date in December was fixed for the reading of the new Bill.[1]

Two incidents, unknown to the world at the time, illustrate the immense difficulty of Grey's position. The very day after the Lords threw out the Bill, the King actually proposed, in the teeth of the popular fury, to dismiss from the service, on account of a Radical speech at Devizes, that modern paladin, Colonel William Napier, then at the height of his fame as the historian of the Peninsular War, in which he had himself played so gallant a part.[2] A fortnight before, William had wanted to cashier Colonel Torrens of the Royal Marines, for saying that ' The House of Lords might be placed in Schedule A.'

Of course Grey would not consent, but the affairs show how little the King understood the temper of his subjects.

It was now that the Prime Minister began to be seriously alarmed at the influence exerted over the King's opinions by the Queen Adelaide, the Ladies of the Court, and the FitzClarences. William had long kept these influences at arm's length, but they were beginning to tell at last. The furious attacks in the Press on the interference of the ' German frow,' always brutal and at first unjust, only made matters worse at Court and aroused the King's strong indignation. The Queen was deeply interested in politics on the Tory side, and though at first she observed discretion, we find her in the end consulting the Duke of Wellington through a third

---

[1] Grey was, no doubt, wrong, because the country would have misunderstood further postponement, but these are his arguments to Holland on October 30: ' After all, it is only a question of a fortnight. Parliament would not meet, any rate, till the first week of December. The sitting then would not last above a fortnight. Is it not better to take the prorogation at once to the 9th or 10th of January, when we may be well prepared with all our measures to go on without further delay or interruption? I am persuaded we should in the end save time.'

[2] The speech can be read in his life by Bruce (1864), i. 353-7. He was, of course, only an officer on half-pay.

person as to whether the King could safely dismiss his Ministers.[1] Already on September 27, 1831, Grey wrote to Holland :

The affair of Torrens convinces me that the people who compose the King's private society have had some effect. [And on October 30] : How can I go to Brighton without an invitation ? I told you how I was received on my last two visits to Windsor : by the King personally with the greatest kindness, but he carefully avoided my coming into the presence of the Queen. The same thing would probably happen if I went uninvited to Brighton. At most I should be asked to dinner, and all the Queen's circle would talk about nothing for the next fortnight but the manner of my reception.

Two months later he reports to his wife : ' The Queen civil, but her civility at the freezing point.'

During the last three days of October 1831 occurred the riots at Bristol. The close Tory corporation had long been at feud with the inhabitants, and particularly with the members of the rather weak Political Union. Forces that in Birmingham were united to preserve order, were in Bristol at bitter enmity. And to make matters worse, the Recorder of the city was Sir Charles Wetherell ; he united that judicial post with his very unjudicial proceedings in the House of Commons, where also an attempt had been made to represent Bristol as hostile to the Bill, in spite of its two Reform members. When it was known that Wetherell was coming down on October 29, to make his state entry into the city, and administer the laws as Judge, all parties foretold trouble. The Mayor and corporation, having enlisted some young Tory ' bloods ' as special constables to guard the procession, showed the utmost incapacity to meet the danger they had done not a little

---

[1] *Wellington Despatches*, viii: 16–56, 169. I do not see how anyone who reads the Queen's letter there, of Jan. 18, 1832, can doubt that she used her influence with the King against his Ministers.

to provoke. Neither can the middle-class Reformers be exempt from blame ; they looked on passively at the triumph of a relatively small body of hooligans, so long as it was a matter of sacking the Mansion House and making Wetherell escape over the roof. Only when it came to opening the prisons and burning down the town, they pressed their services on the magistrates, who were too incapable or sulky to make use of them even then. As ill-luck would have it, the small body of dragoons in the town was commanded by Colonel Brereton, an officer nervous about shedding blood almost to the verge of insanity. Finally, his hand was forced by Major Mackworth, and a series of charges on the morning of the 31st restored order, but not till the Bishop's Palace, several public buildings, and about forty houses had been burnt to the ground. An eye-witness wrote to Lord Melbourne : ' Fifty of our London police would have disposed of any of the assemblages I witnessed.' [1]

The Bristol riots showed everyone on what lava crust they were treading. Each side drew its own obvious political moral, and Reformers and anti-Reformers throughout the country held their own opinions more firmly in the light of the fires of Bristol.

The winter of 1831-2 was in every respect a portentous season. Trade was stagnant, agriculture was depressed. In October the cholera landed for the first time on British soil, in the congenial atmosphere of the slums of Sunderland ; in the course of fifteen months it took a toll of 50,000 victims from the crowded and insanitary hovels of the poor.[2] The terror and religious fanaticism that it caused among an ignorant

---

[1] Grenfell's letter in *H.O. Papers*, 40, 28, where see also letters of the Mayor, Lieut. Claxton, Brereton, and Mackworth ; *Butler*, 305–10. Mr. Stanley Weyman has a spirited and just picture of the riots in his Reform Bill romance of *Chippinge*.

[2] England and Wales, 21,882 deaths ; Ireland, 20,070 ; Scotland, 9592 (Creighton, *Epidemics in Britain*, ii. 816).

population added to the political and social horrors of the time.

In the country districts ' Captain Swing ' reappeared, and ricks blazed night after night. In December the insurance companies raised the premiums on the insurance of farming stock, in the disturbed districts, ' from two to ten shillings per cent.,' and reported that ' the burnings at the present season far outnumber those of last winter '—the winter of the rural revolt ! Near Devizes a pease rick was watched burning by a large crowd, that gave three cheers for the conflagration. One adviser wrote to the Home Office that the only way to stop arson, ' which the better-intentioned among the labourers look upon as venial,' was to ' let the body of the incendiary be consigned to the Surgeon for dissection, as in the case of murder,' since the mere gallows had lost its terror to starving men ![1]

All over the industrial districts of the north and midlands there were strikes, unemployment, and violence, social and political. From Colne in Lancashire the workmen marched over the hills into Yorkshire to burn Gisburne Park, the seat of Lord Ribblesdale, who had voted against the Bill ; they wished to imitate the proceedings in Bristol of which they had read in the papers, but they were stopped in time by the military. In Staffordshire 50,000 miners, brutalised by the slavery of the underground life of that epoch, were roaming the countryside in large bands, armed with staves, a terror to all men. In Shropshire, Reform Bill riots among the colliers were repressed by the Yeomanry.[2] The inhuman conditions under which the working classes had lived during the last half century produced this year some bestial crimes against blacklegs, and fore-

---

[1] *H.O. Papers,* 40, 29. This was the era when the almost superstitious popular horror of dissection was a grave trouble to the medical faculty, and caused the unholy trade of the ' resurrection men ' and the crimes of Burke and Hare.

[2] *H.O. Papers,* 52, 15.

shadowed no rosewater revolution, if revolution should come. In November, at Preston—where the work-men complained that their employers treated them like ' Turkish Bashaws,' too proud to give a civil answer, and not turning their heads to them when they spoke— the distress was acute, and only the soldiers saved the town from the desperation of the people. At Black-burn and elsewhere in the north the working classes were exhorted by their speakers to arm and put down the House of Lords on their own behalf.[1]

It would be wrong to think of all England as united against the Lords ; for though nearly all England was against the Lords, it was not united.

Great and evident as were the dangers impending over property and order, they had for once no effect in rallying the middle class to the conservative side. On the contrary, these dangers became the text of heated letters to Grey and his colleagues, abusing them for not taking a stronger line with the Lords. One captain of industry demands a creation of peers, to prevent ' coal pits being set on fire and gas pipes cut.' Another exhorts the authorities to make peers and carry the Bill, or else the Political Unions will make a revolution and carry universal suffrage—a consummation by no means desired by the correspondent.[2]

More important and more threatening than the Bristol riots was the formation of the ' Low Political Unions ' all over the north that winter. They differed from the Political Unions formed on the Birmingham model ; the latter, strong specially in the west and south-west,[3] contained both middle and lower classes, and were organised under middle-classes leadership, working in the first instance to keep the peace and to demonstrate for the Bill, and intending only in the last

[1] *H.O. Papers*, 52, 13.
[2] Ibid., 49, 29.
[3] *E.g.* the Frome and the Bath Unions did much to prevent the spread of the Bristol disease in that region (*H.O. Papers*, 40, 29).

resort to fight for it. The 'Low Political Unions,' on the other hand, were entirely composed of working men, desiring to combine and expecting soon to fight against the Lords for a programme undefined. They were called into being by the wave of indignation against the Lords for throwing out the Bill ; in some places, as Manchester, where class antagonism was very bitter, the two kinds of Political Union existed side by side, neither of them therefore strong like the Mother of Unions at Birmingham.[1]

In both kinds of Union, drilling and quasi-military organisations were not unusual ; and this tendency increased after the throwing out of the Bill. During October and November the idea of armed resistance became daily more familiar to the middle and lower classes.[2] Arming of the Unions as such was rarely attempted, but members were encouraged to obtain arms as individuals, according to their right in common law, and gun-makers drove a flourishing trade. Now the drilling of men who had arms at home, and their avowed intention of carrying the Bill, or something stronger, by force if necessary, filled the King and the Tories with profound alarm and raised a most difficult problem for the Government.

Grey had to solve the problem of the Political Unions

[1] *H.O. Papers*, 40, 29 ; 40, 30 ; 52, 15 ; 44, 25. I gather from the *H.O. Papers* that the Low Political Unions that winter did not often consist of more than 800 or 1000 members in places like Preston, Oldham, or Macclesfield. But these, if organised and accustomed to act together, could lead the rest of the workmen of the place in the day of crisis.

[2] On November 4, no less respected a person than Carlyle's friend, Charles Buller, M.P., wrote to Colonel William Napier to ask him to ' draw out a plan for the composition and officering of a national guard ; put your name to it, and let it appear in *The Times* ; add a few of your stirring sentences to incite the British spirit of the cockney, and we shall have a national guard, and you at its head, in a fortnight.' The historian of the Peninsular War declined, in a very sensible letter, both for private reasons and on grounds of public policy (Bruce's *Life of Sir W. Napier*, i. 362–5).

or perish. If he gave them their head completely and allowed the drilling and military organisation to proceed unchecked, he would lose the King, who had taken alarm at statements made to him on the subject by the Duke of Wellington and others. Nor, indeed, were the King and the Duke wholly mistaken in their view ; for if the military organisation of the Unions went much further, Grey, with only a few thousand soldiers to back him, would find the arm of the law subjected in fact to the Political Unions, and the magistrates would everywhere be dependent on the goodwill of the Union leaders for the preservation of peace. If, on the other hand, he adopted the full programme of the King and the Duke, and attempted to put down the Political Unions altogether, as Pitt had put down the Corresponding Society and the Trade Unions of his day, the Ministry would fall, the Bill would disappear, and armed revolution or reaction would supervene.

The strong middle course actually adopted saved the situation. On November 22, 1831, a Royal Proclamation was issued denouncing as illegal all Political Unions ' with various divisions and subdivisions, under leaders with a gradation of rank and authority, and distinguished by certain badges, assuming a power of acting independently of the civil magistrates.' ' All such associations so constituted and appointed as aforesaid to be unconstitutional and illegal.'

At first, Wellington thought that the Proclamation was ' a real act,' that the Government had ' broken with the Radicals,' and that his own game was won. But in a few days he found out his mistake.[1] The Unions all over the country, quietly eliminating the quasi-military part of their organisation, declared that they were not the illegal bodies referred to by the Proclamation. The ground had been prudently prepared beforehand with Attwood, to whom Althorp, with the cognisance of

---

[1] *Despatches,* viii. 79, 85, 91, 93-4.

Grey, sent down a personal message through the Birmingham attorney, Joseph Parkes, explaining why Attwood must abandon the ' drilled meeting ' of the Union appointed for November 22, and adjust his methods to the limits set by the Proclamation.[1]

The Proclamation was indeed a most successful act of statesmanship, and sensibly diminished the prospect of revolution or reaction. It was generally welcomed by the middle class, including many of the Unionists themselves, who recognised the growing danger of anarchy and rejoiced that the legal authority of a Liberal Government should be reaffirmed. The country had been drifting, and now a stand had been made.[2]

The strategic genius of Wellington clearly perceived that the relation of the Whig Government with the Political Unions was the key to the whole position. He saw that it governed, among other things, the negotiations of Grey with Lord Wharncliffe. These negotiations were, on the part of the Prime Minister, an attempt to persuade the ' waverers ' among the Peers to support the new Bill, if it was drawn up on agreed lines. The Duke never took any part in these dealings. When the Proclamation about Unions was first issued, on November 22, he thought that Grey was ' breaking with the Radicals ' and would therefore make real concessions to Wharncliffe. But when he found that the Proclamation had caused no such breach, he rightly deduced that Grey would make no concessions of any value to a Tory mind. Thenceforth he had only contempt for the proceedings of Wharncliffe and ' these gentlemen who set about to break up the party.' [3]

If once we grant the Duke's premiss that the people of England were not to count in the matter, he did

---

[1] *Althorp*, 368 ; Torrens' *Melbourne*, i. 386 ; *Butler*, 316, for Grey's cognisance of Parkes' mission.

[2] There are letters to this effect in *H.O. Papers*, 40, 29.

[3] *Despatches*, viii. 79, 93–4, 101–3, 271.

right to be angry with Wharncliffe for selling the pass. He was right in so far as Grey never once contemplated making the new Bill ' less efficient ' than the old. The negotiations themselves, and the new features in the Bill that resulted from them, were only intended to save the face of those Peers and Bishops who would abandon further opposition.

On December 11 one of the Tory negotiators had to confess to the Duke that ' we found all parts of the Bill closed against any concession.' [1] But although the negotiations never resulted in a positive agreement between the parties, they were from Grey's point of view not unsuccessful, and Wellington attributed to them the passage of the Second Reading of the Bill in the Peers next April.[2]

' We had a dreadful scene [wrote Althorp, on December 6] at my Cabinet dinner yesterday. Durham made the most brutal attack on Lord Grey I ever heard in my life, and, I conclude, will instantly resign. He will put this upon alterations in the Bill, most unfairly, because there is no alteration of any consequence in the main principle. And I doubt whether he knows anything about the alterations, as he will not allow anyone to tell him what they are. But if he resigns on this ground it will break up the Government.' [3]

Durham, since his boy's death, had not been able to follow public events with an attentive or a lucid mind.

---

[1] *Despatches*, viii. 125.

[2] *Despatches*, viii. 271. The negotiations are fully recorded in *William's Correspondence*, end of vol. i. Mr. Wallas, in *Place*, 285, and Torrens, in *Melbourne*, i. 396, are mistaken in supposing that Grey ever once meditated ' remodelling the Bill ' in the sense of concession. The Bill was remodelled in the only sense that Grey ever intended, and many Reformers preferred it to the old Bill. Though Grey was at first averse to peer-making, he was at no time in favour of weakening the Bill.

[3] *Althorp*, 374–5, where the date of the letter is wrongly printed December 20, instead of December 6. The evidence of this unhappy scene rests not on *Greville*, who has popularised it, but who had it only at third hand, but on Althorp himself.

When this storm had passed, he seemed to have forgotten about it, and soon ' returned as if nothing had happened.'

The new Reform Bill was introduced into the House of Commons by Lord John Russell on December 12, 1831. The new features, suggested by the Wharncliffe negotiations, gave effect to many of the criticisms made by the Opposition on points of machinery and detail. The disfranchising Schedules A and B were drawn up no longer on the basis of population, but on the basis of the number of houses and the amount of assessed taxes ; and the new census of 1831 was employed. The Government also conceded the principle of the Gascoyne amendment that had been the immediate cause of the dissolution ; [1] the numbers of the House were not to be reduced, and it was therefore possible to take a dozen boroughs out of Schedule B while allotting an equal number more members to centres of population—as, for instance, to Rochdale, which the former Bills had not proposed to enfranchise.

The new Bill was regarded by many advanced Reformers, including Cobbett and Hunt, as better than its predecessor ; while the Tories, from Peel downwards, had the melancholy satisfaction of feeling that their opposition had been justified by the changes made. ' In its details,' Croker wrote to Lord Hertford, ' it is a great triumph for me and our party. But it leaves the great objection just where it was. Nay, by removing anomalies and injustice, it makes the Bill more palatable and therefore more dangerous.' [2]

On December 17 the Second Reading was carried in the Commons by a majority of exactly two to one, indicating Tory abstentions. And then the House adjourned for Christmas.

[1] See p. 294, above.
[2] *Croker*, ii. 141. Owing to the different system of calculation adopted under the new Bill, Calne, for which Macaulay sat, got into Schedule B—a personal triumph for Croker !

The new Bill had done well. Nothing had been lost by it in the country, and something had been gained by it in the Lords ; but not enough. The question of peer-making now took the field as the great controversy of the year 1832, henceforth overshadowing the discussion of the Bill itself.

In the previous autumn, when the cry for peer-making first grew loud, Grey was opposed to it for reasons of principle and for reasons of tactics. The reasons of principle, in the interest of the constitution, were his dislike of an act of violence, for which the twelve Tory peers created in 1711 to carry the Treaty of Utrecht seemed to him a precedent at once unhappy and inexact. He thought the creation of fifty or more peers would ' destroy ' the House of Lords as an independent and self-respecting body. He held also that it would gravely injure the Commons to take out of it so many of the best county members, ' withdrawing from it so great a portion of the property of the country.'

His tactical objections, in the interest of the Bill itself, were two. First, that to create new peers avowedly to carry the Bill would cause some of its previous supporters and all the ' waverers ' to vote against it in protest ; for this reason it was impossible to calculate how many new creations would be wanted—certainly well over fifty. Second, that the King, if he ever consented at all, would insist on calling up the heirs to existing peerages, many of whom were doing good work in the Lower House, sitting for county seats which their family influence had helped to gain. There would have to be a great number of bye-elections under disadvantageous conditions, and the Whigs had recently lost two bye-elections, for Dorset and Cambridgeshire.[1]

These arguments against peer-making would doubtless have continued to weigh with Grey, if the passage

---

[1] See Appendix H, below, ' Peer-making,' letters of Oct. and Nov. 1831.

of the Bill could have been secured by any other means. But when he found that his negotiations with Lord Wharncliffe, and his personal interviews with the leading Bishops,[1] though not entirely unsuccessful, gave little assurance of the passage of the Bill intact through Committee, he began to envisage peer-making as a last resource. Graham, Brougham, Durham, and Holland were those who pressed him hardest on the point in a series of admirably argued letters, and after Christmas the adhesion of the Prime Minister to their doctrine gave them the command of the divided Cabinet.

On New Year's Day, 1832, Grey wrote to Holland and to Brougham,[2] confessing that he had ' come nearer ' to Brougham's ' view of the matter of the Peerage ' than he thought he ever could have done, stating that he accepted Brougham's proposal of 'twelve at once ' in earnest of more to follow if required ; but adding that ' the King would dislike the thing in the greatest degree,' that four of their colleagues in the Cabinet were certainly against creation, and that the resignation of either Lansdowne or Palmerston would be ' fatal.'

When the Cabinet met next day, Althorp expected that several Ministers would resign at the end of it. In discussing the proposal for the immediate creation of a dozen peers, Melbourne, Richmond, Palmerston, and Lansdowne were against, and Stanley ' somewhat averse ' ;[3] while the rest of the Cabinet were for— Grant very doubtfully. Grey went to Brighton on the following day (January 3), to urge the policy of the majority of the Cabinet on the King, but not with the threat of immediate resignation if his request was denied.

The policy of creating twelve peers as earnest of the King's future intentions was a half measure, open to all the objections which Grey had felt as to the probable

---

[1] *William's Correspondence*, i. 443–4.
[2] *Brougham*, iii. 151–66, and Appendix H, below, p. 386.
[3] Parker's *Graham*, i. 134 ; *Brougham*, iii. 455.

bad effect of creations on the waverers. The King very sensibly said that he would rather create twenty-one peers at once than run the risk of requiring a 'second edition.' But Grey would give no assurance that even twenty-one would suffice in the end. After more than a week's negotiations between King and Cabinet, William on January 15, 1832, wrote Grey his famous promise in the following words :

The King will not, after having allowed that the resource should be effectual, and having, indeed, insisted upon the absurdity of incurring any risk by an insufficient addition to the House of Lords, if resorted to at all, *deny to his Ministers the power of acting at once up to the full exigency of the case ;* it being understood that the contemplated addition shall be deferred till it may appear certain that, without such addition, the strength of the Government would be insufficient to bring the measure of Parliamentary Reform to a successful issue.

No limitation of numbers was set. The only reservations were :

That the *creations of new Peers* shall under no circumstances exceed three. That the other additions shall be made by calling up eldest sons, or collateral heirs of Peerages where no direct heirs are likely to succeed, without reference to the objection that has been made, of throwing open the representation of counties or boroughs. If these sources should prove insufficient, recourse may be had to the Scotch and Irish Peerage for promotion to the English Peerage on this occasion.

If, therefore, the King had not in May gone back on his written promise of January 15, there would have been no national crisis ; and when Peel said to Croker on May 14, that the King's case for then refusing to make peers was ' a bad one,' he was doing no injustice to his sovereign.[1]

The letter of January 15 was Grey's most remarkable success in purely personal dealings. His handling

---

[1] *Croker*, ii. 165.

of the King was extraordinary, and knowing what we do of William's opinions and *entourage*, we must wonder more at his promise in January than at his attempt to avoid fulfilling it in May. The long conservative hesitations felt by the Prime Minister himself before making the demand, probably helped to obtain its concession, since the King by January felt assured that Grey was speaking from his heart when he declared that he considered peer-making 'a great evil which nothing would have induced him to think of resorting to, except the danger, or rather the certainty, of incurring one infinitely greater.'[1]

In March 1832, when the new Bill had nearly finished its smooth course through Committee in the Commons, the question of its probable fate in the Lords became too much for the nerves of some of Grey's colleagues. He himself was fairly confident, on account of his personal relations with the waverers, that, if nothing rash was done, it would pass its Second Reading.[2] But his confidence was not shared by the rest of the Cabinet. Holland's calculations foretold a draw ! Even Althorp, 'that most honest, frank, true and stout-hearted of God's creatures,' was so overworked with conducting the Bill through the Commons, and so over-wrought with anxiety for it in the Lords, that he removed the pistols from his bedroom ; on March 3 he said to Hobhouse : ' I do not know whether I ought not to make matters easier by shooting myself.' ' For God's sake, shoot anybody else you like,' was the answer.

Finally, the leading members of the Cabinet— Brougham, Durham, Holland, Althorp, Graham, and

---

[1] *William's Correspondence*, ii. 69. Holland writes to Grey, when the latter goes to ask for the peers : ' I think you will and must succeed. The King knows your own reluctance to the measure so well that he must infer from your urging it, your deep sense of its absolute necessity.'

[2] *Creevey*, ii. 242–3.

Russell—combined to coerce Grey into demanding an immediate creation of peers, rather than take the chance of defeat on the Second Reading. Their resignations, particularly Althorp's, were threatened in case their chief refused.

It was now that Grey's character was put to its supreme test. If he had been a weak man and ' easily led,' as he was sometimes represented by those who only half knew him, he must have yielded against his better judgment to this combination. But he saw clearly that his colleagues were trying to force him to bring about a premature crisis, which would render both King and Lords unmanageable, and would not justify itself to moderate people in the country.

Since January 15 the King stood pledged to make an unlimited number of peers, but only if the creation was deferred till its need was ' certain.'[1] William eventually went back even on that promise ; how much more would he have refused to be better than his word and to create fifty, sixty, or seventy peers on a mere speculation that the Bill would not pass ! If, on such a refusal, the Ministers resigned, many people would think they had acted factiously and in panic. On the other hand, if the King by any chance consented to create at once, a great many of the moderate peers, outraged at an action which they had been prepared to avert by voting for the Bill, would turn against the Ministers with fury and very probably throw out the Bill in spite of the new creations. In that case the Ministers would have played their trump card prematurely and would have lost after all. Grey preferred to trust to the Second Reading being passed, when he could face the Committee stage with the King's promise to create still in his pocket, to be produced, if necessary, as the *ultima ratio*.

Grey's reasoning of the subject, set out in an admirable letter to Althorp,[2] ended with a firm declaration

---

[1] See p. 332, above.
[2] Printed in *Althorp*, 407-13, as well as in *William's Correspondence.*

that he could not do as he was asked, and that if Althorp resigned he could not carry on the Government. The letter was read to the Cabinet on March 11, 1832, and such was the force of its arguments in favour of abiding by the existing arrangement with the King and delaying the creation of peers till a defeat was certain or had taken place, that when a division was called for Grey carried with him the whole Cabinet except Durham. Durham burst away, declaring that he resigned. But he too, when he found that his resignation would involve Russell's and would break up the Ministry, allowed himself to be over-persuaded by Althorp.

Grey, the 'pessimist' of the Napoleonic Wars, the valetudinarian of the long years of opposition conducted from Howick, had become in the hour of supreme domestic danger a pillar of strength among his colleagues. His victory in the Cabinet of March 11 was a victory of character.[1]

Yet he had now put heavy personal stakes on the Bill passing its Second Reading without catastrophe, and when in April the great debate in the Lords began, his family, if not himself, felt a terrible anxiety about the division. Lady Grey writes to her daughter in the spirit of Shakespeare's Portia when her Brutus had gone to the Senate :

Monday, April 9.—Car really seems less alarmed than anybody I see, and his apparent confidence keeps up my spirits though I am very nervous indeed. They do not expect the division till Wednesday.

Tuesday night, or rather Wednesday morning, 1 *o'clock.*— Car is not yet home and I am in a state of extreme nervousness.

---

[1] The authorities for the story of the Cabinet crisis of March are *William's Correspondence*, ii. 195–6, note, 257–72 ; *Althorp*, 402–14 ; *Edinburgh Review*, July 1871, 291–4 ; *Hobhouse*, iv. 180, 188–200 ; *Butler*, 347–9 ; Parker's *Graham*, i. 137–41 ; MS. letter of Durham to Grey, March 12, of which the last paragraph is quoted in Reid's *Durham*, i. 278.

When he went to the House he thought the division would take place to-night, but as Henry left Lord Wharncliffe speaking at 12, they think it will probably be adjourned. I had much rather they would get through it to-night. They all went to the House in spirits, *making sure* of carrying the 2nd reading, tho' by a small majority, but Mr. Wood who came to tea has rather damped my hopes by telling me there is a report of two defections, Lord de Roos and Lord Ravensworth.

Wednesday.—Car came home before 2 this morning, and though very tired, he seemed in good spirits, and he had rather more sleep than usual. Lord de Roos is still with us ; there is doubt of Lord Ravensworth.[1] However, Car thinks the division safe. God grant it.

It was already broad daylight on Saturday, April 14, 1832, before the House divided. Grey's speeches had been conciliatory as well as eloquent, and this was believed to have affected several waverers.[2] He lost no favour with the Peers either temporal or spiritual by a skirmish at close quarters with Phillpotts, the powerful and truculent Bishop of Exeter, to whose invective he replied with warmth that ' the pulses of ambition may beat as strongly under sleeves of lawn as under an ordinary habit.'[3] The Bishops voted fifteen against and twelve for the Bill —a great improvement on their record of twenty-one to two in the previous October. Wharncliffe both spoke and voted for the Second Reading, which was carried by 184 to 175, the majority of nine which Charles Wood had prophesied to his father-in-law.[4]

---

[1] They both voted straight. [2] *Althorp*, 417–18.

[3] Greville, the moderate, describing this episode, wrote of Phillpotts : ' He is carried away by his ambition and alarm, and horrifies his brethren, who feel all the danger in these times of such a colleague.' ' He has a desperate and dreadful countenance, and looks like the man he is.' Greville compared him to Queen Mary's Gardiner !

[4] *Althorp*, 418, note.

CHAPTER V

THE STRUGGLE FOR THE BILL—THE 'DAYS OF MAY'

'Rise like lions after slumber
In unvanquishable number!
Shake your chains to earth, like dew
Which in sleep had fall'n on you:
Ye are many—they are few.'
SHELLEY.

Quoted by Dr. Kay at a meeting in Rochdale during the 'Days of May.'

THE passage of the Second Reading of the Bill in the Lords on April 14, 1832, greatly relieved the situation. If hostile amendments were now carried, they could quickly be reversed as the outcome of a peer-making crisis, whereas if the whole Bill had been again thrown out, the insult of such an act, combined with the prospect of the long delay before yet another Bill could have been brought through all its stages, might well have been too much for the patience of the people, if the King had hesitated a day in the creation of peers. Perhaps therefore the greatest danger was passed on April 14. But the most exciting and memorable popular crisis still lay ahead.

The 'Days of May' were brought about by an attempt, not indeed to destroy the Bill or even perhaps seriously to cut down its provisions, but to reassert the power and prestige of the House of Lords by taking the conduct of the Bill out of the hands of the Ministers and handing it over to the leaders of opposition. One of the motives was a very natural desire to heal the breach

337

in the Tory ranks, caused by the division of April 14, when Wharncliffe and his friends, to save the State, had voted against the party to whose fold they longed to return. But whatever the motives the experiment was ill-timed. If tried at all, it should have been in the previous October, when the Bill first came up to the Lords. Neither the Ministers, the Commons, nor the people were any longer in the mood for such trifling, after all that had come and gone.

On May 7 Lord Lyndhurst moved in Committee to postpone the consideration of the disfranchising clauses of the Bill till after the enfranchising clauses had been taken.[1] Grey, who had already told Wharncliffe in private that the Government could not agree to this procedure,[2] now publicly warned the House that if the amendment was carried he would have ' to consider what course he should take.' But they would not listen. Waverers and Wellington men trooped off together to the division, and carried by thirty-five the postponement of Schedules A and B.

Grey at once saw that his opponents had played into his hands. The real danger, he had long ago foretold, would arise if they pruned down the measure, here a little and there a little, on points each too small to seem a proper case for peer-making, yet collectively injurious to the popular character of the Bill. But now they had defied the Government on a main principle of procedure and he was quick to take advantage of it.[3] As

---

[1] Lyndhurst's speech implied that the Peers intended to cut down the number of towns to be enfranchised, and then correspondingly reduce the number of boroughs in Schedules A and B. On the other hand, Ellenborough's speech, made immediately after the division, implies that the Bill would be swallowed wholesale as to disfranchisement, and be made, if anything, more democratic as to franchise qualification ! The fact was that the Lords who voted for the amendment had very divergent ideas as to what they would make of the Bill when they had taken it out of Grey's hands.   [2] *Greville*, May 12, 1832.

[3] On June 2, after the crisis, Creevey writes : ' In the House of Lords yesterday, Grey, according to his custom, came and talked to me.

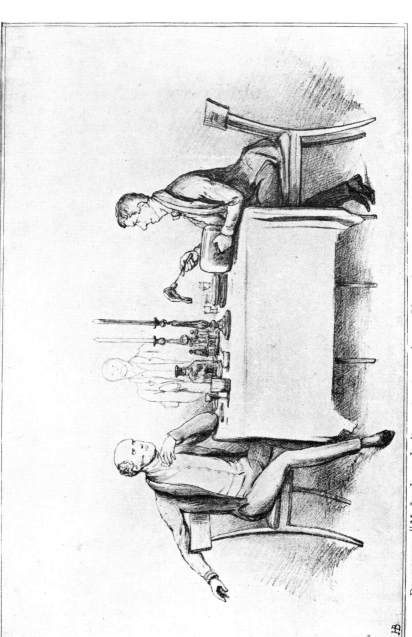

BROUGHAM: "My Lord, you don't seem to eat your chops. I have already placed six in Schedule A, and am about to discuss a seventh, while you have scarcely got through one. Come, cheer up, and all will be well to-morrow."

soon as the House rose, the Cabinet chiefs, without leaving Westminster, met hastily in the Lord Chancellor's room, and decided to resign if the King would not give them power to make peers at once. The full Cabinet next morning confirmed this decision, Richmond alone dissenting. Even Palmerston smelt battle and forgot his doubts about the Bill.

That afternoon (May 8), Grey and Brougham posted down to Windsor and saw the King. They asked for not less than fifty peers. He replied that he would send them an answer next day, but they had no doubt from his manner that it would contain a refusal. They started back to London at once, dining on the way at a public-house at Hounslow on mutton chops ; Brougham's universal appetite added kidneys, but Grey declared that ' he cared not for kidneys.' The meal took hold of the popular imagination, and was immortalised by Doyle in one of the most famous of his ' H.B.' cartoons.[1]

Next day (May 9) arrived the King's letter. Declining to make ' so large an addition to the Peerage,' he accepted their resignations, but asked them to ' continue in discharge of their official functions ' until the new Ministry was formed.

It is important to remember that throughout the ten ' Days of May,' the Whig Ministers were in charge

It is really too much to see his happiness at its being all over and well over. He dwells upon the marvellous luck of Wellington's false move—upon the eternal difficulties he (Grey) would have been involved in had the Opposition not brought it to a crisis when they did. Their blunder he conceives to have been their belief that he would not resign upon his defeat on an apparent question of form. Thank God ! They did not know their man.'

[1] John Doyle, the father of ' Dicky Doyle,' and father also of a less savage style of political cartoon than that of Gillray or Cruikshank. For the mutton chops at Hounslow see *Creevey*, May 9, and *Brougham*, iii. 193. Brougham's posthumous account of the interview with the King is incredible, as regards Grey's alleged self-effacement before his Chancellor, and is generally rejected.

of the ordinary running of the administration, though they were in no position to make decisions of policy. None of them was for an hour superseded by a Tory. The anomalous state of affairs is indicated by a letter which Grey wrote from Downing Street on May 14 to inform Lord Hill, commanding the troops in England, that two privates from the barracks at Birmingham had joined Attwood's Political Union, and had stated that ' the greater part of their comrades are prepared to follow their example.' ' I am no longer in a situation,' adds the fallen Prime Minister, ' to offer any advice, but I cannot help suggesting that the most expedient course would be to remove the regiment immediately from Birmingham to some other quarter, without attracting publick notice to the cause of it at present.' Thus, if the Revolution had broken out that week, there would have been no really responsible Ministers to suppress it or to negotiate with its chiefs.

But in fact the Revolution was timed for the moment of Wellington's taking office, and not before. To some extent, though by no means entirely, the 'Days of May' were due to a misunderstanding. The King's intention was to get the Bill passed unaltered, but, in order to avoid peer-making, to have it passed by the Tories.[1] The people thought that the Bill as well as the Ministry was in danger. William commissioned Lyndhurst to take soundings, and then asked Wellington to form a Government and pass the Bill. The Duke thought it his duty to help his sovereign ' to shake off the trammels of a tyrannical Minister ' at any expense to his own consistency in the matter of Reform.[2] By some queer subtlety in his usually

---

[1] It appears that William tried first of all to persuade Brougham to keep office and help pass the Bill—at least Brougham said so at the time (*Althorp*, 423, note), and not merely years afterwards (*Brougham*, iii. 194–5). [2] *Despatches*, viii. 304.

straightforward mind, he thought that the Lords would be degraded by passing the Bill under threat of peer-making, if the Bill was presented to them by Lord Grey, but not if it was presented to them by himself—although in either case the threat of peer-making would be the compelling force. The point was too subtle for Peel, who refused to take office to pass the Bill, and thereby made the task of Cabinet-making difficult from the start.[1]

A point that was too subtle for Peel was very much too subtle for the mass of Englishmen. All they knew was that the King had refused to make peers, that Grey had therefore resigned, and that the King had sent for Wellington—the man who had stood almost alone in pronouncing against any Reform at all, the soldier who was reported to have said that if the people of England were not quiet, ' there was a way to make them.' Those words, everywhere repeated, were taken up as a challenge. They would show the Duke that English citizens could stand up to the soldiers as well as Frenchmen or Belgians. The middle and working classes were for once united, in the resolve to make forcible resistance to the formation of a Wellington Ministry.

The House of Commons gradually came to believe the amazing truth that the Tories were themselves going to pass ' the Bill, the whole Bill, and nothing but the Bill.'[2] But the people never believed it, and if they had it would have made no difference, they were so angry. ' Every man you met,' said Cobbett, ' seemed

---

[1] In defence of Peel's distinction between the case of 1832 and the cases of 1829 and 1846, it must be remembered that in 1832 the Whigs could and would pass the necessary measure if the Tories declined to take office ; whereas in 1829 they could not have passed Catholic Emancipation, and in 1846 they refused to take office to pass the Corn Law, and ' handed back the poisoned challice to Sir Robert.'

[2] They believed it during the decisive debate of May 14, but had not yet come to believe it fully in the debates of May 9 and 10.

to be convulsed with rage.' When, on May 13, Attwood was informed of the Duke's good intentions as a Reformer, he replied that, whatever sort of Bill the Tories passed, if the House of Lords could, even at the climax of this great popular movement, make and unmake Ministries at will, 'there was an end of popular power in England, and the spirit of the people would be utterly broken.'[1]

Attwood was right in thinking that the coming era would be profoundly affected by the example of Wellington's success or failure. The defeat, upon this issue, of the King and Lords by the Commons and the people was the source from which sprang the peaceful democratic development of the Victorian Age. The 'Days of May' half won beforehand the battle for the Repeal of the Corn Laws, and for the working-class franchise of 1867.

But Grey, the man of an earlier generation, more concerned with winding up the terrible arrears of the age gone by than in foreseeing the distant future, would have been content to have the unaltered Bill passed by the Tories. He and Althorp indulged their too domestic natures in the happy prospect of shuffling off the cares of State. Althorp, 'with bright eye and radiant smile,' went off to oil the locks of his beloved fowling-pieces, which had been rusting for eighteen months. And Grey wrote to Holland on May 13:

Can a new administration be formed? I begin to be *afraid* that the attempt will fail.

And two days later, when Holland had rebuked his want of spirit, replied :

I believe all you say is quite right ; the truth is that never was captive more desirous of escaping from prison than I am from my present situation. But I will do my duty.[2]

[1] Wakefield's *Life of Attwood*.

[2] For more of Grey's correspondence during the ' Days of May,' see Appendix H, below.

The attempt to form a Tory Ministry was frustrated by the House of Commons. The Whig Ministers had tried to render the work of the Cabinet-makers easy, on condition that ' the Bill ' was passed. But the Commons would have none of it. It is true that Althorp and Stanley persuaded a meeting of the Whig party at Brooks's, on May 13, to allow the new Ministry to come in, to pass the Reform Bill, perhaps with democratic additions, and then to turn out the Duke.[1] But in the Commons next evening all manœuvres and subtleties were swept away by a wave of angry distrust, felt by Whig and Tory alike, at the prospect of anti-Reformers passing the Reform Bill as the price of office. When from both sides of the House one private member after another rose to express the abhorrence felt by any plain man at this ridiculous, dangerous, and dishonourable shift, the other Tory chiefs saw that Peel was in the right. Baring was to have had a leading place in the new Ministry. ' I had rather,' he said, after that debate, ' face a thousand devils than such a House of Commons.' [2]

Hearing that the Lower House was unmanageable, Wellington next day (May 15) abandoned the attempt to form a Cabinet, and Grey was again sent for. The Commons, by preventing the formation of a Tory Ministry, had averted an organised insurrection in the great cities of England and Scotland, though if we are to judge by the debates very few members were aware of it. Still less did the Whig and Tory magnates, with whom lay the decision of the Cabinet crisis, discuss their conduct in relation to the impending insurrection. Yet few contingent historical propositions are more

---

[1] *Campbell*, ii. 10; Parker's *Graham*, i. 143; *Althorp*, 429. The Duke, of course, could have passed no Reform Bill not approved by the Whig House of Commons.

[2] *Greville*, May 17. The abortive Cabinet-making is most fully described in *Croker*.

certain than this, that if the Duke had taken office there would have been a rebellion.

The disturbances of the winter had died away at the beginning of the year 1832, though cholera and bad trade continued. But with the return of order came an increasing determination to fight, if necessary, for the Bill. The Proclamation of November 22 [1] had checked the militarisation of the Unions, but had not disarmed them. Those of them that looked to Attwood for orders had indeed kept within the letter of the law, but the law could not prevent their individual members from purchasing arms. And the 'Low Political Unions' of the northern working men sometimes transgressed the proclamation. There was drilling at Manchester in January.[2] In Lancashire and Yorkshire a vigorous trade went on with working-class customers for swords at twelve shillings each, and then by competition at six shillings. At Halifax the Political Union obtained 400 pistols from a Birmingham firm.[3] In Scotland, Jeffrey had written to Grey, in January, that order was perfect, largely owing to the Unions ; that there were ' no burnings, no turbulent assemblies,' but that ' the passion for Reform was more universal than ever,' and that if it was not obtained peaceably, ' the rising would not be confined to the lower orders,' but that ' persons of good estate and character ' would cast in their lot with the rebels.

Such was the state of things in the island when, in the second week of May, the news spread that Wellington was forming a Ministry. The immediate effect was not rioting, as when the Lords threw out the Bill in October, but a general suspension of work and business in the big towns. Men of all classes stood

---

[1] See p. 326, above.

[2] *H.O. Papers*, 40, 30 : General Bouverie's letters of January 25 and 29.

[3] *H.O. Papers*, 40, 30 : Eastham's evidence in Col. Shaw's report.

about in groups to listen for the news, and to await the coming crisis. In Scotland, wrote Cockburn, ' the fearful part of it ' was ' the absence of riot.' In England Sir Robert Heron observed ' no breaking of windows, no trifling expressions of discontent : all seemed reserved for a tremendous explosion.' In the whole of Yorkshire and Lancashire, in the 'Days of May,' there was only one riot—in York.[1] But one of the members for Yorkshire had a letter from some of his leading constituents to say that they were ' tired of signing petitions, and wished to fight it out, and the sooner the better.'[2] Pikes were hammered in Sheffield without concealment. Employers and workmen prepared to act together even in Manchester, where business was suspended. Everywhere that week the Political Unions were swelled by crowds of new members, prepared to obey any commands, lawful or unlawful, that they might receive from their chiefs. If the authority of the Government became paralysed or hostile, here would be the new bulwark against anarchy. The English genius for improvisation, for ordered liberty, and for self-help in a crisis had found expression in Attwood's Political Unions.

In many places the Yeomanry refused to serve under Tory officers. Even in an old-world county like Bucks, ' the respectable classes came to the resolution of not acting as special constables.'[3] The regiments of the gallant little army that had rushed about from place to place, putting down so many local riots, would be alike unwilling and unable to suppress the organised and simultaneous revolt of the principal towns of the country.

Birmingham, during the 'Days of May,' passed morally under the obedience of Attwood's Union.

---

[1] *H.O. Papers*, 40, 30 : General Bouverie's letter of May 21.
[2] *Althorp*, 433.
[3] Ibid., 433.

Its ranks were being swelled by soldiers from the barracks, by Quakers, by Roman Catholic priests, and by 500 conservative-minded citizens, who now joined in a body to avert a social revolution. The police reports for Birmingham, and indeed for the country generally, were no heavier in May than in other months.[1]

'If any accident,' it was said, 'had made resistance begin anywhere, it would have run like an electric shock.' Such being the state of England and Scotland, what were the plans of the popular leaders? Place and Attwood were in complete understanding and close correspondence with each other and with the Union chiefs in all the great cities of the island. Their plan was first to try and prevent the Duke from taking office. For this purpose they created a run on the banks, initiated by Place's famous placard, 'To stop the Duke, go for Gold!' The refusal of taxes also began, and was to continue until Grey was again in the saddle.

But if, in spite of all, the Duke came into office, then, and only then, resort was to be made to the system of 'hostile defence,' as Place termed it. London's part in it would be not to make the revolution, but to demonstrate in such a way that none of the 7000 troops in and around the capital could be moved to the provinces. It was calculated, too optimistically indeed, that then only 4000 troops would be left to coerce the rest of the island. As the City Fathers were at one with the mob and the Unions,[2] there should have been no difficulty

---

[1] Wakefield's *Life of Attwood*. The only exception to the good order and union of classes and the interest in Reform, during the 'Days of May,' was on Tyneside, where an embittered industrial strife was going on between the Reformers themselves. The employers were engaged in breaking the Miners' Union. The Union men and their leader had demonstrated powerfully in favour of the Bill in 1831. See Hammond, *Skilled Labourer*, chap. iii., pp. 35, 41.

[2] On May 23 Attwood received the Freedom of the City of London.

GREY   JOHN BULL   THE KING   WELLINGTON

John Bull intervenes.   May, 1832.   *From "H.B." Political Sketches.*

about London fulfilling its part. Meanwhile, Birmingham and the other great cities were to barricade themselves, to create where necessary new municipal authorities, to close all banks, and then to sit down in a state of armed defence against any action the Government might take. What would happen after that, time and the hour would determine. It was hoped that the Duke would resign.[1]

This programme was not a hole-and-corner conspiracy of fools and fanatics. It was announced in its principles by the *Times* and other newspapers, who declared that the people would pay no taxes till Lord Grey came back, that the middle and working classes were united and prepared to fight if troops were sent against them ; but that till Wellington actually took office the word was ' peace, order, and no taxes.'[2]

It is most strange, that while men were crying from the house-tops that there would be armed resistance if the Duke came in, neither he, Peel, nor Croker, neither Grey, Holland, nor Althorp, discussed it in their letters and speeches as relevant to the question whether the Duke should take office. One cannot but suspect that it secretly influenced their minds, though they thought that ' noblesse ' obliged them to avoid allusion to a subject so indecorous and unconstitutional.

The news that Wellington had on May 15 abandoned his attempt to form a Cabinet spread next day over the land, and for a few hours relaxed the tension. But presently it was discovered that all was still at issue. The King had not really yielded. He had only asked Lord Grey to continue in office and to pass the Bill ; but he still refused to make peers, trusting that Wellington would ease matters by withdrawing his opposition. The Duke, however, refused to do any-

---

[1] The most important passages from the *Place Papers*, B.M., relating to the conspiracy, are published in Mr. Wallas' *Place*.

[2] *Times*, May 12-16, 1832.

thing more than abstain from voting as an individual peer. Even now he would not, as a party leader, call off the opposition, because to do so would be to yield to the unconstitutional threat of peer-making !

On May 17 Grey came down to the House, expecting to hear the Duke deprecate further opposition, and prepared in return to announce the Ministerial crisis at an end. Instead of this, he heard himself fiercely assailed for his unconstitutional conduct by Lyndhurst and Wellington themselves. Taken unawares, he had no declaration of policy to make. The crisis remained as acute as before.

The rage of the people rose high at this fresh disappointment. May 18 was the day when the preparations for revolt were most complete, and the passion that inspired them nearest to breaking-point. Place sent a précis of the conspirators' intentions to his friend Hobhouse, the Minister-at-War, for the instruction of his colleagues. It was now a question of hours. The Cabinet met in Downing Street at noon, and decided to ask for ' full and indisputable security ' for the passage of the Bill. Grey and Brougham took the Cabinet minute across to the King at St. James's Palace. He was in great distress, and most unwilling to comply. The afternoon wore on, and the capital and the country hung on the issue of that prolonged interview. At length William gave way, and wrote the famous words :

His Majesty authorises Earl Grey, if any obstacle should arise during the further progress of the Bill, to submit to him a creation of Peers to such extent as shall be necessary to enable him to carry the Bill.

The battle was won. The country instantly sank to rest with a sigh of profound relief. When the King pressed for a forcible dissolution of the Political Unions, Grey refused with unusual emphasis, adding with truth that they would dissolve of themselves if nothing foolish was done. He had learnt, during the last months of

ALTHORP, RUSSELL.　　　　BURDETT, HOBHOUSE, STANLEY, GRAHAM.
(in top boots)

In front of the throne are the Commissioners with Lord Brougham presiding as Chancellor.
The Duke of Sussex is the stout figure by the curtain on the right.　The benches of
the Tory Peers are vacant.　The Commons are at the bar.

The Reform Bill receiving the Royal Assent in the House of Lords.

*From the engraving by Wm. Walker and S. W. Reynolds, after the painting by
Samuel W. Reynolds.*

the struggle, how much the country owed to these Unions, of which he had at first been distrustful. On May 19 he sent for Attwood, thanked him for his services, and asked if anything could be done for him by way of showing the gratitude of the Ministers. It equally well became Grey to offer and Attwood to refuse.[1]

The Tory lords, privately informed by Taylor of what the King had promised to do if they held out any longer, abandoned their opposition in Committee. On June 4 the Third Reading of the Bill was carried by 106 to 22. On June 7 the Reform Bill received the Royal Assent by Commission ; the scene was in the House of Lords ; the Tory benches were empty, and the six Commissioners were Grey, Holland, Brougham, Wellesley, Lansdowne, and Durham.[2]

[1] Wakefield's *Attwood*, 214.

[2] In the picture opposite some details are very exact, *e.g.* the position of H.R.H. the Duke of Sussex by the curtain. But others are not accurate, as Hobhouse tells us that he really came too late to see the event. The Scottish and Irish Reform Bills were passed in the course of the summer.

CHAPTER VI

'The retirement of Lord Grey in 1834 proved the conclusion of a political career which had extended over more than forty years. For nearly nine-tenths of the period, Grey had been in opposition to the Ministry. He had thus less opportunity of conferring benefit upon his country than almost any of his predecessors. Yet perhaps Britain owes more to him than to any other Minister. . . . He had foreseen at thirty the necessity of the measure which he carried at seventy. Peel was as wise as Grey; but Grey, unlike Peel, was as prescient as he was wise. Grey himself should be judged by the Reform Bill alone. . . . He seemed to be raised up to carry Reform. The passage of the Reform Bill made his own tenure of power an anachronism.'—SPENCER WALPOLE, *History of England*, chap. xiii.

THE Reform Bill laid it down that seats in the House of Commons could no longer be purchased or inherited as private property, but must represent the people. This principle being established once for all, the further definition of the classes who were to be regarded as constituting 'the people,' was sure to be made afresh with each changing generation. The battle for popular control of the House of Commons was won in 1832.

The passage of the Reform Bill also decided, not in law but in fact, that the People, acting on and through the House of Commons, were the dominant power in the State. The Tory efforts at resistance in the House of Lords, aided in their last rally by the Crown, had only served to elicit the irresistible power of the popular will.

After 1832 the Government of Great Britain had become 'representative,' whereas Pitt's Attorney-General in 1794 had declared in Court that 'representative government' was 'the direct contrary of the government which is established here.'[1] The change was so profound that in most countries it would only have been effected by civil war. Therein lies the measure of Lord Grey's achievement.

The new principle was indeed a reassertion of the old popular elements in the English constitution of Stuart times. But it was a reassertion of rights which had long ago decayed, and which, now that they were revived, contained far greater power of democratic development than they could ever have had before the Industrial Revolution. It was from 1832 onwards that the whole spirit of our polity finally diverges from that of aristocratic Germany, just as in 1793 it had diverged from that of Jacobin France. We all rejoice at both divergences. But there was much greater danger under Pitt and Castlereagh of Britain becoming like aristocratic Germany, than there ever had been of her becoming like the France of Robespierre.

With the passage of the Reform Bill the new age had arrived, 'making Grey's continuance in power an anachronism.' But since the leaders of the new age, of whom Peel was one of the first, were not yet ready to step forward, Grey did well to preside for two more years over the divided counsels of the Whig Cabinet. This task he performed better than any other Minister could then have done. But the great legislative programme of those two years—Slavery Abolition, Scottish Burgh Reform, the Factory Act, the India Bill, the new Poor Law—was not like the Reform Bill, Lord Grey's personal affair. The sphere in which his interest was deepest, and his guiding hand most felt, was Foreign

[1] *State Trials*, xxiv. pp. 294-5.

Policy. From 1830 to 1834 he helped Lord Palmerston to ward off a series of dangerous crises from Europe, and to settle for eighty years the question of Belgium, the spot in Europe which in all ages, from the days of Alva to our own, most nearly concerns the security of Britain.

Belgium had yet to make good its recently asserted independence of Holland. The candidature of Louis Philippe's son, the Duke of Nemours, for the new throne of Belgium, had been set aside by the firmness of Grey and Palmerston in February 1831.[1] A more acceptable king was found in Prince Leopold of Saxe-Coburg, whom on June 4, 1831, the Belgian Congress elected by 152 votes to 43. The election proved the happiest possible choice for Belgium and for Europe. Leopold had lived for a long time in England, on familiar terms with the leaders of the more Liberal school of English constitutionalism. He had been the husband of the lamented Princess Charlotte, once heiress to the British throne ; he was the uncle and adviser of the Princess Victoria, who had taken her place. One of his most intimate friends was Lord Durham. And throughout Lord Grey's Ministry, King Leopold kept up a close personal correspondence with the British Premier on every shifting phase of the prolonged Belgian crisis.

Grey sent to Belgium Sir Robert Adair, his own and Fox's friend of thirty and forty years back. Adair further strengthened the close personal contact between Brussels and Downing Street. At the same time our able Ambassador at Paris, Lord Granville, the friend of Canning whom Grey had reappointed to his old post, kept him *au fait* with the changes and chances of French politics, where a war-party was straining at the leash, and striving to revive the dangerous crusading zeal of the old Jacobin type.[2] Grey was in complete agreement

[1] See pp. 259–260, above.
[2] Grey's correspondence with King Leopold, Sir Robert Adair, and Lord Granville are in the papers at Howick.

with Palmerston on Foreign Policy, and with the skilful help of Talleyrand in London [1] the two were able, not without difficulty, to preserve the Anglo-French *entente*. France and England continued to support King Leopold and Belgian independence, against the Dutch backed by the reactionary powers of Europe.

In August and September 1831 the dangers caused by the entry first of Dutch and then of French troops into Belgium were skilfully averted without a quarrel with France.[2] A year later (October–December 1832), Britain and France actually co-operated by sea and land to coerce the Dutch into the surrender of the Citadel of Antwerp. All these delicate operations were carried out under the watchful and hostile eyes of the French war party on one side, and on the other of the English Tories and of the despotic Powers of the East. Russia, Austria, and Prussia, jealous of Belgian independence as a breach in the reactionary system of the Treaties of Vienna, only waited for a misunderstanding between France and England to pounce down on the small rebel Kingdom.

At home and abroad it was generally expected that if the Tories returned to power, a breach between France and England would ensue. King William was hostile to the Whig policy of friendship with France. Lord Aberdeen, Wellington's Foreign Minister, made bitter attacks in the House of Lords, not only on the Belgian Revolution and the separation of Belgium from Holland,[3] but on the person and character of the King of the French.[4] Grey's warm reply on behalf of Louis Philippe was greatly appreciated in the Tuileries, where the King ' put his hand on his heart ' and told Lord Granville that Grey's words ' had made an impression that never could be effaced.'

---

[1] See p. 259, above.
[2] See p. 304, above.
[3] *Hansard*, ix. 841–5, Jan. 26, 1832.
[4] Ibid., v. 798–9, August 5, 1831.

Leopold knew that the Tories were the enemies of Belgian independence. He regarded a change of Government in London as certain to lead to a war between France and England, which his own little Kingdom could only hope to survive as a protectorate of France. He therefore made no secret of his Whig partisanship ; in March 1832 he even wrote to Lord Grey hinting strongly at the need for peer-making. During the 'Days of May' he was in ' deep despondency ' at the prospect of a Wellington Ministry, regarding war as certain, but determined, as Adair reported to Grey, ' to fight to the last for his new Kingdom.' In the end, the peace of Europe and the independence of Belgium were saved, though only by a combination of luck and skill. And when at length, in 1841, the Conservatives attained to real power again in this country, it was no longer the reactionary Toryism of Wellington, but the sage counsels of Peel that directed the policy of Aberdeen, who himself had been made wiser by the passage of years.[1]

In a letter to Grey of April 1832 King Leopold thus sums up the Belgian achievement of Grey and Palmerston:

It has been the policy of Great Britain for centuries never to permit Belgium to fall into the hands of any great Power. Everything is now favourable to the policy. The Belgians are warmly attached to their newly-acquired independency. They hate the Dutch, and they are jealous of the French. The new kingdom is quieter and better settled than many old countries. An object, therefore, on which Great Britain lavished so much blood and money, has been attained without its costing a farthing to that country, or being the cause of the slightest hurt to any Englishman.

It was a logical development of this Belgian policy of the Whigs, that eighty years later France and England should fight side by side to save Belgian independence

---

[1] Appendix H, below, p. 390; and p. 389, Lord Holland's letter of May 14 on Aberdeen.

from the despotisms of Central Europe, which even in 1831 had angrily menaced its birth.

But in Lord Grey's time Russia was even more to the fore than Prussia in threatening the liberty of Belgium. Even in Metternich's Europe, the Czar Nicholas was the most despotic figure of all, suppressing the autonomy of the Kingdom of Poland, which he had pledged himself to respect and which the other powers had guaranteed by the Treaties of Vienna. Grey, who never allowed his friendship with the Princess Lieven to influence his policy in the slightest degree, was, much to the disgust of that clever lady, becoming more and more anti-Russian. On January 1, 1832, he wrote to Brougham that the Russians were 'doing all they can to throw the whole Belgian affair into confusion. It is to be regretted that we had no power of sending a fleet into the Baltic last summer to settle the matter of Poland.'

Russia's Polish and Belgian policy so deeply offended Grey's Liberal instincts, that we notice at this period, even as regards the Turkish question, a tendency away from the Russophil leanings which had been so marked in him during the struggle for Greek independence.[1] In the following letter of Grey's to Lord Holland (January 25, 1833) we see him take one step away from pure Foxite tradition on Russia and Turkey, in the direction of that policy which Palmerston and Russell carried to much greater lengths in the Crimean war.

I certainly have not much more fear than you have of an attack upon India, though this is not to be entirely put out of our view. But with the influence which Russia is likely to obtain in the new Government of Greece—with that which events seem likely to give her in Turkey, the danger of her power in that quarter of the world is not remote. The danger, I agree with you, will be best guarded against by a friendly union with France. But you are aware of the difficulties in high

[1] Pp. 227–8, above.

quarters [1] increased by the [French] possession of Algiers. And if, joining with France to resist the advance of Russia into the Mediterranean, hostilities should follow, would either the Parliament or the people support us in a war which would be generally felt to arise for the sake of a remote and problematical interest?

Another important foreign question of that period was the running sore of the Iberian peninsula, the constant civil wars of Liberal and Reactionary in Spain and Portugal. Here also the Whig and Tory policies were opposed. The Whigs were for supporting the Liberal cause in conjunction with France, while jealousy of Liberal France dominated the attitude of Wellington and Aberdeen. Grey regarded it as a British interest to protect Portugal from the disastrous rule of the cruel, reactionary usurper Dom Miguel. He was indeed under no deceptions as to Miguel's constitutionalist rival, Dom Pedro. In October 1833 he wrote to Lord Holland :

I cannot believe that Pedro will ever do any good in Portugal or anywhere else. On the contrary, I am persuaded that if he remains, the affairs of that unhappy country will never be settled. His Government is that of a faction.

This was very much the opinion of Captain Charles Napier, who in command of British seamen in Pedro's service had just destroyed Miguel's fleet. Nevertheless Miguel was much the worst of the two. In January 1834 Grey resigned, because he could not persuade Althorp and the Cabinet to send an expedition to Portugal to give Dom Miguel the *coup-de-grâce*. He was with difficulty persuaded by King William's remonstrances, and by an affectionate round-robin from the whole Cabinet, to resume the reins of power.[2] All, however, worked out as well as he could have wished

---

[1] King William was becoming very jealous of France, and disliked his Ministers' foreign policy.

[2] The full correspondence about this little-known incident is to be found in the papers at Howick.

in Portugal. In the following May, Dom Miguel was finally overthrown by Palmerston's ' Quadruple Alliance ' of England, France, Portugal, and Spain. And Dom Pedro crowned his services to humanity by dying in the hour of his triumph.

The victorious Whigs, who were able at least to begin the process of amelioration in Great Britain, were helpless in front of the Irish question, which neither they nor any important section of the British public then understood at all. The terrorism and systematic murder in agrarian Ireland in 1832 required firm government, coupled with the programme of Disestablishment and Land Acts, which Gladstone introduced in an age too late. From Stanley, Ireland got a rigid Coercion Act, with court-martial justice, much disliked by Lord Althorp and the British Liberals. But no party in Great Britain contemplated disestablishing the alien Church or touching the relations of landlord and tenant, any more than they contemplated yielding to O'Connell's agitation for Repeal of the Union.

Grey supported Stanley on coercion, and sympathised with his dislike of O'Connell.

The best symptom I see [he wrote to Stanley, on September 10, 1832] is the vulgar violence of O'Connell. The only man who could descend to such appeals to the worst feelings of the lowest of the People, must think that his cause is nearly desperate. I wish you could get hold of him.

The Whig panacea for Ireland was Church Reform, in diminutive doses. In this direction Althorp and Lord John Russell were prepared to go further, and Stanley, Richmond, and Graham less far, than the rest of the Cabinet. The Prime Minister, who had never been a strong Churchman politically, had no personal objection to sequestrating for secular purposes a little of the superfluous revenues of the Protestant Establishment in Ireland. But he was anxious to keep the Cabinet together, and he also believed that British opinion would be very jealous of anything savouring of a sacrifice made to conciliate the Roman Church.[1]

And so, under a running fire of threats of resignation from his colleagues on both sides, Grey steered on as best he could, until the General Election of December 1832 yielded the enormous Whig majority of the first Reformed Parliament, and so gave a fresh lease of life and energy to the divided Cabinet.

That Christmastide election was the moment in history when the Whig party entered into full possession of the promised land, after its forty years in the wilderness. A letter of Lady Grey to her daughter, Lady Caroline Barrington, gives a pleasing picture of the old Northumbrian home, on the day of Lord Howick's election at the Alnwick hustings, five miles away :

I am very cross, as Car *would not* let me go to the election. I had set my heart on it, as I heard the Alnwick people would have taken it well, and still more because I wished to hear Henry speak. However, I really had no choice, for I never saw your Papa so obstinate, and perhaps he was right, and that I might have suffered from the cold. *We are the only two left at home,*[2] and I believe that there is scarcely a servant left in the house.

As they two sat together in the silent rooms till the young people came home from the family triumph, they must have summoned up remembrance of many very different elections long ago, in the years of political darkness that had never obscured for them the light of happiness and love.

[1] On Oct. 29, 1832, he wrote to Lord Holland : ' We have been on the point of breaking-up on the Church question in Ireland. We overcame the desire expressed by Richmond and Stanley to have a declaration that we would not divert the Revenues of the Church to any but Church purposes, and I really believe that we may have the means of affecting a very large measure of Reform by giving a very liberal construction to the phrase " Church purposes." But if we attempt to carry our measures further we shall infallibly break up and throw the whole weight of the Church and all the Protestant feeling of the country into the arms of our enemies.'

[2] Lord Grey, as a peer, could not attend the election.

Shortly after the assembling of the first Reformed Parliament, Lord Grey was able to effect a long-needed change in the Cabinet. Stanley, hating the Irish and hated by them, and aware that his policy over there was too strong for many of his colleagues and for the House of Commons, had long been desirous of some other field for his splendid talents. The difficulty was that no other high Cabinet office was vacant. At length, in March 1833, Durham resigned. Physical pain and mental depression had never let go their grip on him after his boy's death, and since then two of his daughters by his first wife had followed their half-brother to the grave. Disliking Stanley's Irish coercion Bill, and out of touch either personally or politically with all his colleagues, he had long ceased to attend Cabinet Meetings, except on rare occasions. After several attempts to resign, he effected his purpose in March 1833. He retired with the earldom, on which he had laid such inconsequent stress in the middle of his far deeper private tragedies and far higher public aims. Whether in relation to his colleagues Durham had been more sinned against or sinning, he had suffered piteously at the hands of fate.

Durham's departure placed the Privy Seal at Grey's disposition. After ' a most painful scene ' the Prime Minister compelled the incompetent Lord Goderich to take it, and vacate the Colonial Office in favour of Stanley, who had four days before ' positively refused to continue ' as Irish Secretary.[1] This excellent arrangement gave to Stanley's debating power and administrative energy the great task of freeing all the slaves in the British Empire, which Goderich, obeying his own indolence and the obstructionists in the Colonial Office, had persistently refused to set about. Lord Howick, as undersecretary for the Colonies, took a leading part in pressing on his father the urgency of Slavery Abolition ; and by

---

[1] Letters of Grey to Holland, March 24 and 29, 1833.

subsequently resigning office on the introduction of Stanley's Bill, he was instrumental in reducing the period of ' apprenticeship ' for the liberated slaves from twelve to seven years.

The Whigs, and in particular the Grey family, hold a good record in relation to the unhappy negro race. In the one year of office and divided power that they enjoyed between 1782 and 1830, they abolished the Slave Trade in despite of George III. In the first year after they had secured their position by the Reform Bill, they abolished Slavery itself.

Among the Government measures of 1833 was an India Bill of the first importance. The great company's monopoly of trading to India had been taken away in 1813, and the time had now come to put an end to its monopoly of the China trade. The East India Company was wound up as a commercial concern on fair terms to the shareholders. It became a Corporation charged with governing India under revised conditions. Among these conditions was a declaration that all offices were to be open to the natives, irrespective of race, religion, and colour.

In the same year the governing bodies of the Scottish burghs were made elective. The entire absence of any representative principle in Scottish municipal life, deeply resented by a population long the best educated in Europe, and latterly aroused to a keen interest in political affairs, had been one of the worst scandals which the unreformed Parliament had refused to remedy. Jeffrey had declared it dangerous to delay this work of emancipation, even for another year. English municipal reform, which, badly as it was needed, could afford to wait a little longer, was passed in 1835, after Grey had retired to private life.

Another sheaf in the harvest of Reform garnered in 1833 was the Factory Act of that year. Michael Sadler, the Parliamentary champion of the factory children, had, owing to his opposition to the Reform

Bill, failed to obtain the seat he so well deserved in the new House. Lord Ashley (Shaftesbury) took up the cause in his place, and an almost revolutionary agitation in the industrial north made it necessary for the Government to do something. They did not adopt the 'Ten Hours' programme for all workers, and their Bill was very inadequate. But it was a decided step forward in the direction of limiting the labour of children and young persons. Its chief merit was that it set up factory inspectors, in the first instance to the disgust of the working men, but, as it proved, to their immense benefit.

A still larger but less entirely beneficial reform was the new Poor Law of 1834. The pauperisation of the English working class had long been fostered by indiscriminate outdoor relief. Rates in aid of wages kept wages down and sent the birthrate up. The self-respect, independence, and self-help of the 'labouring poor' were systematically annihilated. The unemployed were enslaved and bound down to particular parishes, so that fluidity of labour was stopped, and emigration discouraged. Society was perishing of these diseases, and called for the knife. And the knife was what it got from the Whig Poor Law. The new 'Union' Work Houses, wherein alone poor relief might in future be received by the able-bodied, were horrible to all classes of their inmates. And the sudden withdrawal of outdoor relief from the wage-earner, without any security for the immediate rise of wages, often caused the utmost misery during long years before wages actually rose. Families which had hitherto enjoyed an allowance for every child, were driven to send mother and children to field labour under the terrible conditions of the 'gang system.'[1]

The new Poor Law and the work of the Commission on which it was based, imperfect and harsh as they seem

[1] Dunlop, *The Farm Labourer*, 1913; Hasbach, *English Agricultural Labourer*.

by the more enlightened standards of our day, were the first big attempt to deal scientifically with the evils incident to the industrial revolution. They would have been more truly scientific if they had been more humane. But, taken with the Factory Act, they were at least a hopeful sign of a new era, when the ' condition of the people question ' would receive the serious attention of a reformed Parliament.[1]

Before the Poor Law was through the Upper House, the end of Grey's Cabinet had come—on an Irish question, as was to be expected. In May 1834 Lord John Russell ' upset the coach,' as Stanley wrote, by proclaiming from the ministerial bench that the ' revenues of the Church of Ireland were larger than necessary for the religious and moral instruction of the persons belonging to that Church,' and that he would like to see part of its wealth appropriated for other purposes. The result of Russell's declaration was the resignation of Stanley, Graham, and Richmond, who joined Peel as leaders of the new Conservative party. It was an inevitable and wholesome development of men and parties for the new era.

But to Grey, who was of the old era, the blow seemed politically fatal. He was at the end of his tether. His constitution had enabled him to face the storms of the Reform Bill better than many of his colleagues, but when it was over the effort had left him an old man with broken health. In September 1832 he wrote from Howick : ' I feel a great diminution of my strength, and I am unable to do many things which were a great occupation and

---

[1] The *Howick Papers* and the *H.O. Papers* show that the Government was all this time kept under heavy pressure from many quarters to legislate or act administratively against Trade Unions, then very unpopular and not thoroughly accepted as a normal institution. This course was often debated and always refused, except in the unhappy case of the ' Dorsetshire labourers,' whom Melbourne in 1834 transported for no worse crime than attempting to form an agricultural labourers' union in which they had administered oaths.

amusement to me when I was last here.' In January 1833 he wrote to Lady Durham : ' Young ambition never looked with the same eagerness to place and power, than I do to escape from the burden of both. I have not strength, either of body or mind, to bear it.' No wonder then that in May 1834 he was too old, physically and politically, to give the forward lead to the Liberal party suggested by the retirement of the more Conservative Ministers.

Such was his state of mind when, two months after the departure of Stanley and Graham, an opportunity occurred for his own release, of which he eagerly availed himself.

Stanley's Coercion Act was coming up again for renewal in Parliament. It was agreed to drop the court-martial clauses ; but about the public meeting clauses there were grave differences of opinion in the Cabinet. Littleton, the Irish Secretary, wrote to Lord Wellesley, now Lord-Lieutenant of Ireland, asking him to advise the Prime Minister against their renewal. Wellesley, supposing that Grey and the Cabinet wanted to drop the clauses, and not having a strong opinion on the subject, did as Littleton asked in a letter to Lord Grey of June 21, though he had expressed the opposite view only ten days before. The Prime Minister was much discomposed at Wellesley's *volte face*, but detected that his movement was not spontaneous. Grey, therefore, stood out for the public meeting clauses, and overbore the more Liberal section of the Cabinet on the subject. But meanwhile Littleton, who thought he could ' manage Dan,' had told O'Connell privately that Wellesley, Althorp, and he himself were against the clauses. When, therefore, the clauses were after all retained, O'Connell thought he had been deceived, and told the House the gist of Littleton's ill-placed confidences. Peel took up the case, and a cry was raised in the Parliament for the production of Wellesley's letters. Althorp saw no creditable way out but to resign. On July 8, 1834, Lord Grey resigned with him, and the Government was at an end.

It turned out, contrary to Grey's first expectations, that a Tory Cabinet was still impossible. Althorp was persuaded by the party, greatly against his will, to resume office. But Grey declined to return, while urging Althorp to go back. They all parted friends, and it was not Grey, but only his *clientèle* who considered that he had been ill-treated. He differed from the leading members of the Cabinet on the public meeting clauses, which they struck out after his departure ; he was intensely desirous to quit public life ; his health and strength were no longer adequate, and he had been aware of this for two years past, as his private letters show. Lord Grey's retirement was natural and right, and so was Althorp's unwilling return to office at Grey's request.[1]

To his very old friend, Robert Adair, Grey would have told the whole truth. And to him he wrote, on July 15, 1834 :

I hope that the same administration, in principle and policy, and with little change even in the persons composing it, will continue. It can hardly be necessary for me to add that this is with my entire concurrence and at my desire. In this close of my public life I have the comfort of retaining the confidence and good opinion of those friends, both political and personal, with whom I have been so long united.

So fell Lord Grey, not like the smitten tree, but like the dated leaf.

---

[1] The fullest account of these transactions is in Le Marchant's *Althorp*. But some important letters will be found in Appendix J, ' Lord Grey's Retirement,' pp. 391–2, below. They contain no further direct evidence as to Brougham's conduct, arraigned by Le Marchant. But they prove that Grey himself did not believe that either Brougham or any of his colleagues had intrigued to compass his resignation.

EPILOGUE

THE LAST YEARS—1834 TO 1845

'Let us all be not careful what men will make of these actings.
They, will they, nill they, shall fulfill the good pleasure of God, and
we shall serve our generations. Our rest we expect elsewhere : that
will be durable.'—OLIVER CROMWELL.

THE first use that Lord Grey made of his recovered
leisure was to go to Edinburgh, in September 1834,
to receive the thanks of the Scottish nation. Scotland
owed more even than England to Lord Grey. For the
first time in her political and civic history she had been
endowed with popular institutions. When the inner
warmth of the Scottish nature rises to the top, it rises
to some purpose, and seldom has any man been received
as Grey was received in every town and village that he
passed through on his Scottish tour.

In the speeches at the famous banquet given to
him at Edinburgh, Durham and Brougham quarrelled
over his head ; Brougham, now well on his downward
course to absurdity, tried in vain to set himself beside
Grey as the hero of the hour. The people of Scotland
were for the moment thinking of what Grey had done
for them ; not of what Brougham or Durham had done
or proposed to do, though many of them were in agreement with Durham's advanced Liberal programme,
which frightened Lord Grey.

On the way back through Northumberland, where
the same scenes of popular welcome were repeated,

365

Lady Grey wrote to her daughter, Lady Caroline, describing their experience in Scotland :

> As to the sight, no words can do justice to it, and still less to the feeling that produced it. It was a burst of enthusiasm from a whole nation ! And even Car admits that he would not have conceived it. In the streets [of Edinburgh] they took no notice of the Chancellor [Brougham], and no mention was made of him on any of the banners, tho' there were hundreds in honour of Car, besides those that belonged to the different trades. I tell you this, not because it was a sign of the Chancellor's being unpopular, but as a proof that the dinner was given to your Papa *alone*, tho' the Chancellor is doing all he can to have it supposed it was a joint concern. His arms were not to be seen in any of the devices, while they were painted over Car's chair at the dinner in a way that I thought looked *too* royal. Indeed, I may say that he has been playing the part of King of Scotland, and poor *I*, unworthy as I am, was in consequence like the Queen —applauded every time I came to the window, and shewn up at the ball and dinner exactly as you have seen the poor Queen. It was very annoying to me at the time, tho' gratifying in fact. I had almost as many people to shake hands with as he had, and when we went to the shops we were followed by crowds of people, who put into my hands copies of verses, and presents of trifles—in short it was a degree of homage to him that I could not have conceived, and particularly for an ex-Minister.

Lord Grey was seventy years old when he retired from public life in July 1834. He lived for eleven more years in complete retirement at Howick. His views became more and more conservative as he grew older, but he never again took part in politics, though in April 1835 he was warmly invited by his colleagues, with the King's full concurrence, to return either as Prime Minister, or if he preferred as Foreign Secretary.[1]

He outlived his son-in-law, Lord Durham, whose

---

[1] This correspondence is in the papers at Howick. The invitation is signed by Melbourne, Lansdowne, Holland, Palmerston, and Spring Rice. Althorp had just retired. See also Holland's letter of April 12, in Add. MSS. 37297.

last public service, the famous Canadian Report, helped to lay the foundations of Freedom and Empire.[1]   Grey felt himself an old man, on the August day in 1840, when he stood with Lady Grey outside Lambton Castle, watching the procession of fifty thousand people, on foot and on horseback, set out to carry to his resting-place that fiery lord, who had been both their ancestral chief and the champion of their democratic rights.

Grey's last years at Howick were a long, mellow sunset, tranquil and happy with the sense of labour done.   Lady Georgiana, with the harp on which she played so well the Scottish airs her father loved, was still at Howick.   But most of the great family of children were now scattered, though often returning as guests to the old home.   It was the era of the grand-children, on long visits.   Pictures of Howick and its lord in these latter days, as the most hospitable and homelike of houses and the most pleasant of hosts, have been drawn by many different hands.   ' The very servants are of a breed that makes one feel at home,' wrote one frequent guest.   But the most characteristic portrait of Lord Grey in retirement has been already given to the world in the delightful volumes of Creevey, who had known him so well in years gone by :

Just as I was in the midst of writing the last sentence, Lord Grey stalked into the great library, his spectacles aloft upon his forehead, and I saw at once he was for *jaw*, so I abandoned my letter for you and joined him. . . . It would do you good to see me send him to bed every night at half after eleven o'clock, which is half an hour beyond his usual time.   This I do regu-

---

[1] The legend that Durham did not write his own Report has no historic credentials, though it has most unfairly found its way into the *Dict. of Nat. Biog.*   See Reid's *Life of Durham.*   Grey thought that the conduct of the Melbourne Cabinet to Durham in Canada had been ' very shabby.'   Neither he nor Althorp would ever have treated a colleague so.   Durham on his return from Canada behaved with extraordinary magnanimity to those who had wronged him, in order to facilitate the passage of the Canada Union Bill before he died.

larly, and it amuses him much. He looks about for his book, calls his dog Viper, and out they go, he having been all day as gay as possible, and not an atom of that *gall* he was subject to in earlier life. . . . The same tranquillity and cheerfulness, amounting almost to playfulness, instead of subsiding have rather increased during my stay, and have never been interrupted by a single moment of thoughtfulness or gloom. He could not have felt more pleasure from carrying the Reform Bill, than he does apparently when he picks up half-a-crown from me at cribbage. A curious stranger would discover no out-of-the-way talent in him, no powers of conversation ; a clever man *in discussion*, certainly, but with no fancy, and no judgment (or very little) in works either of fancy or art. A most natural, unaffected, upright man, hospitable and domestic ; far surpassing any man one knows in his noble appearance and beautiful simplicity of manners, and equally surpassing all his contemporaries as a splendid public speaker. Take him all in all, I never saw his fellow ; nor can I see any imitation of him on the stocks.

Lord Grey died on July 17, 1845, and was buried at Howick. Lady Grey survived him until 1861.

Grey had not the genius of Fox or of Gladstone ; yet it was given to him to accomplish the work of Fox, and to succeed more completely than Gladstone. No man mediocre either in mind or character could have achieved that. And while he lacked the highest qualities of his predecessor and successor, he lacked also their faculty for making mistakes.

To understand Grey's paramount influence in the Britain of 1830-1832 is to understand the world of that transition period, buried now beneath the leaves of many years ; it is to understand the position and outlook of those liberal-minded aristocrats peculiar to the history of our island, whose existence was one of the reasons why the political traditions and instincts that the English have inherited differ so profoundly from those of Germany, of France, or even of America.

No statue or monument has been erected to Lord Grey in the precincts of Westminster. The new

Houses of Parliament must serve him for a memorial. Big Ben and the Flag Tower are the symbols of what he did. The old Houses perished by fire, three months after his retirement. In place of the narrow, irregular labyrinth of mediæval Westminster, so famous and so uncomfortable, there rose, in a fortunate hour, the more uniform, less romantic pile, spacious enough to house the new world of ordered progress, obedient to the movements of public opinion. That new world owed it to Lord Grey that it had obtained its political rights without a convulsion. He had interpreted the need of the new, crowding generations, to the old generation of dignity and privilege, to which he himself belonged. He had stood between the living and the dead.

In an age of biographies and memoirs, it chanced that no life of him was written. His tale remained untold. And already in the middle years of the century his widow thought that the world was forgetting the man to whom it owed the Reform Bill. He himself would have cared little. He had not sought the breath of popular applause when alive. Nor was it in pursuit of posthumous fame that he had dragged himself from Howick to Westminster so often and so unwillingly. When the first extravagances of early youth were over, he had asked three things of life : that he might enjoy domestic happiness beside a populous hearth ; that he might prove himself honourable and high-minded in all the relations of life ; and that he might do something lasting for the liberties and for the welfare of his country. The fates, in most abundant measure, granted him all three.

APPENDICES

APPENDIX A

'THE BILL' IN EMBRYO

THE following passages are selected from Lord Grey's letters between 1816 and 1820. From these it will appear that in 1816 he did not favour making Parliamentary Reform a *sine quâ non* of accepting office, but that in December 1820 he had begun to incline to the opposite view; also that he then thought that at least a hundred seats should be taken away from the rotten boroughs (see p. 183, above).

To Lord Holland, December 8, 1816 :

' My political creed is shortly this :
1. Reduction of Establishments⎤
2. Change of Foreign Policy ⎬ *sine quâ non.*
3. Catholic Emancipation ⎦
4. A moderate and gradual Reform of Parliament, not a *sine quâ non*, but to be supported.

' Whether I shall be able to do much to support such a plan of operations remains to be seen. I feel very much below the mark, and am sure I shall disappoint you all. I have no spirit or power left.'

In a letter to George Ponsonby, written three days before this, Grey says just the same at rather greater length, defining the ' change of Foreign Policy ' desirable, as ' abandoning the principle of interference in the government of France.'

December 26, 1819 (*to Lord Holland*) :

' A Reform of Parliament is, from all the information I receive, daily becoming more and more a subject of popular interest, and it will be impossible for any Party, looking to the support of public opinion, to succeed without taking some more direct measure with that view than Lord John Russell's.[1] I was rejoiced at the success of his speech, but a great part of his argument appeared to me to put the principle of Reform far beyond the limit to which he wished to confine it.'

To Holland, April 23, 1820:

' As to Parliamentary Reform, you may be assured that the time is past when any half measures on this subject might have answered the purpose of satisfying the popular feeling, unless they could be accompanied with measures of substantial relief—of which you can have no hope. The general principle of Reform, to be pursued with caution, and gradually and progressively carried into effect, is the language which I should hold, and leave the battle to be fought between the Government and the Reformers, preserving to myself, as far as might be possible, the ground of a mediator between them.'

December 6, 1820:

' My dear Holland,—I have turned it in my mind over and over again, and I am now at last obliged to confess that I have not yet brought myself to any satisfactory conclusion as to the great and preliminary difficulty, whether we ought to make Reform a *sine quâ non*, and if any, what. With respect to stipulating for Reform (*i.e.* Reform of Parliament) at all, we must begin with these admissions. First, that we are not agreed on the principle, some of our most valuable friends and supporters objecting to it *in toto*. Secondly, that we are still less agreed as to the extent to which it should be carried. Thirdly, that we have no data on which we can build any material hope, that any very modified plan, such as that which you suggest, would gain that section of the public which, resting our acceptance of office on some concession of this nature, it must be intended to conciliate.

' I am indeed convinced, as every rational man must be, that our Administration, if we should form one, could only stand upon public confidence and opinion, and that confidence and opinion I am strongly inclined to believe, in the present circumstances of the Country, could not be acquired and certainly not retained, if we were to put aside the question of a Reform of Parliament. But then what is the Reform that would have the effect we desire, and are we likely to be united in our opinions in favour of such a Reform ? I am persuaded that such a very modified plan as you suggest would not do ; it would satisfy nobody ; and, what is worse, it would be impossible to rest upon it as a definitive measure. *With this view I do not think we could hope that less than the following outline would be effectual. Shortening the duration of Parliament at least to five years ; admitting copyholders to vote for*

---

[1] On December 14 Lord John had made a motion for transferring the franchise, from boroughs where there had been proved to be gross bribery, to populous cities.

counties, and adding 100 *members to be divided between the large Towns and the most extensive and populous Counties ; taking away the same number from the representation of the most obnoxious boroughs.*[1] Less than this I feel quite convinced would do little to conciliate public opinion, as far as that opinion depends upon Reform, and in demanding a Reform to this extent as a *sine quâ non,* we should have the concurrence of the great body of our friends ; or would our exclusion for a time, which would certainly be the consequence of our insisting on it, have the effect of giving us so much strength in public opinion as to enable us to force the Court before it is too late to carry this or any other measure ?

'The more I write and the more I think the more I involve myself in doubt and perplexity, and am very anxious to collect the opinions of those whose opinions ought to have the greatest weight with us. Have you ever talked this matter over with Lansdowne ? can you tell me what he thinks ? or have you ever, as I think you once said you would, proposed to McIntosh to make out a project on this most difficult question ? My own feelings, if I had nothing but my own feelings and interests to consider, would be to insist upon such a Reform as I have stated, rather than incur all the labour, anxiety, and danger of undertaking the Government in a moment of such embarrassment, and with the certainty of being counteracted from the beginning, and ultimately betrayed and sacrificed by the Court on the first favourable opportunity.'

For other quotations already published from Grey's political correspondence, 1817–22, see Butler, *Reform Bill,* pp. 31–7, *passim* ; Reid's *Life of Durham,* chapter v. ; *The Wellesley Papers,* ii. 135–7 ; Brougham, *Memoirs,* ii. 444, 454.

APPENDIX B

GREY'S VIEWS OF CANNING'S POLICY, 1822–1827

IN 1822–3 Grey writes to Lord Holland expressing deep sympathy with the cause of the Liberal Spaniards against the aggression of the French reactionaries ; he thinks our Government ought to take more decided measures to protect Spain from invasion, repeal the Foreign Enlistment Act, ' make a naval demonstration and send a message to Parliament.'

---

[1] It is to be noted that this is the degree of disfranchisement proposed by Lord John Russell in his famous motion of April 1822—a great advance on his motion of 1819, which Grey had criticised as too meagre in principle.

On February 19, 1823, he writes to his son Charles:

'Any modification of the present Constitution of Spain, however slight, if made in compliance with the demands of the Allied Powers, would be a fatal admission of the right of interference, which, averse as I am to War (nobody can fear it more than I do), I would resist at any hazard. If we had held a firm and direct language at Verona, I cannot believe that the Allies would have ventured upon the measures to which they have now committed themselves.'

To Lord Holland, January 2, 1824:

'Are you not delighted with the American speech?[1] What a contrast to the conduct and language of our Government last year! I have no doubt it will be decisive in the question of South American Independence, with respect to which, after having bound Spain in the chains of France, Canning will have the glory of following in the wake of the President of the United States!'

All through 1824, Grey in his letters acknowledges the good change in our foreign policy, but always wants Canning's actions to come sooner and to go further than they do, for example the recognition of South American Independence, actually made February 1825.

To Holland, February 7, 1825:

'I do not mean that there was any resemblance between Canning and Castlereagh in personal character and conduct—God knows there cannot exist a greater difference between any two men, and I think it is in favour of Castlereagh. What I meant was that the result of their policy to the Country was much the same: witness Spain and Ireland. The sacrifice of Spain is justified by its having saved us from a War, and now the tardy and ungracious and uncertain recognition of America [viz. of the independence of the South American Republics] is also recommended by the hope of preserving peace. America [viz. the U.S.] has pursued an honourable, generous and direct policy and has found war neither to the right nor left.'

To Lord Howick, February 19, 1827 (after Lord Liverpool's illness):

'If Canning was in health and vigour, and could establish his ascendency, I think it would produce overtures to some of the opposition, and *nommément* to Lansdowne, which I do not think it would be discreditable for them to accept, *if a fair assurance were given them of a determined and bonâ fide support of the Catholic question; by which I mean that it should be brought forward as a measure of the government.*'

---

[1] President Monroe's message to Congress, *December* 2, 1823, containing the original 'Monroe Doctrine.'

To Holland, March 13, 1827 :

' If Canning should be allowed to form a new Administration *with a firm assurance of carrying the Catholic question*, I should be disposed to give him a fair support, and even not to press him prematurely on that subject.'

To Holland, April 14, 1827 :

' I certainly have a rooted distrust of Canning, which can only be cured by " experience and the evidence of facts," and I certainly would take no place in an Administration of which he is the head ; much less in one in which, having already received the appointment, he comes, not to negotiate on equal terms, but to offer places in his Government—this would have been my feeling if I had been still engaged in active politics. But I am out of the question, and it will be for those who remain to consider, quite independently of me, what is right both for themselves and the Public ; *and if they can come in, on terms creditable to themselves, and with a full assurance that the Catholic question is to be brought forward as a measure of Government, I do not say instanter, but within a convenient and reasonable time, I should not disapprove. To a Government not formed upon this principle I can give no support.*'

The Catholic question was however again shelved, so Grey could not approve Canning's administration. While it lasted the correspondence of Grey and Holland is suspended.

To Holland, September 16, 1827 (*after Canning's death*) :

' I received your letter on Friday evening. I did not, either to Tavistock or Lord John, express my surprise at your not having written. When asked by others whether I had heard from you or Lord Lansdowne I have simply stated the fact, that I had not ; or at most may have lamented, as that certainly has been my feeling, the circumstances which, after so many years of the most confidential intercourse, had so entirely broken off all communication on political subjects between us.

' It is too true that I cannot at all agree with you in your views either of the past or present state of the Administration. Barring the Catholic question—and from a passage in your letter even you appear to consider that question as given up for the present, virtually for ever, an opinion expressed by nobody more strongly than by Lord Lansdowne—barring the Catholic question I never could understand what the difference was between Peel and his followers and the present Tory Ministers which could make the re-appointment of the latter the least of all evils. There certainly is one evil greater, much greater, in my estimation, and that is the dissolution of the Whig party and the total destruction of its consequence and character.'

APPENDIX C

THE QUESTION OF GREY TAKING OFFICE UNDER WELLINGTON, 1828–1830

' His Majesty told me that he wished me to form a Government.'
Lyndhurst must be Chancellor. ' Everything else is open to all mankind,
except one person, Lord Grey.'—Wellington to Peel, January 9, 1828
(Parker's *Peel*, ii. 27). See also *Creevey Papers*, ii. 151, February 7, 1828.

Lady Grey to Lord Grey, August 25, 1828:

' My dearest Charles,—After we had taken our drive on Saturday
Me. de Lieven arrived. Lambton was out riding. George ran away,
and poor Louisa who was that day very unwell was just gone to her room,
so that she found nobody but me. She was very gracious, and conse-
quently very agreeable. But I could perceive that she was full of
curiosity about you, having heard the reports of your joining the Administration, and very much bent upon squeezing out of me whatever I might
know. You may imagine she got but little from me, for the best possible
reason, that I had nothing to tell. Having convinced her of this fact,
she then began to express her opinions how impossible it must be for you
to leave your party, to abandon your old principles, etc., etc, adding
" *Lord Grey m'a dit lui même tout recemment—'je ne suis pas un individu,
mais chef de parti, et tout offre à moi seul serait une insulte.*' " I think she
must have misunderstood you, for though I have no doubt you disclaimed
all idea of coming into office yourself, I do not believe you assigned as a
reason delicacy towards your former friends ! I could not help saying
that, though I believed your coming into the Administration was quite
out of the question, and that as far as I was concerned, I sincerely wished
it might be so, yet after what happened last year I considered you as
standing alone and perfectly free to support or oppose the Government as
appeared best for the Country ; and that you must consider *Measures*
and not the *persons* who proposed them. She caught at this, and said,
" Ah, *je vois qu'il est déjà dans le Ministère.*" However, I believe I at
last convinced her that *I* at least knew of no such arrangement.'

Lady Grey to Lord Howick, January 1829:

' My dearest Henry,—I have just had a long conversation with Lord
Rosslyn which, after all, tells us no more than what we had before heard,
viz., that he believes perfectly in the D. of W.'s sincerity that he is anxious
to gain your father's support, to his Govt., or rather that he should form
a part of it, but that he has at present no hope of obtaining the King's

consent to offer him any place which he could accept. He [D. of W.]
talked of him [Grey] in the highest terms and expressed himself as anxious
to consult his wishes upon all points where he could serve him without
appearing to compromise him, and added that while things remained in this
state he could not with any delicacy authorise any person to mention the
subject to Lord Grey, feeling, as he did, uncertain of ever being able to
act as he wished. In the course of this conversation with Lord Rosslyn the
Duke said (what you may recollect we were told before) that it was very
possible the King might consent to take Lord Grey, provided he could
turn him [D. of W.] himself out. I questioned Lord Rosslyn as to his own
opinion on all this, and he assured me that he felt perfect confidence in the
Duke, that he was certain his esteem and admiration for your father was
unfeigned, and besides that he must feel how much strength he would gain
by his accession. He seems to think, indeed he said so, that nothing can be
more insecure than the Duke's situation. The King scarcely attempts to
conceal his dislike to him, and every appointment however trifling is the
cause of dispute, and may prove the cause of the dissolution of the Ministry.
Much of this may be attributed to the Duke of Cumberland, but more
to the King's own disposition—at present he seems to hate all public men,
and perhaps that feeling being so general, is the reason why he goes on
with his present Ministry. Under all these circumstances, Lord Rosslyn
is anxious that your father should stay here out of the way till the course
of events is seen—were he to attend the opening of the session, many
things might occur to force him, even against his will, into an active opposition to the Duke, of which all the Canning party would be too happy to
avail themselves to try to get him over to their party, and we know that
when people act eagerly on the same side, it is not always easy to keep a
line of separation. You say I am vindictive. I am afraid I am so, if
feeling more averse to ever acting with those by whom he was so ill-used
can be reckoned so. Besides I firmly believe that it would not answer
even in an ambitious view. He might assist Lord Lansdowne and the
Huskissons to overthrow the Duke, but it would be to bring *them* into
power, from which they would again exclude him, and I see no reason to
play their game.'

Grey to Brougham (*Howick, February* 5, 1830):
    ' I sincerely wish to support the Duke of Wellington's Administration,
but every day adds to my doubts : more especially when I consider the
sort of recruits that are sought for and the manner of enlisting them.'

May 3, 1830. *Lord Howick's private diary :*
    ' I remained talking politics to my father. He is, I am happy to say,
getting quite as much inclined to oppose the Duke as I can be.'

Wellington to Fitzgerald, December 26, 1830 (*Despatches*, vii. 383):
    ' Lord Grey's conduct from the time he came to town last spring

rendered it impossible to make an offer to him and to some of his friends upon the accession of the present king.'

The belief expressed by Palmerston (*Life*, i. 381) that an offer was made to take in Grey in the summer of 1830 is, therefore, incorrect.

In Ellenborough's *Diary*, ii. 438, November 17, 1830, at the time of the Duke's resignation, we read :

' The King (William IV) asked the Duke's opinion of Lord Grey, and whether he had ever had any communication with him. The Duke said No. The King knew the personal objections the late King had to Lord Grey, and he (the Duke) could not, though often pressed by Lord Grey's friends, have any communication with him without either deceiving him or deceiving the King ; and he would not do either. The King asked what sort of a man Lord Grey was. The Duke said he really did not know. He had the reputation of being an ill-tempered, violent man, but he knew very little of him. He had never had any political conversation with him. The King was much agitated and distressed.'

See also *Life of Disraeli*, i. 388, Lord Lyndhurst's recollections :

' Once the intention of the Duke to admit the Grey party. Took a sudden prejudice to Grey. Something happened on a coal committee. Told L. afterwards he had seen enough of Grey that morning to have nothing to do with him.'

APPENDIX D

FORMATION OF THE GREY MINISTRY

' *Private.* *Thursday morning* [*November* 18, 1830].

' My dear Grey,—I have no engagement that can prevent my receiving you and the other members of your Cabinet at nine this evening. But as you are to see Brougham at four, I should be glad to have a few minutes' conversation with you on that *vital* point, if possible, before. I would call at any time when you can see me alone for a moment.

' Since we met yesterday I have thought over the subject of the Foreign Office, which you pressed so kindly upon me, and which I owed it to you and to myself not to decline without full consideration. But indeed I must do so. Looking back to the experience of the last few years, I am *certain* that a long continuance of sedentary employment would disqualify me from doing myself justice, and make me a less efficient member of your Government in other respects than I should be if you chuse [*sic*] to give me the Presidency of the Council, with the comparative freedom belonging to it. And Holland would, I believe, be quite as well satisfied with the Chancellorship of the Dutchy [*sic*], the salary of which is not inferior, with some Church and other patronage.

'Would not Palmerston suit the Foreign Office better than the Home Office? And might not Sir J. Graham do for the Home? I venture merely to throw this out, as I do anything else that occurs to me, for your consideration.—Ever yours,

'Lansdowne.'

'*Thursday* [*Nov.* 18, 1830].

'Dear Holland,—So much had passed in repeated conversations with Lansdowne, that I had no longer any hopes of effecting anything by my powers of persuasion; and his written determination this morning was so positive that I considered the matter as absolutely concluded, and Palmerston has the Office.

'Lansdowne, then, is to be President, which he desired; and you must be Chancellor of the Duchy—a thing suggested by the King himself yesterday—and there is some very nice Patronage.

'I have not time for more, as I am now going to St. James's. But what is omitted may keep till Lansdowne House, where I shall hope to meet you punctually at nine. I wanted to call this morning, but I have not had a single moment. Brougham has just left me *couleur de rose*. It was my unfortunate note to you, delivered in his presence, that did all the mischief.

'Ever yours, Grey.'

It is said (*Quarterly Review*, cxxvi. 48) that Grey at first intended to offer the Chancellorship to Lord Lyndhurst, but was dissuaded by Althorp. Lyndhurst had served Canning, Goderich, and Wellington as Chancellor, and was supposed to have adaptable views on politics. The story is not improbable, for Grey liked Lyndhurst, and was anxious to avert his opposition; but the evidence is not first hand.

The greatest searchings of heart, except on the Brougham question, were on the question whether to have Lord Carnarvon in the Cabinet—the alternative apparently being Durham, whom Grey wisely preferred, to the disgust of some of his colleagues and some even of his own family. In one of his letters of these Cabinet-making days, Grey writes : 'Carnarvon goes between me and my rest.' Lord Carnarvon was very angry at his omission, but as he became a leader of the opposition to the Reform Bill, Grey's preference of Durham was doubly justified.

Lord Grey's correspondence during the making of his Government affords many side-lights on human nature, on the whole not too discreditable. Two very great noblemen, not counting Carnarvon, applied for places in his Cabinet, but in vain; they did not subsequently support the Reform Bill. The Duke of Devonshire, on the other hand, accepts the post of Lord Chamberlain in a very unselfish and friendly letter, asking Grey to think again if the post might not be better bestowed to secure the support of some less staunch adherent.

Pathetic interest attaches to the letters of Sir Sidney Smith, Admiral of the White, the same age as Grey and long in retirement. He writes, on November 17, asking first to be a Lord of the Admiralty, and when Grey refuses that, writes again, on November 25, asking to be made Master-General of the Ordnance, on the ground of his having shown his knowledge of land fortification and artillery when in 1799 he repulsed Buonaparte at Acre. ' I was opposed to an officer supposed to be a consummate master of the art, and enabled sailors, marines, and Turks to foil him, sustaining twelve formidable assaults, and *literally constructing outworks according to modern rules* under a constant fire at duel distance, our neutral ground never having been more than ten yards.' Grey, however, replies that the post cannot be held by a naval officer, however distinguished.

A brother-squire of Northumberland, Fenwick of Longwitton, writes ' to call your Lordship's attention to my son, Captain William Fenwick, of the Welsh Fusiliers.' The interest lies in Grey's reply that ' I have not the power of interfering with the Patronage of the Army, and advancement, now very difficult in that way, is only to be obtained by purchase. It is only by paying very largely that I can hope to obtain promotion for my own sons.' The latter statement was only too true.

APPENDIX E

THE FRAMING OF THE REFORM BILL

Lord Durham to Lord John Russell, Oct. 22, 1834 (Lambton MSS. Being an answer to Russell's letter to Durham, Oct. 19, 1834, printed in Russell, *Early Correspondence.* ii. 51–4) :

' Shortly after the formation of the Government, Lord Grey asked me, in the House of Lords, if I would assist him in preparing a Reform Bill. I answered that I would do so with the greatest pleasure. He then said, " You can have no objection to consult Lord John Russell ? " I replied, " Certainly not, but the reverse." In consequence of this conversation, I mentioned the subject to you. We then agreed to associate with ourselves Sir James Graham and Lord Duncannon. The Committee thus formed met regularly at my house in Cleveland Row.

I acted as Chairman, and in that capacity signed the daily minutes of our proceedings.' [I have failed to find any trace of these minutes.] 'Lord Grey referred to me all the Memorials from different Towns and Bodies, Deputations from whom I received, in consequence, in Cleveland Row.

'I proposed that you should be requested to give in a plan, because, as it was a measure which must necessarily originate in the House of Commons, you of all its members had the best right to be entrusted with it, having been last in possession of the question.

'You did so. [This original 'plan' of Lord John Russell's is printed in his *English Constitution*, pp. xxxvi-xxxviii.] It was carefully discussed, and after many alterations, to some of which you have referred [in letter of October 19, 1834], the Measure as finally agreed upon was submitted to Lord Grey. [For official synopsis of the measure as submitted to Lord Grey by the Committee of Four on January 14, see Reid's *Durham*, i. 238–43, or *William IV's Correspondence*, i. 461–3.]

'What you state respecting the qualification and the ballot is quite correct [J. R.'s letter of October 19]. I proposed Triennial Parliaments, which at your suggestion were made quinquennial. When the plan was submitted to the Cabinet, I was confined to my room by severe illness. I heard, however, from Sir James Graham, and also from Lord Grey, that Ballot had been struck out.'

Durham then states that Sir James Graham asked him to attend the next Cabinet, as he feared Brougham was to oppose abolishing of Rotten Boroughs. However, Brougham said nothing on that, but tried to have Althorp instead of Lord John as proposer of the Bill in the Commons.

A letter of Sir James Graham's to Durham on his sick bed, dated January 25, 1831 (*Lambton MSS.*), refers to one of these Reform Bill Cabinets: 'The measure on the whole well received, Brougham alone dissentient, and disposed to carp by raising little points when he found no real objections, and very much inclined to defend the nomination Boroughs. We have another Cabinet to-day at four on the grand question.' January 27 : 'Pray come to the Cabinet to-morrow. Althorp and others wish to lower the qualification. I am afraid I foresee difficulties.'

The borough qualification was eventually lowered from £20 to £10 householders, to compensate for the rejection of the Ballot, but not till the middle of February, and then chiefly as a result of Lord John Russell's strong letter of February 13, 1831, printed in *Butler*, 190, note. That letter of Russell's fully bears out the following statement in a letter of Durham to Grey, October 18, 1834 : 'My recommendation of the Jury or £20 qualification [instead of £10] was dependent on the adoption of the Ballot, which, as you know, was proposed in the report which I drew up and delivered to you, signed by myself as Chairman of the Committee, and by Lord John Russell, Sir James Graham, and Lord Duncannon, who composed it.'

All other important documents that I know of on the framing of the Bill have been already printed, and will be found in the passages already referred to in this Appendix and in *Butler*, 179 (Althorp's plan of Reform, December 1830); Lord John Russell's *English Constitution* (1865), pp. xxiii-xli; Parker's *Graham*, i. 117–22; also *Butler*, 173, note 1, on Graham; *William IV's Correspondence*, i. 81–2, note; *Brougham Memoirs*, iii. 92–3, 523–4.

APPENDIX F

THE DISSOLUTION OF APRIL 1831

THE following letter of Grey to Wellesley (Add. MSS., B.M., 37297), not printed in the *Wellesley Papers*, shows that the King's consent to dissolve surprised Grey.

'April 21, 1831.

'My dear Lord,—When I received your Lordship's very kind letter yesterday, I did not expect that I should have been able to answer it as one of the King's Ministers.

'A proposal had then been sent to His Majesty to dissolve the Parliament, and from all the previous communications on this subject there seemed great reason to expect a decided opposition on his part to this measure. Indeed, when, yesterday, I laid before him the Cabinet Minute, the seriousness of his manner, and the cordial distress which he experienced, tho' nothing could exceed his kindness, did not lessen that apprehension.

'He desired the time necessary to consider so important a question, and I have this morning received his answer in an admirably drawn paper, stating all the objections he had felt, and all the difficulties which he still feared; but concluding with an expression of his consent, and of his undiminished confidence in his Ministers. Nothing can be more entitled to the highest praise than this conduct.

'A Dissolution therefore is resolved upon; and the question has been, whether it should be immediate, or that it should wait till certain measures, of some urgency, should be completed. There are difficulties on both courses, but those of delay seem to preponderate, and the final determination, which will be taken to-night, will probably be for immediate dissolution.'

The story told in Roebuck's *History of the Whig Ministry* (ii. 148–51), drawn from talks with Brougham in later years, is entirely fictitious as regards the interview on April 22, between the King, Grey, and Brougham. It represents Brougham as saving a desperate situation by hardly persuading the King to dissolve, whereas he had already agreed to dissolve in his letter to Grey of the day before. The only questions on April 22 related to the day and the mode of the prorogation to dissolve, and even on those points Grey told his son that the King needed no persuasion, either by himself or Brougham. The evidence of all this was published in 1867, in *William's Correspondence*, i. 229 and 234–6, note by Henry, third Earl Grey; and it is confirmed by the above letter to Wellesley. But the following further note by the third Earl Grey has never yet been published :

Note by Henry, third Earl Grey.

' Some extracts from Croker's diary which have been lent by Mr. Giffard to Frederick have been shown to me. These extracts contain accounts of conversations Croker had with Brougham in January 1839 and 1843. In the first there is an entirely untrue account of what passed with the King, when my father and Brougham went to him at Windsor, respecting the creation of peers in May 1832, but into that I need not now enter. What is more material is the account Brougham then gave of the dissolution of 1831. This story is quite different from that given in Roebuck's and Molesworth's books on Brougham's authority. In these books it is said that the King was only asked to dissolve by Brougham in my father's presence on the morning of the 22nd of April, and it is on the question of dissolution or no dissolution that he represents himself as having so successfully worked upon the King, when my father was afraid to speak to him. In his conversation with Croker, on the other hand, he says what is true—that the only point discussed in the audience given to Brougham and my father by the King before the Council for the dissolution of Parliament on the morning of April 22nd, was whether the King should go down to the House of Lords in person.

' I have no doubt, from the information contained in a letter I lately received from Wm. Bathurst, that it was for the first time proposed to the King in this audience that he should go to the House of Lords in person, instead of sending Commissioners to prorogue Parliament, with a view to its dissolution. I also think it probable that Brougham's account of the manner in which this change in the mode of proceeding was brought about may be true. He says that the evening before, or that morning early (I cannot clearly make out which), the Ministers learned from Courtenay (then Clerk of the House of Lords and afterwards Lord Devon) that a consultation was going on, in the room Lord Wyndford had as Dep^y. Speaker at the House of Lords, between the D. of Wellington, Eldon, Lyndhurst, and a few others, and that they had sent for two volumes of the *Journals*. It was ascertained (so Brougham says) that they had discovered that Commiss^{ners.} to prorogue Parlt. can only be called in on a question being put, so that the House would have had the power of adjourning, which Brougham says would have defeated the Govt. In this he is wrong; for as Follett observed in the conversation Croker records, the dissolution might have been effected by proclamation—and I remember that what it was really desired to prevent, was the carrying of an address against the dissolution, which might have had a bad effect in the country, though it would not have stopped the measure.'

APPENDIX G

'BEAR' ELLICE AS WHIP DURING THE REFORM BILL

THE appointment of Ellice as Whip proved very fortunate in the public interest. A letter of Charles Wood to Lord Grey, on July 3, 1832, after the passing of the Reform Bill, records the reasons why Ellice's continuance as Whip is 'indispensable.' ' Perhaps the greatest fault in conducting the affairs of the Government in the House of Commons has been the ignorance of the Cabinet of the feelings of their supporters in the House. Stanley has had the Irishmen disgusted the greater part of the session for want of this. Palmerston, Grant, Graham, and J. Russell are seldom in the House.

' But Ellice has great influence *with the old Whig party* to whom he belongs ; *with city men and merchants* from his mercantile connexion ; *with the radicals* whom on many points he agrees with ; *with the Scotchmen* as a countryman ; *with the Irishmen* whom he feeds. Besides being the most good-natured man alive, conciliatory and familiar with everybody. I will say nothing of his knowledge of business, his experience of the H. of C., his intimacy with Sir H. Taylor, Hardinge, the Speaker, etc.'

No wonder, therefore, that Campbell, who complained on January 22, 1831, that Ellice's appointment ' did not bode well,' afterwards admitted that ' he had more to do with carrying the Bill than any other man.'

APPENDIX H

APPENDIX H

PEER-MAKING AND THE 'DAYS OF MAY'

THE following quotations from MS. letters, together with those given in the text above, or already published in *William's Correspondence*, *Brougham's Memoirs*, Butler's *Passing of the Great Reform Bill*, Le Marchant's *Althorp*, and Parker's *Graham*, will make clear to students the various stages of Grey's thought and conduct, in the matter of peer-making, and during the 'Days of May.'

Grey to Holland, October 30, 1831 :

'With respect to the creation of Peers, it is urged without any knowledge or consideration of the circumstances of the case. It is obviously impossible, with a view to the number that would be required, to counteract the majority. A few may be made, if there is thought to be advantage in it; but even in a limited number, may there not be some inconvenience, as in Dorsetshire and Cambridgeshire, in the new elections which they would occasion, which we have no friends to support, or for which our rich adversaries are ready to contribute anything ? I will endeavour to open a communication with the Bishop of London. But he will of course want modifications and we can offer none that would satisfy him. This is the great difficulty in the way of any attempt at conciliation. I don't believe, however, that the Lords will, a second time, commit the mistake of throwing out the Bill on the 2nd reading. They will probably endeavour to alter it in Committee, which may prove more embarrassing to us.' *November* 3, 1831 : 'I return McCaulay's [*sic*] letter. I acknowledge all the right that is due to his opinion, but it would have had more influence with me if it had been expressed more temperately.' *November* 15, 1831 : 'I received your letter and Allen's paper, which, like everything that comes from him, is very good. But he overlooks the effect of taking at once 50 or 60 great landed proprietors out of the House of Commons and the inconvenience of so many elections.'

Grey to Sir Francis Burdett, November 24, 1831 :

'Supposing the majority of 41 to remain unshaken, is it possible to counteract it by a new creation ? Who can say how many more would be required ? Certainly more than 41. For you may be assured that such an attempt would lose us many of those by whom we have hitherto been supported. It is a question then which goes to the absolute destruction of the House of Lords, an event which I certainly did not contemplate in endeavouring to reform the House of Commons. And the effect on the H. of C. itself would scarcely be less pernicious, by withdrawing from it so great a portion of the property of the country. I must therefore say *quieta prius tentanda*, and that time and confidence ought to be given us for this purpose. If all is unsuccessful and the measure cannot be carried, without what would be as bad as losing it, my lot is cast. Having done all I can constitutionally do, I must retire. But I hope it will not come to this.'

Grey's change of view at Christmas time in favour of peer-making has been described in the text above (p. 331).

Grey to Holland, January 1, 1832 :

' There are two particular points to be settled, the concurrence of the Cabinet and the King : from Lansdowne's letter to me I am afraid he will positively oppose ; the objections of Palmerston are, I hear, scarcely less strong. Melbourne will be adverse, but I should think more reconcileable and so also the Duke of Richmond. The King as you are aware would dislike the thing to the greatest degree ; and I have less hope of overcoming his repugnance, which will be confirmed by the concurrence in his opinion of some of the most important members of the Government, since a conversation which he had on this subject with Sir Herbert Taylor has been reported to me by the Duke of Richmond. If Lansdowne and Palmerston, or one of them, should resign it would in the present circumstances of the Government be fatal.

' I enclose letters which I have had from Brougham, Lambton, and Coke, on the subject. The course advised by the first ' [' twelve at once,' as an earnest of more] ' is that to which I most incline. But the difficulties I have stated may very likely make it impossible.'

Grey to Holland, Pavilion, Brighton, January 4, 1832 :

' My conversation with the King has been very satisfactory, tho' he evidently feels great anxiety with respect to the subject of it. His kindness, confidence and fair dealing were such as I have always experienced from him. I cannot say more. I can have no doubt that he will do what we advise, but he desires to have it in writing. This must therefore be the subject of our deliberation on Saturday. I do not think the King well. He has a cold, which is of no consequence, but his drowsiness exceeds anything I have before seen. He really cannot keep himself awake for five minutes when you are talking to him, except on such a subject as we had to discuss to-day. Don't repeat what I have said about the King. The Queen civil, but her civility as cold as the weather.' *January 5* : ' I have nothing material to add to what I said yesterday. I have drawn up a minute of what passed between the King and me, which he says is perfectly correct, but to which he intends to add some observations. I never saw him in such a state of anxiety; but there can be no doubt of the sincerity of his desire to support the present Government, and he has evidently made up his mind to do the needful—tho' accompanied with an *if*; he said to me to-day that he saw no other alternative. He is also more inclined to a good batch at once, than to a small one, with one after. But he wishes new creations to be avoided, with the exceptions of the two, and the addition to be confined to Eldest Sons—creations of heirs to Barrens, and Scotch and Irish Peers.'

[' Barrens ' means peers with no children—a mild joke started by Holland.]

On January 15 the King, as a result of these negotiations, gave Grey the written promise quoted above (p. 332).

Grey to Holland, February 25, 1832 :

' Certainly our prospects in the Lords are not satisfactory, and I am quite overpowered by the responsibility of deciding between opposite courses, both of which are exposed to so much difficulty and danger.'

Holland to Grey, February 26, 1832 :

' From my observation of Wharncliffe, I suspect you would not lose his vote, though he might lose his temper, if 10, 15, 20, 25 or 30 were created to-morrow. And it is very possible that many of the 14 or 23 converts might do like him—pout at the creation, but yet not venture to vote against the 2nd reading after all.' Grey, however, continued to differ from Holland on this point, partly, no doubt, because he knew that Wharncliffe had a fortnight before told Sir Herbert Taylor that he and his friends would oppose the Bill at every stage if peers were made (*William's Correspondence*, ii. 193).

In an undated letter (of January 1832, I think) Holland suggests to Grey constitutional arguments to use with the King :

' If he does not agree, exclusive of immediate consequences, which are so terrible that they overwhelm and supersede all other considerations, there is one which may possibly escape him, and which no King would or ought to contemplate with satisfaction : by waiving the exercise of a prerogative at a moment of such urgency, and when it would be so grateful to the people, he waives it in truth for ever, he spikes at once the gun which was reserved for extraordinary occasions, and by avowing that he will or can never revert to it, places practically the House of Lords in a state of independence of the Crown, or rather of authority over it, in which they never have been.'

All through March the King, Grey, and Holland are in constant communication as to the chances of the Second Reading in the Peers, making out and comparing their lists of promises, etc.—*e.g. March* 16, 1832, *Holland to Grey* : ' The King bade me compare my list with others, and give him the result before next Thursday.' In the list he attaches, Holland prophesies a draw—185 to 185. (It was actually 184 for, and 175 against.)

But in April, as the crisis approaches, the King gets colder, as evinced in his letter of April 5, printed in his *Correspondence.*

Grey to Holland, April 6, 1832 :

' On the King's letter there cannot be two opinions. I have written, *"en attendant"* Cabinet, to say that we did not press for a decision on a contingent event, except under the inevitable necessity of acting instantly, if the Bill should be rejected, on one or other of the alternatives which had been submitted to him. If he prefers our resignation, the question is settled, and that, certainly, is what I should prefer.'

Grey to Brougham, April 14, 1832 :

' The King seemed pleased with the result [the Second Reading of the Bill in the Peers]. But I am not quite easy about him. I suspect he is tormented to death by all the people about him. He told me that the Duke of Cumberland was loud in his praises of you. This must please you—*laudari a laudato viro.*'

I fear the Prime Minister is here venturing to be satirical about H.R.H.

Grey to Holland, April 26, 1832 :

' I received your letter yesterday. I really do not see how I can have more frequent intercourse with the King, could it even do any good. He does not ask me to Windsor, and I have no business to take me there. Brougham has been, but was not asked to dinner. Anglesey was there on Tuesday, and both had long conversations with him, which equally indicated the strong impression that has been made upon him by constant opportunity, and I am not without suspicion that the opponents of the Government contrive, unsuspected by him, to convey to him their versions through the numerous channels which his constant entourage opens to them.'

May 9, 1832 : ' Dear Holland, our resignations are accepted. Yours, Grey. Wednesday.'

Holland to Grey, May 12, 1832 :

' Is it possible that the King has announced his adhesion to the Bill, the whole Bill, and nothing but the Bill ? We should well consider our line and act up to it in entire concert. As to the publick, if they are really to get the Bill, there may be some inclination in them not to look further, but they should be made aware that nothing but a creation of Peers would relieve them from the permanent influence of the Lords.'

Holland to Grey, May 13, 1832 :

' If the Bill is moved and supported by Wellington, *et sunt qui credere possunt*, what is to be our tone ? Silence, forbearance ? Acquiescence and good wishes mixed with apprehension ? Invective ? Or ridicule ? The last would be to me the most natural, for I really can hardly refrain from laughing when I think of a change beyond any farce, except perhaps a harlequin farce, exhibited in the grave assembly about whose honour and dignity I have heard so much, and played by the great hero of the age.'

Grey to Holland, May 13, 1832 :

' I know nothing positive. The reports which abound will, of course, have reached you. I begin to be afraid the attempt may fail. But I trust the Duke's obstinacy and pride, to risk anything rather than submit to the disgrace of being obliged to give up the task assigned to him, after having thrown the whole country into confusion, acknowledging his inability to perform it. In the meantime the language of the people about the Court is very high :—*The Government is now in the hands of those who have wise heads and stout hearts, and the King, tho' he sees his difficulties, will meet them with unflinching determination.*'

Holland to Grey, May 14, 1832 :

' I think somehow or another Wellington will have the sense to avoid appointing Aberdeen ' [to the Foreign Office, which he had held in the Duke's last Ministry], ' and though it would do him mischief to place him there, I cannot wish him to do so, for, much as I hate, dread and despise the D. of W.'s ministry, I am not sure I do not hate and dread *war* still more.

' I highly approve one opinion in Joseph Hume's speech : If the Whigs *are in*, the people will be satisfied with *this* reform ; if *not*, they must have more. Let them hold and act up to that language, and we shall beat the rascals in a month.'

Grey to Holland, May 14 (*late*), 1832 :

' I have heard nothing of arrangements, but what has passed in the House of Commons makes me fear that they may not be complete. I wish to God they were fairly in office ; but I still depend, as I told you yesterday, on the pride and obstinacy of the Duke.'

May 15 : ' I believe all you say is quite right ; the truth is that never was a captive more desirous of escaping from prison than I am from my present situation. But I will do my duty. Many of the things, however, which you urge will require consideration. We must not be found wanting, but we must be careful not to push matters too far. I have heard nothing since this morning, but I still believe the Duke will persevere, and that an administration *tale quale* will be formed in the course of the day.'

May 15 (*later*) : ' I have heard nothing more. I have ordered the Cabinet to be summoned for *two* to-morrow.'

(For Holland's letter to Grey of May 15–16, see *Butler*, 405, note.)

I do not think it necessary to discuss the absurd charge which Brougham in his old age gradually evolved against himself and Grey, that they would have been afraid to act on the King's permission of May 18, to make Peers, if the Peers had at the last moment turned refractory. Such criminal poltroonery, which must have plunged the country, without leadership, into a welter of blood and confusion, was far indeed from the Grey or the Brougham of 1832. The question is well treated in *Butler*, 413–14. And the evidence of Grey's son Henry, as to his father's views and intentions (*Edinburgh Review*, 1871, July, p. 291), is worth much more than one of Brougham's variable imaginings.

Two letters from very exalted personages, in favour of peer-making, are not without interest. Early in March 1832 the Duke of Sussex, in whose veins the blood of George III flowed commingled with a very sturdy Liberalism, wrote to Grey :

' I am morally convinced that without such a creation of Peers, you will not be able to succeed. Should any objection be started, my answer is that the Whigs have been out of office for upwards of seventy years ; that for the worst of purposes the Tory Party have during that period doubled the Peerage, an evil to be deeply deplored, but which can now only be counteracted by making a copious and proportionate addition of popular and independent men to the aristocracy of the country.'

Leopold, King of the Belgians, who was in close personal correspondence with Grey about Belgian affairs from 1830–1834, wrote to him on March 9, 1832 : ' It appears by reports on which I can rely that the King of Holland still clings to the hope that a defeat of the Reform Bill would give him new chances, and that he has recommended to his agents in this country not to relax in their efforts till this is settled. This shows you of what importance this Reform Bill is, not only to England but to Europe in general. The opposition to this Bill is unfortunately headed by men of uncommon bad faith. I think every measure which *will ensure its success ought to be adopted.*'

The careful underlining of the last eight words makes it clear that His Majesty meant something very special and very definite—obviously peer-making.

APPENDIX J

LORD GREY'S RETIREMENT

LORD WELLESLEY's famous letter to Lord Grey of June 21, 1834 (see p. 363, above), begins as follows:

'My dear Lord,—Understanding from some communications with Mr. Littleton, that the omission of those clauses in Protective Act which confer extensive and extraordinary powers of preventing meetings, etc. on the Lord Lieutenant of Ireland, would facilitate other measures of importance in their progress through Parliament, and would also secure the re-enactment of other important provisions of the Act; I think it may be convenient to your Lordship to receive an early statement of my sentiments on the subject. . . . I cannot therefore state that I consider the preservation of the clauses respecting Meetings, as they now stand in the Act, to be essential to the public tranquillity of Ireland.'

Grey to Wellesley, July 8, 1834:

'My dear Lord,—When I wrote last to your Excellency I was in hopes that the effects of Mr. Littleton's indiscretion would have blown over. But it appears to have been greater than I had imagined, and its consequences have become more serious.

'Any communication with Mr. O'Connell, even of the most general nature, I should have thought discreditable to the Government, and highly objectionable. But when it went the length of exposing to him the secrets of the Government, and the opinions of your Excellency, what but the result, which has followed, could be expected? That such a confidential communication, with a person so little to be trusted, should be made without even a hint of it being given to the Person who, however unworthily, is placed at the head of the Government, or with the Secretary for the Home Department, is still more surprising.

'I acquit Mr. Littleton of everything but imprudence, and hoping that the effect of this would be got over, I had, when he offered his resignation, desired that he would retain his office. In doing this I was actuated not less by personal regard for him, and by a desire not to separate, than by the feeling that, at this moment, his retirement from a situation, the duties of which he had so ably discharged, would be of great detriment to the Public: more particularly when so many important measures, and *imprimis* the Tithe Bill, were in progress.

'All these considerations, however, have been set aside, by what

passed last night in the House of Commons, of which the best explanation will be found in the published debates. The consequence is that Althorp finds himself placed in so disagreeable a situation, that he feels it impossible for him to continue in the Administration. He has, therefore, this morning sent to me his resignation, which I have transmitted with my own, as the necessary and unavoidable consequence, to the King. I had no alternative, as without Lord Althorp it would be impossible for me to form a Treasury Bench, equal to the conduct of public affairs, in the House of Commons.'

Grey to Wellesley, July 12, 1834 :

' My resignation was inevitable after Lord Althorp's and I am not inclined to blame him for resigning. After the double attack from O'Connell and Peel, both falling upon the Government and urging the production of your private letters, there was no hope of carrying the Protective Bill through the House of Commons ; at least without omitting the three first clauses ; and this would have broken up the Government in another and more disadvantageous way.

' Two great errors were committed. The first in writing to your Excellency, without my knowledge and with views entirely at variance with those which I entertained, to urge the expediency of omitting the Meeting Clauses. This produced the letters from your Excellency to me, which, being laid before the Cabinet, as my duty required, produced a division there. This, however, was got over, and those who differed with me, on the sole ground of your Excellency's declaration that the re-enactment of the three clauses, which could only rest on necessity, were not essential to the safety of Ireland, having acquiesced, the Bill was brought in, and the difficulty seemed to be at an end.

' But then came the effect of Mr. Littleton's inconceivable confidence in O'Connell, who, of course, seized the advantage which it gave him, and the inevitable consequences ensued. What is to be the result, I know not. Only one thing is certain—viz., that I, happen what may, never will return to office. The King wishes to bring about an union of Parties. This is simply and absolutely impossible. The only practicable alternative that I can see is the formation of a Tory Administration, under the Duke of Wellington or Sir Robert Peel.'

Grey to Brougham, November 4, 1834 :

' My dear Chancellor,—. . . I have at all times disdained all suspicion and belief, though these things had made my immediate retirement unavoidable, that they were intended to produce that result. Of such an intention, whatever share you might have had in the previous transactions, I entirely acquitted you, having in my possession what I consider as the strongest proof of your wish for my continuance in office.'

INDEX

ABERDEEN, 4th Earl of (afterwards Premier), 174, 225 and note, 236, 353-4, 356, 389

Acre, St. Jean d', 380

Adair, Robert (Sir), 108, 229, 352, 354; Fox's letters to, 61-62; Grey's letters to, 229, 364

Adam, William, M.P., 65

Adam Smith, 14

Addington (1st Viscount Sidmouth, in 1805), 15, 138, 146; his Ministry, 122-8, 130-6; in All the Talents, 142-4

Adelaide, Queen of William IV, 277, 320-1, 386

Adkin, Thomas, 9-10

Albany, the, 213

Albemarle, Earl of, 248

Alexander, Czar, 140

Alexander, spy, 84-5

Algiers, 356

All the Talents, Ministry of (1806-1807), 142-59, 169, 183

Allen, of Holland House, 25, 385

Aln, river, 191

Alnmouth, 3, 109 note, 191

Alnwick, 121, 162, 196, 200, 222, 358

Althorp, Lord, John Charles Spencer, became 3rd Earl Spencer and retired Nov. 1834 (died 1845), 163, 167, 176; opposes junction with Canning, 204, 207; chosen leader of Whigs in Commons, 213; in crises of Nov. 1830, 234, 242-4, 247-8; budget failure, 256; part in Reform Bill, 240 note, 263-4, 268, 271, 275 note, 276, 294, 298, 314, 326-8, 381; conducts Bill in House, 302-3; Peer-making controversy, 331, 333-5; in 'Days of May,' 342-3, 347; relations with Grey, 213-5, 243, 364; after Reform Bill, 356-7, 363-4, 392; retires finally, 366 note; character of, 213-5, 252, 257, 303, 333, 367 note

America, South, 152, 177, 204, 374

America (U.S.), 72, 204, 265, 368, 374

Amiens, Peace of, 118, 127-31

André, Major, 8

Anglesey, Marquis of, 241 note, 249-250, 299, 388

Anne, Queen, 264

Anti-Jacobin, the, 107

Appleby, representation of, 162

Arnold, Dr., of Rugby, 262 note

Arta-Volo boundary, the, 229-30

Ashley, Lord, *see* Shaftesbury, 7th Earl

Attwood, Thomas, founds Birmingham Political Union, 216, 268 note; prepares resistance to Belgian War, 235; supports Reform Bill, 286-7, 314, 326-7; his plans in the 'Days of May,' 220, 340, 342, 344-7, 349